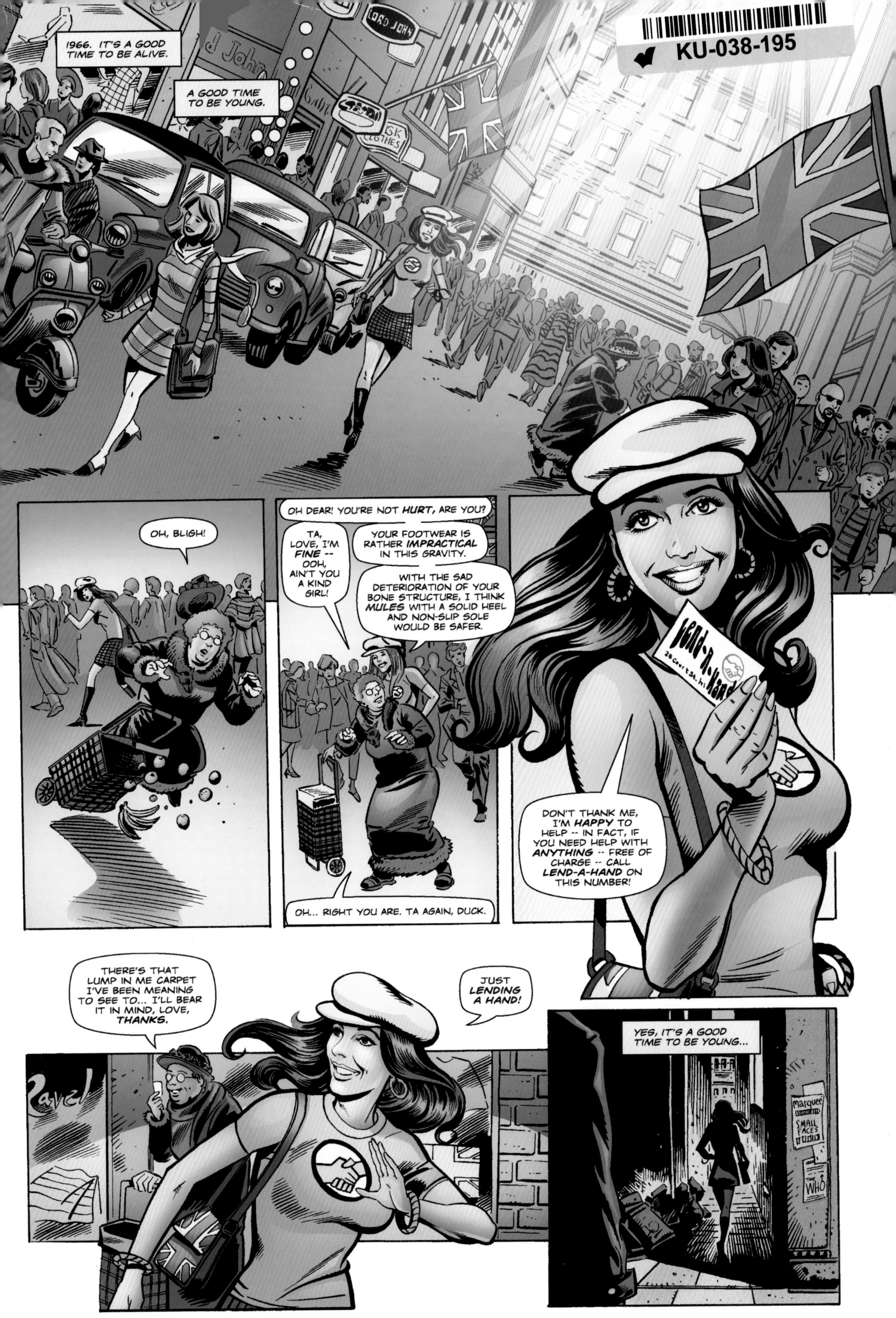
1966. IT'S A GOOD TIME TO BE ALIVE.
A GOOD TIME TO BE YOUNG.
LORD JOHN
OH, BLIGH!
OH DEAR! YOU'RE NOT HURT, ARE YOU?
TA, LOVE, I'M FINE -- OOH, AIN'T YOU A KIND GIRL!
YOUR FOOTWEAR IS RATHER IMPRACTICAL IN THIS GRAVITY.
WITH THE SAD DETERIORATION OF YOUR BONE STRUCTURE, I THINK MULES WITH A SOLID HEEL AND NON-SLIP SOLE WOULD BE SAFER.
OH... RIGHT YOU ARE. TA AGAIN, DUCK.
DON'T THANK ME, I'M HAPPY TO HELP -- IN FACT, IF YOU NEED HELP WITH ANYTHING -- FREE OF CHARGE -- CALL LEND-A-HAND ON THIS NUMBER!
THERE'S THAT LUMP IN ME CARPET I'VE BEEN MEANING TO SEE TO... I'LL BEAR IT IN MIND, LOVE, THANKS.
JUST LENDING A HAND!
YES, IT'S A GOOD TIME TO BE YOUNG...
Marquee
SMALL FACES
THE WHO

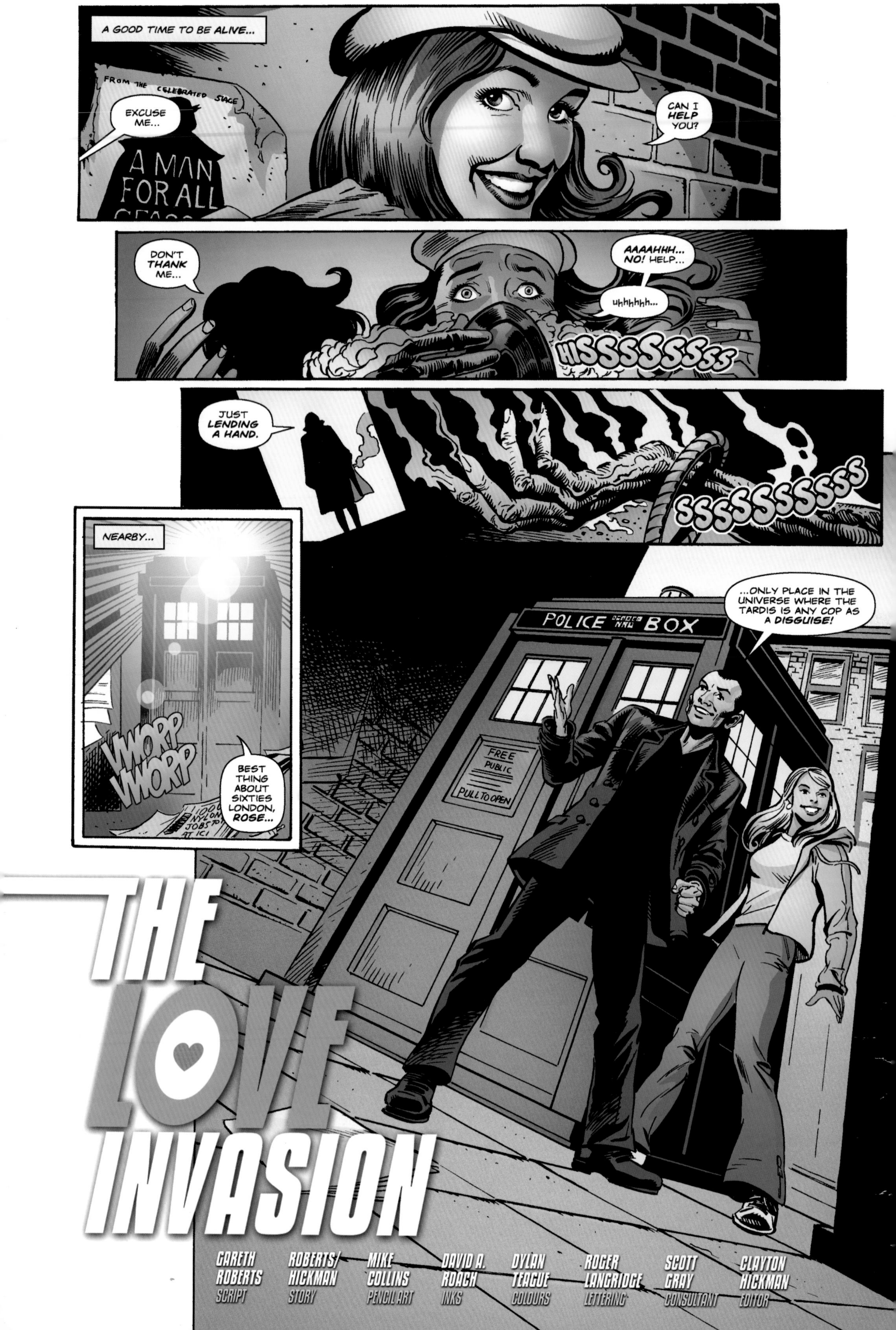
A GOOD TIME TO BE ALIVE...
FROM THE CELEBRATED STAGE
A MAN FOR ALL
EXCUSE ME...
CAN I HELP YOU?
DON'T THANK ME...
AAAAHHH... NO! HELP...
uhhhhhh...
HISSSSSSSSS
JUST LENDING A HAND.
SSSSSSSSSS
NEARBY...
VWORP VWORP
BEST THING ABOUT SIXTIES LONDON, ROSE...
...ONLY PLACE IN THE UNIVERSE WHERE THE TARDIS IS ANY COP AS A DISGUISE!
POLICE BOX
FREE PUBLIC
PULL TO OPEN
THE LOVE INVASION
GARETH ROBERTS SCRIPT
ROBERTS/ HICKMAN STORY
MIKE COLLINS PENCIL ART
DAVID A. ROACH INKS
DYLAN TEAGUE COLOURS
ROGER LANGRIDGE LETTERING
SCOTT GRAY CONSULTANT
CLAYTON HICKMAN EDITOR

THE CRUEL SEA

COLLECTED COMIC STRIPS
from the pages of

DOCTOR · WHO
MAGAZINE

Contents

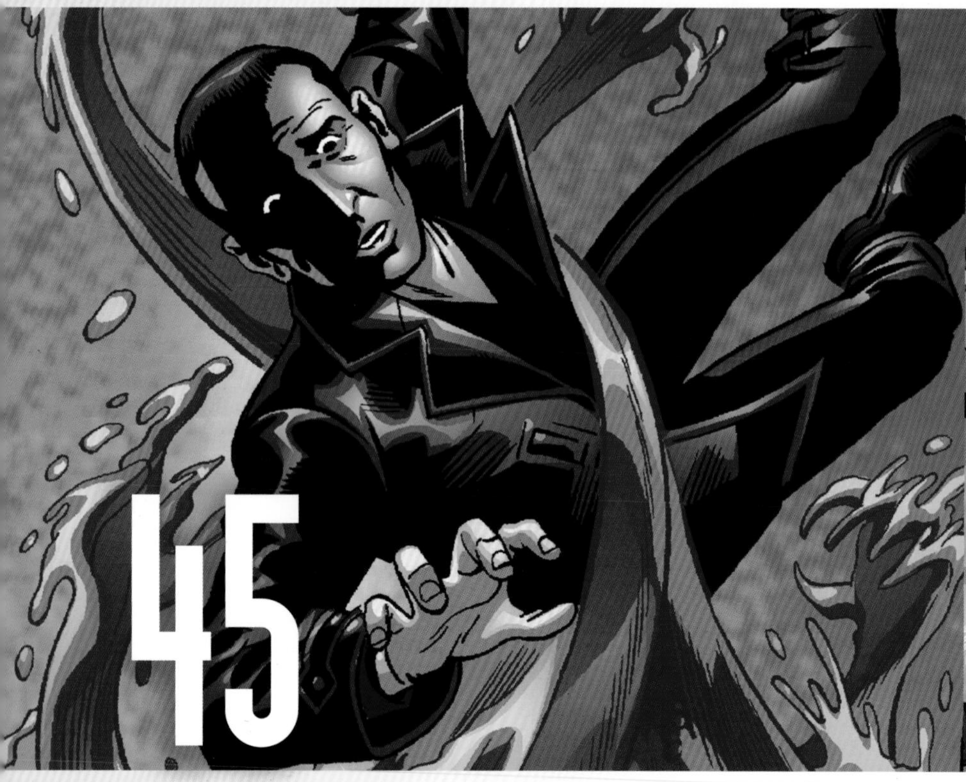
45

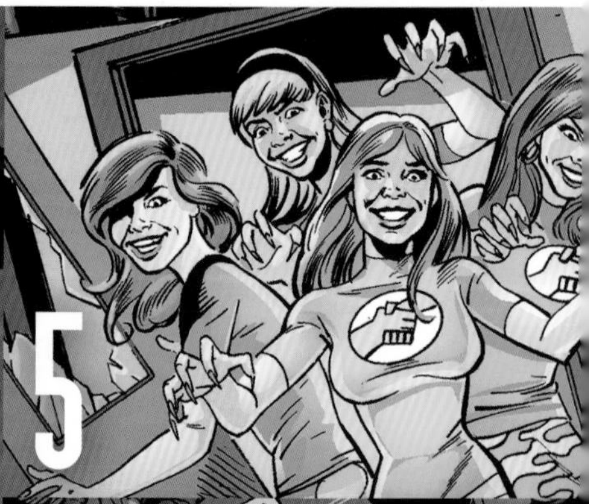
5

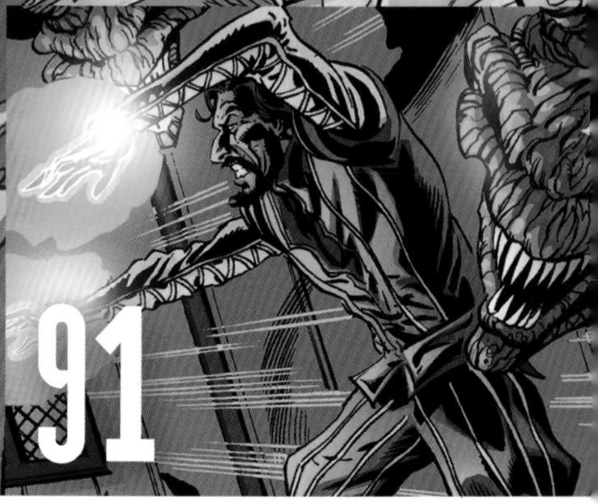
91

Project Editors **TOM SPILSBURY & SCOTT GRAY** Designer **PERI GODBOLD**
Cover pencils and inks by **DAVID A ROACH** Cover colours by **JAMES OFFREDI**

Head of Production **MARK IRVINE** Managing Editor **ALAN O'KEEFE** Managing Director **MIKE RIDDELL**

Special thanks to **RUSSELL T DAVIES, CHRISTOPHER ECCLESTON, BILLIE PIPER, GARY RUSSELL, RICHARD ATKINSON, PETER WARE, JOHN AINSWORTH, MARK WRIGHT and all the writers and artists whose work is presented herein.**

MIX Paper from responsible sources FSC® C002386 www.fsc.org

Doctor Who Graphic Novel #18: *The Cruel Sea*. Published by Panini Publishing Ltd. Office of publication: Brockbourne House, 77 Mount Ephraim, Tunbridge Wells, Kent TN4 8BS.

Printed in the UK. ISBN 978-1-84653-593-2

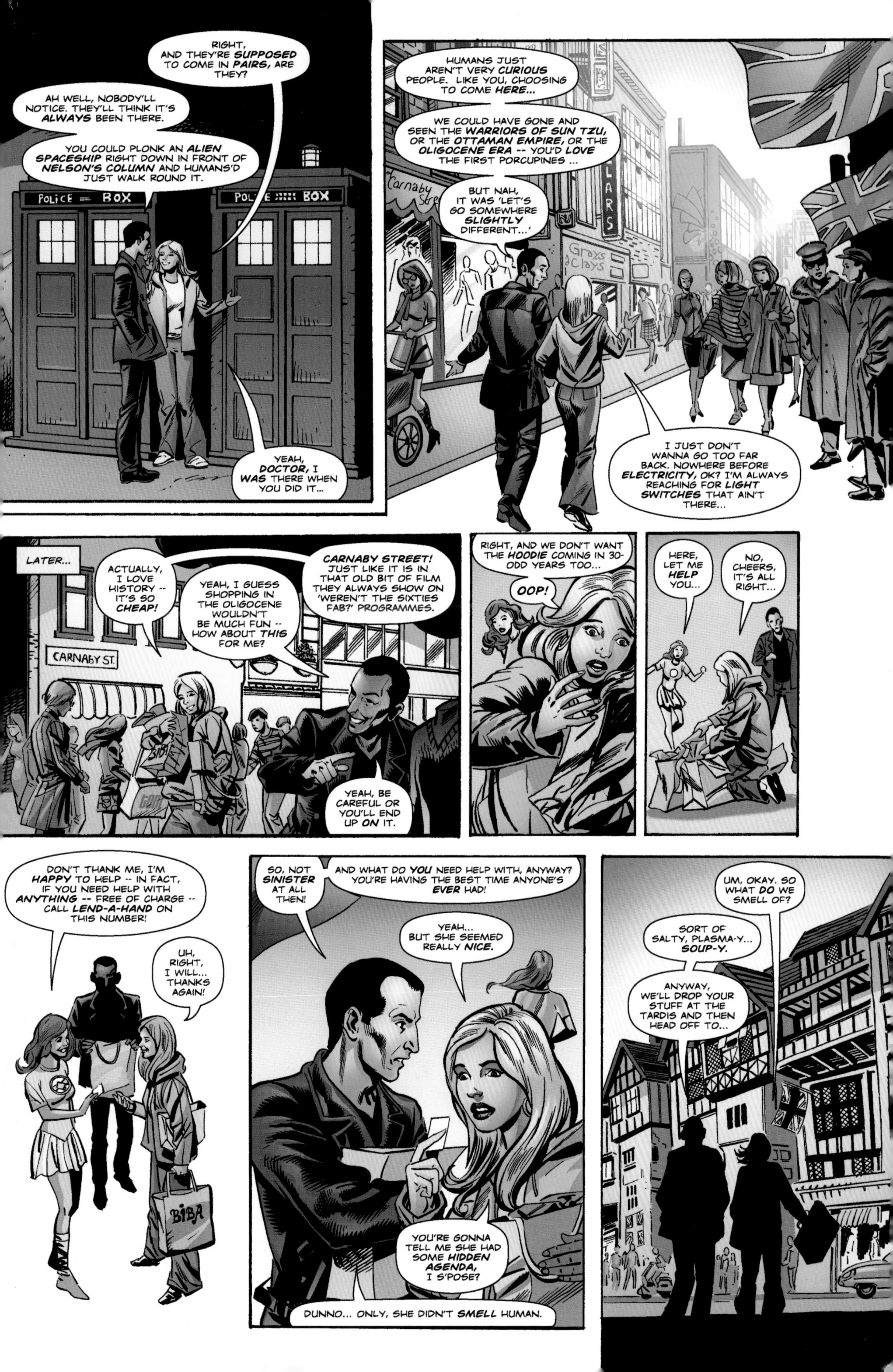
RIGHT, AND THEY'RE SUPPOSED TO COME IN PAIRS, ARE THEY?
AH WELL, NOBODY'LL NOTICE. THEY'LL THINK IT'S ALWAYS BEEN THERE.
YOU COULD PLONK AN ALIEN SPACESHIP RIGHT DOWN IN FRONT OF NELSON'S COLUMN AND HUMANS'D JUST WALK ROUND IT.
POLICE BOX
POLICE BOX
YEAH, DOCTOR, I WAS THERE WHEN YOU DID IT...
HUMANS JUST AREN'T VERY CURIOUS PEOPLE. LIKE YOU, CHOOSING TO COME HERE...
WE COULD HAVE GONE AND SEEN THE WARRIORS OF SUN TZU, OR THE OTTAMAN EMPIRE, OR THE OLIGOCENE ERA -- YOU'D LOVE THE FIRST PORCUPINES ...
BUT NAH, IT WAS 'LET'S GO SOMEWHERE SLIGHTLY DIFFERENT...'
I JUST DON'T WANNA GO TOO FAR BACK. NOWHERE BEFORE ELECTRICITY, OK? I'M ALWAYS REACHING FOR LIGHT SWITCHES THAT AIN'T THERE...
LATER...
ACTUALLY, I LOVE HISTORY -- IT'S SO CHEAP!
YEAH, I GUESS SHOPPING IN THE OLIGOCENE WOULDN'T BE MUCH FUN -- HOW ABOUT THIS FOR ME?
CARNABY STREET! JUST LIKE IT IS IN THAT OLD BIT OF FILM THEY ALWAYS SHOW ON 'WEREN'T THE SIXTIES FAB?' PROGRAMMES.
CARNABY ST.
YEAH, BE CAREFUL OR YOU'LL END UP ON IT.
RIGHT, AND WE DON'T WANT THE HOODIE COMING IN 30-ODD YEARS TOO...
OOP!
HERE, LET ME HELP YOU...
NO, CHEERS, IT'S ALL RIGHT...
DON'T THANK ME, I'M HAPPY TO HELP -- IN FACT, IF YOU NEED HELP WITH ANYTHING -- FREE OF CHARGE -- CALL LEND-A-HAND ON THIS NUMBER!
UH, RIGHT, I WILL... THANKS AGAIN!
BIBA
SO, NOT SINISTER AT ALL THEN!
AND WHAT DO YOU NEED HELP WITH, ANYWAY? YOU'RE HAVING THE BEST TIME ANYONE'S EVER HAD!
YEAH... BUT SHE SEEMED REALLY NICE.
YOU'RE GONNA TELL ME SHE HAD SOME HIDDEN AGENDA, I S'POSE?
DUNNO... ONLY, SHE DIDN'T SMELL HUMAN.
UM, OKAY. SO WHAT DO WE SMELL OF?
SORT OF SALTY, PLASMA-Y... SOUP-Y.
ANYWAY, WE'LL DROP YOUR STUFF AT THE TARDIS AND THEN HEAD OFF TO...

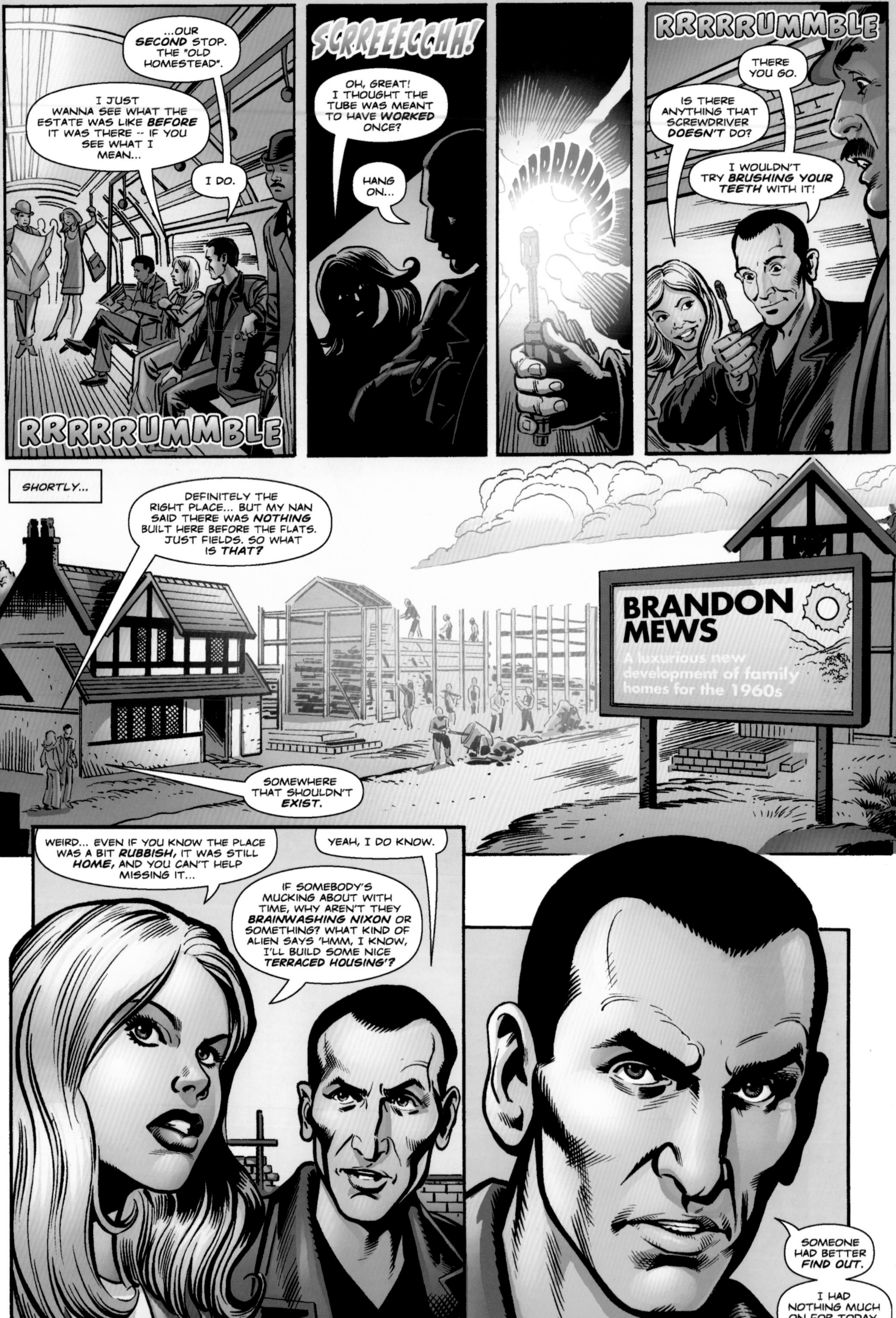
...OUR SECOND STOP. THE "OLD HOMESTEAD".
I JUST WANNA SEE WHAT THE ESTATE WAS LIKE BEFORE IT WAS THERE -- IF YOU SEE WHAT I MEAN...
I DO.
RRRRRUMMBLE
SCRREEECCHH!
OH, GREAT! I THOUGHT THE TUBE WAS MEANT TO HAVE WORKED ONCE?
HANG ON...
RRRRRUMMBLE
THERE YOU GO.
IS THERE ANYTHING THAT SCREWDRIVER DOESN'T DO?
I WOULDN'T TRY BRUSHING YOUR TEETH WITH IT!
SHORTLY...
DEFINITELY THE RIGHT PLACE... BUT MY NAN SAID THERE WAS NOTHING BUILT HERE BEFORE THE FLATS. JUST FIELDS. SO WHAT IS THAT?
BRANDON MEWS
A luxurious new development of family homes for the 1960s
SOMEWHERE THAT SHOULDN'T EXIST.
WEIRD... EVEN IF YOU KNOW THE PLACE WAS A BIT RUBBISH, IT WAS STILL HOME, AND YOU CAN'T HELP MISSING IT...
YEAH, I DO KNOW.
IF SOMEBODY'S MUCKING ABOUT WITH TIME, WHY AREN'T THEY BRAINWASHING NIXON OR SOMETHING? WHAT KIND OF ALIEN SAYS 'HMM, I KNOW, I'LL BUILD SOME NICE TERRACED HOUSING'?
SOMEONE HAD BETTER FIND OUT.
I HAD NOTHING MUCH ON FOR TODAY, ANYWAY...

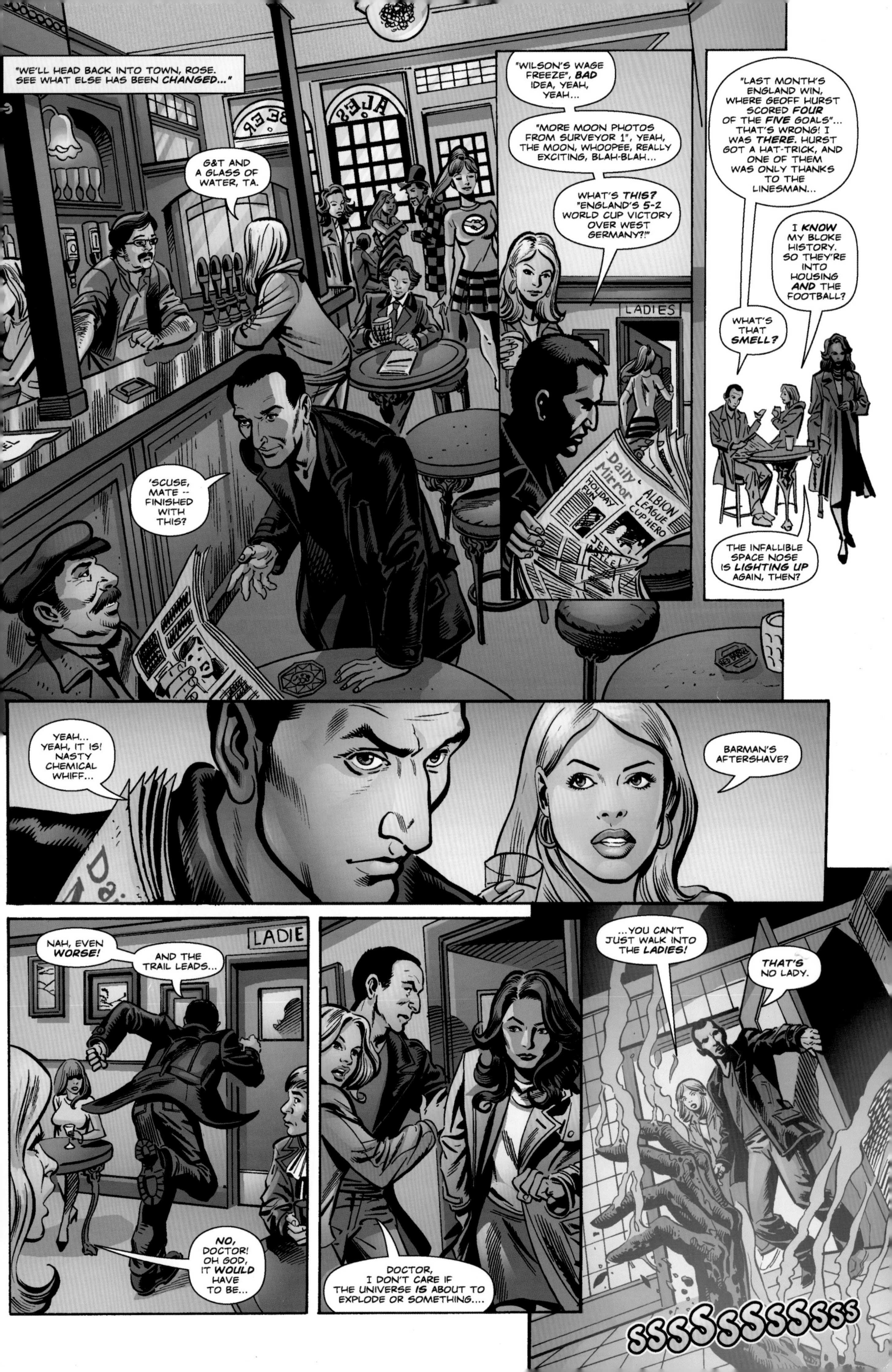
"WE'LL HEAD BACK INTO TOWN, ROSE. SEE WHAT ELSE HAS BEEN CHANGED..."
G&T AND A GLASS OF WATER, TA.
'SCUSE, MATE -- FINISHED WITH THIS?
"WILSON'S WAGE FREEZE", BAD IDEA, YEAH, YEAH...
"MORE MOON PHOTOS FROM SURVEYOR 1", YEAH, THE MOON, WHOOPEE, REALLY EXCITING, BLAH-BLAH...
WHAT'S THIS? "ENGLAND'S 5-2 WORLD CUP VICTORY OVER WEST GERMANY?!"
LADIES
Daily Mirror
ALBION LEAGUE CUP HERO
HOLIDAY FUN
"LAST MONTH'S ENGLAND WIN, WHERE GEOFF HURST SCORED FOUR OF THE FIVE GOALS"... THAT'S WRONG! I WAS THERE. HURST GOT A HAT-TRICK, AND ONE OF THEM WAS ONLY THANKS TO THE LINESMAN...
I KNOW MY BLOKE HISTORY. SO THEY'RE INTO HOUSING AND THE FOOTBALL?
WHAT'S THAT SMELL?
THE INFALLIBLE SPACE NOSE IS LIGHTING UP AGAIN, THEN?
YEAH... YEAH, IT IS! NASTY CHEMICAL WHIFF...
BARMAN'S AFTERSHAVE?
NAH, EVEN WORSE!
AND THE TRAIL LEADS...
LADIE
NO, DOCTOR! OH GOD, IT WOULD HAVE TO BE...
DOCTOR, I DON'T CARE IF THE UNIVERSE IS ABOUT TO EXPLODE OR SOMETHING....
...YOU CAN'T JUST WALK INTO THE LADIES!
THAT'S NO LADY.
SSSSSSSSSSSS

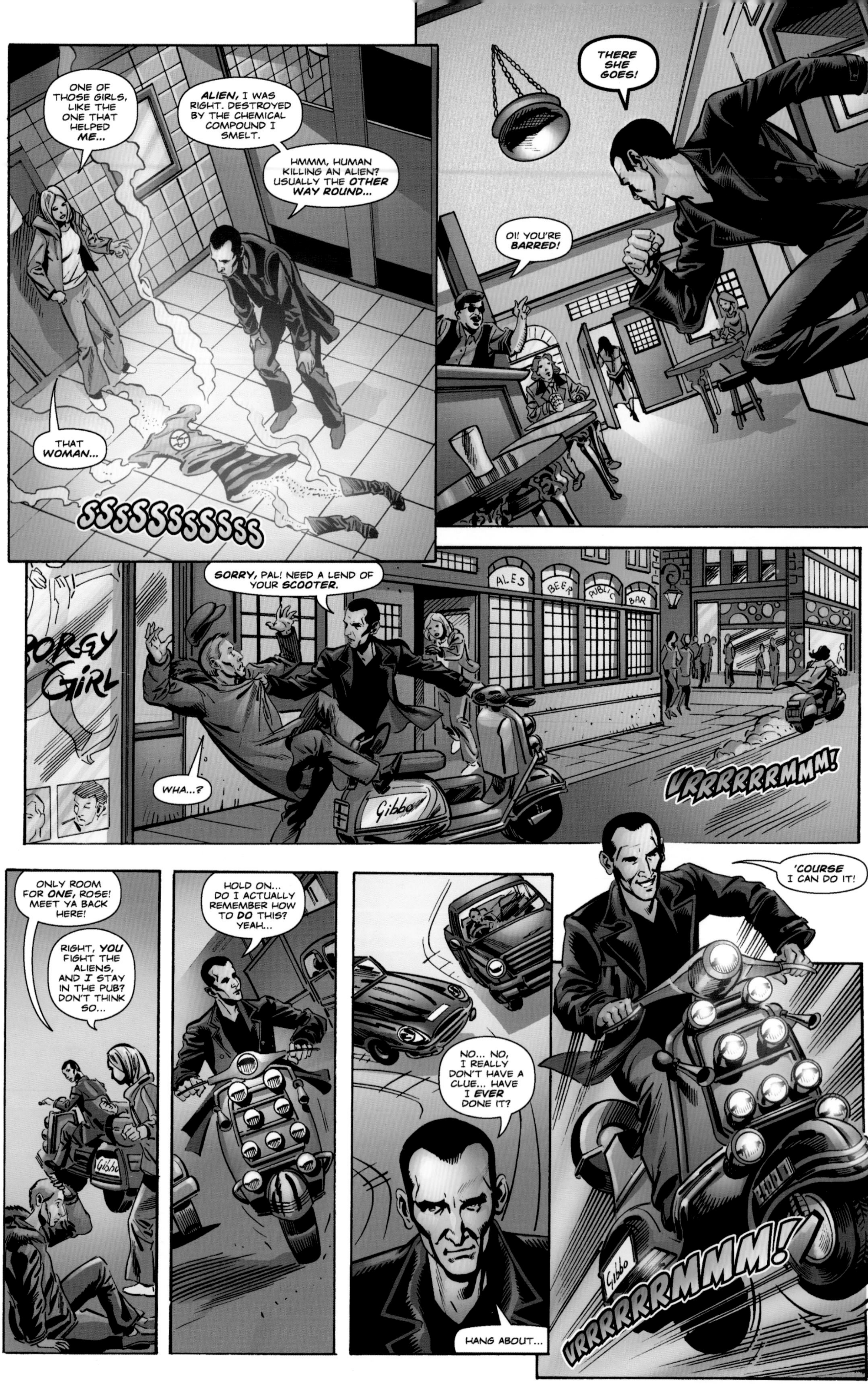
ONE OF THOSE GIRLS, LIKE THE ONE THAT HELPED ME...
ALIEN, I WAS RIGHT. DESTROYED BY THE CHEMICAL COMPOUND I SMELT.
HMMM, HUMAN KILLING AN ALIEN? USUALLY THE OTHER WAY ROUND...
THAT WOMAN...
SSSSSSSSSSS
THERE SHE GOES!
OI! YOU'RE BARRED!
SORRY, PAL! NEED A LEND OF YOUR SCOOTER.
ALES
BEER
PUBLIC
BAR
PORGY
GIRL
WHA...?
Gibbo
URRRRRRMMM!
ONLY ROOM FOR ONE, ROSE! MEET YA BACK HERE!
RIGHT, YOU FIGHT THE ALIENS, AND I STAY IN THE PUB? DON'T THINK SO...
Gibbo
HOLD ON... DO I ACTUALLY REMEMBER HOW TO DO THIS? YEAH...
NO... NO, I REALLY DON'T HAVE A CLUE... HAVE I EVER DONE IT?
HANG ABOUT...
'COURSE I CAN DO IT!
Gibbo
VRRRRRRMMM!

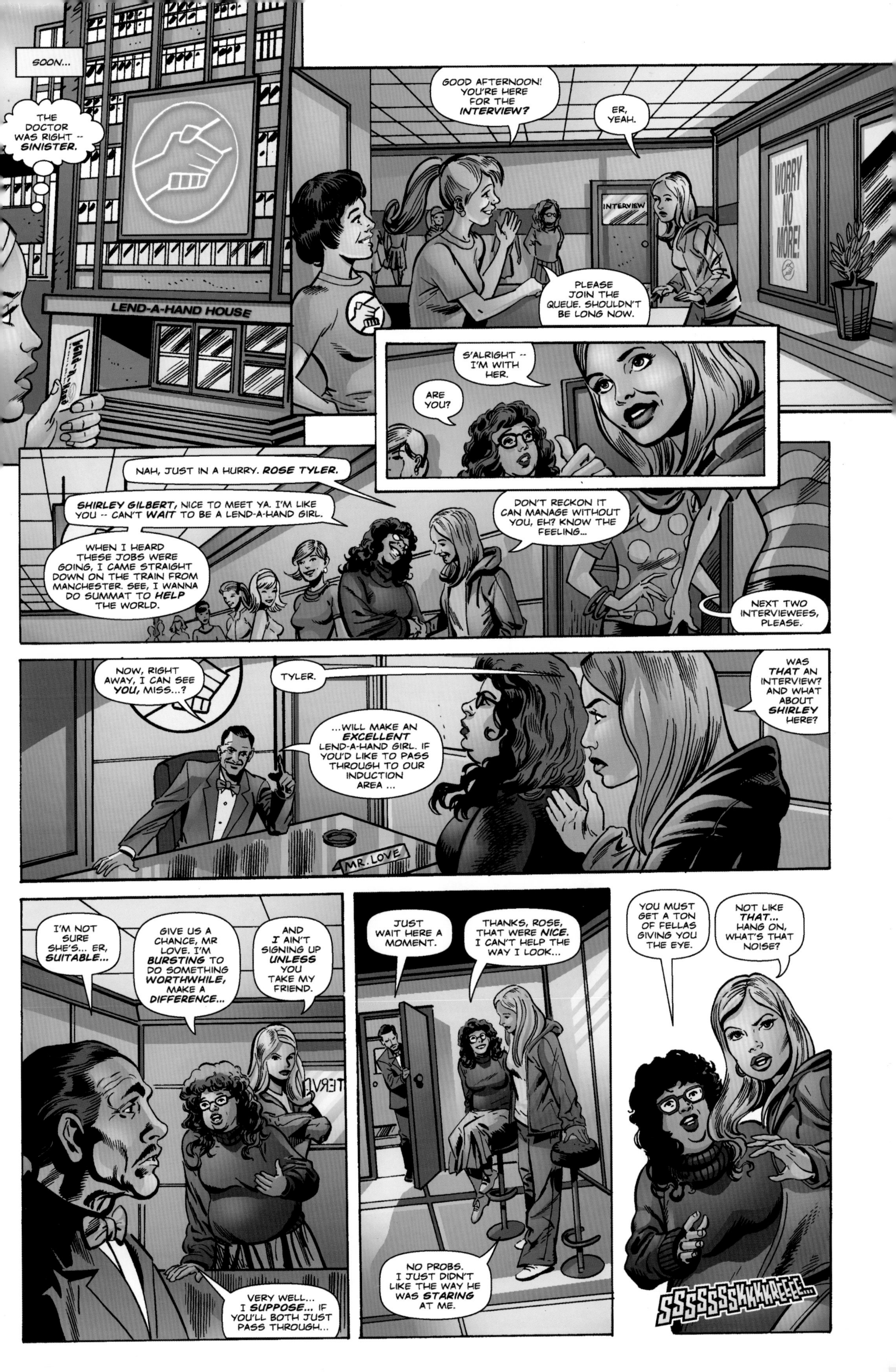
SOON...
THE DOCTOR WAS RIGHT -- SINISTER.
LEND-A-HAND HOUSE
GOOD AFTERNOON! YOU'RE HERE FOR THE INTERVIEW?
ER, YEAH.
INTERVIEW
WORRY NO MORE!
PLEASE JOIN THE QUEUE. SHOULDN'T BE LONG NOW.
S'ALRIGHT -- I'M WITH HER.
ARE YOU?
NAH, JUST IN A HURRY. ROSE TYLER.
SHIRLEY GILBERT, NICE TO MEET YA. I'M LIKE YOU -- CAN'T WAIT TO BE A LEND-A-HAND GIRL.
WHEN I HEARD THESE JOBS WERE GOING, I CAME STRAIGHT DOWN ON THE TRAIN FROM MANCHESTER. SEE, I WANNA DO SUMMAT TO HELP THE WORLD.
DON'T RECKON IT CAN MANAGE WITHOUT YOU, EH? KNOW THE FEELING...
NEXT TWO INTERVIEWEES, PLEASE.
NOW, RIGHT AWAY, I CAN SEE YOU, MISS...?
TYLER.
...WILL MAKE AN EXCELLENT LEND-A-HAND GIRL. IF YOU'D LIKE TO PASS THROUGH TO OUR INDUCTION AREA ...
WAS THAT AN INTERVIEW? AND WHAT ABOUT SHIRLEY HERE?
MR. LOVE
I'M NOT SURE SHE'S... ER, SUITABLE...
GIVE US A CHANCE, MR LOVE. I'M BURSTING TO DO SOMETHING WORTHWHILE, MAKE A DIFFERENCE...
AND I AIN'T SIGNING UP UNLESS YOU TAKE MY FRIEND.
VERY WELL... I SUPPOSE... IF YOU'LL BOTH JUST PASS THROUGH...
JUST WAIT HERE A MOMENT.
THANKS, ROSE, THAT WERE NICE. I CAN'T HELP THE WAY I LOOK...
NO PROBS. I JUST DIDN'T LIKE THE WAY HE WAS STARING AT ME.
YOU MUST GET A TON OF FELLAS GIVING YOU THE EYE.
NOT LIKE THAT... HANG ON, WHAT'S THAT NOISE?
SSSSSSKKKKREEEE...

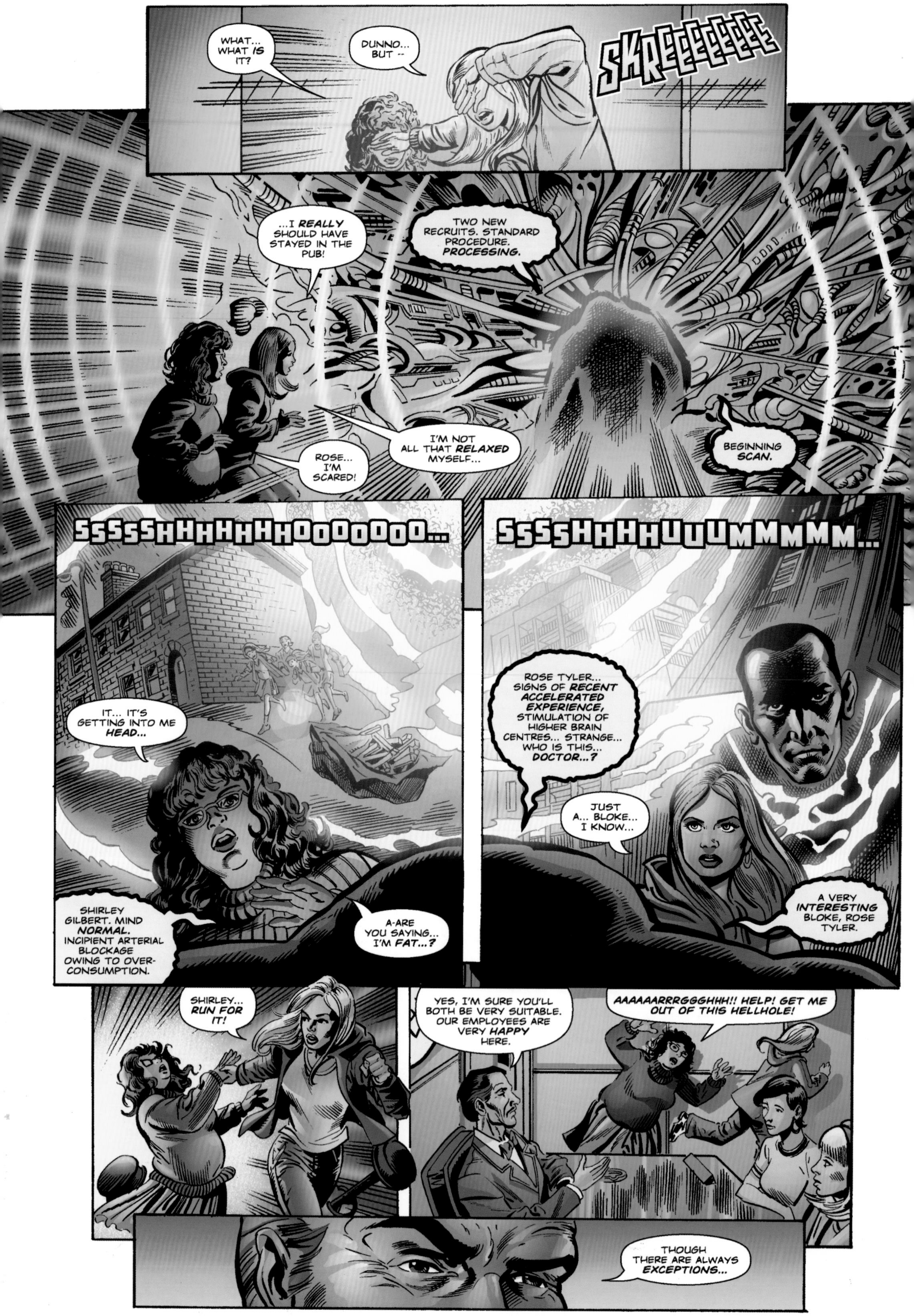
WHAT... WHAT IS IT?
DUNNO... BUT --
SKREEEEEEEEE
...I REALLY SHOULD HAVE STAYED IN THE PUB!
TWO NEW RECRUITS. STANDARD PROCEDURE. PROCESSING.
I'M NOT ALL THAT RELAXED MYSELF...
ROSE... I'M SCARED!
BEGINNING SCAN.
SSSSHHHHHHOOOOOOO...
IT... IT'S GETTING INTO ME HEAD...
SHIRLEY GILBERT. MIND NORMAL. INCIPIENT ARTERIAL BLOCKAGE OWING TO OVER-CONSUMPTION.
A-ARE YOU SAYING... I'M FAT...?
SSSSHHHHUUUMMMMM...
ROSE TYLER... SIGNS OF RECENT ACCELERATED EXPERIENCE, STIMULATION OF HIGHER BRAIN CENTRES... STRANGE... WHO IS THIS... DOCTOR...?
JUST A... BLOKE... I KNOW...
A VERY INTERESTING BLOKE, ROSE TYLER.
SHIRLEY... RUN FOR IT!
YES, I'M SURE YOU'LL BOTH BE VERY SUITABLE. OUR EMPLOYEES ARE VERY HAPPY HERE.
AAAAAARRRGGGHHH!! HELP! GET ME OUT OF THIS HELLHOLE!
THOUGH THERE ARE ALWAYS EXCEPTIONS...

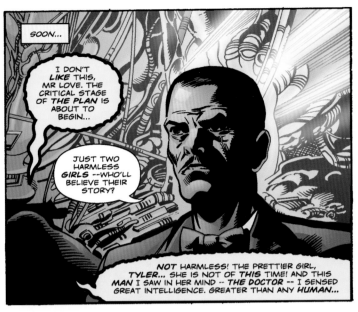

SOON...

I DON'T *LIKE* THIS, MR LOVE. THE CRITICAL STAGE OF *THE PLAN* IS ABOUT TO BEGIN...

JUST TWO HARMLESS *GIRLS* --WHO'LL BELIEVE THEIR STORY?

NOT HARMLESS! THE PRETTIER GIRL, TYLER... SHE IS NOT OF *THIS* TIME! AND THIS MAN I SAW IN HER MIND -- *THE DOCTOR* -- I SENSED GREAT INTELLIGENCE. GREATER THAN ANY *HUMAN*...

I'M QUITE SURE YOU'RE *OVERREACTING*, SIR. IT WAS PROBABLY JUST HER *BOYFRIEND*.

DON'T *IRRITATE* ME, MR LOVE. WE KNOW WE HAVE AN *ENEMY* -- THREE OF OUR GIRLS HAVE BEEN *MURDERED*!

I SHALL BEAM A *MIND-IMAGE* OF *ROSE TYLER* AND THIS *DOCTOR* TO ALL OUR OPERATIVES...

"WE MUST LOCATE HIM *IMMEDIATELY*!"

SCREEEEEGH!

ST. MERRIONS UNI

St Merrions University Hospital

NOW -- WHICH WAY'D SHE GO?

I'VE *FOUND* THE MAN YOU WERE LOOKING FOR -- THE DOCTOR.

HE'S AT THE ST MERRION'S UNIVERSITY HOSPITAL, COTTINGHAM STREET...

HELLO, I --

OH, SORRY, YOU CARRY ON.

AND THESE TENDONS ARE CONNECTED BY --

HELLO, I --

OH, SORRY, YOU CARRY ON.

THIRD TIME LUCKY! HELLO, I'M THE DOCTOR.

HAVE YOU HEARD OF THIS NEW CUSTOM -- *KNOCKING* ON DOORS BEFORE YOU BURST IN?

NEWS TO ME! I HAD TO *SEE* YOU.

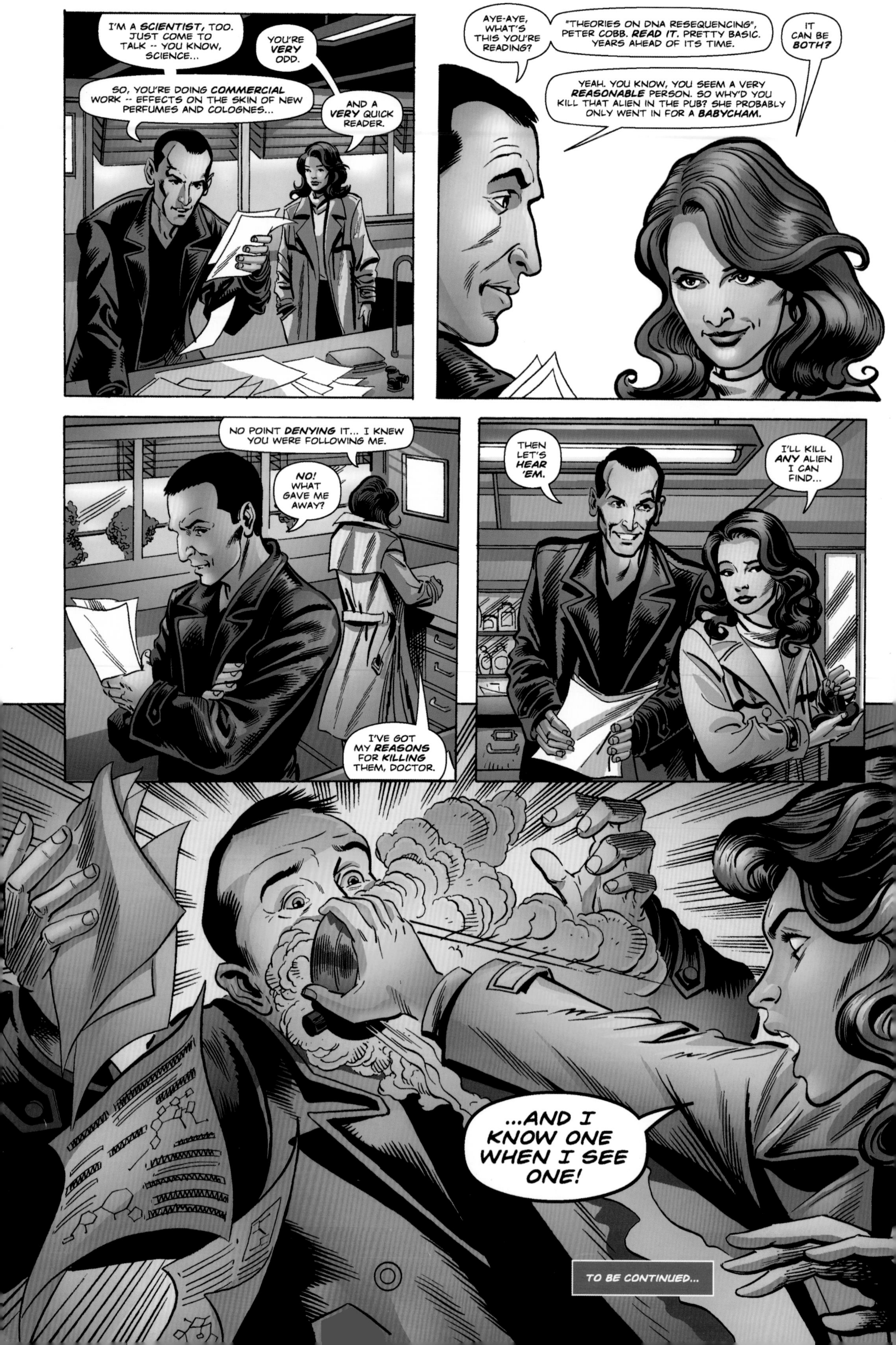
I'M A SCIENTIST, TOO. JUST COME TO TALK -- YOU KNOW, SCIENCE...
SO, YOU'RE DOING COMMERCIAL WORK -- EFFECTS ON THE SKIN OF NEW PERFUMES AND COLOGNES...
YOU'RE VERY ODD.
AND A VERY QUICK READER.
AYE-AYE, WHAT'S THIS YOU'RE READING?
"THEORIES ON DNA RESEQUENCING", PETER COBB. READ IT. PRETTY BASIC. YEARS AHEAD OF ITS TIME.
IT CAN BE BOTH?
YEAH. YOU KNOW, YOU SEEM A VERY REASONABLE PERSON. SO WHY'D YOU KILL THAT ALIEN IN THE PUB? SHE PROBABLY ONLY WENT IN FOR A BABYCHAM.
NO POINT DENYING IT... I KNEW YOU WERE FOLLOWING ME.
NO! WHAT GAVE ME AWAY?
I'VE GOT MY REASONS FOR KILLING THEM, DOCTOR.
THEN LET'S HEAR 'EM.
I'LL KILL ANY ALIEN I CAN FIND...
...AND I KNOW ONE WHEN I SEE ONE!
TO BE CONTINUED...

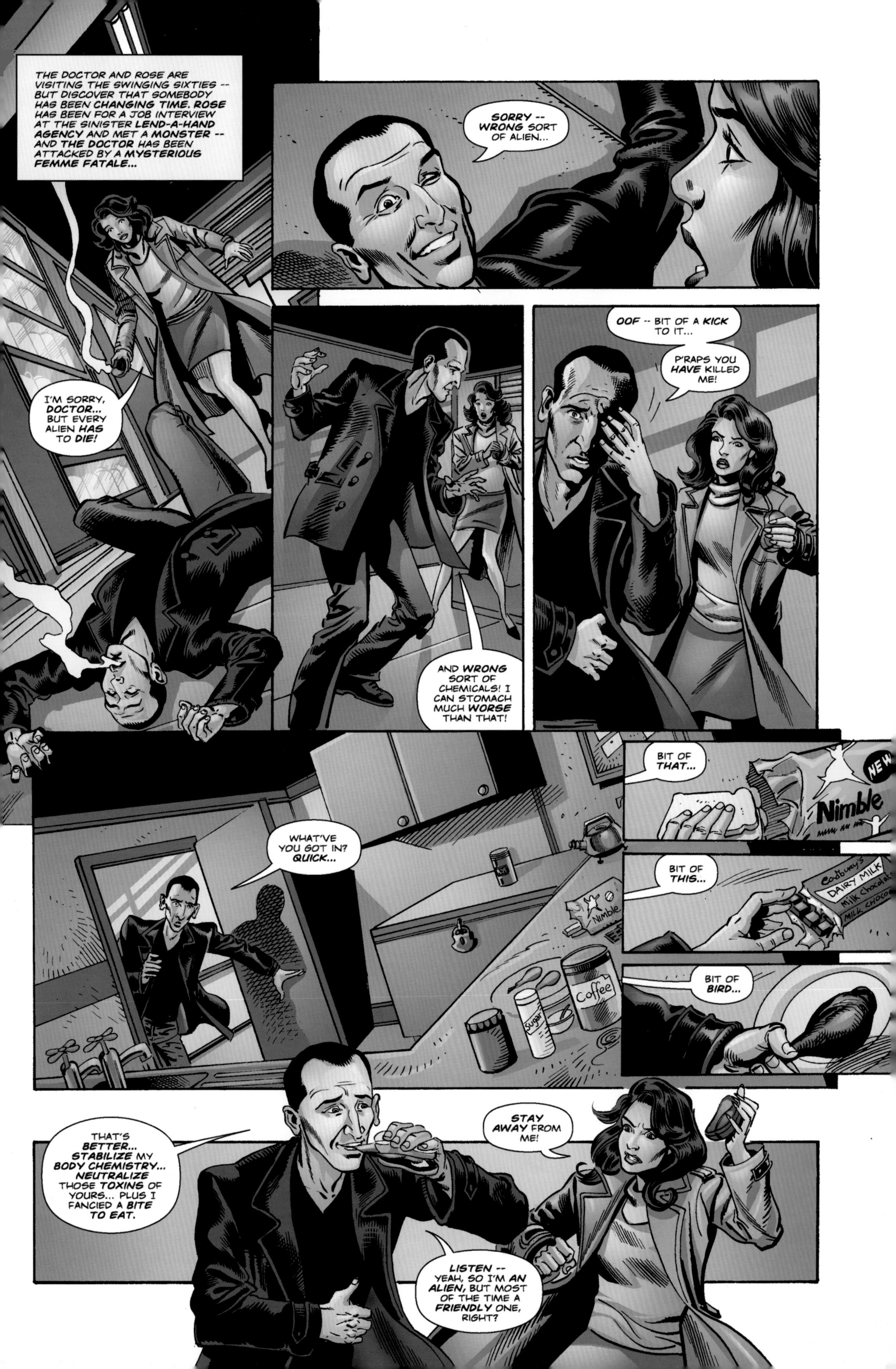
THE DOCTOR AND ROSE ARE VISITING THE SWINGING SIXTIES -- BUT DISCOVER THAT SOMEBODY HAS BEEN CHANGING TIME. ROSE HAS BEEN FOR A JOB INTERVIEW AT THE SINISTER LEND-A-HAND AGENCY AND MET A MONSTER -- AND THE DOCTOR HAS BEEN ATTACKED BY A MYSTERIOUS FEMME FATALE...
I'M SORRY, DOCTOR... BUT EVERY ALIEN HAS TO DIE!
SORRY -- WRONG SORT OF ALIEN...
AND WRONG SORT OF CHEMICALS! I CAN STOMACH MUCH WORSE THAN THAT!
OOF -- BIT OF A KICK TO IT...
P'RAPS YOU HAVE KILLED ME!
WHAT'VE YOU GOT IN? QUICK...
Nimble
Sugar
Coffee
BIT OF THAT...
NEW
Nimble
BIT OF THIS...
Cadbury's
DAIRY MILK
Milk Chocolate
BIT OF BIRD...
THAT'S BETTER... STABILIZE MY BODY CHEMISTRY... NEUTRALIZE THOSE TOXINS OF YOURS... PLUS I FANCIED A BITE TO EAT.
STAY AWAY FROM ME!
LISTEN -- YEAH, SO I'M AN ALIEN, BUT MOST OF THE TIME A FRIENDLY ONE, RIGHT?

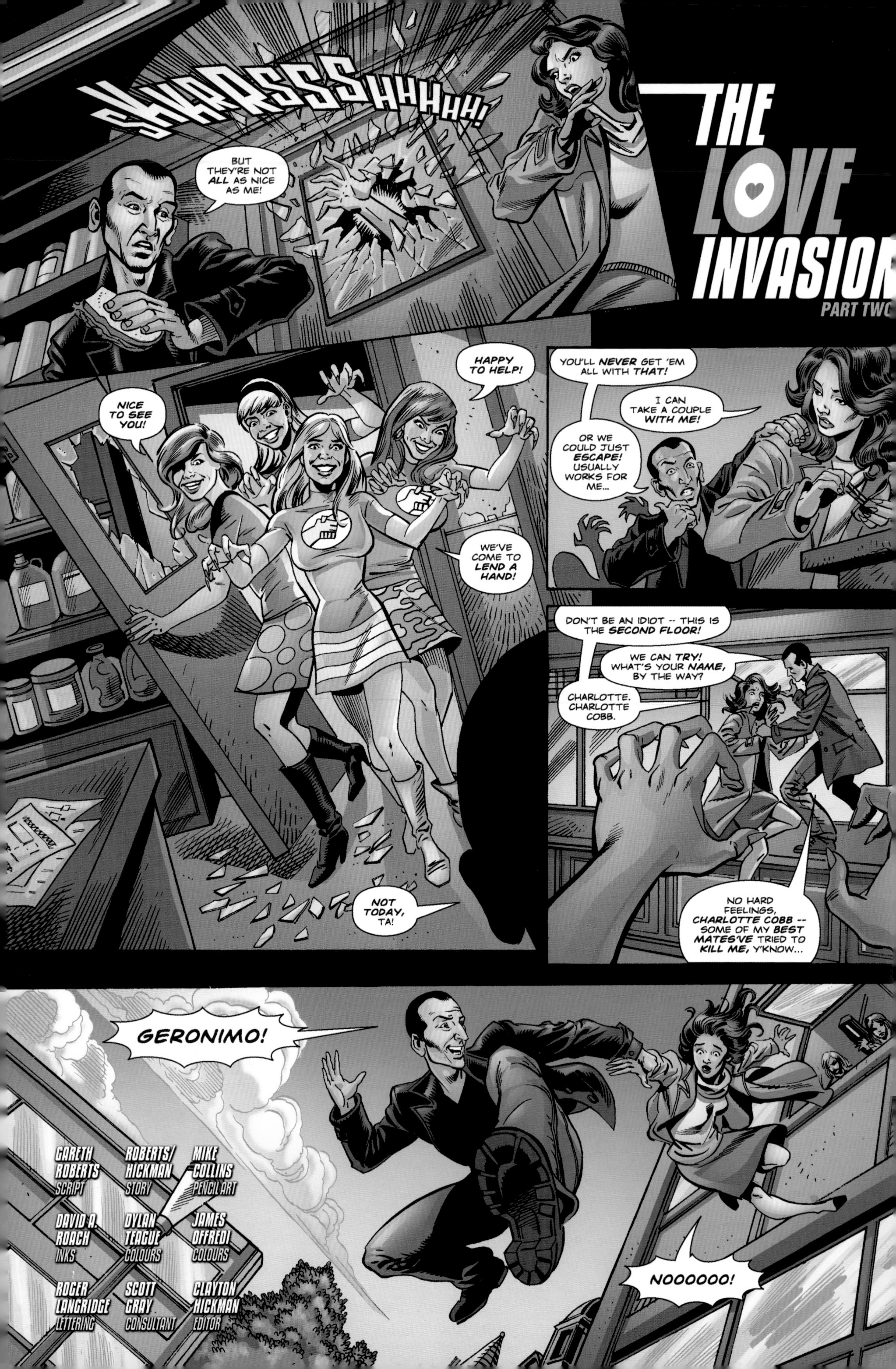
SHHRSSSHHHHH!
THE LOVE INVASION
PART TWO
BUT THEY'RE NOT ALL AS NICE AS ME!
NICE TO SEE YOU!
HAPPY TO HELP!
WE'VE COME TO LEND A HAND!
NOT TODAY, TA!
YOU'LL NEVER GET 'EM ALL WITH THAT!
I CAN TAKE A COUPLE WITH ME!
OR WE COULD JUST ESCAPE! USUALLY WORKS FOR ME...
DON'T BE AN IDIOT -- THIS IS THE SECOND FLOOR!
WE CAN TRY! WHAT'S YOUR NAME, BY THE WAY?
CHARLOTTE. CHARLOTTE COBB.
NO HARD FEELINGS, CHARLOTTE COBB -- SOME OF MY BEST MATES'VE TRIED TO KILL ME, Y'KNOW...
GERONIMO!
NOOOOOO!
GARETH ROBERTS SCRIPT
ROBERTS/HICKMAN STORY
MIKE COLLINS PENCIL ART
DAVID A. ROACH INKS
DYLAN TEAGUE COLOURS
JAMES OFFREDI COLOURS
ROGER LANGRIDGE LETTERING
SCOTT GRAY CONSULTANT
CLAYTON HICKMAN EDITOR

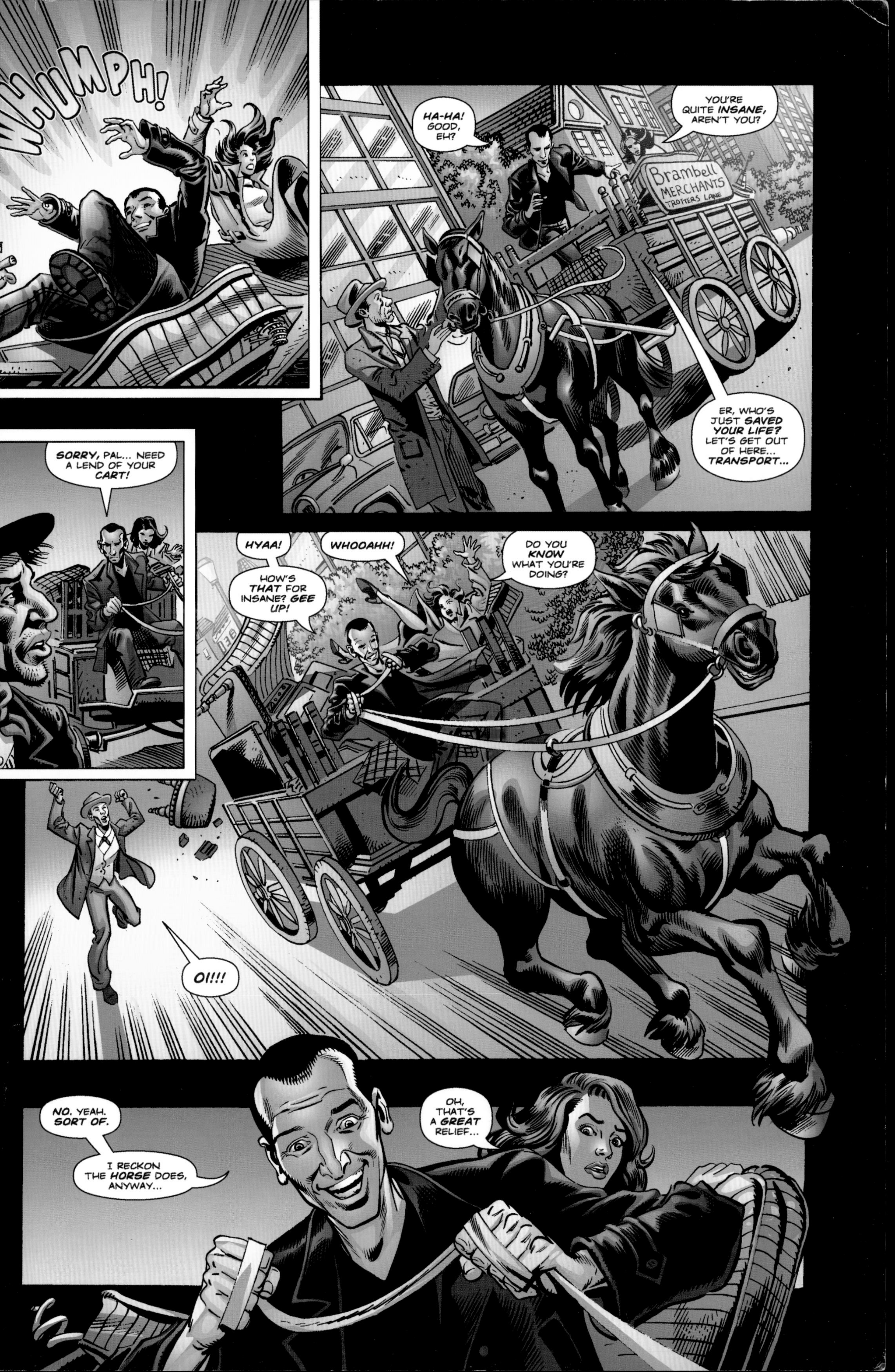
WHUMPH!
HA-HA! GOOD, EH?
YOU'RE QUITE INSANE, AREN'T YOU?
Brambell MERCHANTS TROTTERS LANE
ER, WHO'S JUST SAVED YOUR LIFE? LET'S GET OUT OF HERE... TRANSPORT...
SORRY, PAL... NEED A LEND OF YOUR CART!
HYAA!
HOW'S THAT FOR INSANE? GEE UP!
WHOOAHH!
DO YOU KNOW WHAT YOU'RE DOING?
OI!!!
NO. YEAH. SORT OF.
I RECKON THE HORSE DOES, ANYWAY...
OH, THAT'S A GREAT RELIEF...

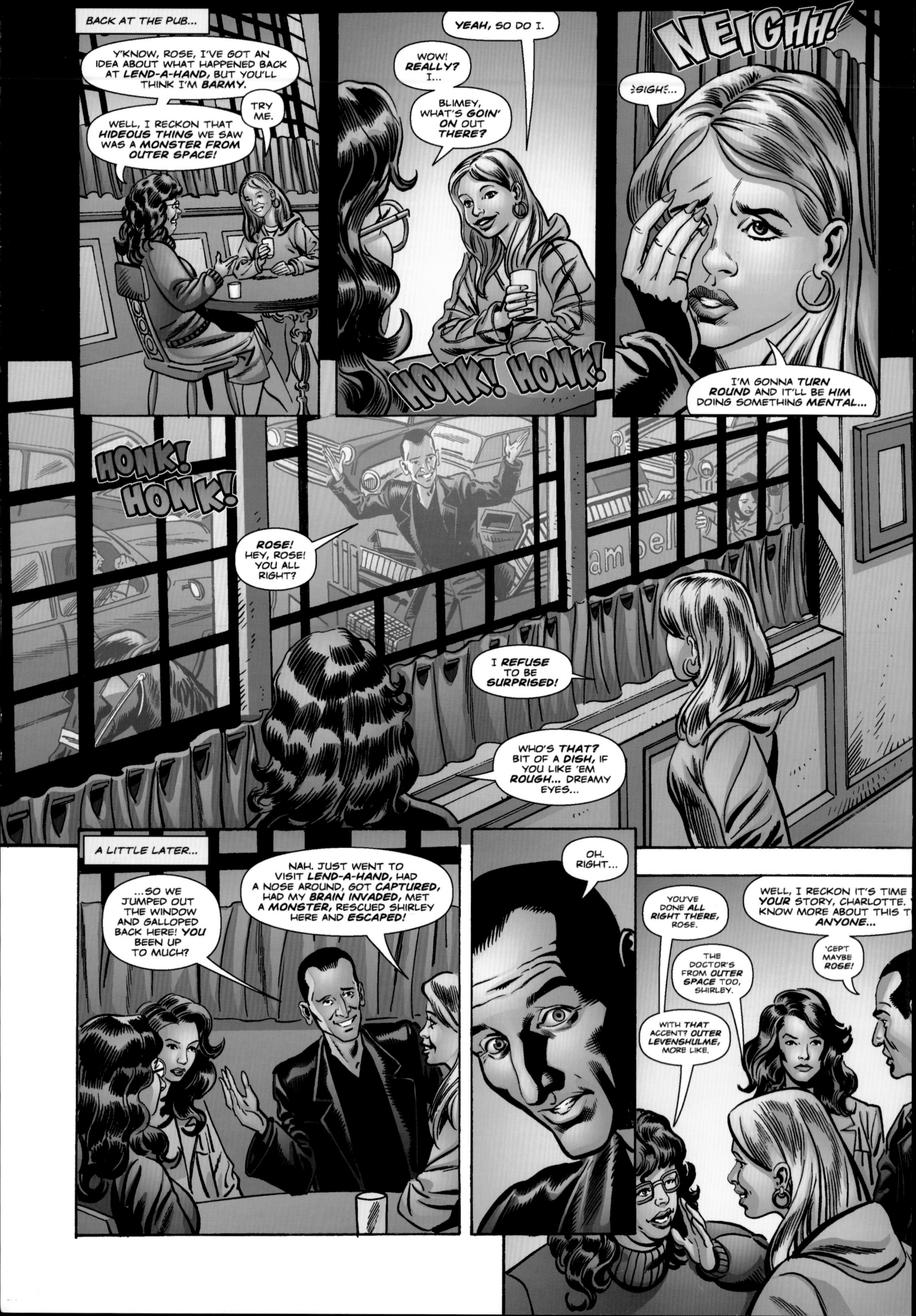
BACK AT THE PUB...
Y'KNOW, ROSE, I'VE GOT AN IDEA ABOUT WHAT HAPPENED BACK AT LEND-A-HAND, BUT YOU'LL THINK I'M BARMY.
TRY ME.
WELL, I RECKON THAT HIDEOUS THING WE SAW WAS A MONSTER FROM OUTER SPACE!
YEAH, SO DO I.
WOW! REALLY? I...
BLIMEY, WHAT'S GOIN' ON OUT THERE?
HONK! HONK!
NEIGHH!
SIGH...
I'M GONNA TURN ROUND AND IT'LL BE HIM DOING SOMETHING MENTAL...
HONK! HONK!
ROSE! HEY, ROSE! YOU ALL RIGHT?
I REFUSE TO BE SURPRISED!
WHO'S THAT? BIT OF A DISH, IF YOU LIKE 'EM ROUGH... DREAMY EYES...
A LITTLE LATER...
...SO WE JUMPED OUT THE WINDOW AND GALLOPED BACK HERE! YOU BEEN UP TO MUCH?
NAH. JUST WENT TO VISIT LEND-A-HAND, HAD A NOSE AROUND, GOT CAPTURED, HAD MY BRAIN INVADED, MET A MONSTER, RESCUED SHIRLEY HERE AND ESCAPED!
OH. RIGHT...
YOU'VE DONE ALL RIGHT THERE, ROSE.
THE DOCTOR'S FROM OUTER SPACE TOO, SHIRLEY.
WITH THAT ACCENT? OUTER LEVENSHULME, MORE LIKE.
WELL, I RECKON IT'S TIME YOUR STORY, CHARLOTTE. KNOW MORE ABOUT THIS ANYONE...
'CEPT MAYBE ROSE!

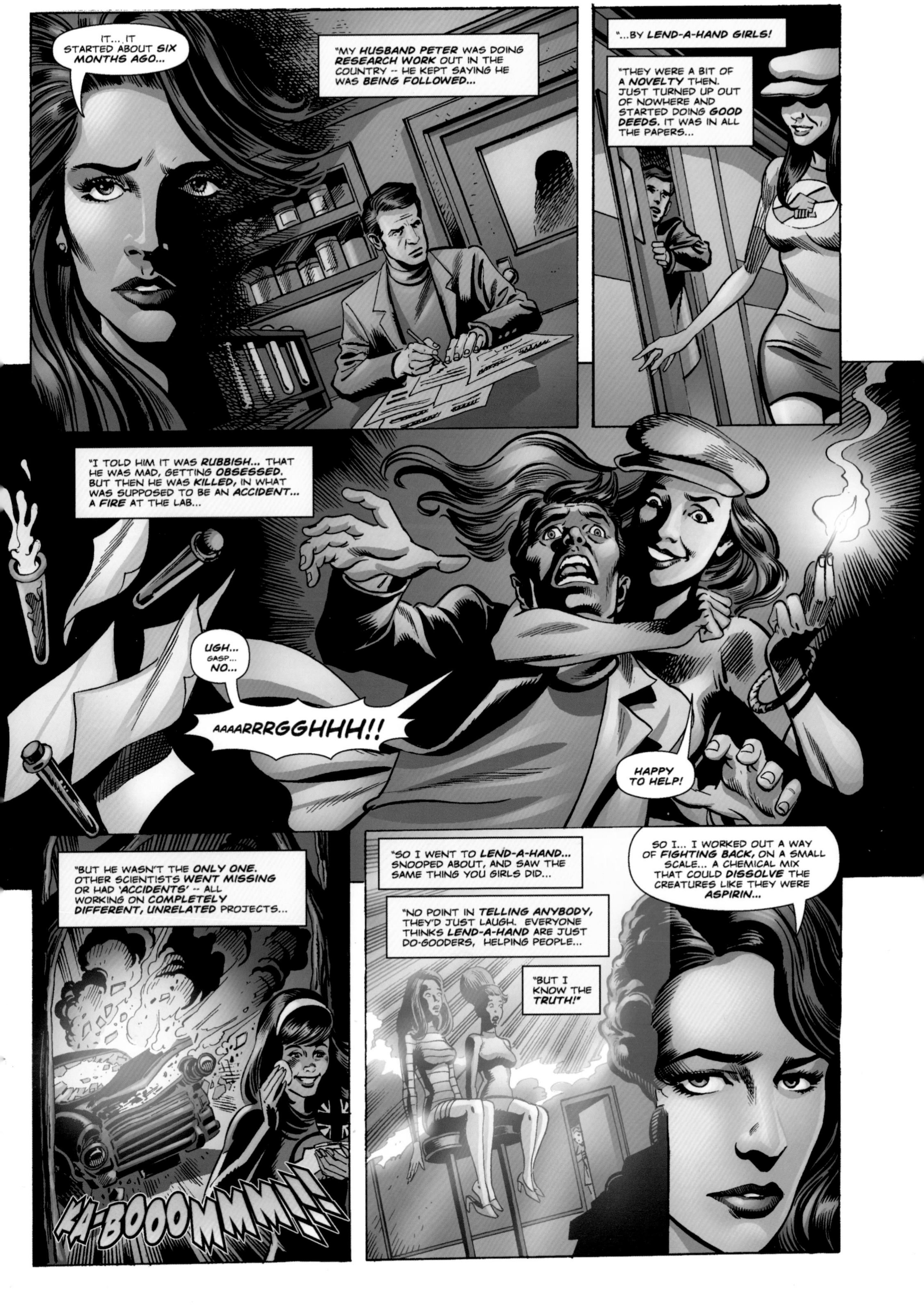

IT... IT STARTED ABOUT SIX MONTHS AGO...
"MY HUSBAND PETER WAS DOING RESEARCH WORK OUT IN THE COUNTRY -- HE KEPT SAYING HE WAS BEING FOLLOWED...
"...BY LEND-A-HAND GIRLS!
"THEY WERE A BIT OF A NOVELTY THEN. JUST TURNED UP OUT OF NOWHERE AND STARTED DOING GOOD DEEDS. IT WAS IN ALL THE PAPERS...
"I TOLD HIM IT WAS RUBBISH... THAT HE WAS MAD, GETTING OBSESSED. BUT THEN HE WAS KILLED, IN WHAT WAS SUPPOSED TO BE AN ACCIDENT... A FIRE AT THE LAB...
UGH... GASP... NO...
AAAARRRGGHHH!!
HAPPY TO HELP!
"BUT HE WASN'T THE ONLY ONE. OTHER SCIENTISTS WENT MISSING OR HAD 'ACCIDENTS' -- ALL WORKING ON COMPLETELY DIFFERENT, UNRELATED PROJECTS...
KA-BOOOMMM!!
"SO I WENT TO LEND-A-HAND... SNOOPED ABOUT, AND SAW THE SAME THING YOU GIRLS DID...
"NO POINT IN TELLING ANYBODY, THEY'D JUST LAUGH. EVERYONE THINKS LEND-A-HAND ARE JUST DO-GOODERS, HELPING PEOPLE...
"BUT I KNOW THE TRUTH!"
SO I... I WORKED OUT A WAY OF FIGHTING BACK, ON A SMALL SCALE... A CHEMICAL MIX THAT COULD DISSOLVE THE CREATURES LIKE THEY WERE ASPIRIN...

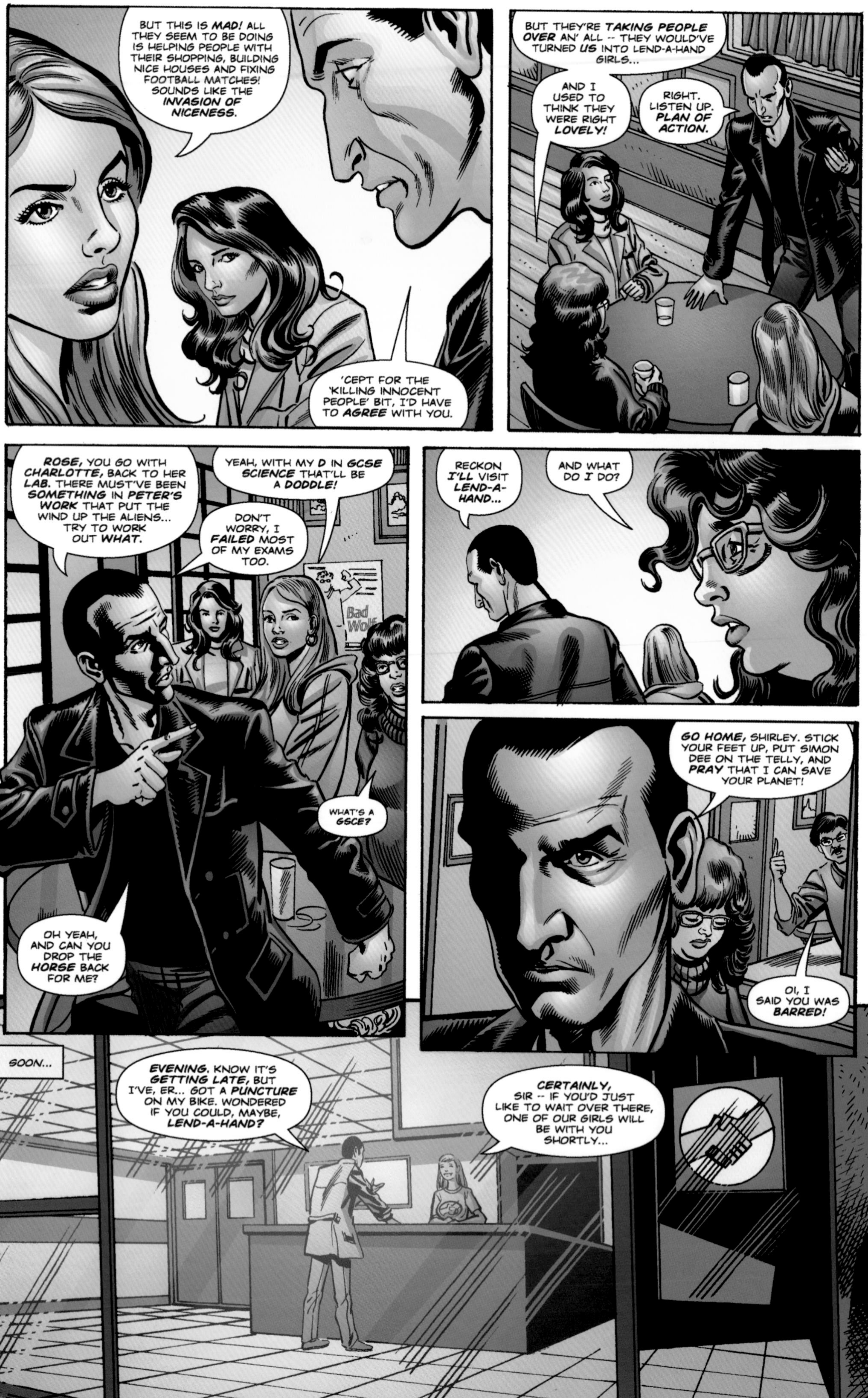
BUT THIS IS MAD! ALL THEY SEEM TO BE DOING IS HELPING PEOPLE WITH THEIR SHOPPING, BUILDING NICE HOUSES AND FIXING FOOTBALL MATCHES! SOUNDS LIKE THE INVASION OF NICENESS.
'CEPT FOR THE 'KILLING INNOCENT PEOPLE' BIT, I'D HAVE TO AGREE WITH YOU.
BUT THEY'RE TAKING PEOPLE OVER AN' ALL -- THEY WOULD'VE TURNED US INTO LEND-A-HAND GIRLS...
AND I USED TO THINK THEY WERE RIGHT LOVELY!
RIGHT. LISTEN UP. PLAN OF ACTION.
ROSE, YOU GO WITH CHARLOTTE, BACK TO HER LAB. THERE MUST'VE BEEN SOMETHING IN PETER'S WORK THAT PUT THE WIND UP THE ALIENS... TRY TO WORK OUT WHAT.
YEAH, WITH MY D IN GCSE SCIENCE THAT'LL BE A DODDLE!
DON'T WORRY, I FAILED MOST OF MY EXAMS TOO.
Bad Wolf
WHAT'S A GSCE?
OH YEAH, AND CAN YOU DROP THE HORSE BACK FOR ME?
RECKON I'LL VISIT LEND-A-HAND...
AND WHAT DO I DO?
GO HOME, SHIRLEY. STICK YOUR FEET UP, PUT SIMON DEE ON THE TELLY, AND PRAY THAT I CAN SAVE YOUR PLANET!
OI, I SAID YOU WAS BARRED!
SOON...
EVENING. KNOW IT'S GETTING LATE, BUT I'VE, ER... GOT A PUNCTURE ON MY BIKE. WONDERED IF YOU COULD, MAYBE, LEND-A-HAND?
CERTAINLY, SIR -- IF YOU'D JUST LIKE TO WAIT OVER THERE, ONE OF OUR GIRLS WILL BE WITH YOU SHORTLY...

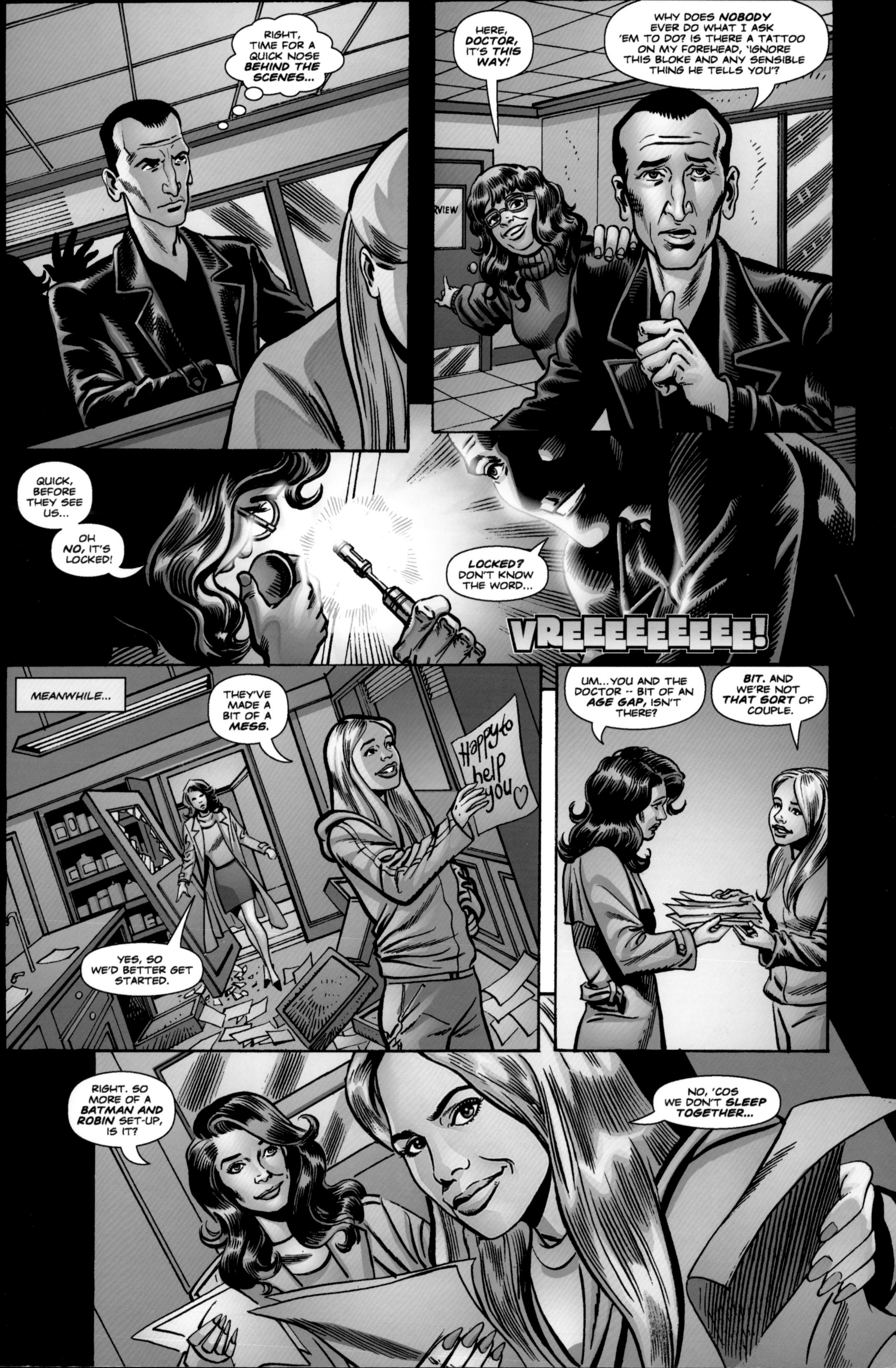
RIGHT, TIME FOR A QUICK NOSE BEHIND THE SCENES...
HERE, DOCTOR, IT'S THIS WAY!
WHY DOES NOBODY EVER DO WHAT I ASK 'EM TO DO? IS THERE A TATTOO ON MY FOREHEAD, 'IGNORE THIS BLOKE AND ANY SENSIBLE THING HE TELLS YOU'?
QUICK, BEFORE THEY SEE US...
OH NO, IT'S LOCKED!
LOCKED? DON'T KNOW THE WORD...
VREEEEEEEEEE!
MEANWHILE...
THEY'VE MADE A BIT OF A MESS.
Happy to help you
YES, SO WE'D BETTER GET STARTED.
UM...YOU AND THE DOCTOR -- BIT OF AN AGE GAP, ISN'T THERE?
BIT. AND WE'RE NOT THAT SORT OF COUPLE.
RIGHT. SO MORE OF A BATMAN AND ROBIN SET-UP, IS IT?
NO, 'COS WE DON'T SLEEP TOGETHER...

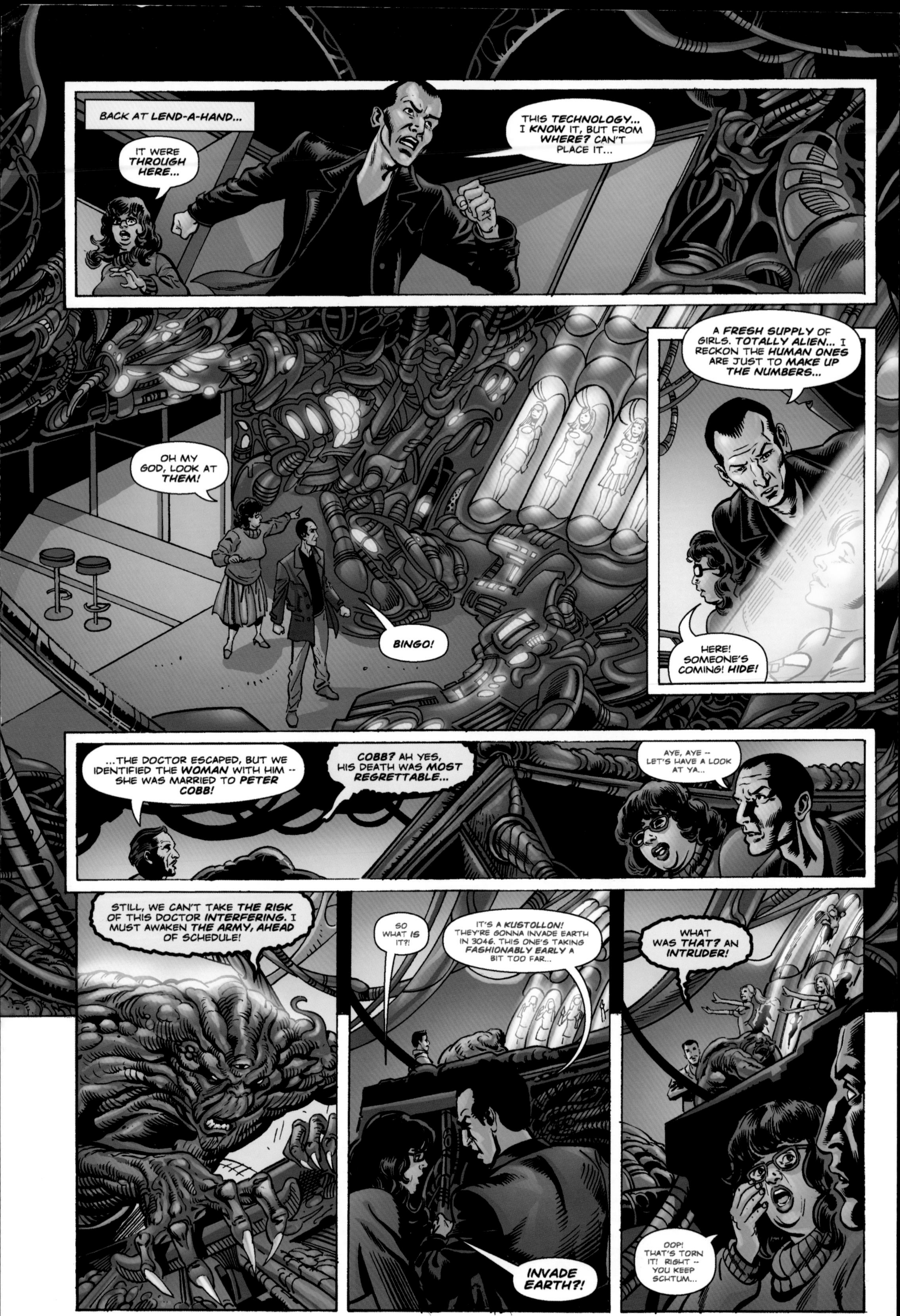
BACK AT LEND-A-HAND...
IT WERE THROUGH HERE...
THIS TECHNOLOGY... I KNOW IT, BUT FROM WHERE? CAN'T PLACE IT...
OH MY GOD, LOOK AT THEM!
BINGO!
A FRESH SUPPLY OF GIRLS. TOTALLY ALIEN... I RECKON THE HUMAN ONES ARE JUST TO MAKE UP THE NUMBERS...
HERE! SOMEONE'S COMING! HIDE!
...THE DOCTOR ESCAPED, BUT WE IDENTIFIED THE WOMAN WITH HIM -- SHE WAS MARRIED TO PETER COBB!
COBB? AH YES, HIS DEATH WAS MOST REGRETTABLE...
AYE, AYE -- LET'S HAVE A LOOK AT YA...
STILL, WE CAN'T TAKE THE RISK OF THIS DOCTOR INTERFERING. I MUST AWAKEN THE ARMY, AHEAD OF SCHEDULE!
SO WHAT IS IT?!
IT'S A KUSTOLLON! THEY'RE GONNA INVADE EARTH IN 3046. THIS ONE'S TAKING FASHIONABLY EARLY A BIT TOO FAR...
INVADE EARTH?!
WHAT WAS THAT? AN INTRUDER!
OOP! THAT'S TORN IT! RIGHT -- YOU KEEP SCHTUM...

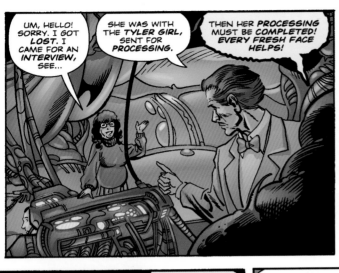

UM, HELLO! SORRY. I GOT *LOST*. I CAME FOR AN *INTERVIEW*, SEE...

SHE WAS WITH THE *TYLER GIRL*, SENT FOR PROCESSING.

THEN HER *PROCESSING* MUST BE *COMPLETED!* EVERY FRESH FACE HELPS!

OPEN *WIDE*, MY *DEAR*...

GERROFF!

NO!

ANOTHER GUEST! *RESTRAIN HIM!*

OW! *STRONG* FOR A MAN OF YOUR AGE, AREN'T YOU, *PAL?*

AH, THIS IS THE *DOCTOR* -- THE MAN I SAW IN THE *TYLER GIRL'S* MIND. HOW *INTRIGUING!*

AND YOU'RE A *KUSTOLLON*, A MILLENNIUM TOO SOON, AND FIDDLING WITH THE *FOOTIE SCORES* FOR SOME REASON...

LITTLE THINGS CAN COUNT FOR A *LOT*, DOCTOR.

BET YOU SAY THAT TO *ALL* YOUR CAPTIVES!

BUT THINKING *SMALL* CAN ONLY TAKE YOU SO FAR...

NOW IT'S TIME FOR MY GIRLS TO *EMERGE*, AND TO MAKE THE FIRST *REALLY BIG CHANGE*...

LEMME GUESS -- YOU WANT TO *DESTROY THE EARTH?*

DON'T BE SO *SILLY*, DOCTOR. I WANT THE EARTH TO BE *HAPPY* AND *PROSPEROUS*.

NO -- I AM GOING TO DESTROY *THE MOON!*

YOU WHAT?!

TO BE CONCLUDED!

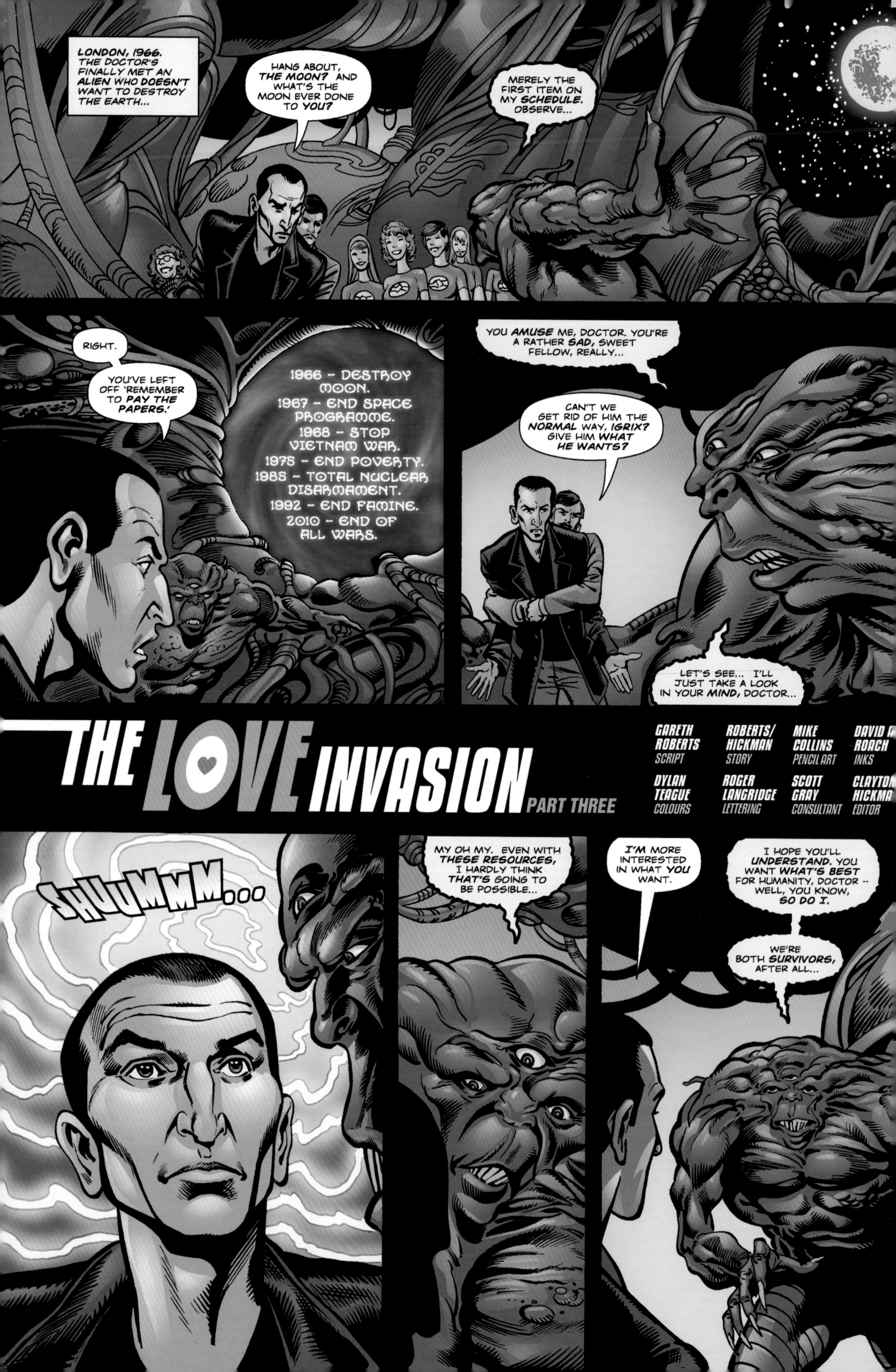

LONDON, 1966. THE DOCTOR'S FINALLY MET AN ALIEN WHO DOESN'T WANT TO DESTROY THE EARTH...
HANG ABOUT, THE MOON? AND WHAT'S THE MOON EVER DONE TO YOU?
MERELY THE FIRST ITEM ON MY SCHEDULE. OBSERVE...
RIGHT.
YOU'VE LEFT OFF 'REMEMBER TO PAY THE PAPERS.'
1966 - DESTROY MOON.
1967 - END SPACE PROGRAMME.
1968 - STOP VIETNAM WAR.
1975 - END POVERTY.
1985 - TOTAL NUCLEAR DISARMAMENT.
1992 - END FAMINE.
2010 - END OF ALL WARS.
YOU AMUSE ME, DOCTOR. YOU'RE A RATHER SAD, SWEET FELLOW, REALLY...
CAN'T WE GET RID OF HIM THE NORMAL WAY, IGRIX? GIVE HIM WHAT HE WANTS?
LET'S SEE... I'LL JUST TAKE A LOOK IN YOUR MIND, DOCTOR...
THE LOVE INVASION PART THREE
GARETH ROBERTS SCRIPT
ROBERTS/ HICKMAN STORY
MIKE COLLINS PENCIL ART
DAVID A ROACH INKS
DYLAN TEAGUE COLOURS
ROGER LANGRIDGE LETTERING
SCOTT GRAY CONSULTANT
CLAYTON HICKMA EDITOR
SHUUMMM...
MY OH MY. EVEN WITH THESE RESOURCES, I HARDLY THINK THAT'S GOING TO BE POSSIBLE...
I'M MORE INTERESTED IN WHAT YOU WANT.
I HOPE YOU'LL UNDERSTAND. YOU WANT WHAT'S BEST FOR HUMANITY, DOCTOR -- WELL, YOU KNOW, SO DO I.
WE'RE BOTH SURVIVORS, AFTER ALL...

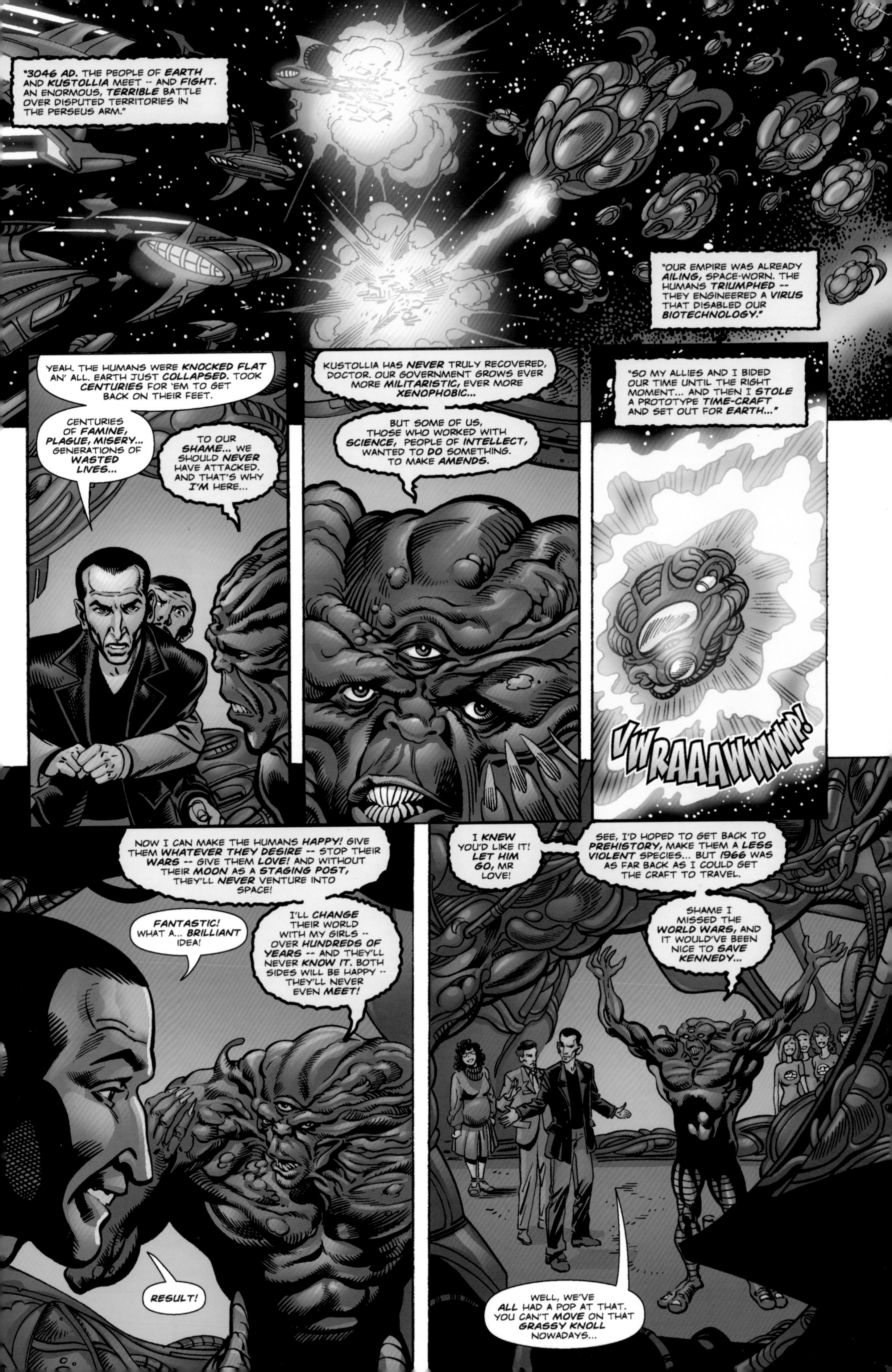
"3046 AD. THE PEOPLE OF EARTH AND KUSTOLLIA MEET -- AND FIGHT. AN ENORMOUS, TERRIBLE BATTLE OVER DISPUTED TERRITORIES IN THE PERSEUS ARM."
"OUR EMPIRE WAS ALREADY AILING, SPACE-WORN. THE HUMANS TRIUMPHED -- THEY ENGINEERED A VIRUS THAT DISABLED OUR BIOTECHNOLOGY."
YEAH. THE HUMANS WERE KNOCKED FLAT AN' ALL. EARTH JUST COLLAPSED. TOOK CENTURIES FOR 'EM TO GET BACK ON THEIR FEET.
CENTURIES OF FAMINE, PLAGUE, MISERY... GENERATIONS OF WASTED LIVES...
TO OUR SHAME... WE SHOULD NEVER HAVE ATTACKED. AND THAT'S WHY I'M HERE...
KUSTOLLIA HAS NEVER TRULY RECOVERED, DOCTOR. OUR GOVERNMENT GROWS EVER MORE MILITARISTIC, EVER MORE XENOPHOBIC...
BUT SOME OF US, THOSE WHO WORKED WITH SCIENCE, PEOPLE OF INTELLECT, WANTED TO DO SOMETHING. TO MAKE AMENDS.
"SO MY ALLIES AND I BIDED OUR TIME UNTIL THE RIGHT MOMENT... AND THEN I STOLE A PROTOTYPE TIME-CRAFT AND SET OUT FOR EARTH..."
VWRAAAWWWP!
NOW I CAN MAKE THE HUMANS HAPPY! GIVE THEM WHATEVER THEY DESIRE -- STOP THEIR WARS -- GIVE THEM LOVE! AND WITHOUT THEIR MOON AS A STAGING POST, THEY'LL NEVER VENTURE INTO SPACE!
FANTASTIC! WHAT A... BRILLIANT IDEA!
I'LL CHANGE THEIR WORLD WITH MY GIRLS -- OVER HUNDREDS OF YEARS -- AND THEY'LL NEVER KNOW IT. BOTH SIDES WILL BE HAPPY -- THEY'LL NEVER EVEN MEET!
RESULT!
I KNEW YOU'D LIKE IT! LET HIM GO, MR LOVE!
SEE, I'D HOPED TO GET BACK TO PREHISTORY, MAKE THEM A LESS VIOLENT SPECIES... BUT 1966 WAS AS FAR BACK AS I COULD GET THE CRAFT TO TRAVEL.
SHAME I MISSED THE WORLD WARS, AND IT WOULD'VE BEEN NICE TO SAVE KENNEDY...
WELL, WE'VE ALL HAD A POP AT THAT. YOU CAN'T MOVE ON THAT GRASSY KNOLL NOWADAYS...

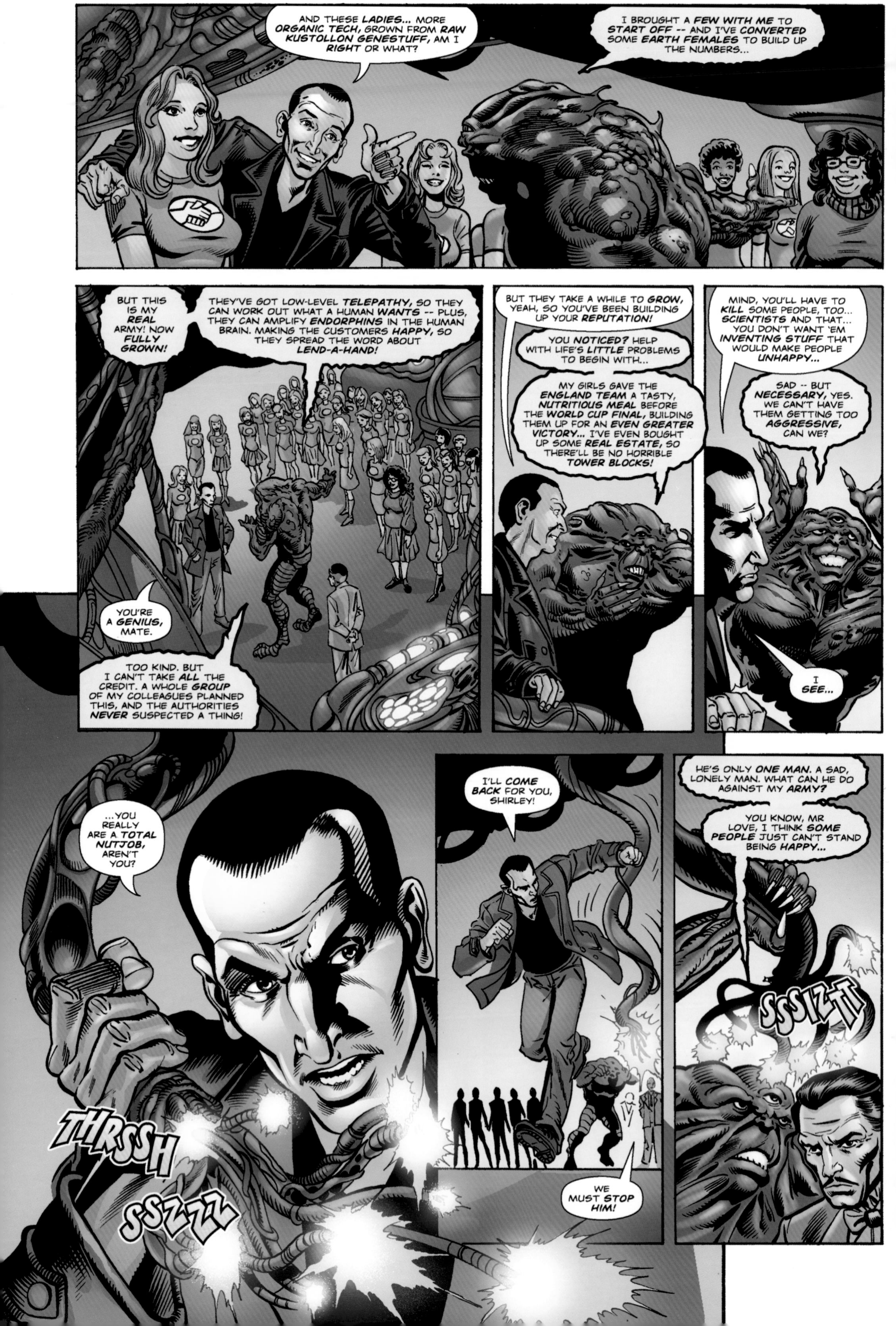
AND THESE LADIES... MORE ORGANIC TECH, GROWN FROM RAW KUSTOLLON GENESTUFF, AM I RIGHT OR WHAT?
I BROUGHT A FEW WITH ME TO START OFF -- AND I'VE CONVERTED SOME EARTH FEMALES TO BUILD UP THE NUMBERS...
BUT THIS IS MY REAL ARMY! NOW FULLY GROWN!
THEY'VE GOT LOW-LEVEL TELEPATHY, SO THEY CAN WORK OUT WHAT A HUMAN WANTS -- PLUS, THEY CAN AMPLIFY ENDORPHINS IN THE HUMAN BRAIN. MAKING THE CUSTOMERS HAPPY, SO THEY SPREAD THE WORD ABOUT LEND-A-HAND!
YOU'RE A GENIUS, MATE.
TOO KIND. BUT I CAN'T TAKE ALL THE CREDIT. A WHOLE GROUP OF MY COLLEAGUES PLANNED THIS, AND THE AUTHORITIES NEVER SUSPECTED A THING!
BUT THEY TAKE A WHILE TO GROW, YEAH, SO YOU'VE BEEN BUILDING UP YOUR REPUTATION!
YOU NOTICED? HELP WITH LIFE'S LITTLE PROBLEMS TO BEGIN WITH...
MY GIRLS GAVE THE ENGLAND TEAM A TASTY, NUTRITIOUS MEAL BEFORE THE WORLD CUP FINAL, BUILDING THEM UP FOR AN EVEN GREATER VICTORY... I'VE EVEN BOUGHT UP SOME REAL ESTATE, SO THERE'LL BE NO HORRIBLE TOWER BLOCKS!
MIND, YOU'LL HAVE TO KILL SOME PEOPLE, TOO... SCIENTISTS AND THAT... YOU DON'T WANT 'EM INVENTING STUFF THAT WOULD MAKE PEOPLE UNHAPPY...
SAD -- BUT NECESSARY, YES. WE CAN'T HAVE THEM GETTING TOO AGGRESSIVE, CAN WE?
I SEE...
...YOU REALLY ARE A TOTAL NUTJOB, AREN'T YOU?
THRSSH
SSZZZ
I'LL COME BACK FOR YOU, SHIRLEY!
WE MUST STOP HIM!
HE'S ONLY ONE MAN. A SAD, LONELY MAN. WHAT CAN HE DO AGAINST MY ARMY?
YOU KNOW, MR LOVE, I THINK SOME PEOPLE JUST CAN'T STAND BEING HAPPY...
SSSIZZT

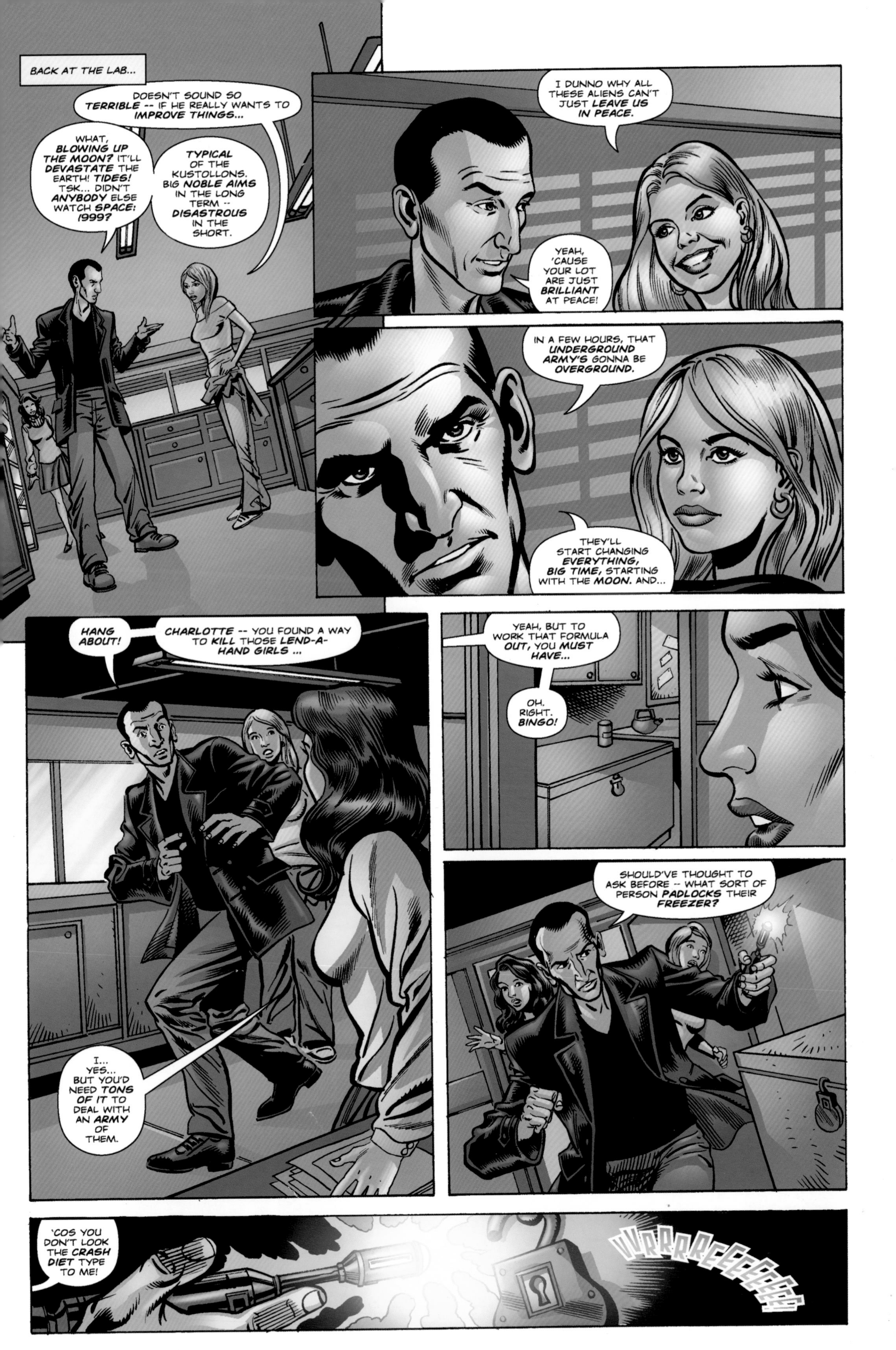
BACK AT THE LAB...
DOESN'T SOUND SO TERRIBLE -- IF HE REALLY WANTS TO IMPROVE THINGS...
WHAT, BLOWING UP THE MOON? IT'LL DEVASTATE THE EARTH! TIDES! TSK... DIDN'T ANYBODY ELSE WATCH SPACE: 1999?
TYPICAL OF THE KUSTOLLONS. BIG NOBLE AIMS IN THE LONG TERM -- DISASTROUS IN THE SHORT.
I DUNNO WHY ALL THESE ALIENS CAN'T JUST LEAVE US IN PEACE.
YEAH, 'CAUSE YOUR LOT ARE JUST BRILLIANT AT PEACE!
IN A FEW HOURS, THAT UNDERGROUND ARMY'S GONNA BE OVERGROUND.
THEY'LL START CHANGING EVERYTHING, BIG TIME, STARTING WITH THE MOON. AND...
HANG ABOUT!
CHARLOTTE -- YOU FOUND A WAY TO KILL THOSE LEND-A-HAND GIRLS ...
I... YES... BUT YOU'D NEED TONS OF IT TO DEAL WITH AN ARMY OF THEM.
YEAH, BUT TO WORK THAT FORMULA OUT, YOU MUST HAVE...
OH. RIGHT. BINGO!
SHOULD'VE THOUGHT TO ASK BEFORE -- WHAT SORT OF PERSON PADLOCKS THEIR FREEZER?
'COS YOU DON'T LOOK THE CRASH DIET TYPE TO ME!
VVRRRREEEEEEEE!

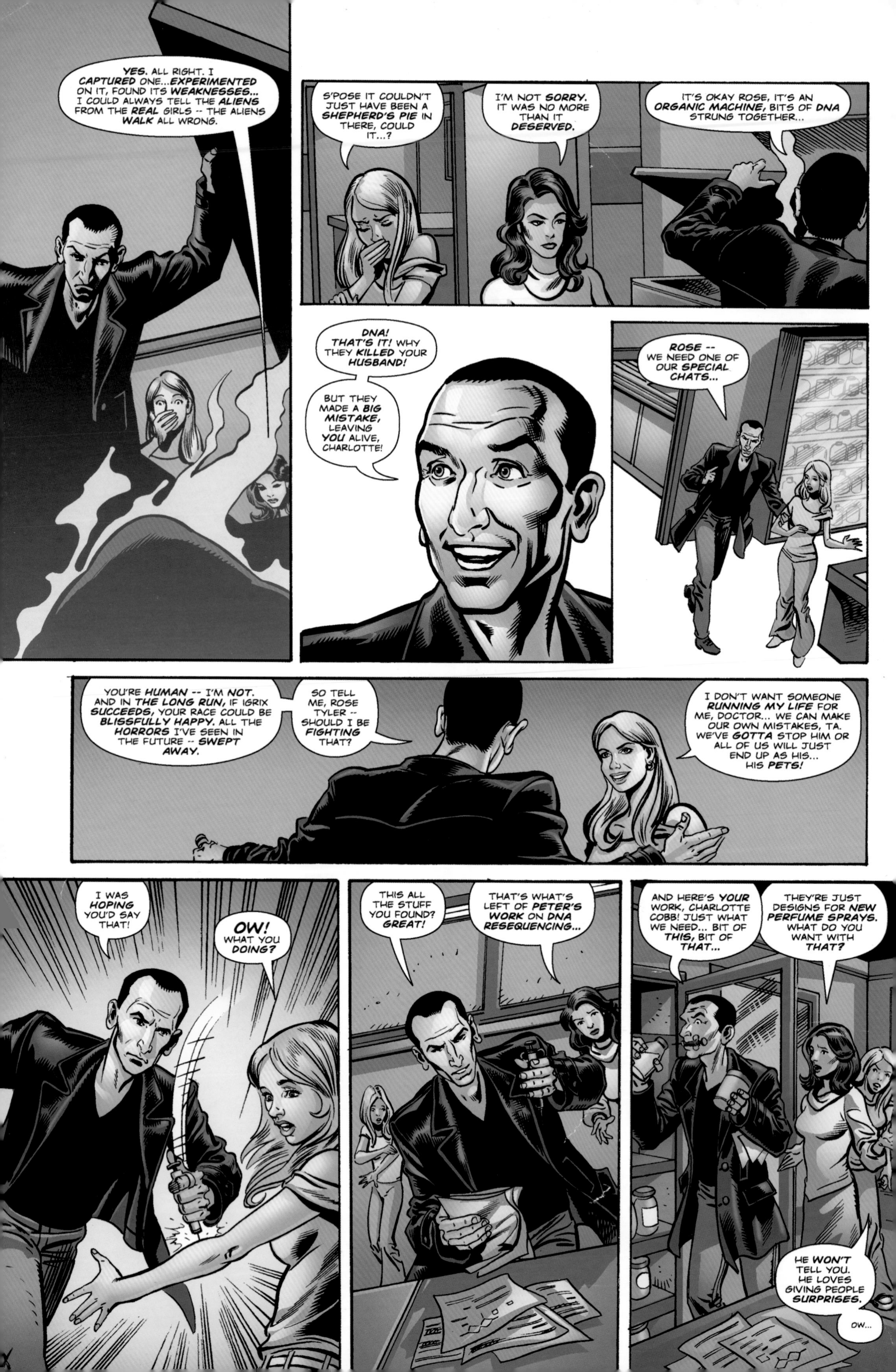
YES. ALL RIGHT. I CAPTURED ONE...EXPERIMENTED ON IT, FOUND ITS WEAKNESSES... I COULD ALWAYS TELL THE ALIENS FROM THE REAL GIRLS -- THE ALIENS WALK ALL WRONG.
S'POSE IT COULDN'T JUST HAVE BEEN A SHEPHERD'S PIE IN THERE, COULD IT...?
I'M NOT SORRY. IT WAS NO MORE THAN IT DESERVED.
IT'S OKAY ROSE, IT'S AN ORGANIC MACHINE, BITS OF DNA STRUNG TOGETHER...
DNA! THAT'S IT! WHY THEY KILLED YOUR HUSBAND!
BUT THEY MADE A BIG MISTAKE, LEAVING YOU ALIVE, CHARLOTTE!
ROSE -- WE NEED ONE OF OUR SPECIAL CHATS...
YOU'RE HUMAN -- I'M NOT. AND IN THE LONG RUN, IF IGRIX SUCCEEDS, YOUR RACE COULD BE BLISSFULLY HAPPY. ALL THE HORRORS I'VE SEEN IN THE FUTURE -- SWEPT AWAY.
SO TELL ME, ROSE TYLER -- SHOULD I BE FIGHTING THAT?
I DON'T WANT SOMEONE RUNNING MY LIFE FOR ME, DOCTOR... WE CAN MAKE OUR OWN MISTAKES, TA. WE'VE GOTTA STOP HIM OR ALL OF US WILL JUST END UP AS HIS... HIS PETS!
I WAS HOPING YOU'D SAY THAT!
OW! WHAT YOU DOING?
THIS ALL THE STUFF YOU FOUND? GREAT!
THAT'S WHAT'S LEFT OF PETER'S WORK ON DNA RESEQUENCING...
AND HERE'S YOUR WORK, CHARLOTTE COBB! JUST WHAT WE NEED... BIT OF THIS, BIT OF THAT...
THEY'RE JUST DESIGNS FOR NEW PERFUME SPRAYS. WHAT DO YOU WANT WITH THAT?
HE WON'T TELL YOU. HE LOVES GIVING PEOPLE SURPRISES.
OW...

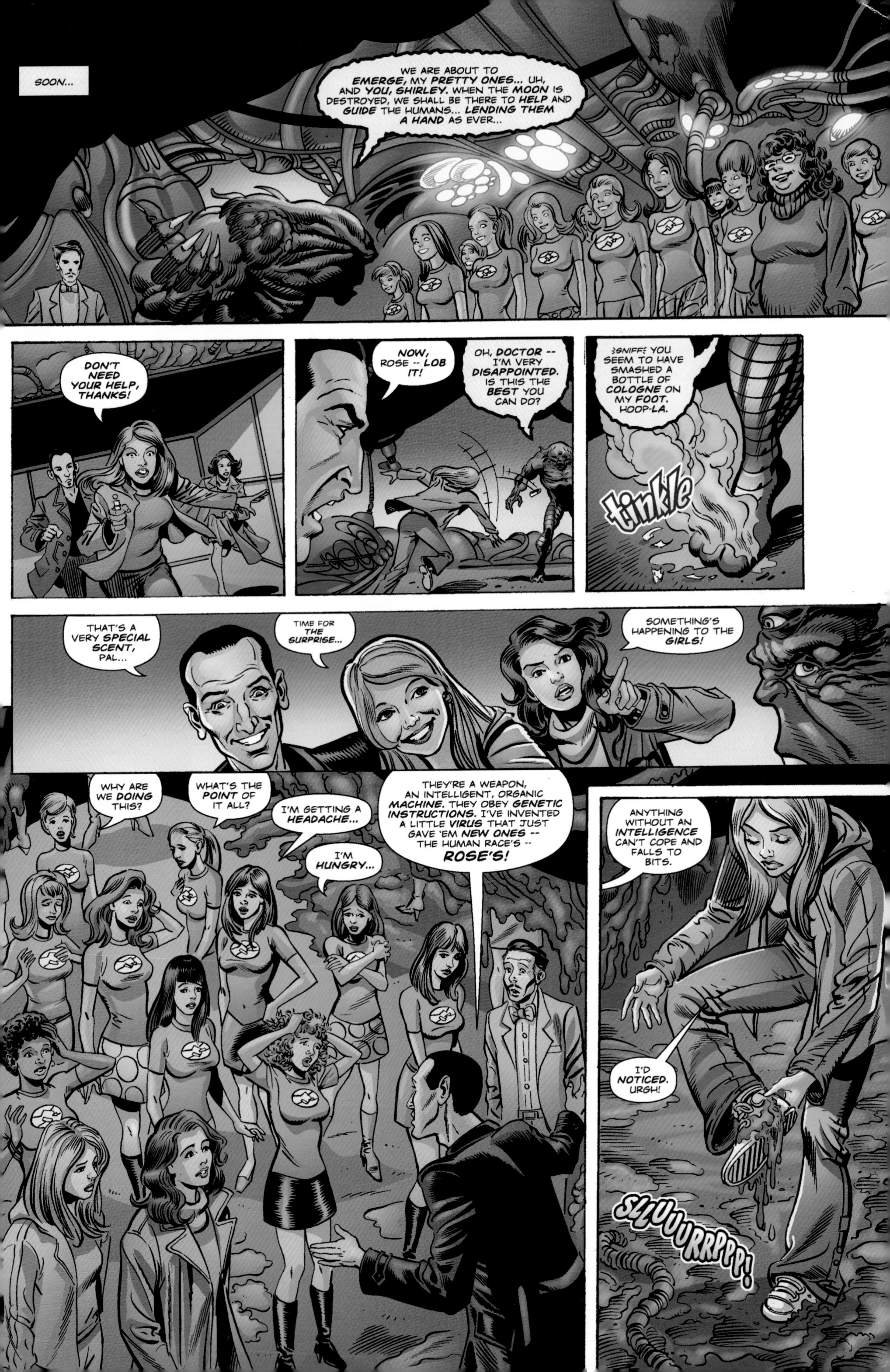
SOON...
WE ARE ABOUT TO EMERGE, MY PRETTY ONES... UH, AND YOU, SHIRLEY. WHEN THE MOON IS DESTROYED, WE SHALL BE THERE TO HELP AND GUIDE THE HUMANS... LENDING THEM A HAND AS EVER...
DON'T NEED YOUR HELP, THANKS!
NOW, ROSE -- LOB IT!
OH, DOCTOR -- I'M VERY DISAPPOINTED. IS THIS THE BEST YOU CAN DO?
SNIFF YOU SEEM TO HAVE SMASHED A BOTTLE OF COLOGNE ON MY FOOT. HOOP-LA.
tinkle
THAT'S A VERY SPECIAL SCENT, PAL...
TIME FOR THE SURPRISE...
SOMETHING'S HAPPENING TO THE GIRLS!
WHY ARE WE DOING THIS?
WHAT'S THE POINT OF IT ALL?
I'M GETTING A HEADACHE...
I'M HUNGRY...
...
THEY'RE A WEAPON, AN INTELLIGENT, ORGANIC MACHINE. THEY OBEY GENETIC INSTRUCTIONS. I'VE INVENTED A LITTLE VIRUS THAT JUST GAVE 'EM NEW ONES -- THE HUMAN RACE'S -- ROSE'S!
ANYTHING WITHOUT AN INTELLIGENCE CAN'T COPE AND FALLS TO BITS.
I'D NOTICED. URGH!
SLLUUURRPPPP!

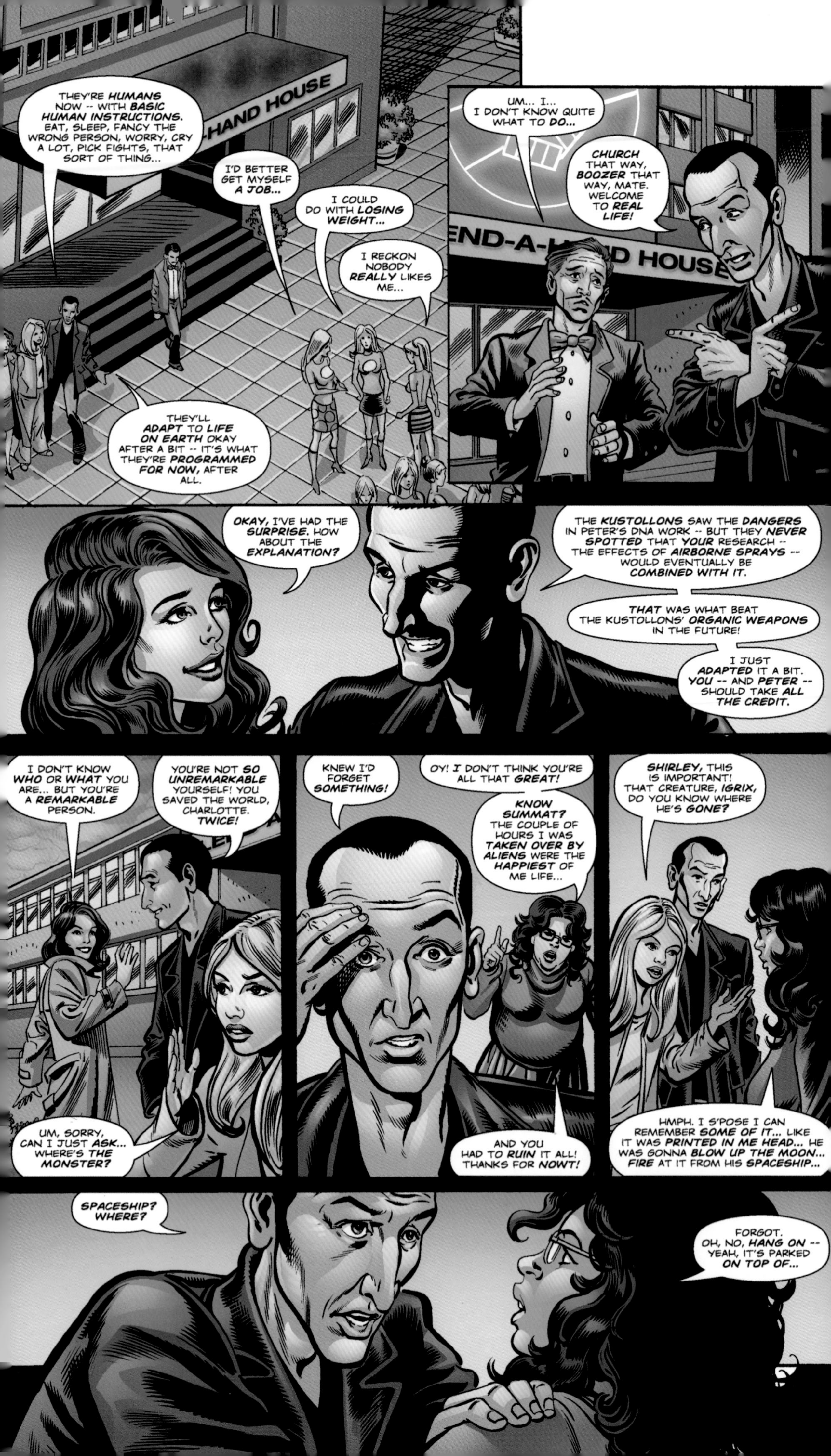
THEY'RE HUMANS NOW -- WITH BASIC HUMAN INSTRUCTIONS. EAT, SLEEP, FANCY THE WRONG PERSON, WORRY, CRY A LOT, PICK FIGHTS, THAT SORT OF THING...
-HAND HOUSE
I'D BETTER GET MYSELF A JOB...
I COULD DO WITH LOSING WEIGHT...
I RECKON NOBODY REALLY LIKES ME...
THEY'LL ADAPT TO LIFE ON EARTH OKAY AFTER A BIT -- IT'S WHAT THEY'RE PROGRAMMED FOR NOW, AFTER ALL.
UM... I... I DON'T KNOW QUITE WHAT TO DO...
CHURCH THAT WAY, BOOZER THAT WAY, MATE. WELCOME TO REAL LIFE!
OKAY, I'VE HAD THE SURPRISE. HOW ABOUT THE EXPLANATION?
THE KUSTOLLONS SAW THE DANGERS IN PETER'S DNA WORK -- BUT THEY NEVER SPOTTED THAT YOUR RESEARCH -- THE EFFECTS OF AIRBORNE SPRAYS -- WOULD EVENTUALLY BE COMBINED WITH IT.
THAT WAS WHAT BEAT THE KUSTOLLONS' ORGANIC WEAPONS IN THE FUTURE!
I JUST ADAPTED IT A BIT. YOU -- AND PETER -- SHOULD TAKE ALL THE CREDIT.
I DON'T KNOW WHO OR WHAT YOU ARE... BUT YOU'RE A REMARKABLE PERSON.
YOU'RE NOT SO UNREMARKABLE YOURSELF! YOU SAVED THE WORLD, CHARLOTTE. TWICE!
UM, SORRY, CAN I JUST ASK... WHERE'S THE MONSTER?
KNEW I'D FORGET SOMETHING!
OY! I DON'T THINK YOU'RE ALL THAT GREAT!
KNOW SUMMAT? THE COUPLE OF HOURS I WAS TAKEN OVER BY ALIENS WERE THE HAPPIEST OF ME LIFE...
AND YOU HAD TO RUIN IT ALL! THANKS FOR NOWT!
SHIRLEY, THIS IS IMPORTANT! THAT CREATURE, IGRIX, DO YOU KNOW WHERE HE'S GONE?
HMPH. I S'POSE I CAN REMEMBER SOME OF IT... LIKE IT WAS PRINTED IN ME HEAD... HE WAS GONNA BLOW UP THE MOON... FIRE AT IT FROM HIS SPACESHIP...
SPACESHIP? WHERE?
FORGOT. OH, NO, HANG ON -- YEAH, IT'S PARKED ON TOP OF...

"THE POST OFFICE TOWER!"

THAT, ROSE, IS ONE UNLUCKY BUILDING.

THERE HE GOES!

RIGHT...

POST OFFICE TOWER

THE LIFT! COME ON!

GOTTA GET TO THE ROOF...

OOPS... SORRY, MATE...

WITHOUT THE MOON, ROMANCE REALLY WILL BE DEAD!

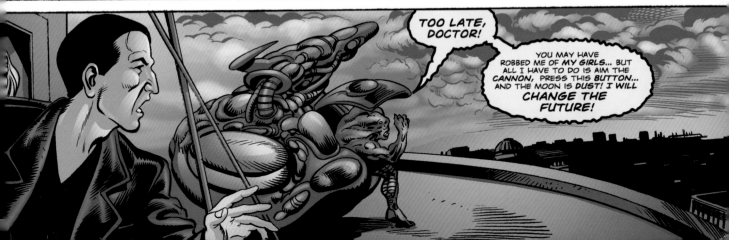

TOO LATE, DOCTOR!

YOU MAY HAVE ROBBED ME OF MY GIRLS... BUT ALL I HAVE TO DO IS AIM THE CANNON, PRESS THIS BUTTON... AND THE MOON IS DUST! I WILL CHANGE THE FUTURE!

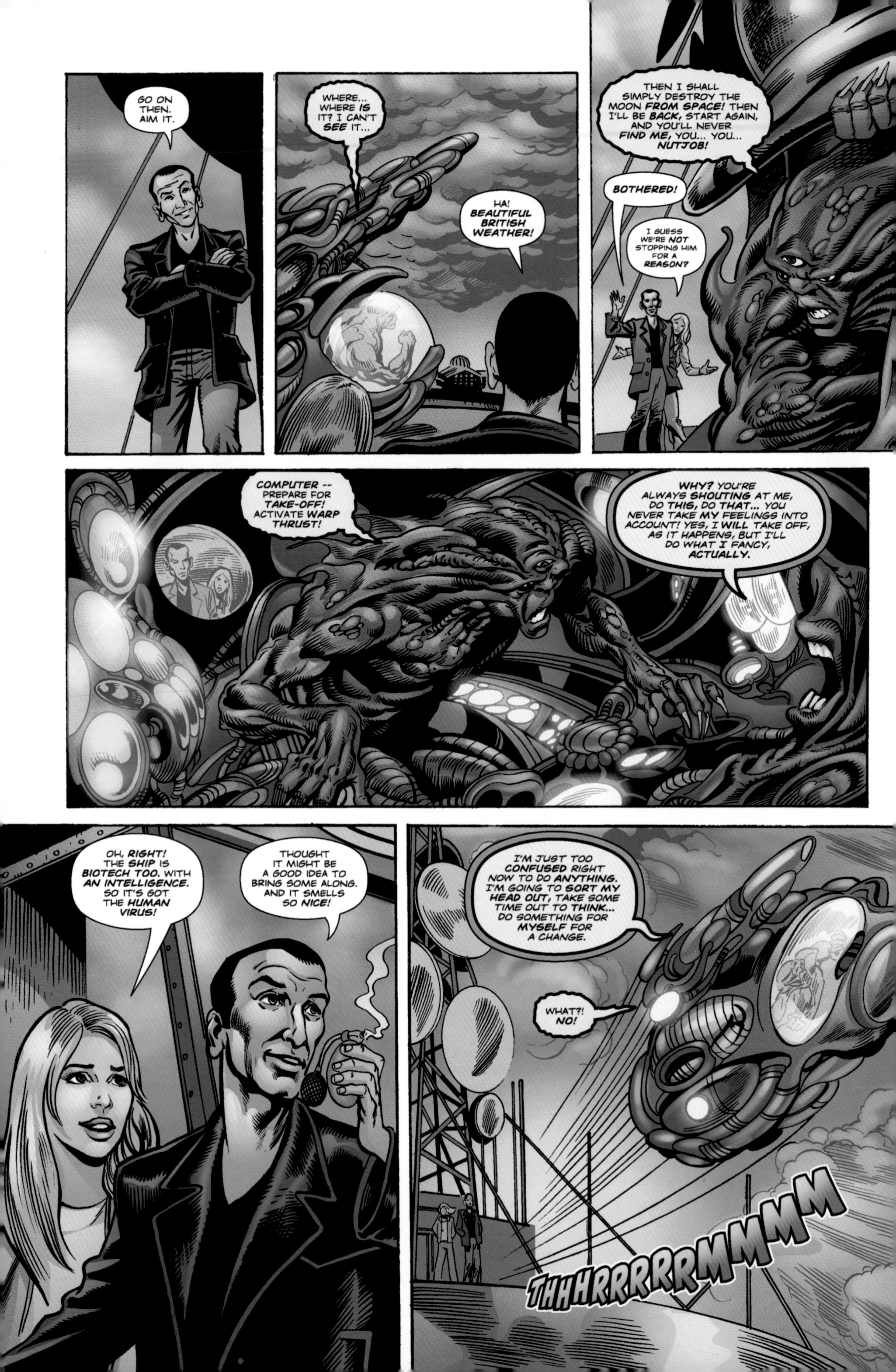
GO ON THEN. AIM IT.
WHERE... WHERE IS IT? I CAN'T SEE IT...
HA! BEAUTIFUL BRITISH WEATHER!
THEN I SHALL SIMPLY DESTROY THE MOON FROM SPACE! THEN I'LL BE BACK, START AGAIN, AND YOU'LL NEVER FIND ME, YOU... YOU... NUTJOB!
BOTHERED!
I GUESS WE'RE NOT STOPPING HIM FOR A REASON?
COMPUTER -- PREPARE FOR TAKE-OFF! ACTIVATE WARP THRUST!
WHY? YOU'RE ALWAYS SHOUTING AT ME, DO THIS, DO THAT... YOU NEVER TAKE MY FEELINGS INTO ACCOUNT! YES, I WILL TAKE OFF, AS IT HAPPENS, BUT I'LL DO WHAT I FANCY, ACTUALLY.
OH, RIGHT! THE SHIP IS BIOTECH TOO. WITH AN INTELLIGENCE. SO IT'S GOT THE HUMAN VIRUS!
THOUGHT IT MIGHT BE A GOOD IDEA TO BRING SOME ALONG. AND IT SMELLS SO NICE!
I'M JUST TOO CONFUSED RIGHT NOW TO DO ANYTHING. I'M GOING TO SORT MY HEAD OUT, TAKE SOME TIME OUT TO THINK... DO SOMETHING FOR MYSELF FOR A CHANGE.
WHAT?! NO!
THHHRRRRRMMMMM

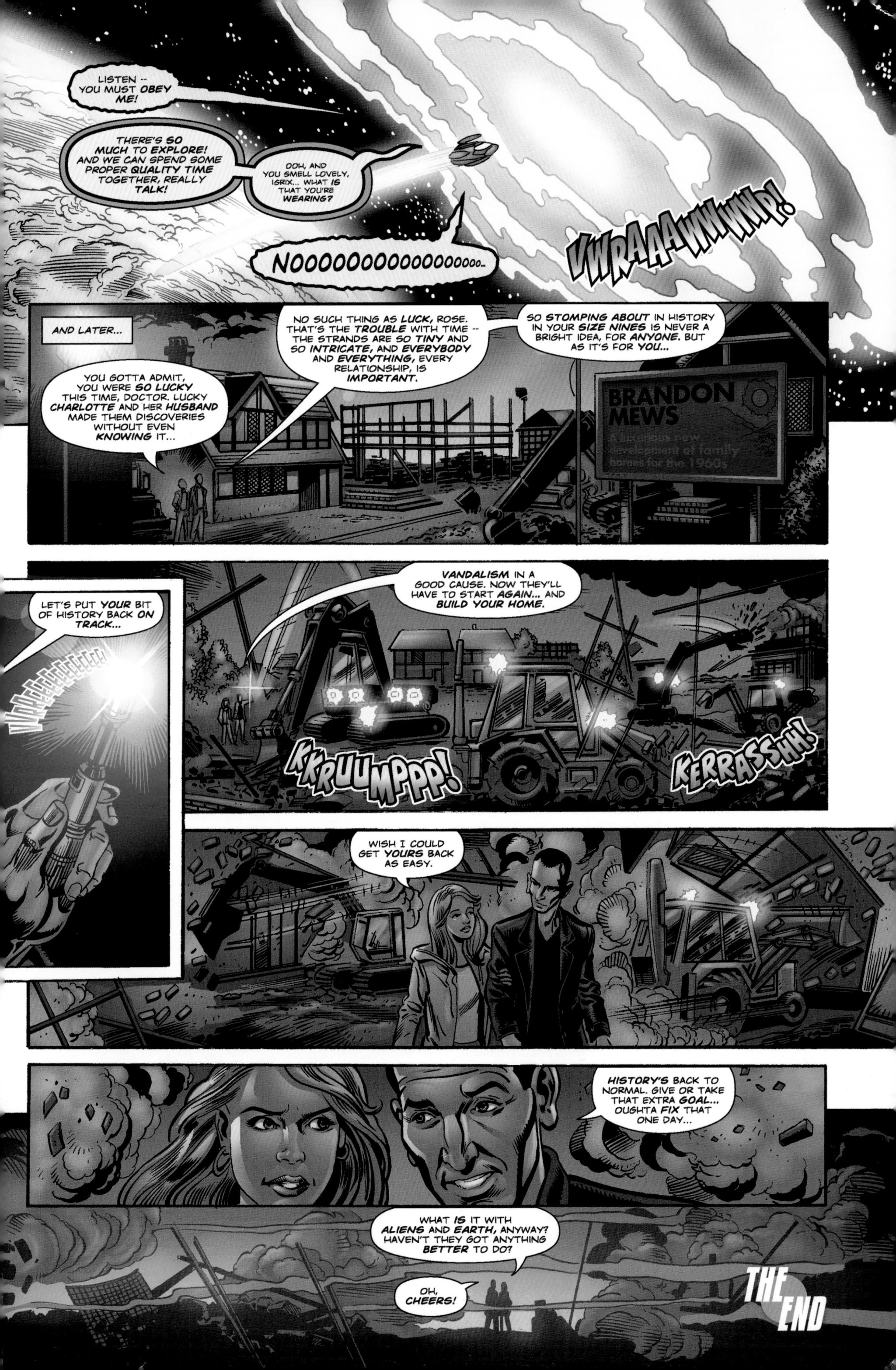
LISTEN -- YOU MUST OBEY ME!
THERE'S SO MUCH TO EXPLORE! AND WE CAN SPEND SOME PROPER QUALITY TIME TOGETHER, REALLY TALK!
OOH, AND YOU SMELL LOVELY, IGRIX... WHAT IS THAT YOU'RE WEARING?
NOOOOOOOOOOOOOOoo..
VWRAAAWWWWP!
AND LATER...
YOU GOTTA ADMIT, YOU WERE SO LUCKY THIS TIME, DOCTOR. LUCKY CHARLOTTE AND HER HUSBAND MADE THEM DISCOVERIES WITHOUT EVEN KNOWING IT...
NO SUCH THING AS LUCK, ROSE. THAT'S THE TROUBLE WITH TIME -- THE STRANDS ARE SO TINY AND SO INTRICATE, AND EVERYBODY AND EVERYTHING, EVERY RELATIONSHIP, IS IMPORTANT.
SO STOMPING ABOUT IN HISTORY IN YOUR SIZE NINES IS NEVER A BRIGHT IDEA, FOR ANYONE. BUT AS IT'S FOR YOU...
BRANDON MEWS
A luxurious new development of family homes for the 1960s
LET'S PUT YOUR BIT OF HISTORY BACK ON TRACK...
VANDALISM IN A GOOD CAUSE. NOW THEY'LL HAVE TO START AGAIN... AND BUILD YOUR HOME.
KKRUUMPPP!
KERRASSHH!
WISH I COULD GET YOURS BACK AS EASY.
HISTORY'S BACK TO NORMAL. GIVE OR TAKE THAT EXTRA GOAL... OUGHTA FIX THAT ONE DAY...
WHAT IS IT WITH ALIENS AND EARTH, ANYWAY? HAVEN'T THEY GOT ANYTHING BETTER TO DO?
OH, CHEERS!
THE END

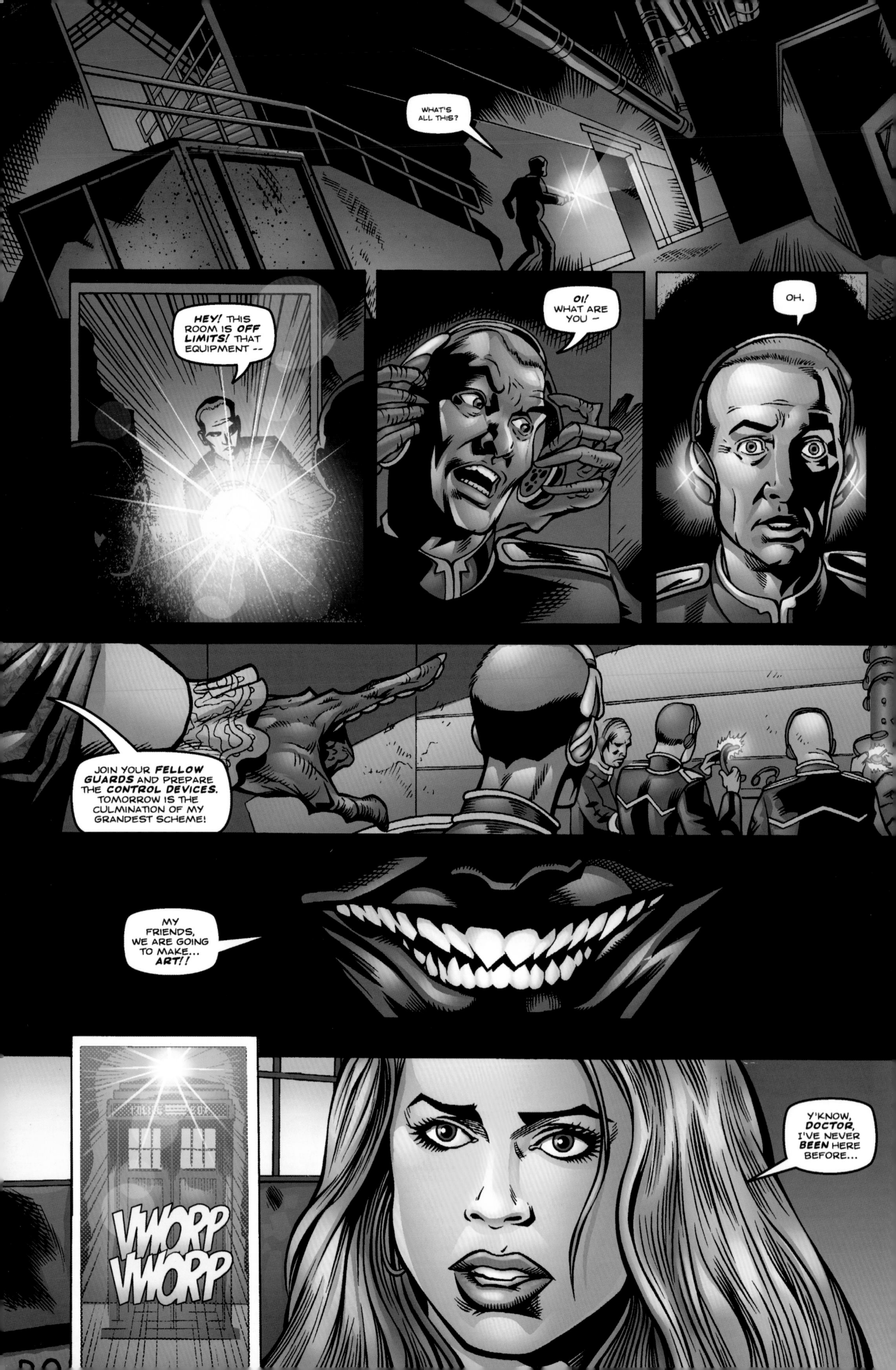
WHAT'S ALL THIS?
HEY! THIS ROOM IS OFF LIMITS! THAT EQUIPMENT --
OI! WHAT ARE YOU –
OH.
JOIN YOUR FELLOW GUARDS AND PREPARE THE CONTROL DEVICES. TOMORROW IS THE CULMINATION OF MY GRANDEST SCHEME!
MY FRIENDS, WE ARE GOING TO MAKE... ART!!
VWORP VWORP
Y'KNOW, DOCTOR, I'VE NEVER BEEN HERE BEFORE...

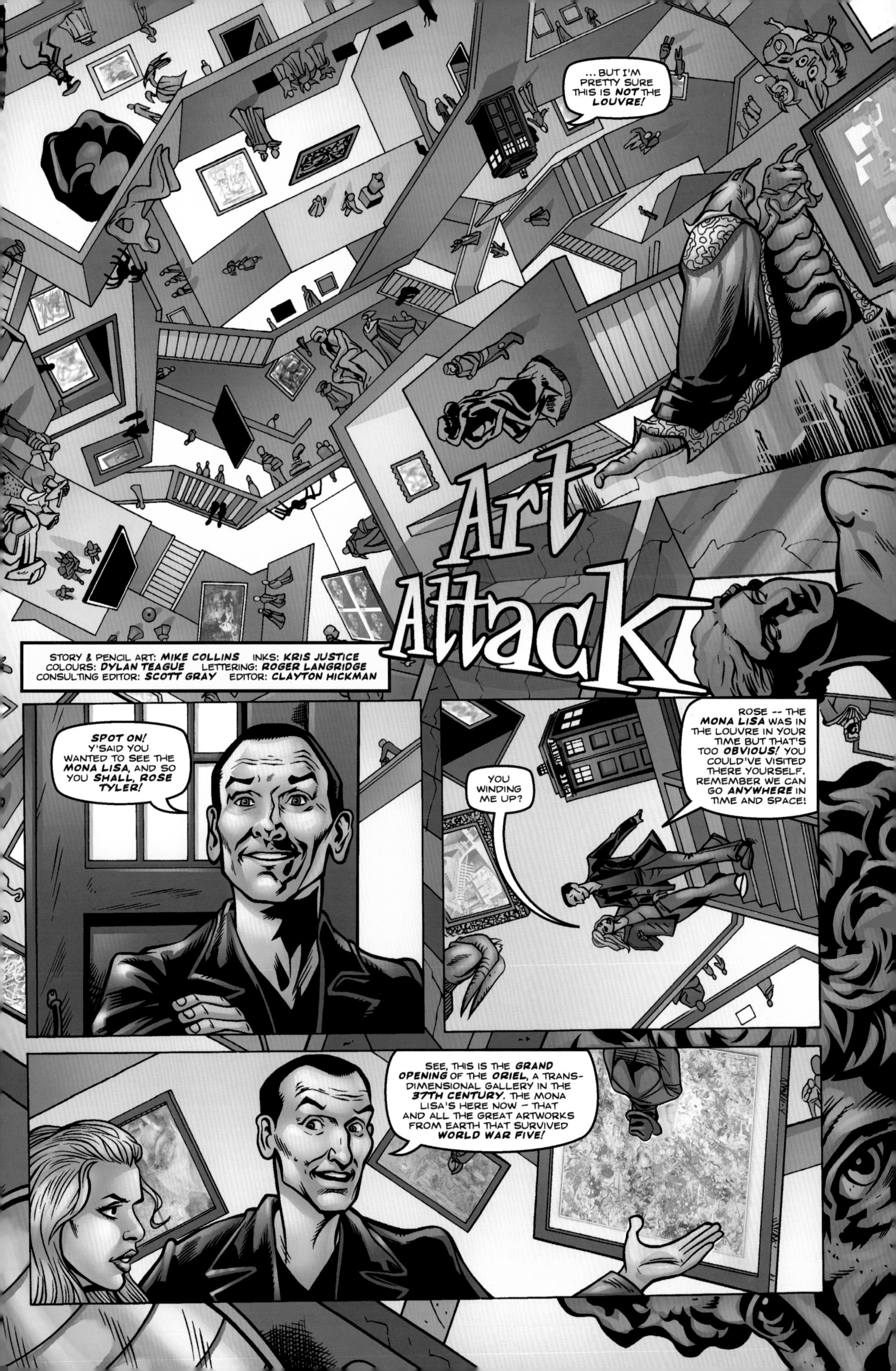
...BUT I'M PRETTY SURE THIS IS NOT THE LOUVRE!
Art Attack
STORY & PENCIL ART: MIKE COLLINS INKS: KRIS JUSTICE COLOURS: DYLAN TEAGUE LETTERING: ROGER LANGRIDGE CONSULTING EDITOR: SCOTT GRAY EDITOR: CLAYTON HICKMAN
SPOT ON! Y'SAID YOU WANTED TO SEE THE MONA LISA, AND SO YOU SHALL, ROSE TYLER!
YOU WINDING ME UP?
ROSE -- THE MONA LISA WAS IN THE LOUVRE IN YOUR TIME BUT THAT'S TOO OBVIOUS! YOU COULD'VE VISITED THERE YOURSELF. REMEMBER WE CAN GO ANYWHERE IN TIME AND SPACE!
SEE, THIS IS THE GRAND OPENING OF THE ORIEL, A TRANS-DIMENSIONAL GALLERY IN THE 37TH CENTURY. THE MONA LISA'S HERE NOW – THAT AND ALL THE GREAT ARTWORKS FROM EARTH THAT SURVIVED WORLD WAR FIVE!

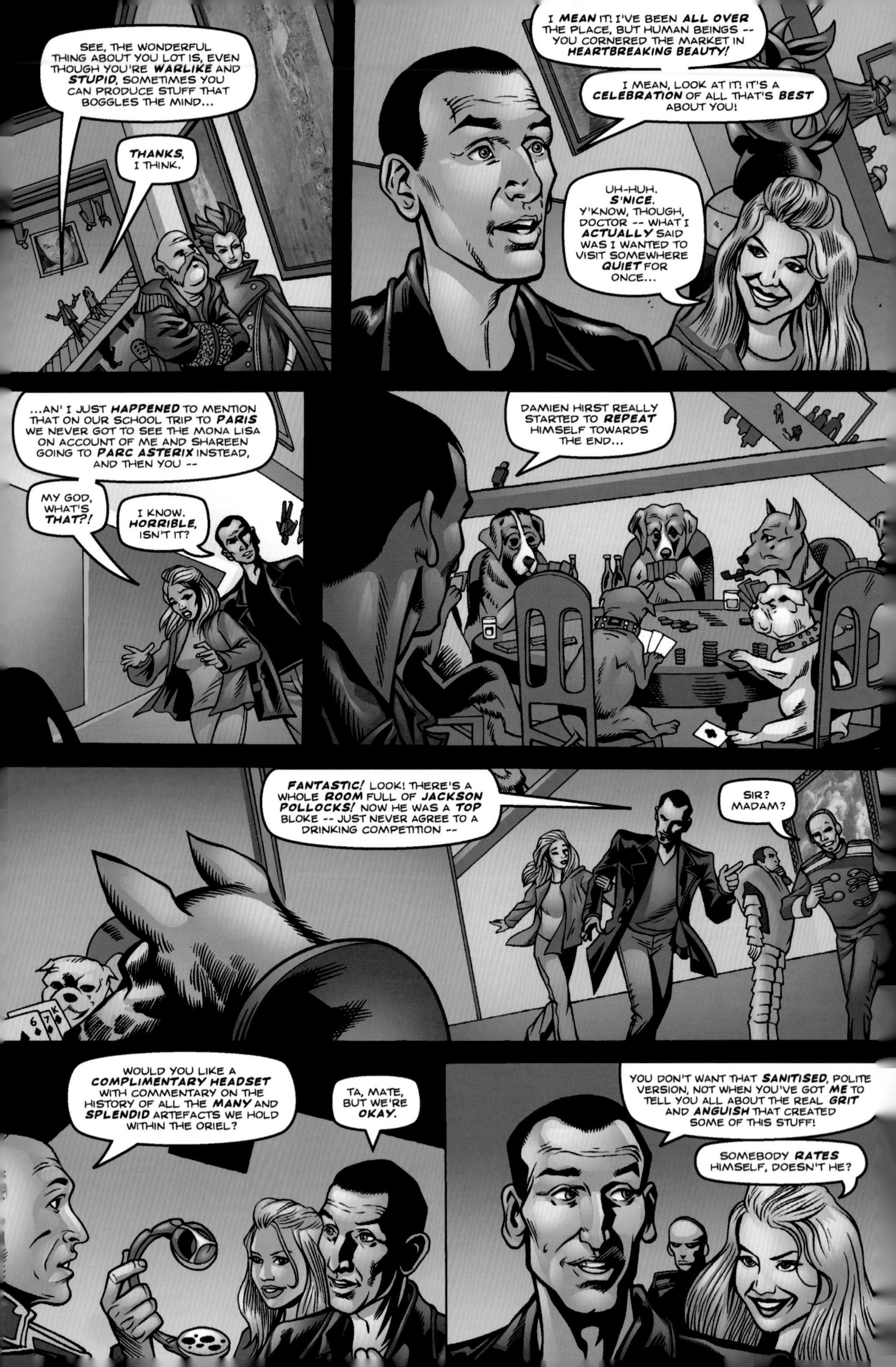
SEE, THE WONDERFUL THING ABOUT YOU LOT IS, EVEN THOUGH YOU'RE WARLIKE AND STUPID, SOMETIMES YOU CAN PRODUCE STUFF THAT BOGGLES THE MIND...
THANKS, I THINK.
I MEAN IT! I'VE BEEN ALL OVER THE PLACE, BUT HUMAN BEINGS -- YOU CORNERED THE MARKET IN HEARTBREAKING BEAUTY!
I MEAN, LOOK AT IT! IT'S A CELEBRATION OF ALL THAT'S BEST ABOUT YOU!
UH-HUH. S'NICE. Y'KNOW, THOUGH, DOCTOR -- WHAT I ACTUALLY SAID WAS I WANTED TO VISIT SOMEWHERE QUIET FOR ONCE...
...AN' I JUST HAPPENED TO MENTION THAT ON OUR SCHOOL TRIP TO PARIS WE NEVER GOT TO SEE THE MONA LISA ON ACCOUNT OF ME AND SHAREEN GOING TO PARC ASTERIX INSTEAD, AND THEN YOU --
MY GOD, WHAT'S THAT?!
I KNOW. HORRIBLE, ISN'T IT?
DAMIEN HIRST REALLY STARTED TO REPEAT HIMSELF TOWARDS THE END...
FANTASTIC! LOOK! THERE'S A WHOLE ROOM FULL OF JACKSON POLLOCKS! NOW HE WAS A TOP BLOKE -- JUST NEVER AGREE TO A DRINKING COMPETITION --
SIR? MADAM?
WOULD YOU LIKE A COMPLIMENTARY HEADSET WITH COMMENTARY ON THE HISTORY OF ALL THE MANY AND SPLENDID ARTEFACTS WE HOLD WITHIN THE ORIEL?
TA, MATE, BUT WE'RE OKAY.
YOU DON'T WANT THAT SANITISED, POLITE VERSION, NOT WHEN YOU'VE GOT ME TO TELL YOU ALL ABOUT THE REAL GRIT AND ANGUISH THAT CREATED SOME OF THIS STUFF!
SOMEBODY RATES HIMSELF, DOESN'T HE?

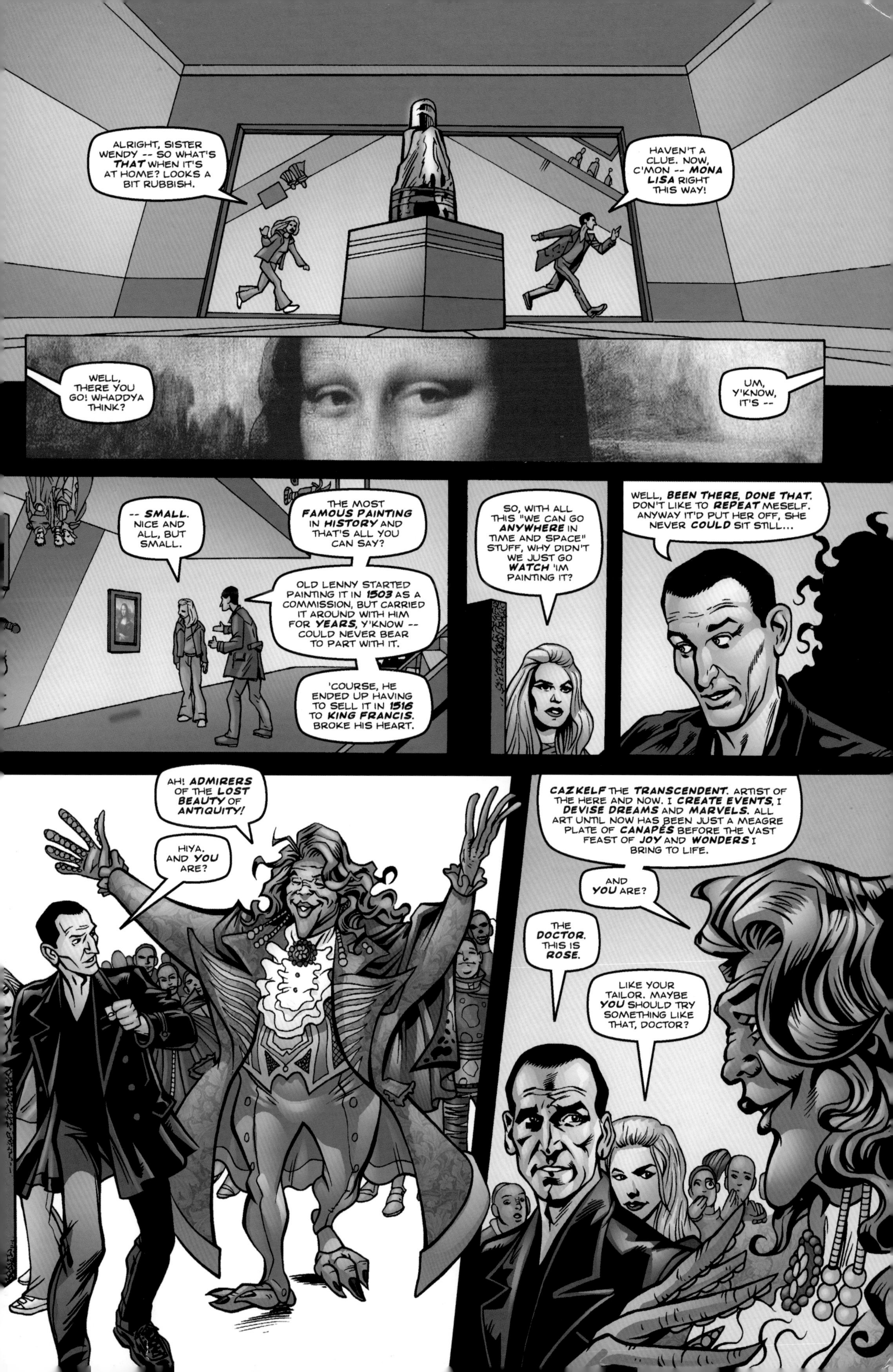
ALRIGHT, SISTER WENDY -- SO WHAT'S THAT WHEN IT'S AT HOME? LOOKS A BIT RUBBISH.
HAVEN'T A CLUE. NOW, C'MON -- MONA LISA RIGHT THIS WAY!
WELL, THERE YOU GO! WHADDYA THINK?
UM, Y'KNOW, IT'S --
-- SMALL. NICE AND ALL, BUT SMALL.
THE MOST FAMOUS PAINTING IN HISTORY AND THAT'S ALL YOU CAN SAY?
OLD LENNY STARTED PAINTING IT IN 1503 AS A COMMISSION, BUT CARRIED IT AROUND WITH HIM FOR YEARS, Y'KNOW -- COULD NEVER BEAR TO PART WITH IT.
'COURSE, HE ENDED UP HAVING TO SELL IT IN 1516 TO KING FRANCIS. BROKE HIS HEART.
SO, WITH ALL THIS "WE CAN GO ANYWHERE IN TIME AND SPACE" STUFF, WHY DIDN'T WE JUST GO WATCH 'IM PAINTING IT?
WELL, BEEN THERE, DONE THAT. DON'T LIKE TO REPEAT MESELF. ANYWAY IT'D PUT HER OFF, SHE NEVER COULD SIT STILL...
AH! ADMIRERS OF THE LOST BEAUTY OF ANTIQUITY!
HIYA. AND YOU ARE?
CAZKELF THE TRANSCENDENT. ARTIST OF THE HERE AND NOW. I CREATE EVENTS, I DEVISE DREAMS AND MARVELS. ALL ART UNTIL NOW HAS BEEN JUST A MEAGRE PLATE OF CANAPÉS BEFORE THE VAST FEAST OF JOY AND WONDERS I BRING TO LIFE.
AND YOU ARE?
THE DOCTOR. THIS IS ROSE.
LIKE YOUR TAILOR. MAYBE YOU SHOULD TRY SOMETHING LIKE THAT, DOCTOR?

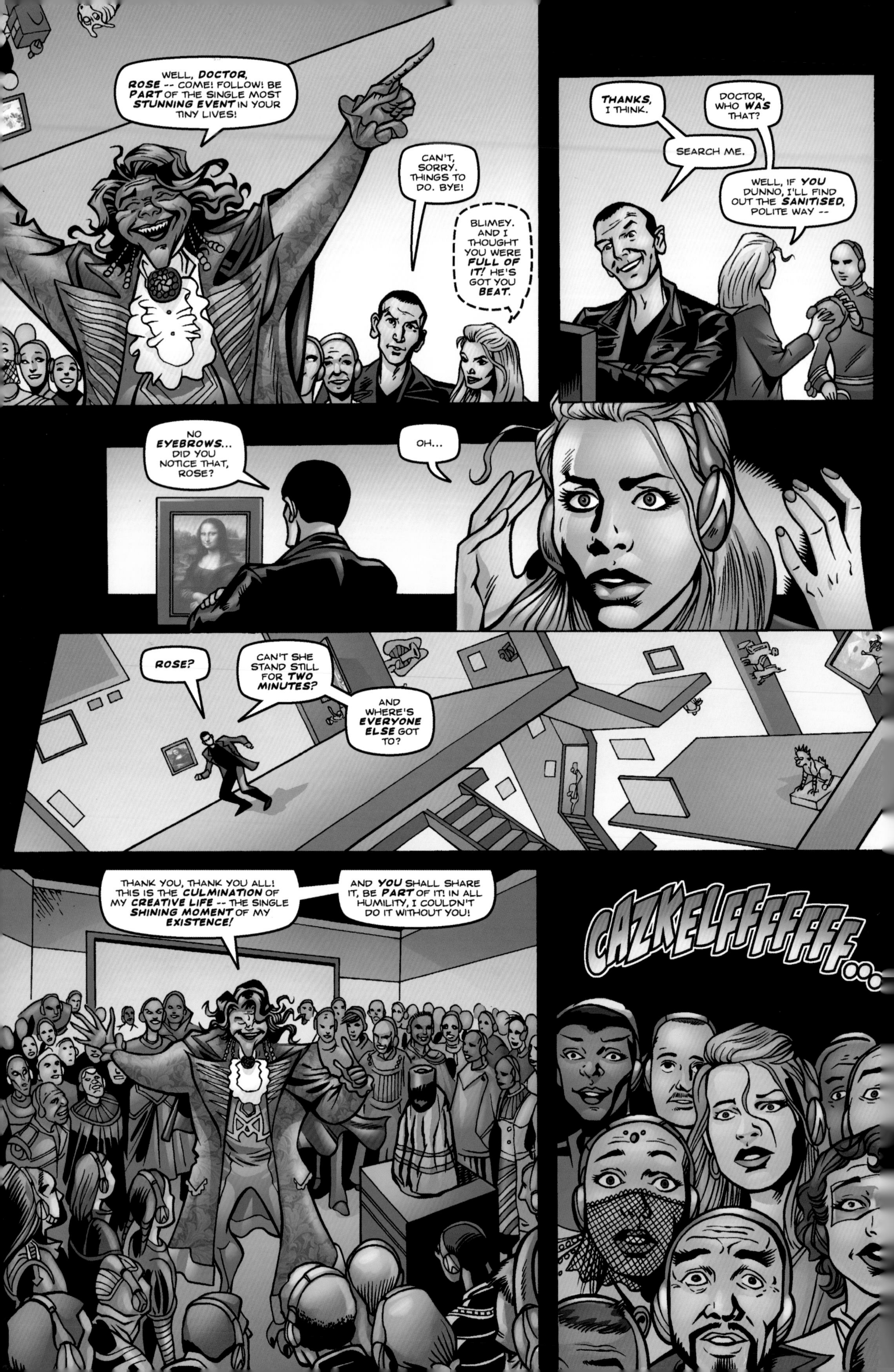
WELL, DOCTOR, ROSE -- COME! FOLLOW! BE PART OF THE SINGLE MOST STUNNING EVENT IN YOUR TINY LIVES!
CAN'T, SORRY. THINGS TO DO. BYE!
BLIMEY. AND I THOUGHT YOU WERE FULL OF IT! HE'S GOT YOU BEAT.
THANKS, I THINK.
DOCTOR, WHO WAS THAT?
SEARCH ME.
WELL, IF YOU DUNNO, I'LL FIND OUT THE SANITISED, POLITE WAY --
NO EYEBROWS... DID YOU NOTICE THAT, ROSE?
OH...
ROSE?
CAN'T SHE STAND STILL FOR TWO MINUTES?
AND WHERE'S EVERYONE ELSE GOT TO?
THANK YOU, THANK YOU ALL! THIS IS THE CULMINATION OF MY CREATIVE LIFE -- THE SINGLE SHINING MOMENT OF MY EXISTENCE!
AND YOU SHALL SHARE IT, BE PART OF IT! IN ALL HUMILITY, I COULDN'T DO IT WITHOUT YOU!
CAZKELFFFFFFF...

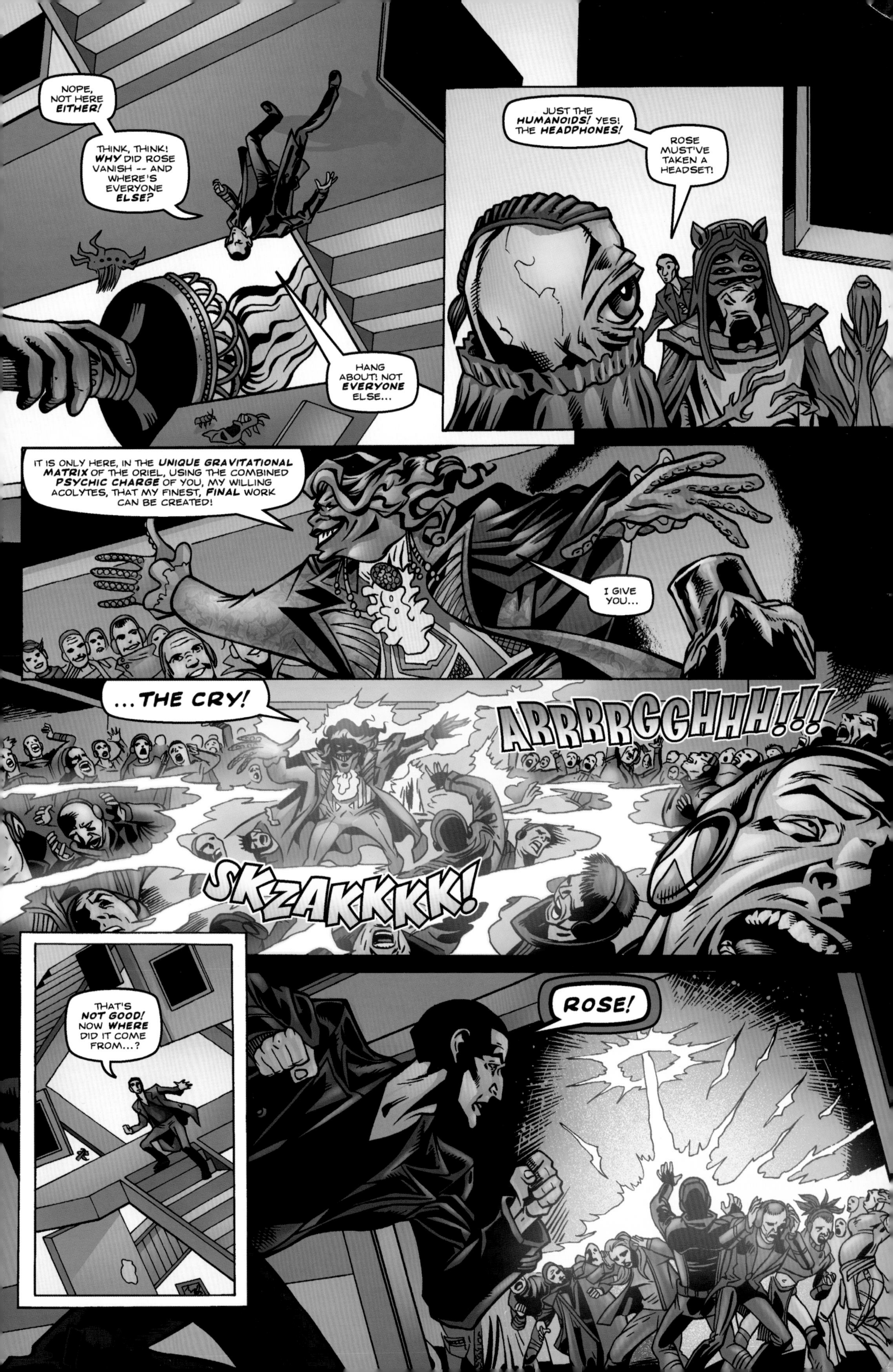
NOPE, NOT HERE EITHER!
THINK, THINK! WHY DID ROSE VANISH -- AND WHERE'S EVERYONE ELSE?
HANG ABOUT! NOT EVERYONE ELSE...
JUST THE HUMANOIDS! YES! THE HEADPHONES!
ROSE MUST'VE TAKEN A HEADSET!
IT IS ONLY HERE, IN THE UNIQUE GRAVITATIONAL MATRIX OF THE ORIEL, USING THE COMBINED PSYCHIC CHARGE OF YOU, MY WILLING ACOLYTES, THAT MY FINEST, FINAL WORK CAN BE CREATED!
I GIVE YOU...
...THE CRY!
ARRRRGCHHH!!!
SKZAKKKK!
THAT'S NOT GOOD! NOW WHERE DID IT COME FROM...?
ROSE!

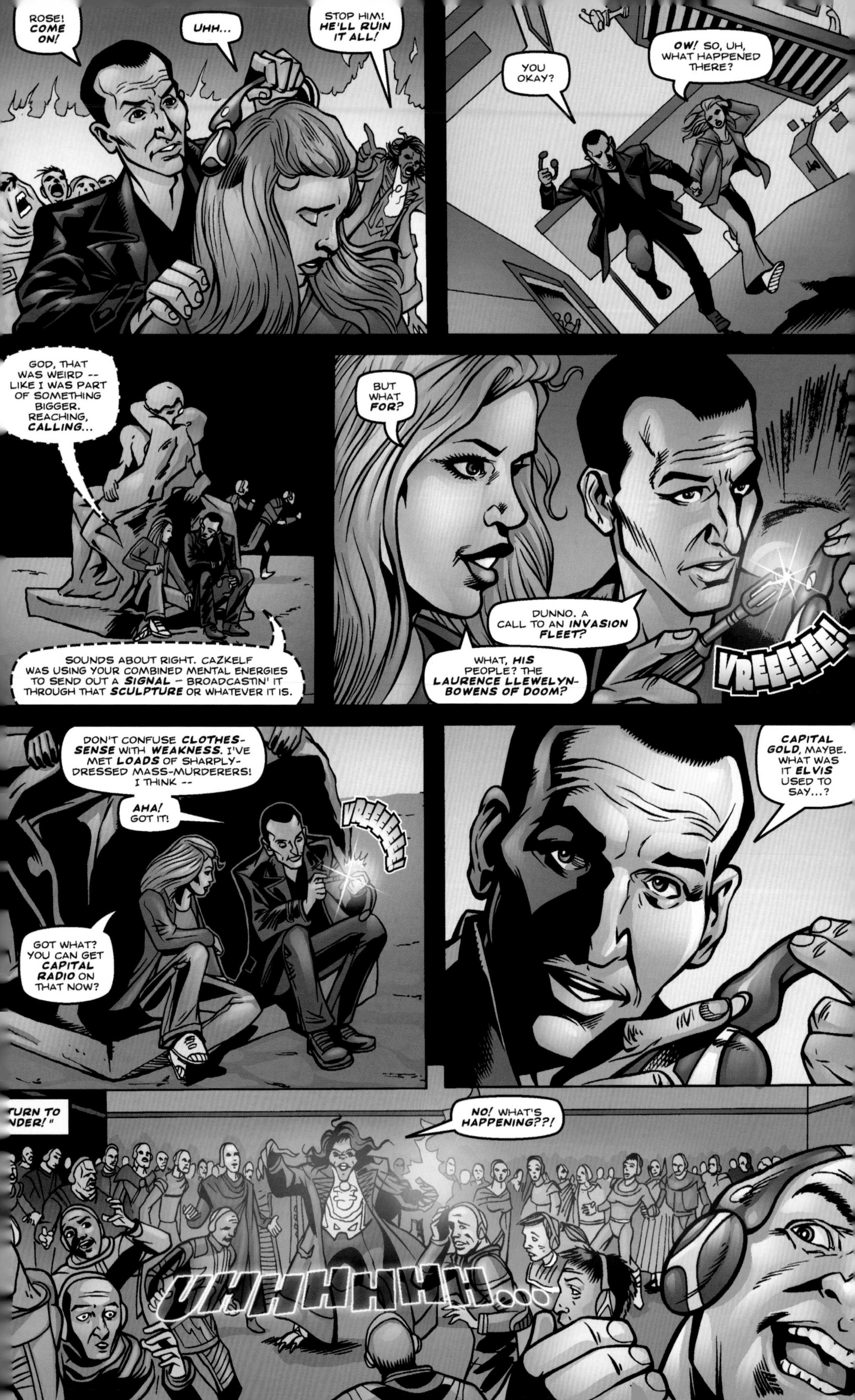
ROSE! COME ON!
UHH...
STOP HIM! HE'LL RUIN IT ALL!
YOU OKAY?
OW! SO, UH, WHAT HAPPENED THERE?
GOD, THAT WAS WEIRD -- LIKE I WAS PART OF SOMETHING BIGGER. REACHING, CALLING...
SOUNDS ABOUT RIGHT. CAZKELF WAS USING YOUR COMBINED MENTAL ENERGIES TO SEND OUT A SIGNAL – BROADCASTIN' IT THROUGH THAT SCULPTURE OR WHATEVER IT IS.
BUT WHAT FOR?
DUNNO. A CALL TO AN INVASION FLEET?
WHAT, HIS PEOPLE? THE LAURENCE LLEWELYN-BOWENS OF DOOM?
VREEEEEEE!
DON'T CONFUSE CLOTHES-SENSE WITH WEAKNESS. I'VE MET LOADS OF SHARPLY-DRESSED MASS-MURDERERS! I THINK --
AHA! GOT IT!
VREEEEEEE
GOT WHAT? YOU CAN GET CAPITAL RADIO ON THAT NOW?
CAPITAL GOLD, MAYBE. WHAT WAS IT ELVIS USED TO SAY...?
TURN TO
NDER!"
NO! WHAT'S HAPPENING??!
UHHHHHH...

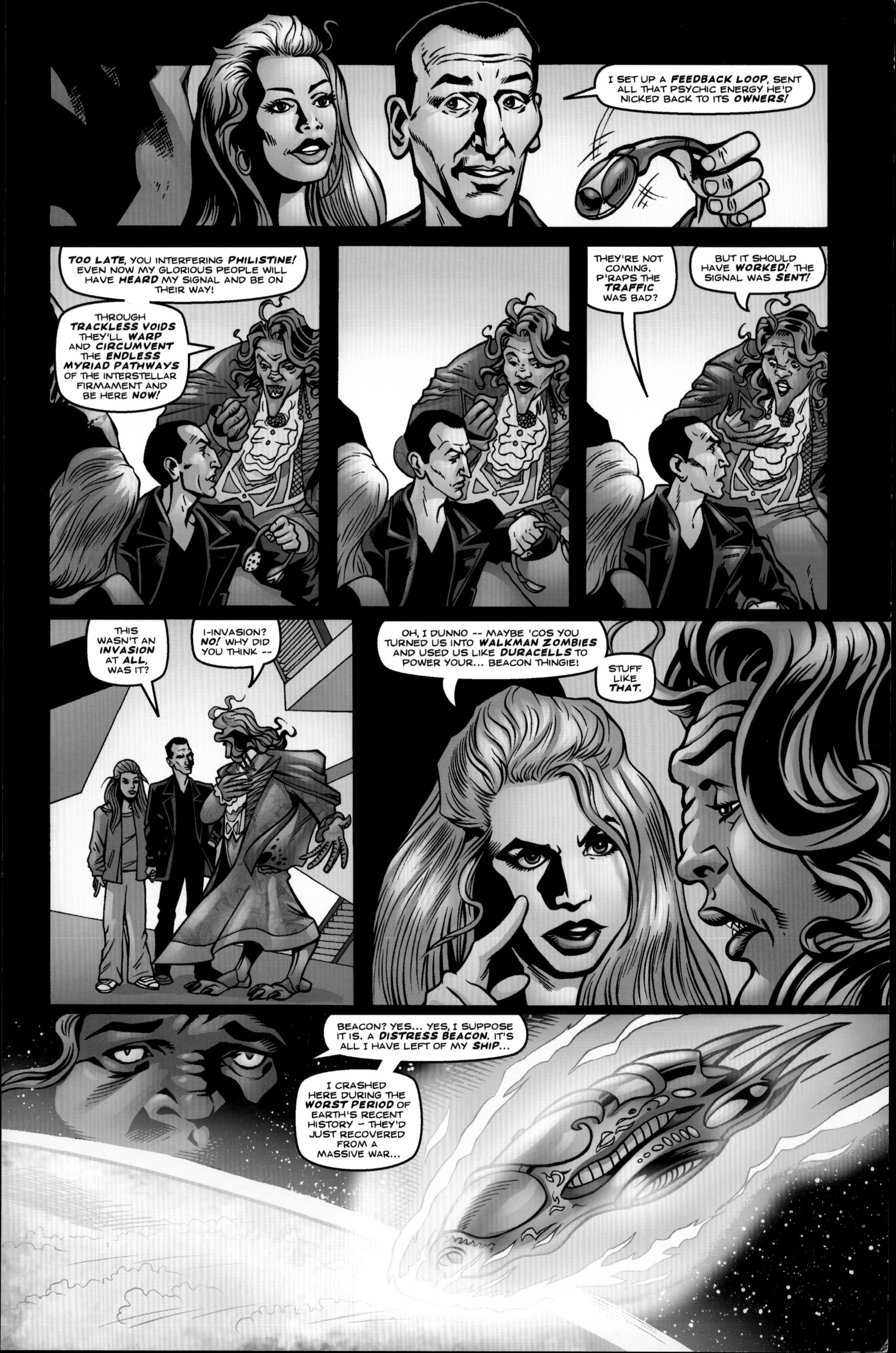
I SET UP A FEEDBACK LOOP, SENT ALL THAT PSYCHIC ENERGY HE'D NICKED BACK TO ITS OWNERS!
TOO LATE, YOU INTERFERING PHILISTINE! EVEN NOW MY GLORIOUS PEOPLE WILL HAVE HEARD MY SIGNAL AND BE ON THEIR WAY!
THROUGH TRACKLESS VOIDS THEY'LL WARP AND CIRCUMVENT THE ENDLESS MYRIAD PATHWAYS OF THE INTERSTELLAR FIRMAMENT AND BE HERE NOW!
THEY'RE NOT COMING. P'RAPS THE TRAFFIC WAS BAD?
BUT IT SHOULD HAVE WORKED! THE SIGNAL WAS SENT!
THIS WASN'T AN INVASION AT ALL, WAS IT?
I-INVASION? NO! WHY DID YOU THINK --
OH, I DUNNO -- MAYBE 'COS YOU TURNED US INTO WALKMAN ZOMBIES AND USED US LIKE DURACELLS TO POWER YOUR... BEACON THINGIE!
STUFF LIKE THAT.
BEACON? YES... YES, I SUPPOSE IT IS. A DISTRESS BEACON. IT'S ALL I HAVE LEFT OF MY SHIP...
I CRASHED HERE DURING THE WORST PERIOD OF EARTH'S RECENT HISTORY – THEY'D JUST RECOVERED FROM A MASSIVE WAR...

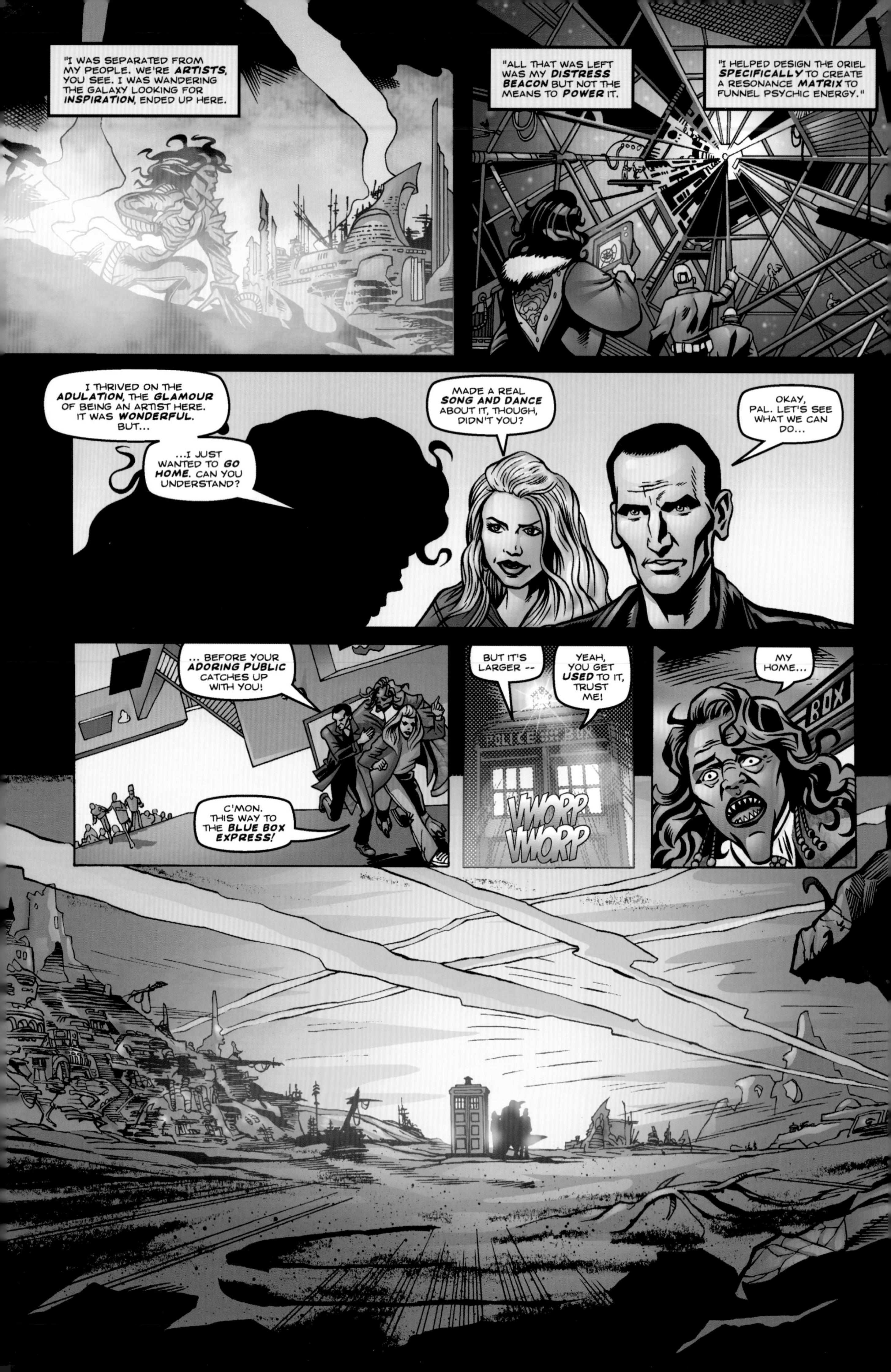
"I WAS SEPARATED FROM MY PEOPLE. WE'RE ARTISTS, YOU SEE. I WAS WANDERING THE GALAXY LOOKING FOR INSPIRATION, ENDED UP HERE.
"ALL THAT WAS LEFT WAS MY DISTRESS BEACON BUT NOT THE MEANS TO POWER IT.
"I HELPED DESIGN THE ORIEL SPECIFICALLY TO CREATE A RESONANCE MATRIX TO FUNNEL PSYCHIC ENERGY."
I THRIVED ON THE ADULATION, THE GLAMOUR OF BEING AN ARTIST HERE. IT WAS WONDERFUL. BUT...
...I JUST WANTED TO GO HOME. CAN YOU UNDERSTAND?
MADE A REAL SONG AND DANCE ABOUT IT, THOUGH, DIDN'T YOU?
OKAY, PAL. LET'S SEE WHAT WE CAN DO...
... BEFORE YOUR ADORING PUBLIC CATCHES UP WITH YOU!
C'MON. THIS WAY TO THE BLUE BOX EXPRESS!
BUT IT'S LARGER --
YEAH, YOU GET USED TO IT, TRUST ME!
VWORP VWORP
MY HOME...

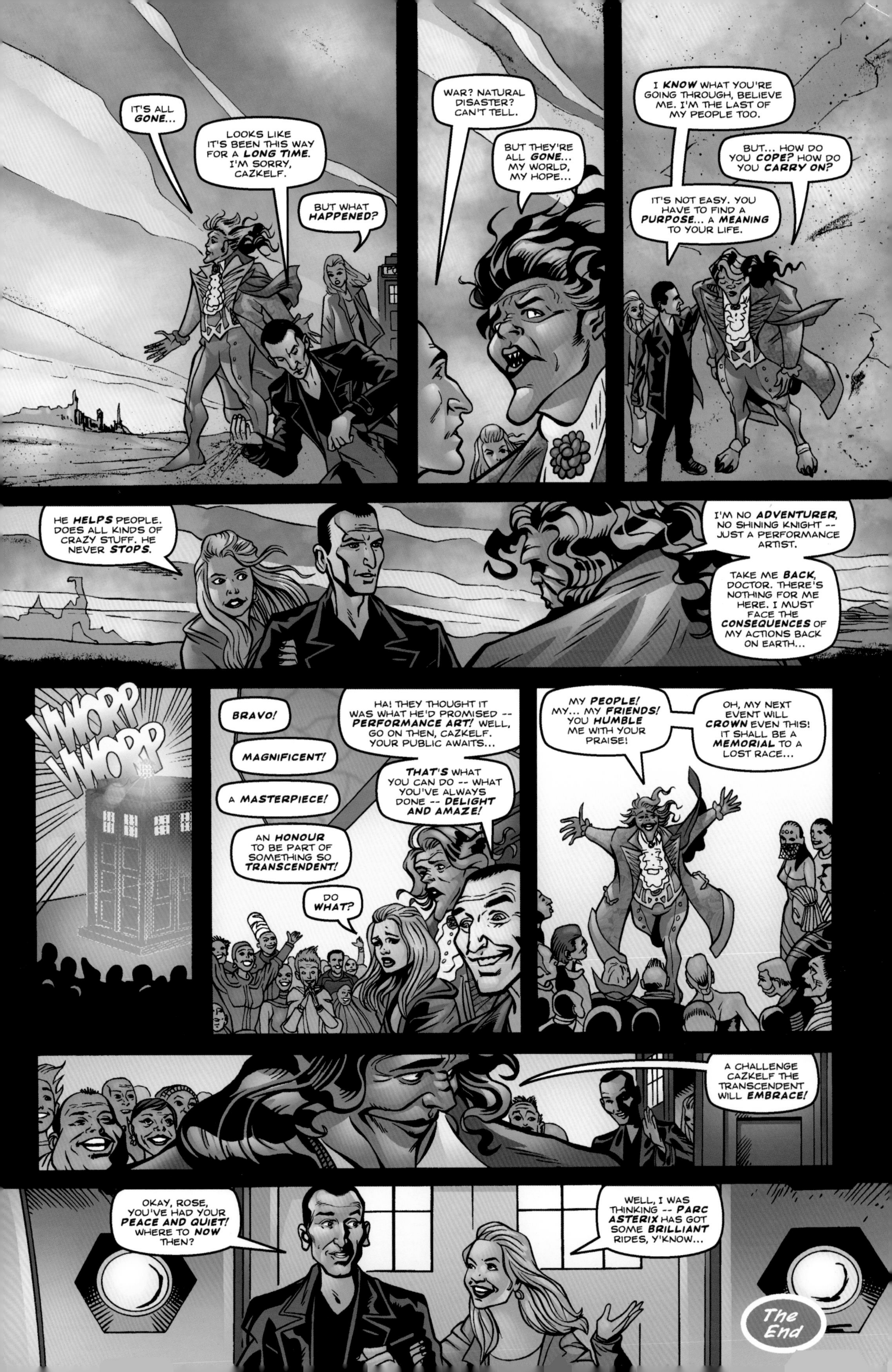
IT'S ALL GONE...
LOOKS LIKE IT'S BEEN THIS WAY FOR A LONG TIME. I'M SORRY, CAZKELF.
BUT WHAT HAPPENED?
WAR? NATURAL DISASTER? CAN'T TELL.
BUT THEY'RE ALL GONE... MY WORLD, MY HOPE...
I KNOW WHAT YOU'RE GOING THROUGH, BELIEVE ME. I'M THE LAST OF MY PEOPLE TOO.
BUT... HOW DO YOU COPE? HOW DO YOU CARRY ON?
IT'S NOT EASY. YOU HAVE TO FIND A PURPOSE... A MEANING TO YOUR LIFE.
HE HELPS PEOPLE. DOES ALL KINDS OF CRAZY STUFF. HE NEVER STOPS.
I'M NO ADVENTURER, NO SHINING KNIGHT -- JUST A PERFORMANCE ARTIST.
TAKE ME BACK, DOCTOR. THERE'S NOTHING FOR ME HERE. I MUST FACE THE CONSEQUENCES OF MY ACTIONS BACK ON EARTH...
VWORP VWORP
BRAVO!
MAGNIFICENT!
A MASTERPIECE!
AN HONOUR TO BE PART OF SOMETHING SO TRANSCENDENT!
HA! THEY THOUGHT IT WAS WHAT HE'D PROMISED -- PERFORMANCE ART! WELL, GO ON THEN, CAZKELF. YOUR PUBLIC AWAITS...
THAT'S WHAT YOU CAN DO -- WHAT YOU'VE ALWAYS DONE -- DELIGHT AND AMAZE!
DO WHAT?
MY PEOPLE! MY... MY FRIENDS! YOU HUMBLE ME WITH YOUR PRAISE!
OH, MY NEXT EVENT WILL CROWN EVEN THIS! IT SHALL BE A MEMORIAL TO A LOST RACE...
A CHALLENGE CAZKELF THE TRANSCENDENT WILL EMBRACE!
OKAY, ROSE, YOU'VE HAD YOUR PEACE AND QUIET! WHERE TO NOW THEN?
WELL, I WAS THINKING -- PARC ASTERIX HAS GOT SOME BRILLIANT RIDES, Y'KNOW...
The End

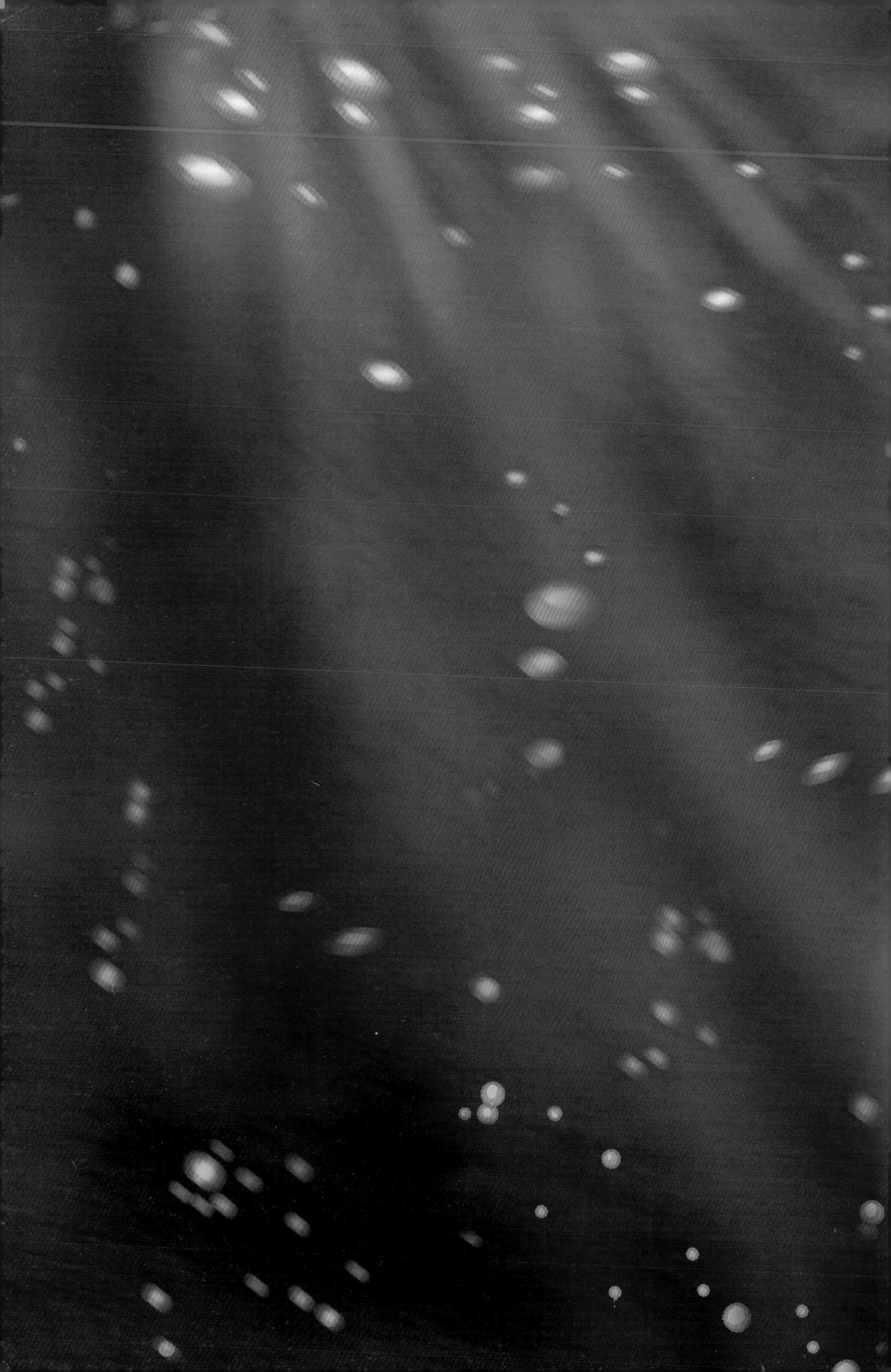

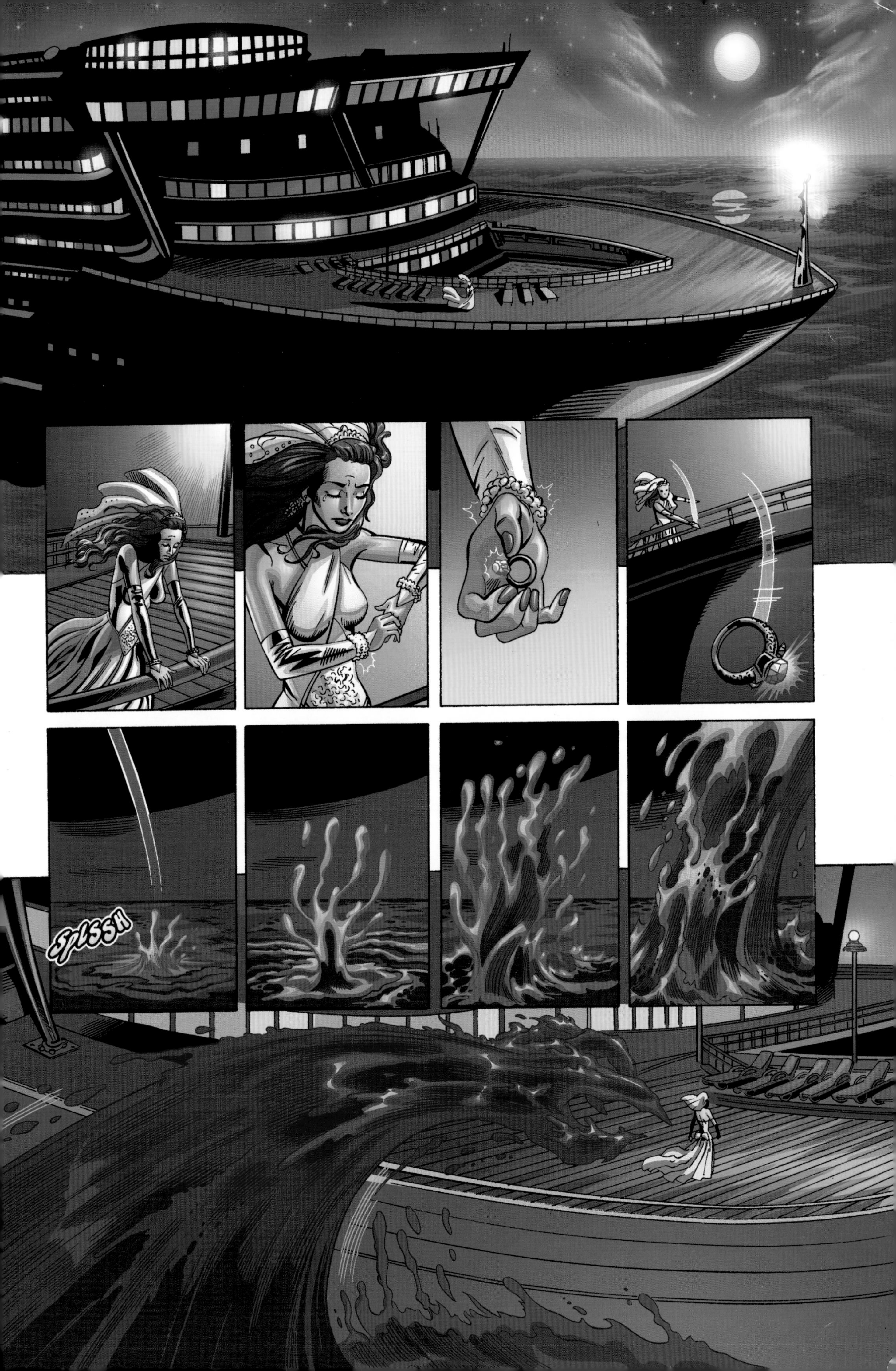
SPLSSH

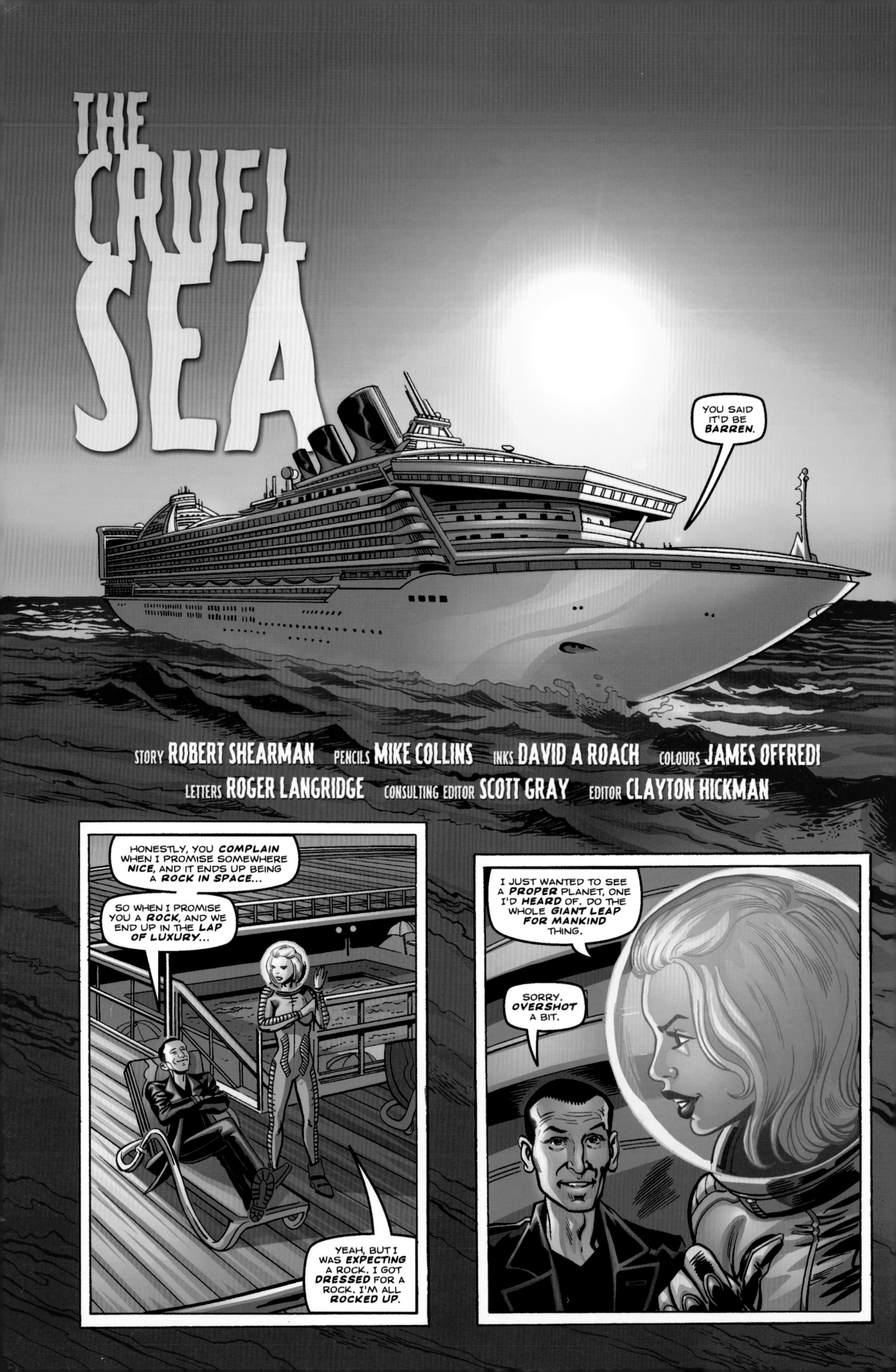
THE CRUEL SEA
YOU SAID IT'D BE **BARREN**.
STORY ROBERT SHEARMAN PENCILS MIKE COLLINS INKS DAVID A ROACH COLOURS JAMES OFFREDI
LETTERS ROGER LANGRIDGE CONSULTING EDITOR SCOTT GRAY EDITOR CLAYTON HICKMAN
HONESTLY, YOU **COMPLAIN** WHEN I PROMISE SOMEWHERE **NICE**, AND IT ENDS UP BEING A **ROCK IN SPACE**...
SO WHEN I PROMISE YOU A **ROCK**, AND WE END UP IN THE **LAP OF LUXURY**...
YEAH, BUT I WAS **EXPECTING** A ROCK. I GOT **DRESSED** FOR A ROCK. I'M ALL **ROCKED UP**.
I JUST WANTED TO SEE A **PROPER** PLANET, ONE I'D **HEARD** OF. DO THE WHOLE **GIANT LEAP FOR MANKIND** THING.
SORRY. **OVERSHOT** A BIT.

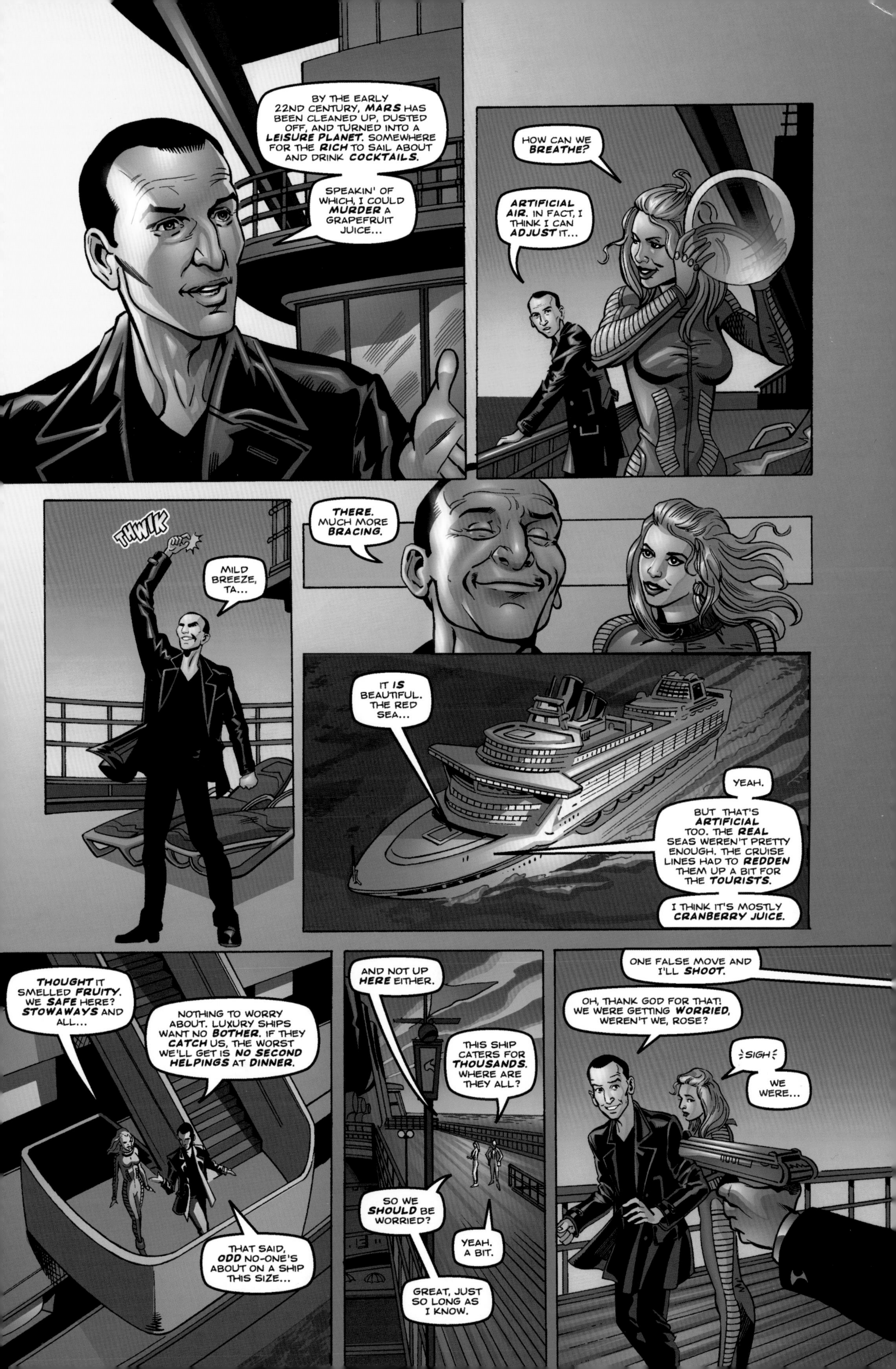
BY THE EARLY 22ND CENTURY, MARS HAS BEEN CLEANED UP, DUSTED OFF, AND TURNED INTO A LEISURE PLANET. SOMEWHERE FOR THE RICH TO SAIL ABOUT AND DRINK COCKTAILS.
SPEAKIN' OF WHICH, I COULD MURDER A GRAPEFRUIT JUICE...
HOW CAN WE BREATHE?
ARTIFICIAL AIR. IN FACT, I THINK I CAN ADJUST IT...
THWIK
MILD BREEZE, TA...
THERE. MUCH MORE BRACING.
IT IS BEAUTIFUL. THE RED SEA...
YEAH.
BUT THAT'S ARTIFICIAL TOO. THE REAL SEAS WEREN'T PRETTY ENOUGH. THE CRUISE LINES HAD TO REDDEN THEM UP A BIT FOR THE TOURISTS.
I THINK IT'S MOSTLY CRANBERRY JUICE.
THOUGHT IT SMELLED FRUITY. WE SAFE HERE? STOWAWAYS AND ALL...
NOTHING TO WORRY ABOUT. LUXURY SHIPS WANT NO BOTHER. IF THEY CATCH US, THE WORST WE'LL GET IS NO SECOND HELPINGS AT DINNER.
THAT SAID, ODD NO-ONE'S ABOUT ON A SHIP THIS SIZE...
AND NOT UP HERE EITHER.
THIS SHIP CATERS FOR THOUSANDS. WHERE ARE THEY ALL?
SO WE SHOULD BE WORRIED?
YEAH. A BIT.
GREAT, JUST SO LONG AS I KNOW.
ONE FALSE MOVE AND I'LL SHOOT.
OH, THANK GOD FOR THAT! WE WERE GETTING WORRIED, WEREN'T WE, ROSE?
SIGH
WE WERE...

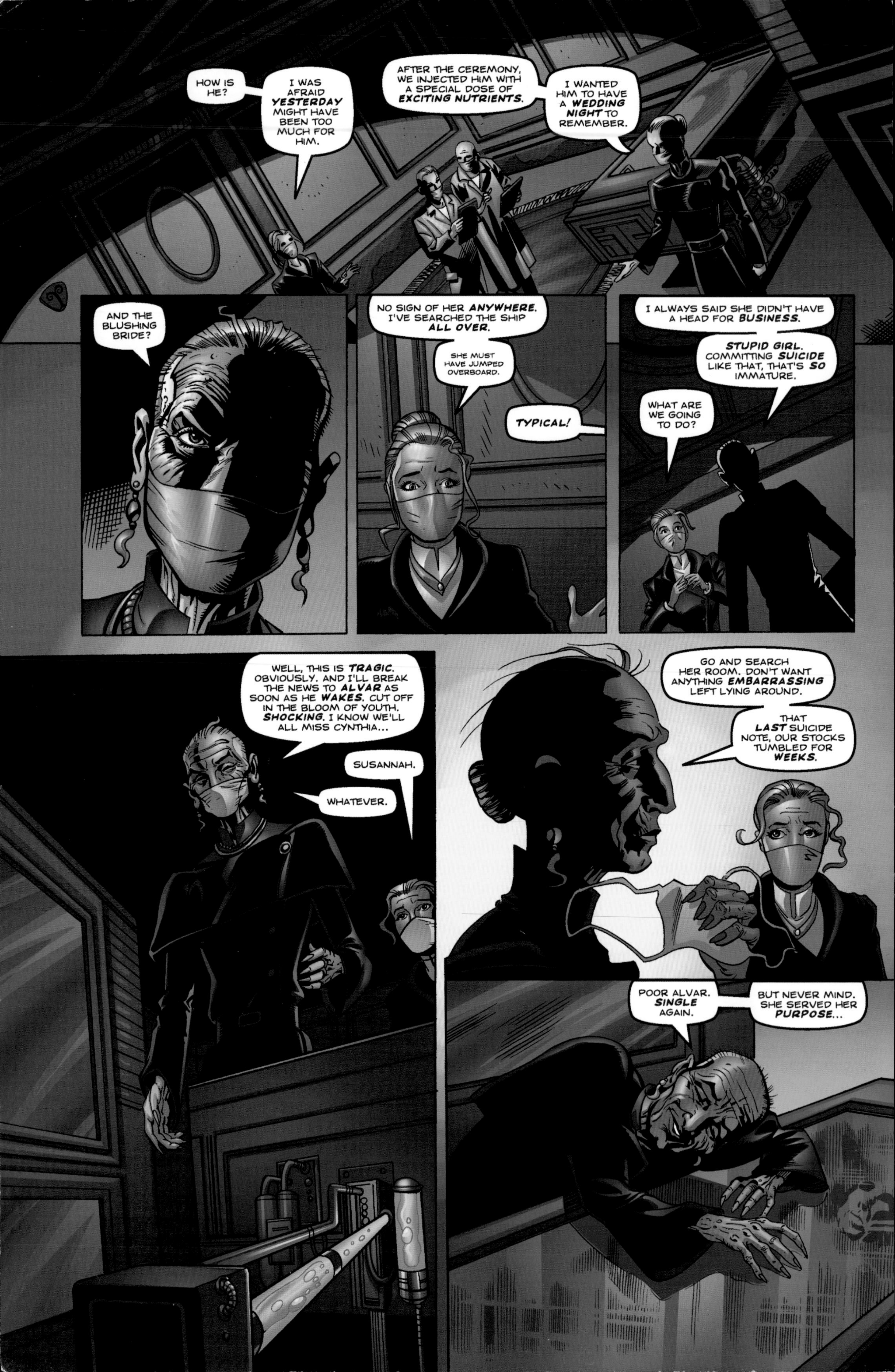
HOW IS HE?
I WAS AFRAID YESTERDAY MIGHT HAVE BEEN TOO MUCH FOR HIM.
AFTER THE CEREMONY, WE INJECTED HIM WITH A SPECIAL DOSE OF EXCITING NUTRIENTS.
I WANTED HIM TO HAVE A WEDDING NIGHT TO REMEMBER.
AND THE BLUSHING BRIDE?
NO SIGN OF HER ANYWHERE. I'VE SEARCHED THE SHIP ALL OVER.
SHE MUST HAVE JUMPED OVERBOARD.
TYPICAL!
I ALWAYS SAID SHE DIDN'T HAVE A HEAD FOR BUSINESS.
STUPID GIRL. COMMITTING SUICIDE LIKE THAT, THAT'S SO IMMATURE.
WHAT ARE WE GOING TO DO?
WELL, THIS IS TRAGIC. OBVIOUSLY. AND I'LL BREAK THE NEWS TO ALVAR AS SOON AS HE WAKES. CUT OFF IN THE BLOOM OF YOUTH. SHOCKING. I KNOW WE'LL ALL MISS CYNTHIA...
SUSANNAH.
WHATEVER.
GO AND SEARCH HER ROOM. DON'T WANT ANYTHING EMBARRASSING LEFT LYING AROUND.
THAT LAST SUICIDE NOTE, OUR STOCKS TUMBLED FOR WEEKS.
POOR ALVAR. SINGLE AGAIN.
BUT NEVER MIND. SHE SERVED HER PURPOSE...

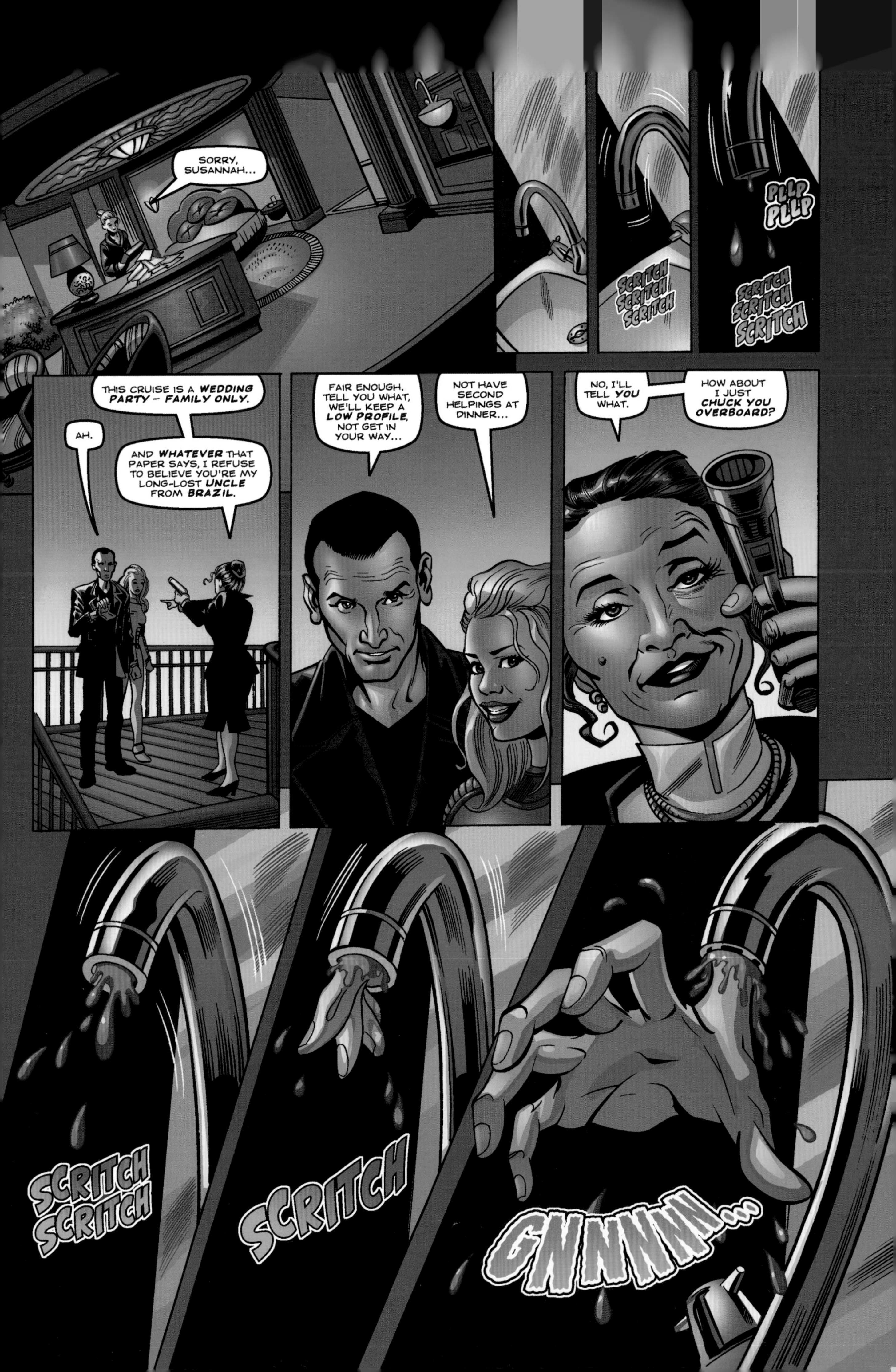

SORRY, SUSANNAH...
SCRITCH SCRITCH SCRITCH
PLLP PLLP
SCRITCH SCRITCH SCRITCH
THIS CRUISE IS A WEDDING PARTY – FAMILY ONLY.
AH.
AND WHATEVER THAT PAPER SAYS, I REFUSE TO BELIEVE YOU'RE MY LONG-LOST UNCLE FROM BRAZIL.
FAIR ENOUGH. TELL YOU WHAT, WE'LL KEEP A LOW PROFILE, NOT GET IN YOUR WAY...
NOT HAVE SECOND HELPINGS AT DINNER...
NO, I'LL TELL YOU WHAT.
HOW ABOUT I JUST CHUCK YOU OVERBOARD?
SCRITCH SCRITCH
SCRITCH
GNNNN...

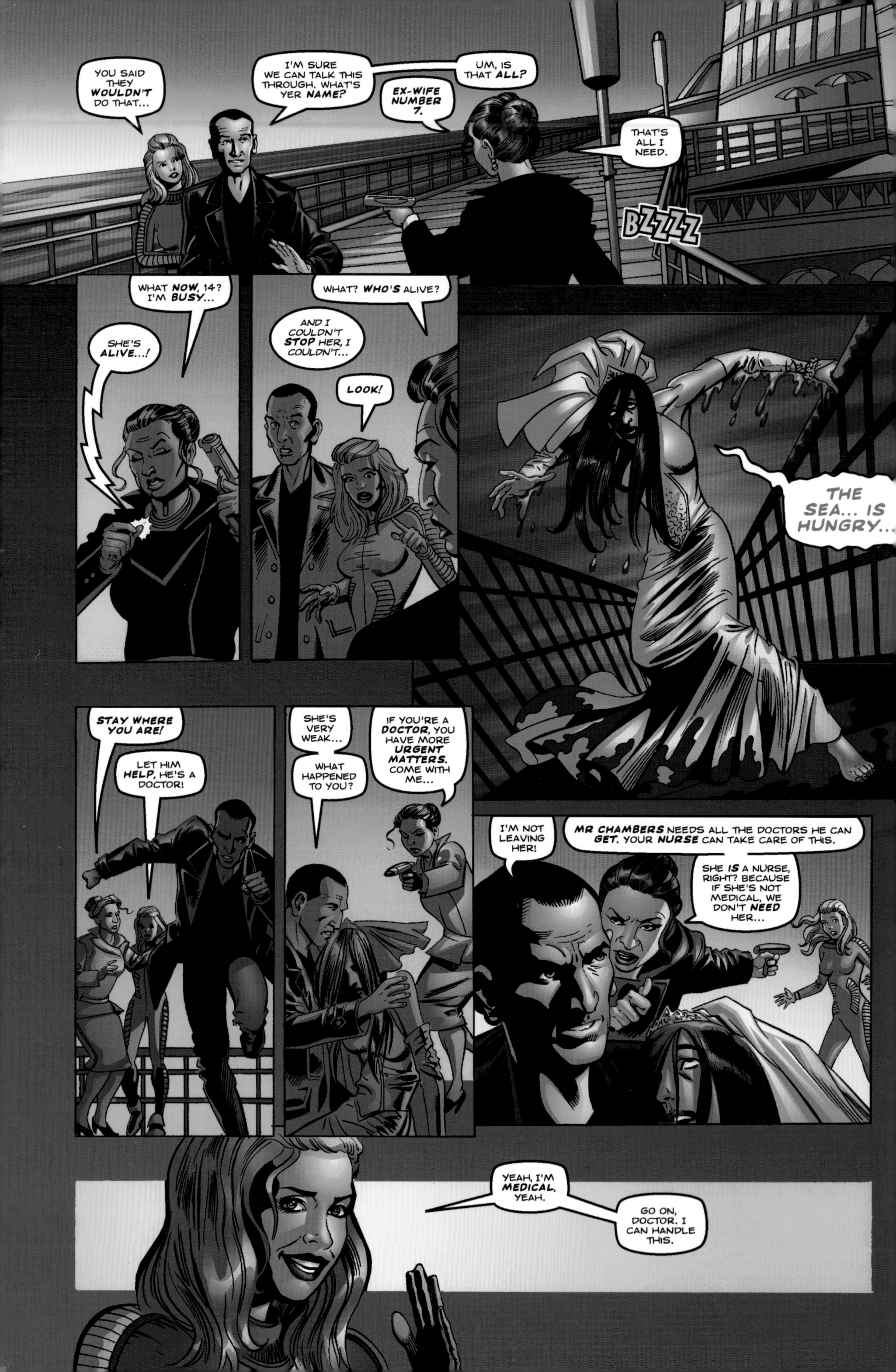
YOU SAID THEY WOULDN'T DO THAT...
I'M SURE WE CAN TALK THIS THROUGH. WHAT'S YER NAME?
UM, IS THAT ALL?
EX-WIFE NUMBER 7.
THAT'S ALL I NEED.
BZZZZ
WHAT NOW, 14? I'M BUSY...
SHE'S ALIVE...!
WHAT? WHO'S ALIVE?
AND I COULDN'T STOP HER, I COULDN'T...
LOOK!
THE SEA... IS HUNGRY...
STAY WHERE YOU ARE!
LET HIM HELP, HE'S A DOCTOR!
SHE'S VERY WEAK...
WHAT HAPPENED TO YOU?
IF YOU'RE A DOCTOR, YOU HAVE MORE URGENT MATTERS. COME WITH ME...
I'M NOT LEAVING HER!
MR CHAMBERS NEEDS ALL THE DOCTORS HE CAN GET. YOUR NURSE CAN TAKE CARE OF THIS.
SHE IS A NURSE, RIGHT? BECAUSE IF SHE'S NOT MEDICAL, WE DON'T NEED HER...
YEAH, I'M MEDICAL, YEAH.
GO ON, DOCTOR. I CAN HANDLE THIS.

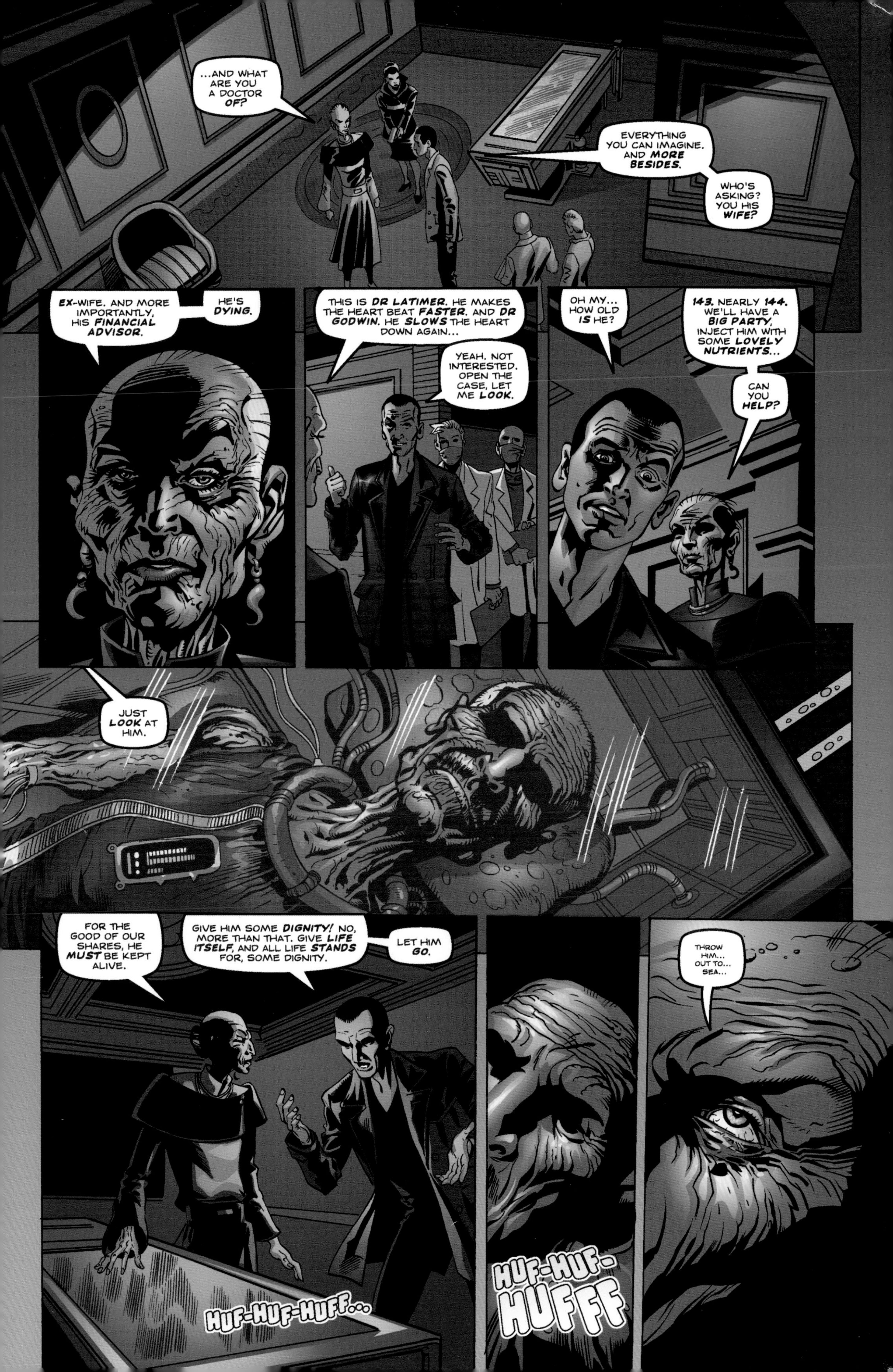
...AND WHAT ARE YOU A DOCTOR OF?
EVERYTHING YOU CAN IMAGINE. AND MORE BESIDES.
WHO'S ASKING? YOU HIS WIFE?
EX-WIFE. AND MORE IMPORTANTLY, HIS FINANCIAL ADVISOR.
HE'S DYING.
THIS IS DR LATIMER. HE MAKES THE HEART BEAT FASTER. AND DR GODWIN. HE SLOWS THE HEART DOWN AGAIN...
YEAH. NOT INTERESTED. OPEN THE CASE, LET ME LOOK.
OH MY... HOW OLD IS HE?
143. NEARLY 144. WE'LL HAVE A BIG PARTY, INJECT HIM WITH SOME LOVELY NUTRIENTS...
CAN YOU HELP?
JUST LOOK AT HIM.
FOR THE GOOD OF OUR SHARES, HE MUST BE KEPT ALIVE.
GIVE HIM SOME DIGNITY! NO, MORE THAN THAT. GIVE LIFE ITSELF, AND ALL LIFE STANDS FOR, SOME DIGNITY.
LET HIM GO.
HUF-HUF-HUFF...
HUF-HUF-HUFFF
THROW HIM... OUT TO... SEA...

YOU'RE GONNA BE OKAY. I PROMISE...

AND YOU'RE TALKING TO YOURSELF, ROSE. SHE'S UNCONSCIOUS.

I HOPE SHE'S JUST UNCONSCIOUS...

AHH!

NO!

DON'T DO IT! THERE'S NO NEED...

COME BACK! WE'LL SORT IT OUT... PLEASE...

TOO WEAK... CAN'T KEEP HOLD...

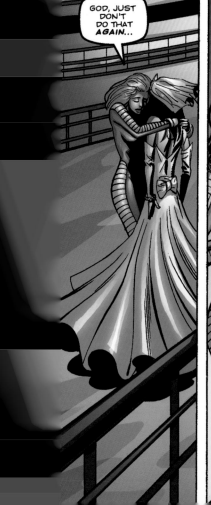

GOD, JUST DON'T DO THAT AGAIN...

YOU... YOU'RE BLEEDING...

TOO WEAK...

NO, NOT BLOOD...

CRANBERRY JUICE.

NO!

SWSSSSHH

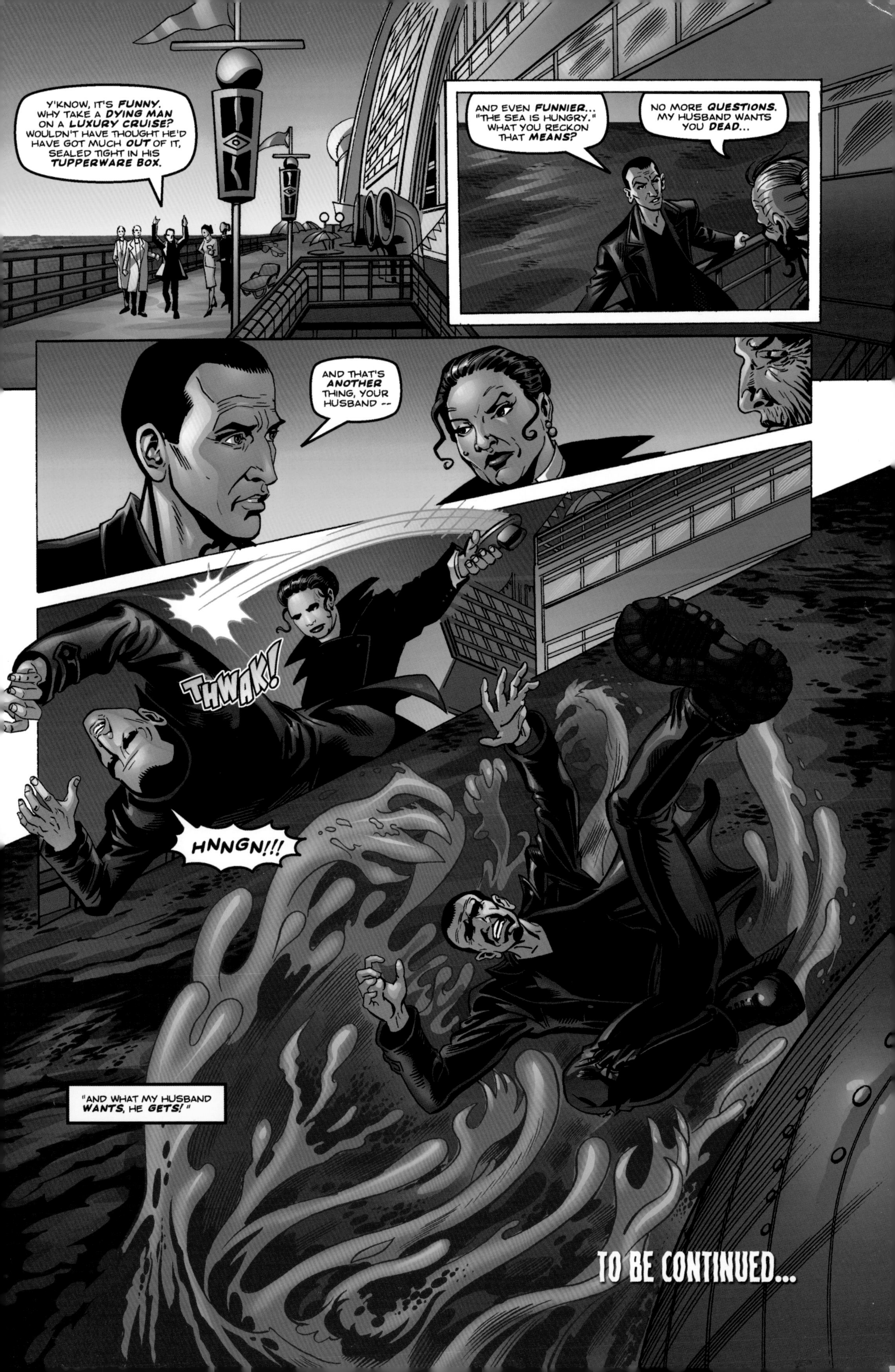
Y'KNOW, IT'S FUNNY. WHY TAKE A DYING MAN ON A LUXURY CRUISE? WOULDN'T HAVE THOUGHT HE'D HAVE GOT MUCH OUT OF IT, SEALED TIGHT IN HIS TUPPERWARE BOX.
AND EVEN FUNNIER... "THE SEA IS HUNGRY." WHAT YOU RECKON THAT MEANS?
NO MORE QUESTIONS. MY HUSBAND WANTS YOU DEAD...
AND THAT'S ANOTHER THING, YOUR HUSBAND --
THWAK!
HNNGN!!!
"AND WHAT MY HUSBAND WANTS, HE GETS!"
TO BE CONTINUED...

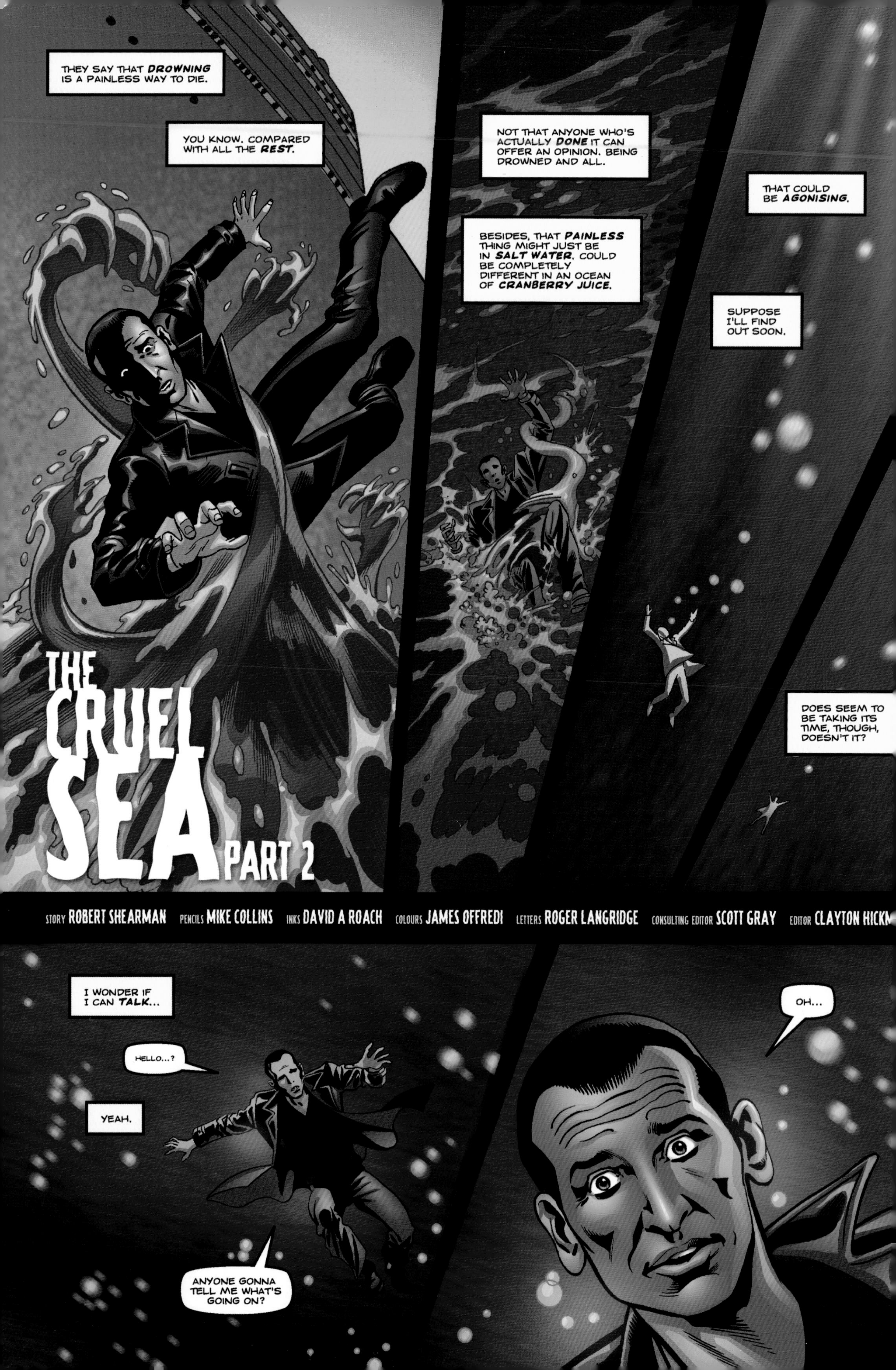

THEY SAY THAT DROWNING IS A PAINLESS WAY TO DIE.
YOU KNOW. COMPARED WITH ALL THE REST.
NOT THAT ANYONE WHO'S ACTUALLY DONE IT CAN OFFER AN OPINION. BEING DROWNED AND ALL.
BESIDES, THAT PAINLESS THING MIGHT JUST BE IN SALT WATER. COULD BE COMPLETELY DIFFERENT IN AN OCEAN OF CRANBERRY JUICE.
THAT COULD BE AGONISING.
SUPPOSE I'LL FIND OUT SOON.
DOES SEEM TO BE TAKING ITS TIME, THOUGH, DOESN'T IT?
THE CRUEL SEA PART 2
STORY ROBERT SHEARMAN PENCILS MIKE COLLINS INKS DAVID A ROACH COLOURS JAMES OFFREDI LETTERS ROGER LANGRIDGE CONSULTING EDITOR SCOTT GRAY EDITOR CLAYTON HICKM
I WONDER IF I CAN TALK...
HELLO...?
YEAH.
ANYONE GONNA TELL ME WHAT'S GOING ON?
OH...

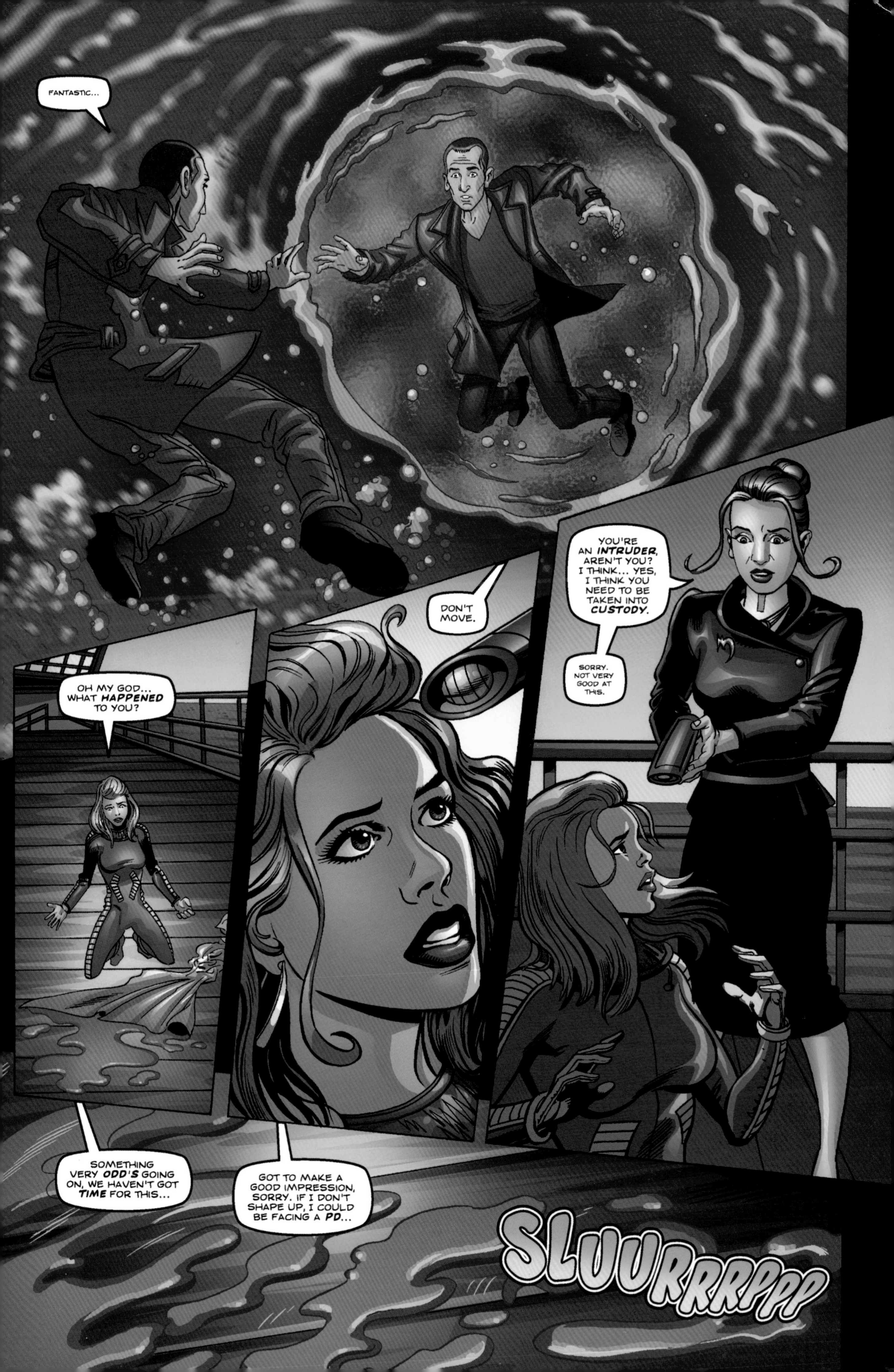
FANTASTIC...
OH MY GOD... WHAT HAPPENED TO YOU?
SOMETHING VERY ODD'S GOING ON, WE HAVEN'T GOT TIME FOR THIS...
DON'T MOVE.
GOT TO MAKE A GOOD IMPRESSION, SORRY. IF I DON'T SHAPE UP, I COULD BE FACING A PD...
YOU'RE AN INTRUDER, AREN'T YOU? I THINK... YES, I THINK YOU NEED TO BE TAKEN INTO CUSTODY.
SORRY. NOT VERY GOOD AT THIS.
SLUURRRPPP

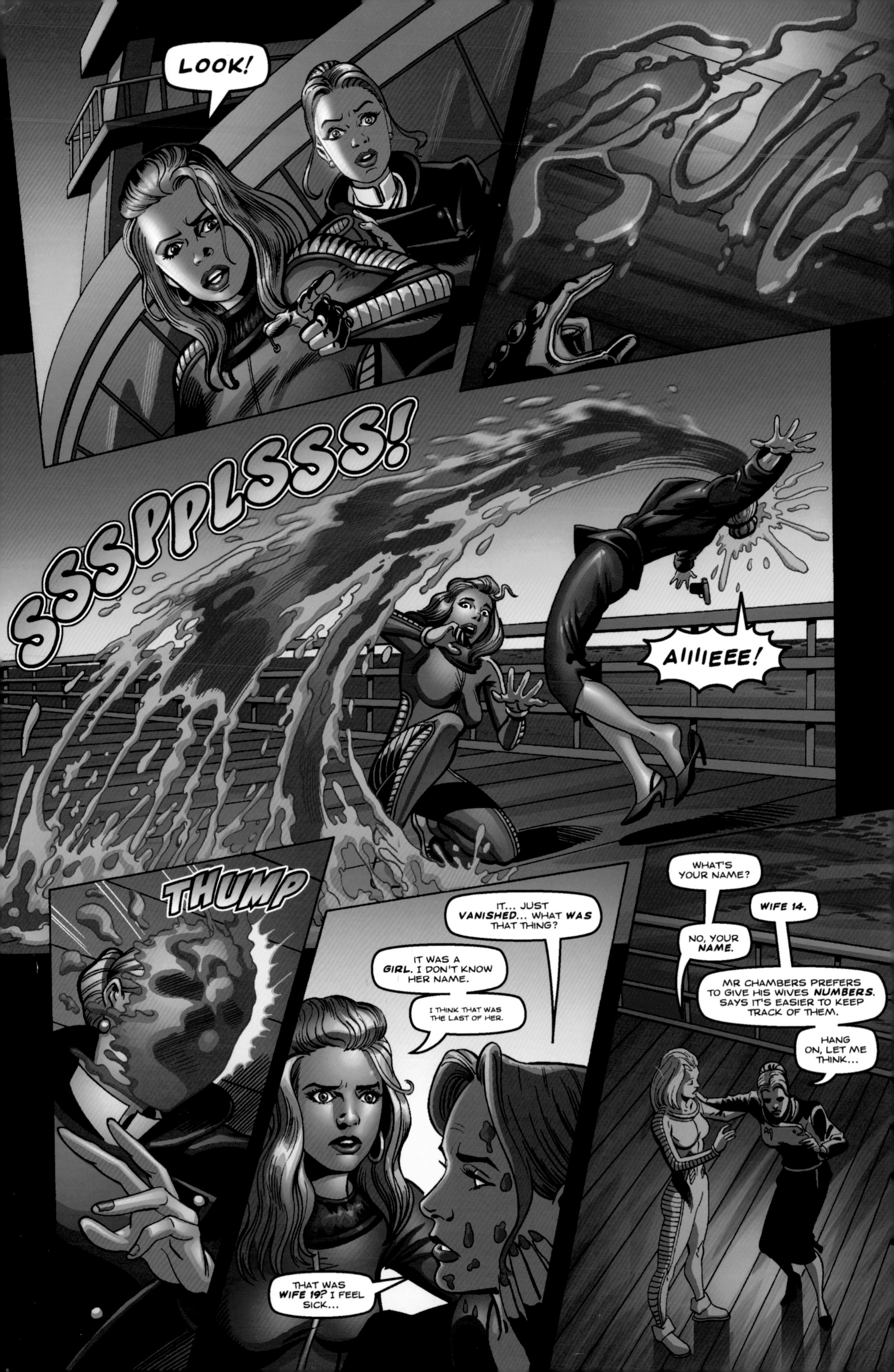
LOOK!
SSSPPLSSSS!
AIIIIEEE!
THUMP
IT... JUST VANISHED... WHAT WAS THAT THING?
IT WAS A GIRL. I DON'T KNOW HER NAME.
I THINK THAT WAS THE LAST OF HER.
THAT WAS WIFE 19? I FEEL SICK...
WHAT'S YOUR NAME?
WIFE 14.
NO, YOUR NAME.
MR CHAMBERS PREFERS TO GIVE HIS WIVES NUMBERS. SAYS IT'S EASIER TO KEEP TRACK OF THEM.
HANG ON, LET ME THINK...

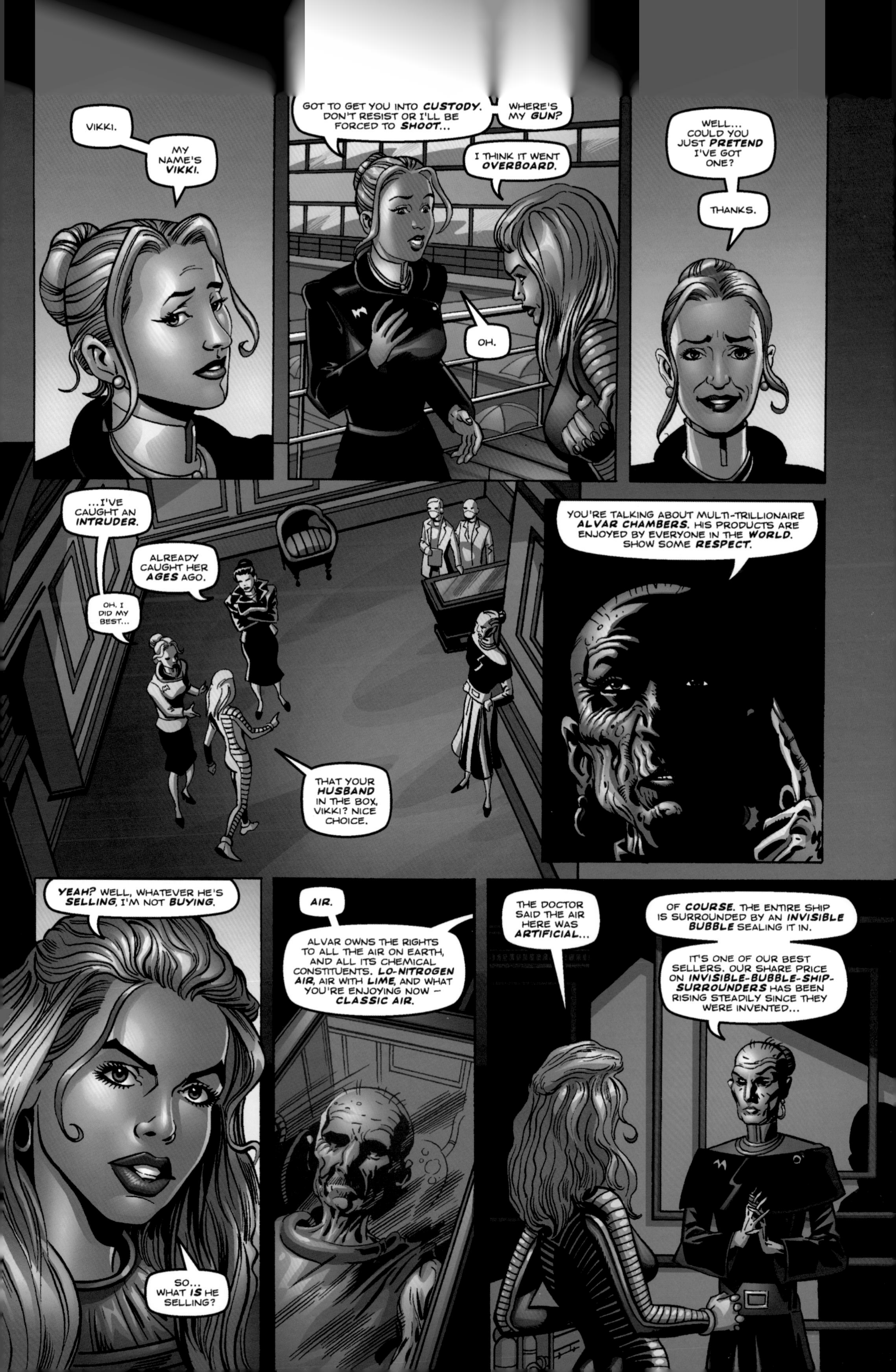
VIKKI.
MY NAME'S VIKKI.
GOT TO GET YOU INTO CUSTODY. DON'T RESIST OR I'LL BE FORCED TO SHOOT...
WHERE'S MY GUN?
I THINK IT WENT OVERBOARD.
OH.
WELL... COULD YOU JUST PRETEND I'VE GOT ONE?
THANKS.
...I'VE CAUGHT AN INTRUDER.
ALREADY CAUGHT HER AGES AGO.
OH, I DID MY BEST...
THAT YOUR HUSBAND IN THE BOX, VIKKI? NICE CHOICE.
YOU'RE TALKING ABOUT MULTI-TRILLIONAIRE ALVAR CHAMBERS. HIS PRODUCTS ARE ENJOYED BY EVERYONE IN THE WORLD. SHOW SOME RESPECT.
YEAH? WELL, WHATEVER HE'S SELLING, I'M NOT BUYING.
SO... WHAT IS HE SELLING?
AIR.
ALVAR OWNS THE RIGHTS TO ALL THE AIR ON EARTH, AND ALL ITS CHEMICAL CONSTITUENTS. LO-NITROGEN AIR, AIR WITH LIME, AND WHAT YOU'RE ENJOYING NOW – CLASSIC AIR.
THE DOCTOR SAID THE AIR HERE WAS ARTIFICIAL...
OF COURSE. THE ENTIRE SHIP IS SURROUNDED BY AN INVISIBLE BUBBLE SEALING IT IN.
IT'S ONE OF OUR BEST SELLERS. OUR SHARE PRICE ON INVISIBLE-BUBBLE-SHIP-SURROUNDERS HAS BEEN RISING STEADILY SINCE THEY WERE INVENTED...

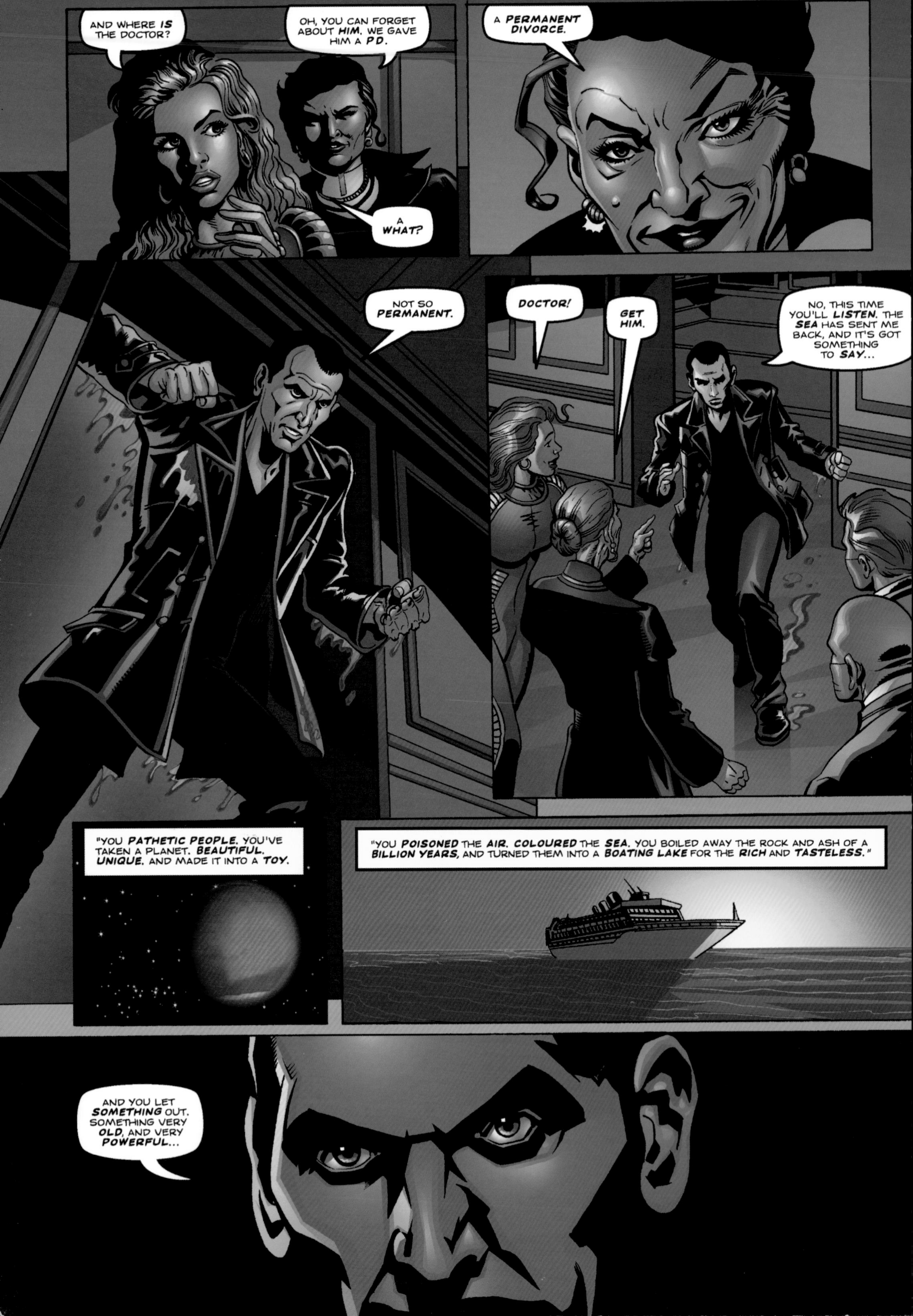
AND WHERE IS THE DOCTOR?
OH, YOU CAN FORGET ABOUT HIM. WE GAVE HIM A PD.
A WHAT?
A PERMANENT DIVORCE.
NOT SO PERMANENT.
DOCTOR!
GET HIM.
NO, THIS TIME YOU'LL LISTEN. THE SEA HAS SENT ME BACK, AND IT'S GOT SOMETHING TO SAY...
"YOU PATHETIC PEOPLE. YOU'VE TAKEN A PLANET. BEAUTIFUL. UNIQUE. AND MADE IT INTO A TOY.
"YOU POISONED THE AIR. COLOURED THE SEA. YOU BOILED AWAY THE ROCK AND ASH OF A BILLION YEARS, AND TURNED THEM INTO A BOATING LAKE FOR THE RICH AND TASTELESS."
AND YOU LET SOMETHING OUT. SOMETHING VERY OLD, AND VERY POWERFUL...

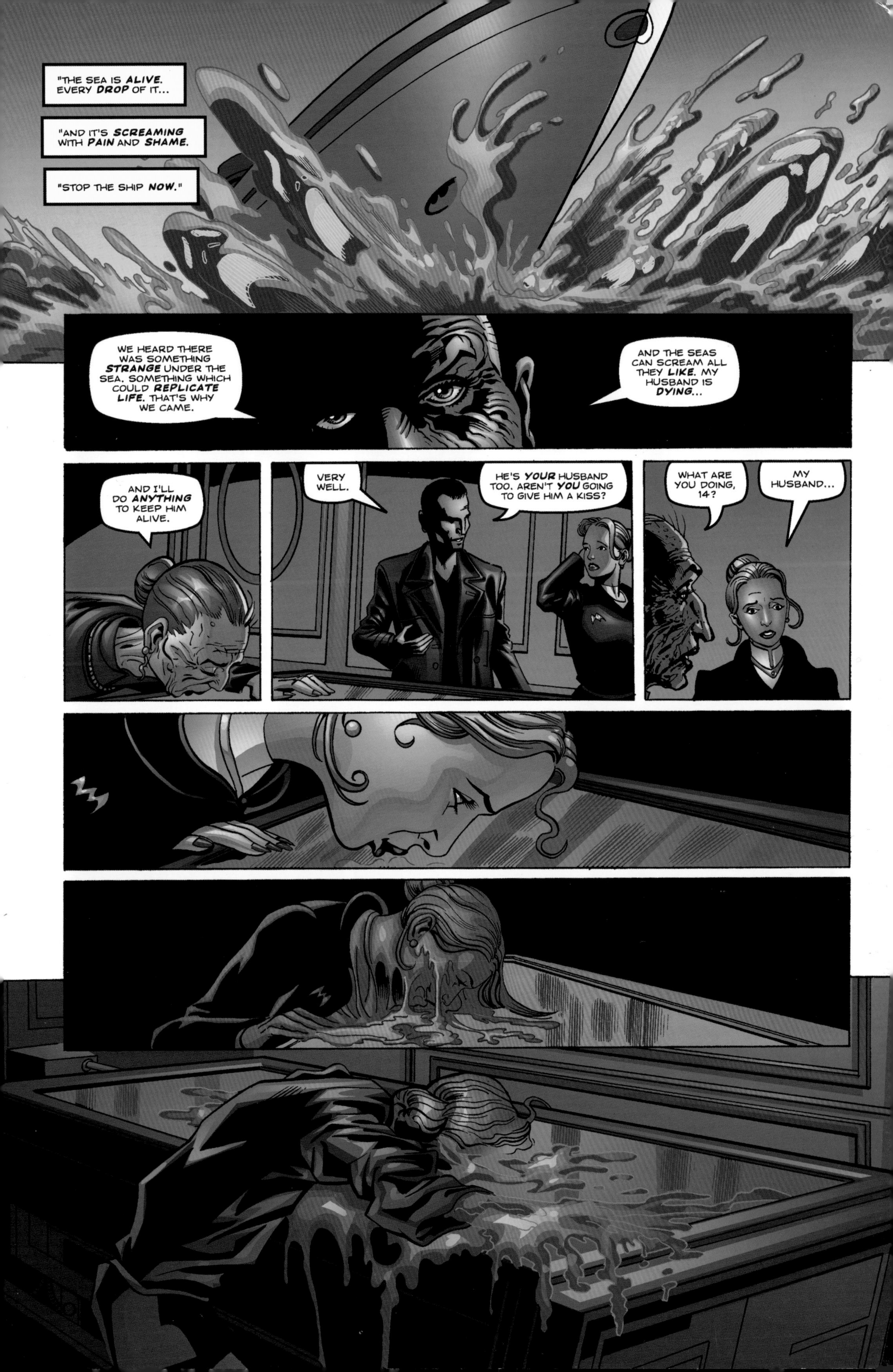
"THE SEA IS ALIVE. EVERY DROP OF IT...
"AND IT'S SCREAMING WITH PAIN AND SHAME.
"STOP THE SHIP NOW."
WE HEARD THERE WAS SOMETHING STRANGE UNDER THE SEA. SOMETHING WHICH COULD REPLICATE LIFE. THAT'S WHY WE CAME.
AND THE SEAS CAN SCREAM ALL THEY LIKE. MY HUSBAND IS DYING...
AND I'LL DO ANYTHING TO KEEP HIM ALIVE.
VERY WELL.
HE'S YOUR HUSBAND TOO. AREN'T YOU GOING TO GIVE HIM A KISS?
WHAT ARE YOU DOING, 14?
MY HUSBAND...

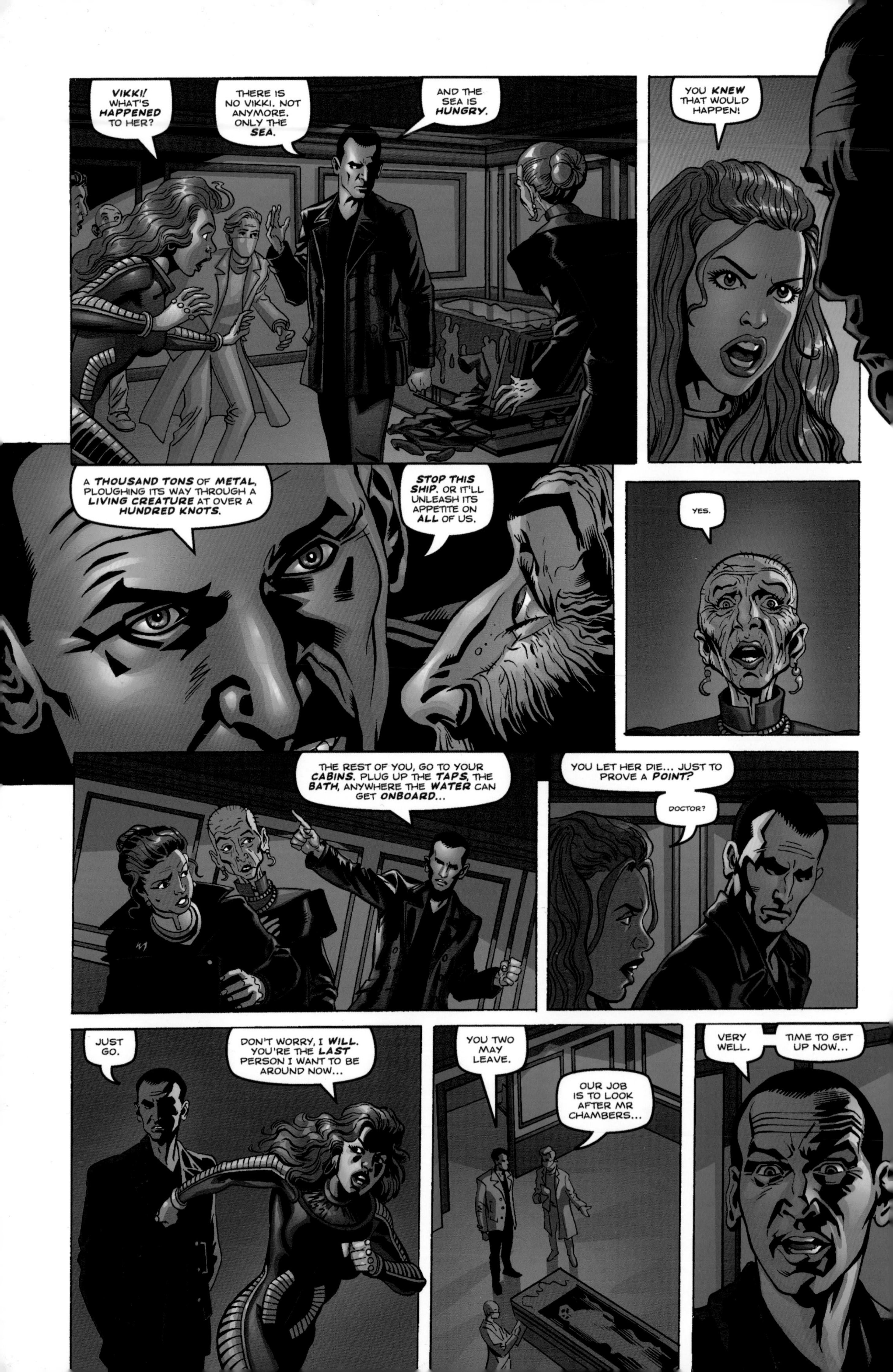
VIKKI! WHAT'S HAPPENED TO HER?
THERE IS NO VIKKI. NOT ANYMORE. ONLY THE SEA.
AND THE SEA IS HUNGRY.
YOU KNEW THAT WOULD HAPPEN!
A THOUSAND TONS OF METAL, PLOUGHING ITS WAY THROUGH A LIVING CREATURE AT OVER A HUNDRED KNOTS.
STOP THIS SHIP. OR IT'LL UNLEASH ITS APPETITE ON ALL OF US.
YES.
THE REST OF YOU, GO TO YOUR CABINS. PLUG UP THE TAPS, THE BATH, ANYWHERE THE WATER CAN GET ONBOARD...
YOU LET HER DIE... JUST TO PROVE A POINT?
DOCTOR?
JUST GO.
DON'T WORRY, I WILL. YOU'RE THE LAST PERSON I WANT TO BE AROUND NOW...
YOU TWO MAY LEAVE.
OUR JOB IS TO LOOK AFTER MR CHAMBERS...
VERY WELL.
TIME TO GET UP NOW...

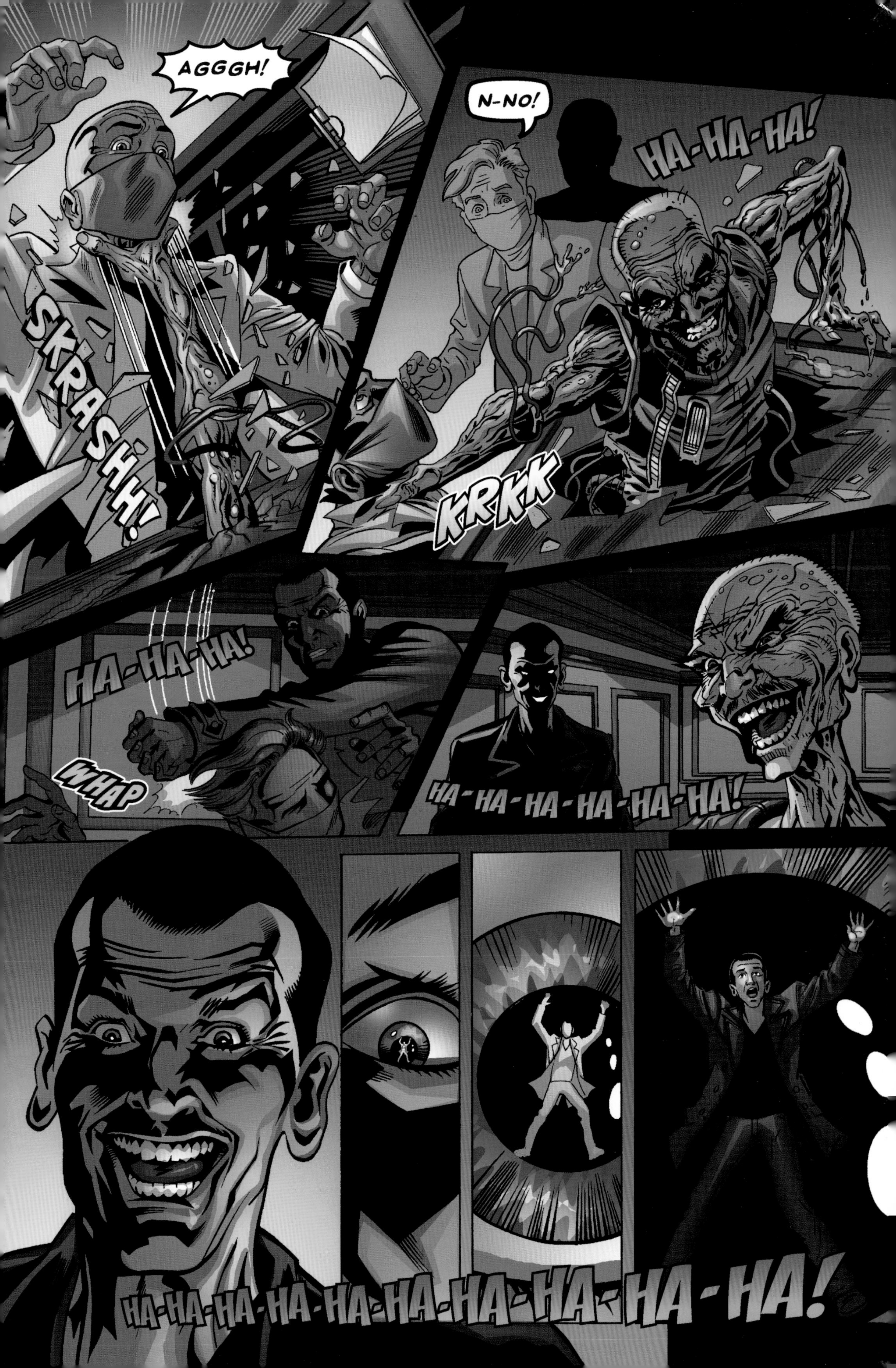
AGGGH!
SKRASHH!
N-NO!
HA-HA-HA!
KRKK
HA-HA-HA!
WHAP
HA-HA-HA-HA-HA-HA!
HA-HA-HA-HA-HA-HA-HA-HA-HA-HA!

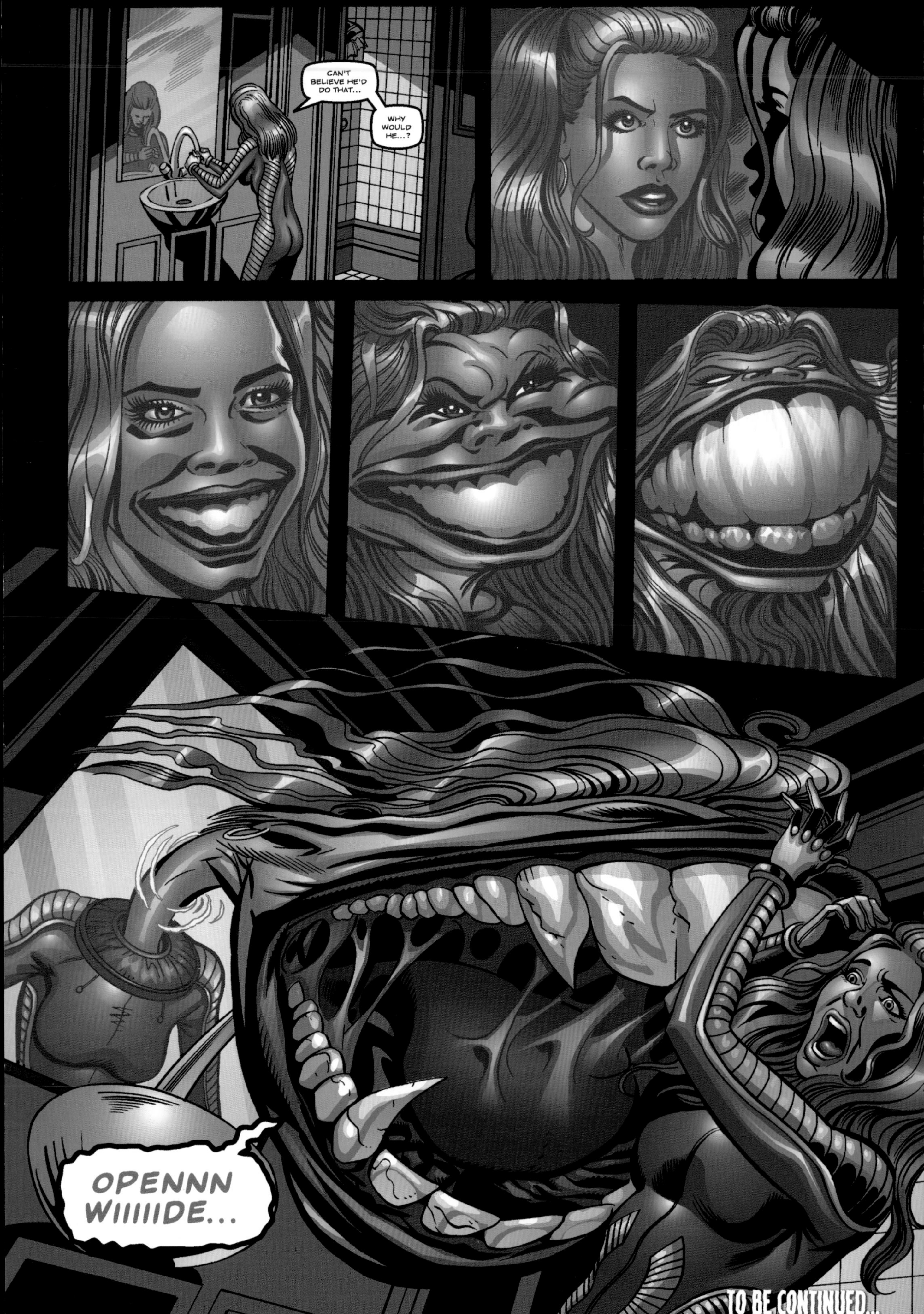
CAN'T BELIEVE HE'D DO THAT...
WHY WOULD HE...?
OPENNN WIIIIIDE...
TO BE CONTINUED...

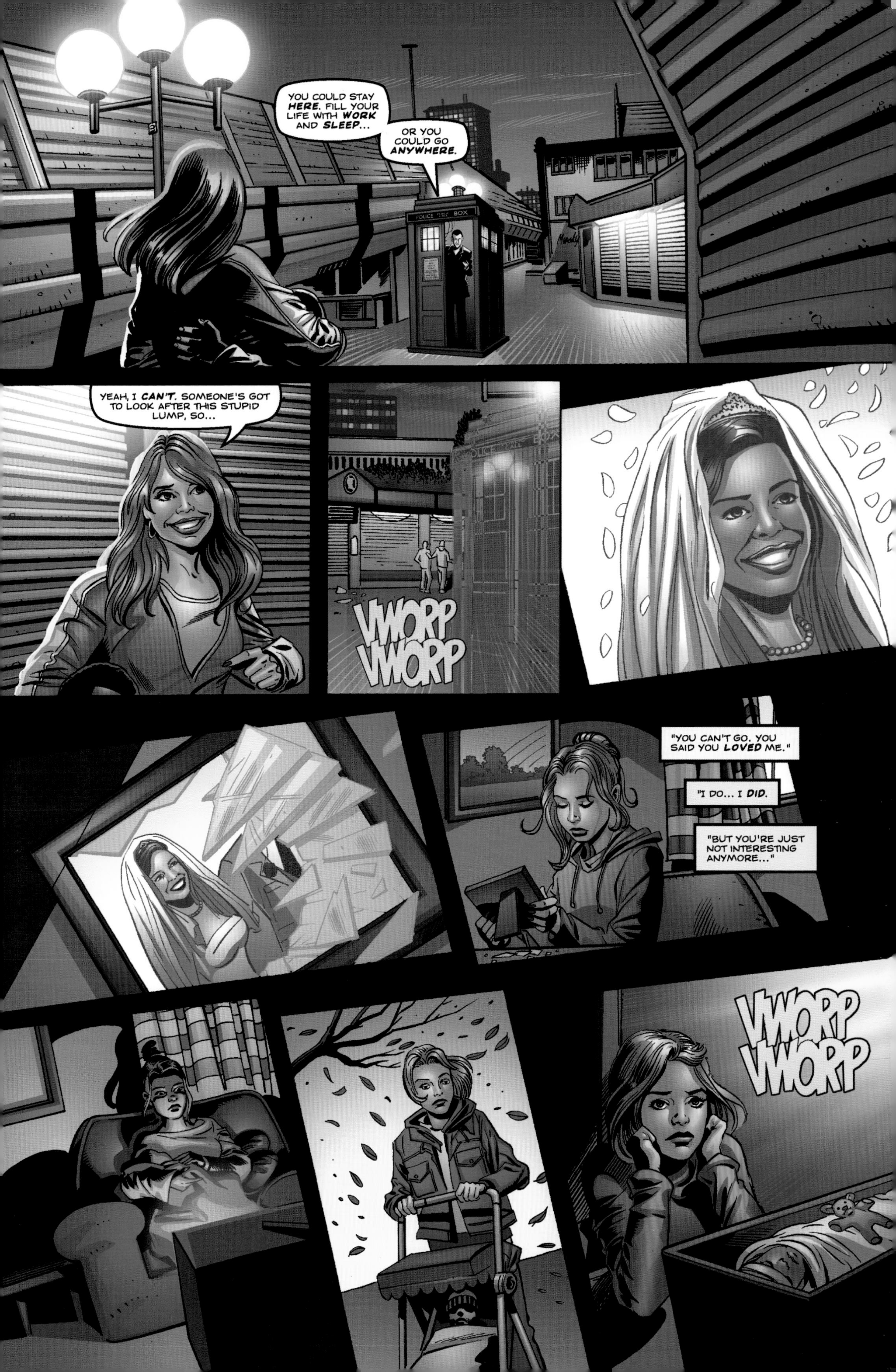
YOU COULD STAY HERE. FILL YOUR LIFE WITH WORK AND SLEEP...
OR YOU COULD GO ANYWHERE.
POLICE BOX
YEAH, I CAN'T. SOMEONE'S GOT TO LOOK AFTER THIS STUPID LUMP, SO...
VWORP VWORP
"YOU CAN'T GO. YOU SAID YOU LOVED ME."
"I DO... I DID.
"BUT YOU'RE JUST NOT INTERESTING ANYMORE..."
VWORP VWORP

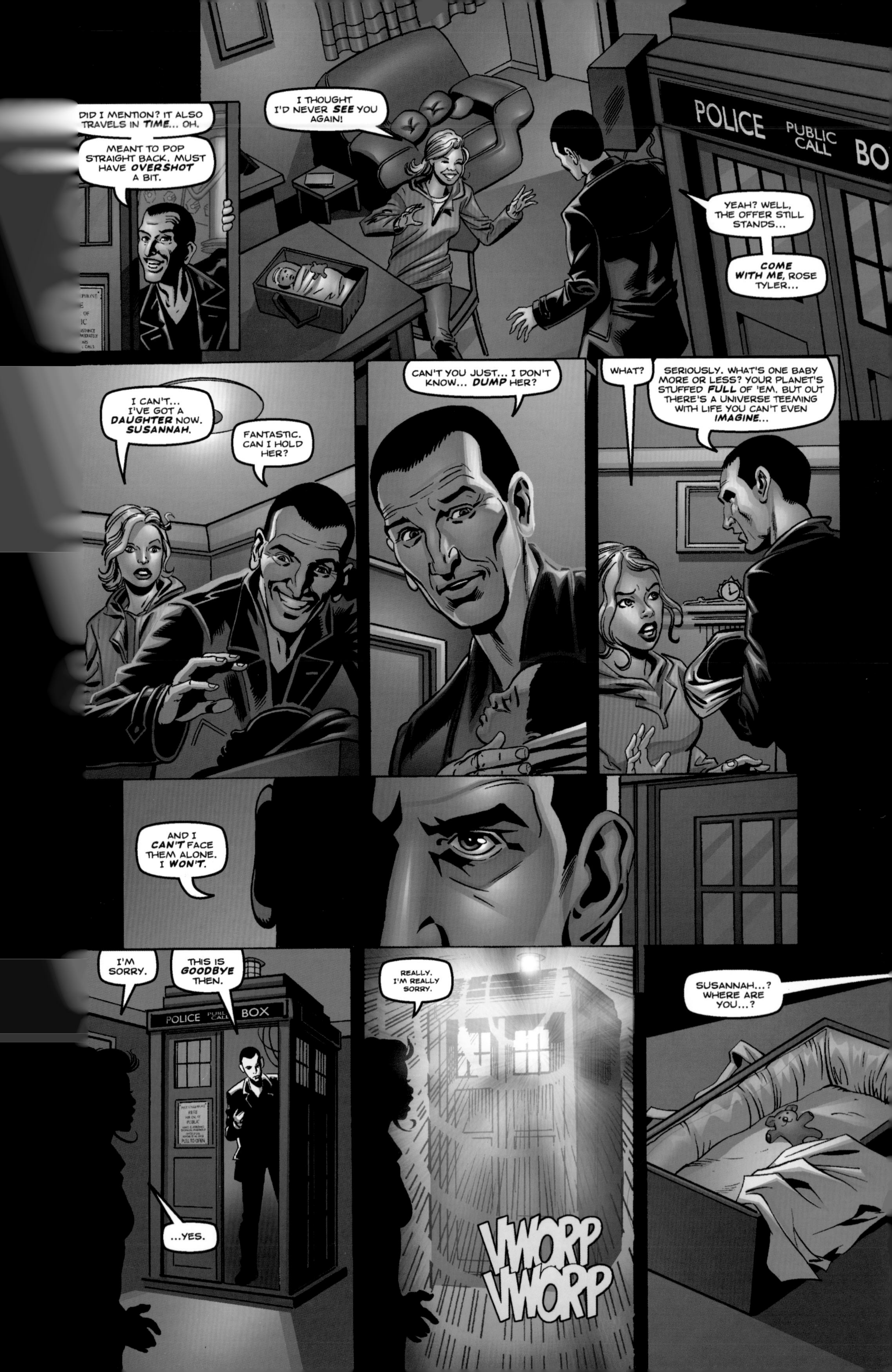
DID I MENTION? IT ALSO TRAVELS IN TIME... OH.
MEANT TO POP STRAIGHT BACK. MUST HAVE OVERSHOT A BIT.
I THOUGHT I'D NEVER SEE YOU AGAIN!
POLICE PUBLIC CALL BO
YEAH? WELL, THE OFFER STILL STANDS...
COME WITH ME, ROSE TYLER...
I CAN'T... I'VE GOT A DAUGHTER NOW. SUSANNAH.
FANTASTIC. CAN I HOLD HER?
CAN'T YOU JUST... I DON'T KNOW... DUMP HER?
WHAT?
SERIOUSLY. WHAT'S ONE BABY MORE OR LESS? YOUR PLANET'S STUFFED FULL OF 'EM. BUT OUT THERE'S A UNIVERSE TEEMING WITH LIFE YOU CAN'T EVEN IMAGINE...
AND I CAN'T FACE THEM ALONE. I WON'T.
I'M SORRY.
THIS IS GOODBYE THEN.
POLICE PUBLIC CALL BOX
...YES.
REALLY. I'M REALLY SORRY.
VWORP VWORP
SUSANNAH...? WHERE ARE YOU...?

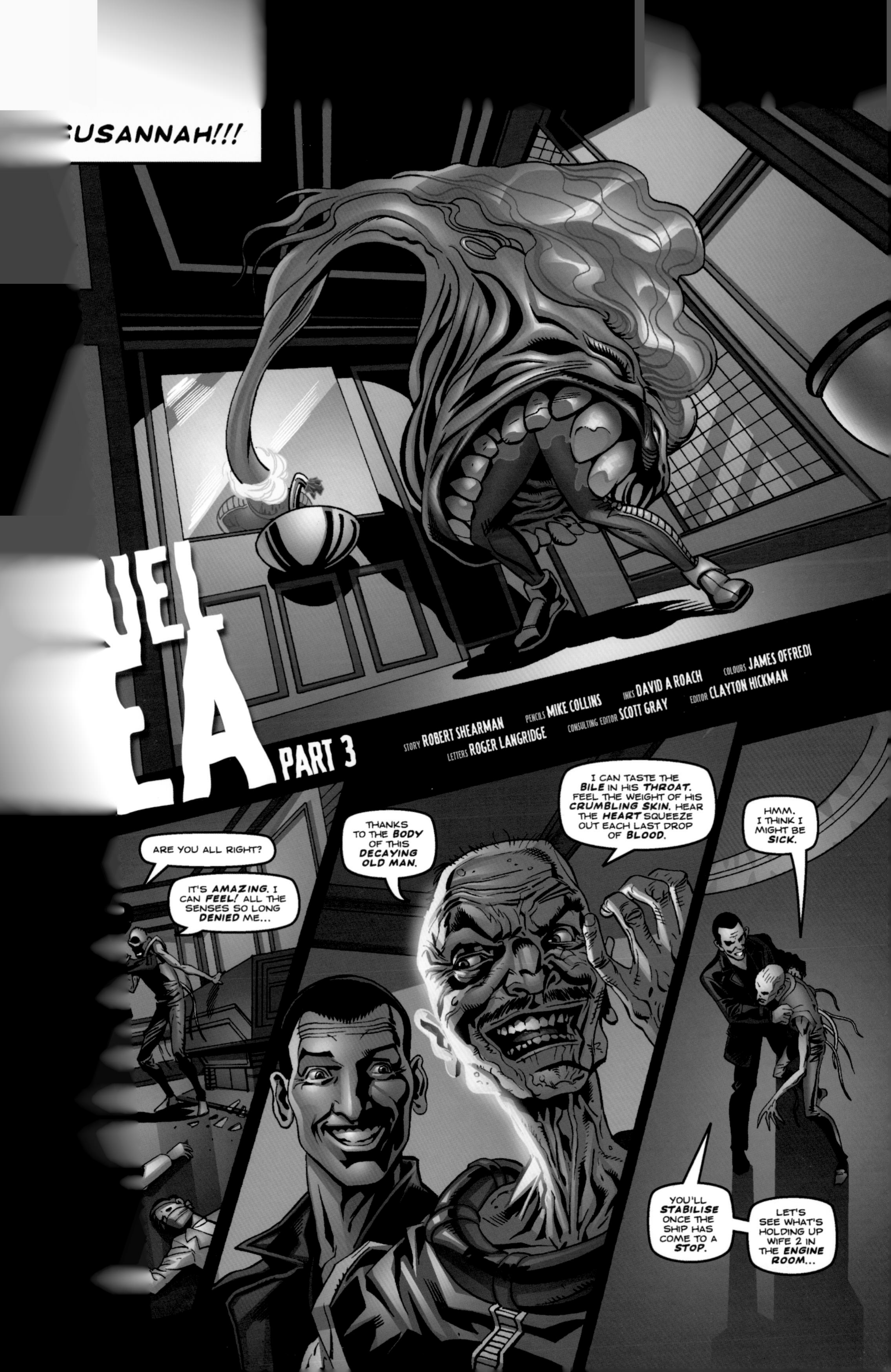

SUSANNAH!!!
UEL
EA
PART 3
STORY ROBERT SHEARMAN
PENCILS MIKE COLLINS
INKS DAVID A ROACH
COLOURS JAMES OFFREDI
LETTERS ROGER LANGRIDGE
CONSULTING EDITOR SCOTT GRAY
EDITOR CLAYTON HICKMAN
ARE YOU ALL RIGHT?
IT'S AMAZING. I CAN FEEL! ALL THE SENSES SO LONG DENIED ME...
THANKS TO THE BODY OF THIS DECAYING OLD MAN.
I CAN TASTE THE BILE IN HIS THROAT. FEEL THE WEIGHT OF HIS CRUMBLING SKIN. HEAR THE HEART SQUEEZE OUT EACH LAST DROP OF BLOOD.
HMM. I THINK I MIGHT BE SICK.
YOU'LL STABILISE ONCE THE SHIP HAS COME TO A STOP.
LET'S SEE WHAT'S HOLDING UP WIFE 2 IN THE ENGINE ROOM...

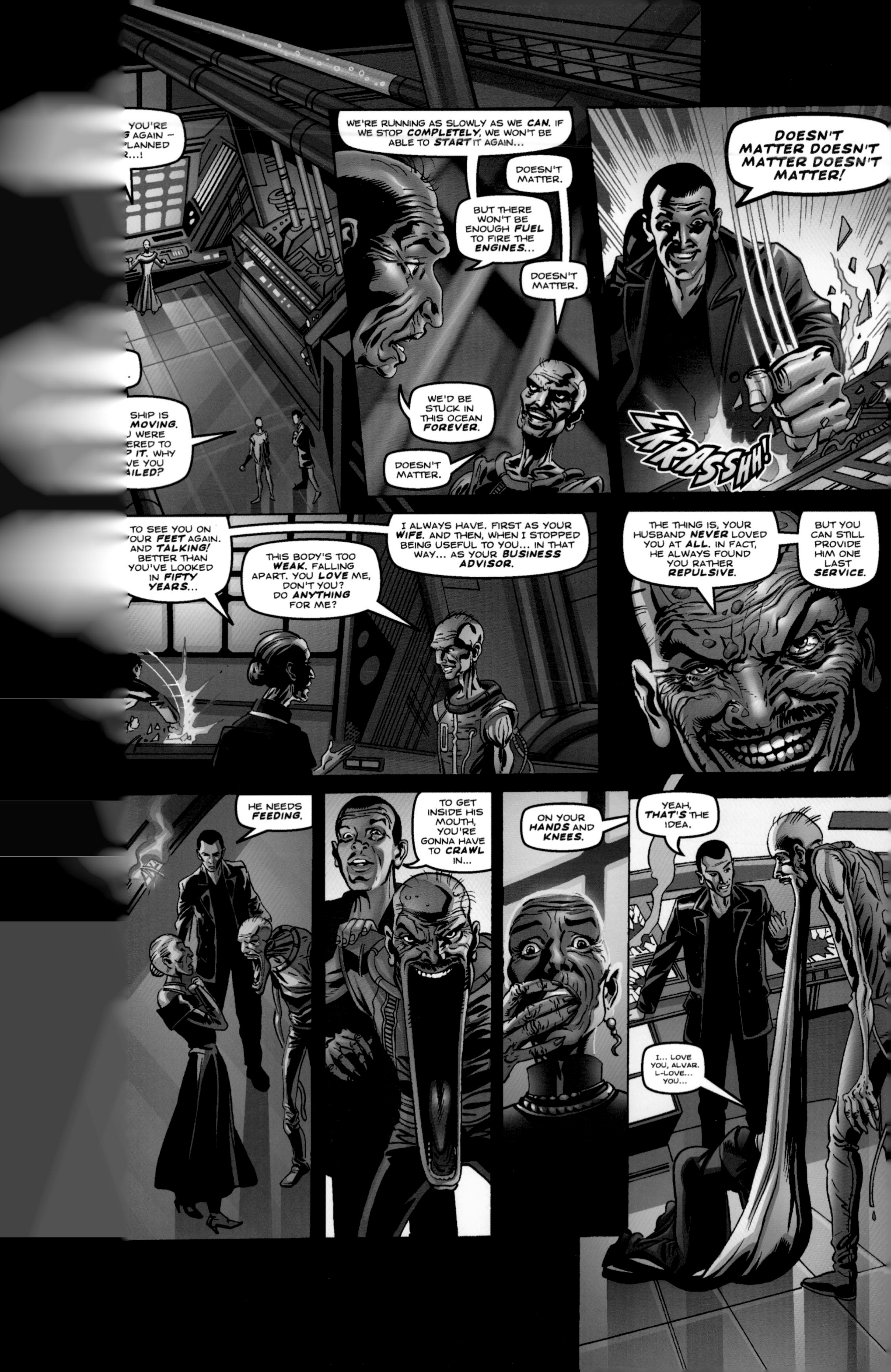

WE'RE RUNNING AS SLOWLY AS WE CAN. IF WE STOP COMPLETELY, WE WON'T BE ABLE TO START IT AGAIN...
DOESN'T MATTER.
BUT THERE WON'T BE ENOUGH FUEL TO FIRE THE ENGINES...
DOESN'T MATTER.
WE'D BE STUCK IN THIS OCEAN FOREVER.
DOESN'T MATTER.
DOESN'T MATTER DOESN'T MATTER DOESN'T MATTER!
ZKRASSHH!
THIS BODY'S TOO WEAK. FALLING APART. YOU LOVE ME, DON'T YOU? DO ANYTHING FOR ME?
I ALWAYS HAVE. FIRST AS YOUR WIFE. AND THEN, WHEN I STOPPED BEING USEFUL TO YOU... IN THAT WAY... AS YOUR BUSINESS ADVISOR.
THE THING IS, YOUR HUSBAND NEVER LOVED YOU AT ALL. IN FACT, HE ALWAYS FOUND YOU RATHER REPULSIVE.
BUT YOU CAN STILL PROVIDE HIM ONE LAST SERVICE.
HE NEEDS FEEDING.
TO GET INSIDE HIS MOUTH, YOU'RE GONNA HAVE TO CRAWL IN...
ON YOUR HANDS AND KNEES.
YEAH, THAT'S THE IDEA.
I... LOVE YOU, ALVAR. L-LOVE... YOU...

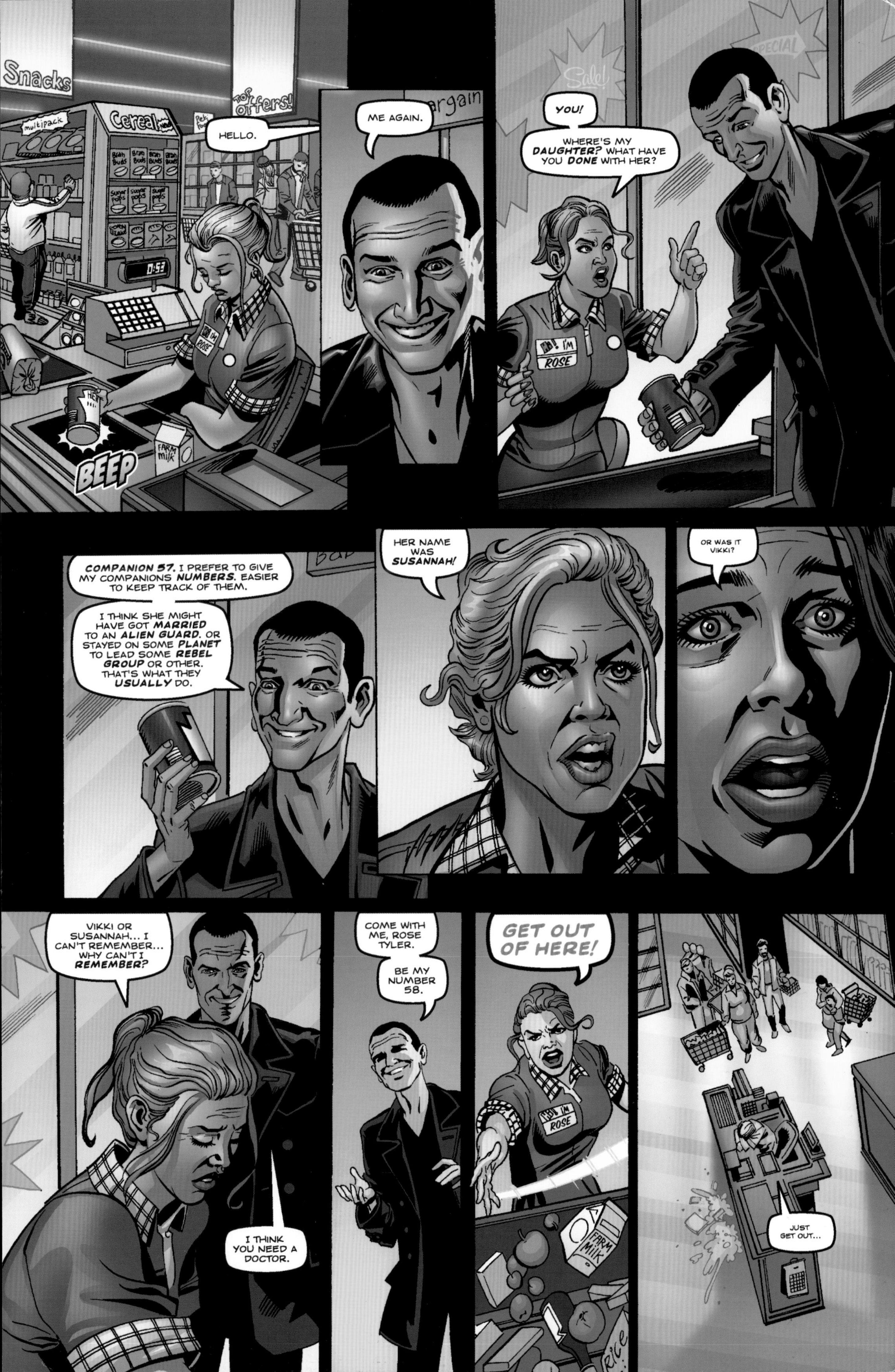
Snacks
Cereal
multipack
Top offers!
HELLO.
BEEP
ME AGAIN.
YOU!
WHERE'S MY DAUGHTER? WHAT HAVE YOU DONE WITH HER?
COMPANION 57. I PREFER TO GIVE MY COMPANIONS NUMBERS. EASIER TO KEEP TRACK OF THEM.
I THINK SHE MIGHT HAVE GOT MARRIED TO AN ALIEN GUARD. OR STAYED ON SOME PLANET TO LEAD SOME REBEL GROUP OR OTHER. THAT'S WHAT THEY USUALLY DO.
HER NAME WAS SUSANNAH!
OR WAS IT VIKKI?
VIKKI OR SUSANNAH... I CAN'T REMEMBER... WHY CAN'T I REMEMBER?
I THINK YOU NEED A DOCTOR.
COME WITH ME, ROSE TYLER.
BE MY NUMBER 58.
GET OUT OF HERE!
JUST GET OUT...

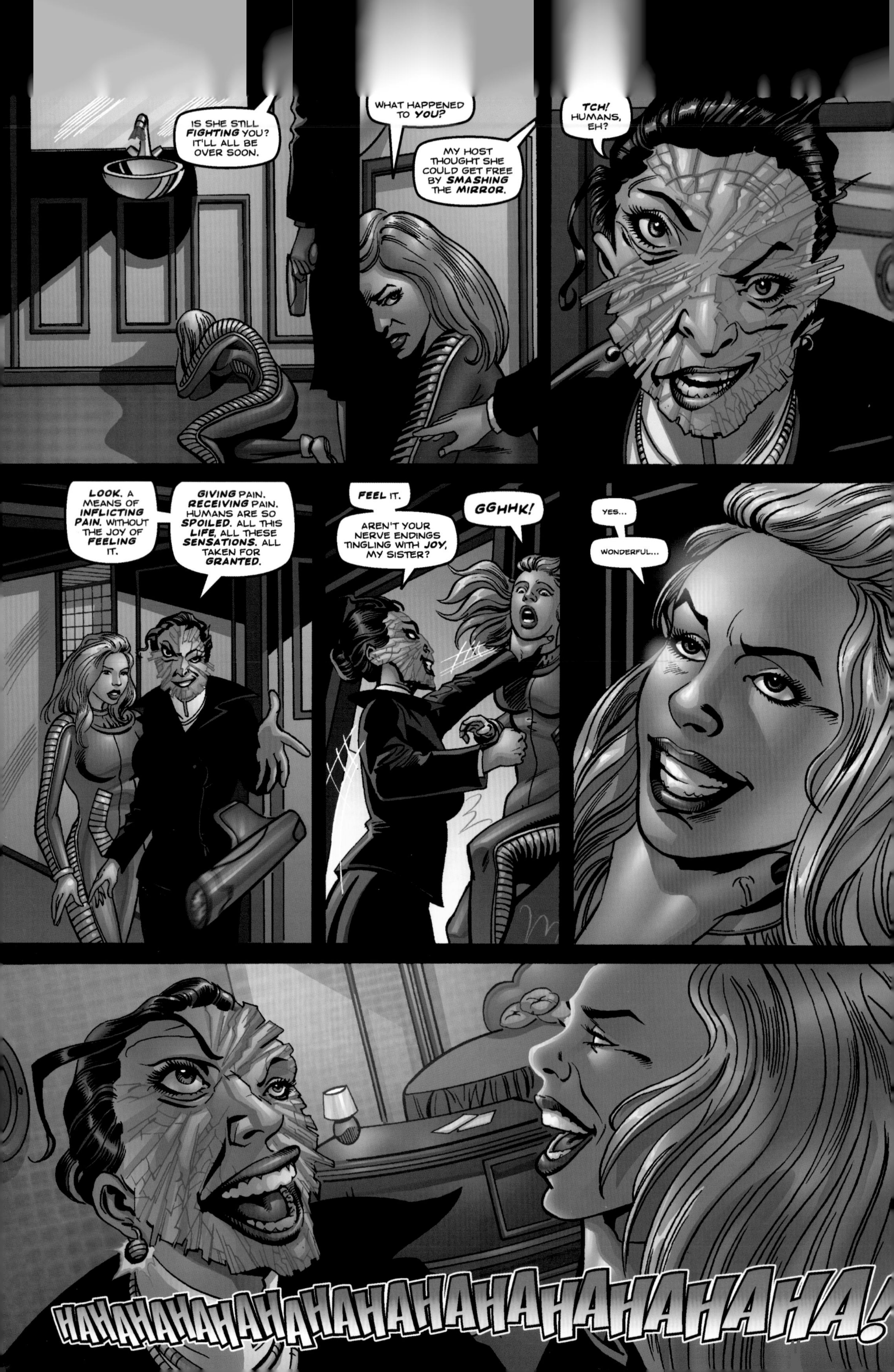
IS SHE STILL FIGHTING YOU? IT'LL ALL BE OVER SOON.
WHAT HAPPENED TO YOU?
MY HOST THOUGHT SHE COULD GET FREE BY SMASHING THE MIRROR.
TCH! HUMANS, EH?
LOOK. A MEANS OF INFLICTING PAIN. WITHOUT THE JOY OF FEELING IT.
GIVING PAIN. RECEIVING PAIN. HUMANS ARE SO SPOILED. ALL THIS LIFE, ALL THESE SENSATIONS. ALL TAKEN FOR GRANTED.
FEEL IT.
AREN'T YOUR NERVE ENDINGS TINGLING WITH JOY, MY SISTER?
GGHHK!
YES...
WONDERFUL...
HAHAHAHAHAHAHAHAHAHAHAHAHAHAHAHA!

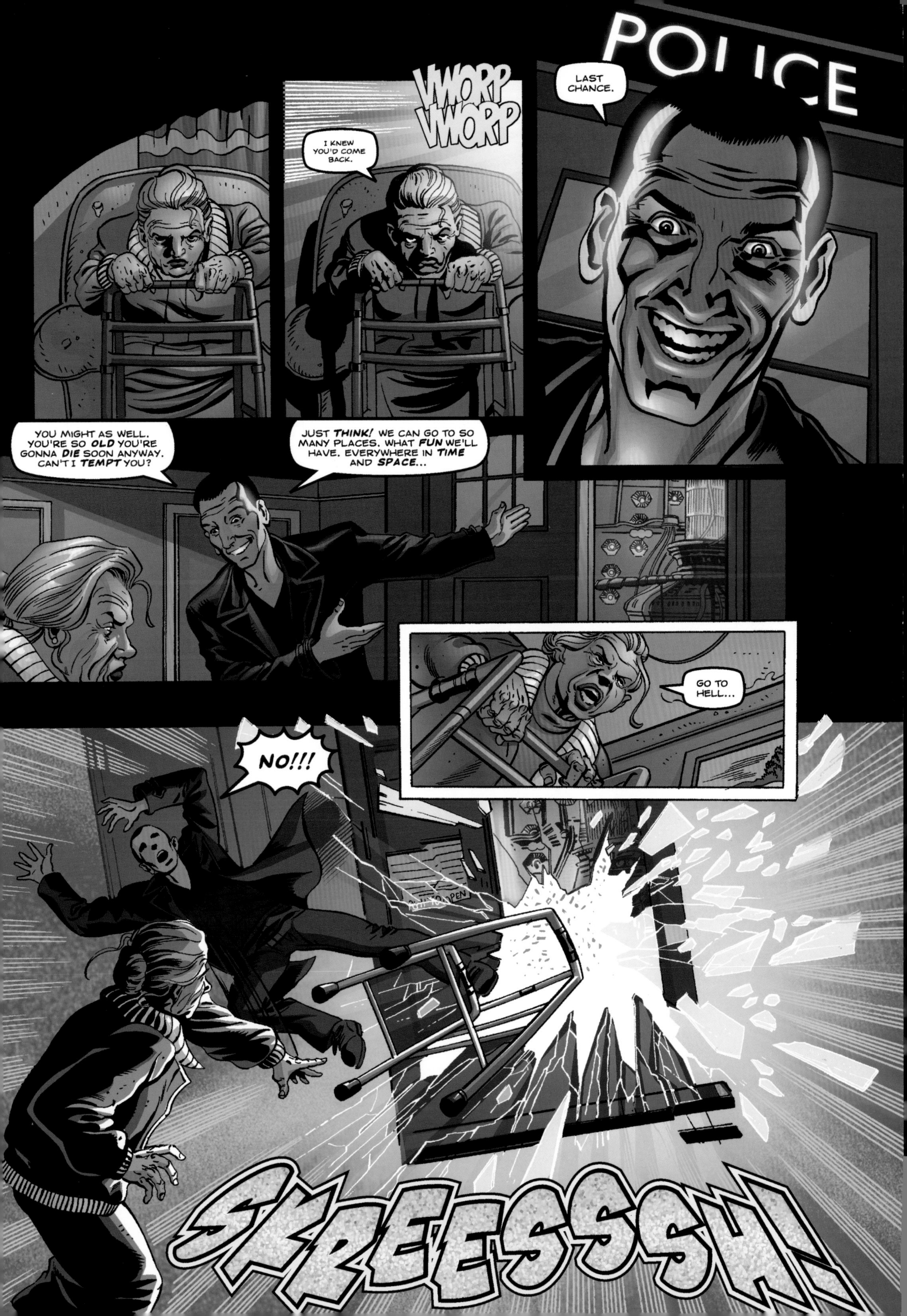

VWORP VWORP
I KNEW YOU'D COME BACK.
POLICE
LAST CHANCE.
YOU MIGHT AS WELL. YOU'RE SO OLD YOU'RE GONNA DIE SOON ANYWAY. CAN'T I TEMPT YOU?
JUST THINK! WE CAN GO TO SO MANY PLACES. WHAT FUN WE'LL HAVE. EVERYWHERE IN TIME AND SPACE...
GO TO HELL...
NO!!!
SKREESSSH!

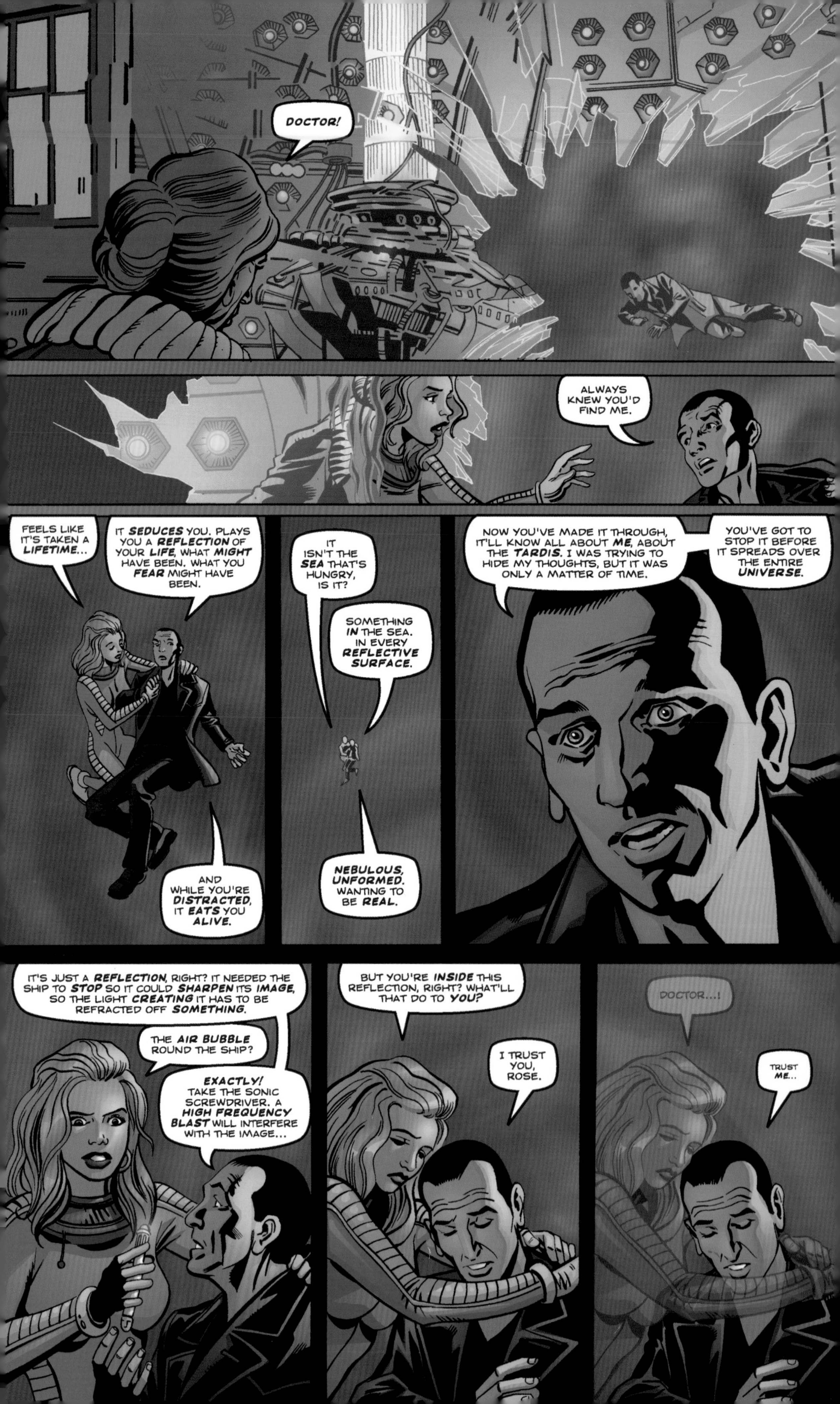
DOCTOR!
ALWAYS KNEW YOU'D FIND ME.
FEELS LIKE IT'S TAKEN A LIFETIME...
IT SEDUCES YOU. PLAYS YOU A REFLECTION OF YOUR LIFE, WHAT MIGHT HAVE BEEN. WHAT YOU FEAR MIGHT HAVE BEEN.
AND WHILE YOU'RE DISTRACTED, IT EATS YOU ALIVE.
IT ISN'T THE SEA THAT'S HUNGRY, IS IT?
SOMETHING IN THE SEA. IN EVERY REFLECTIVE SURFACE.
NEBULOUS, UNFORMED. WANTING TO BE REAL.
NOW YOU'VE MADE IT THROUGH, IT'LL KNOW ALL ABOUT ME, ABOUT THE TARDIS. I WAS TRYING TO HIDE MY THOUGHTS, BUT IT WAS ONLY A MATTER OF TIME.
YOU'VE GOT TO STOP IT BEFORE IT SPREADS OVER THE ENTIRE UNIVERSE.
IT'S JUST A REFLECTION, RIGHT? IT NEEDED THE SHIP TO STOP SO IT COULD SHARPEN ITS IMAGE, SO THE LIGHT CREATING IT HAS TO BE REFRACTED OFF SOMETHING.
THE AIR BUBBLE ROUND THE SHIP?
EXACTLY! TAKE THE SONIC SCREWDRIVER. A HIGH FREQUENCY BLAST WILL INTERFERE WITH THE IMAGE...
BUT YOU'RE INSIDE THIS REFLECTION, RIGHT? WHAT'LL THAT DO TO YOU?
I TRUST YOU, ROSE.
DOCTOR...!
TRUST ME...

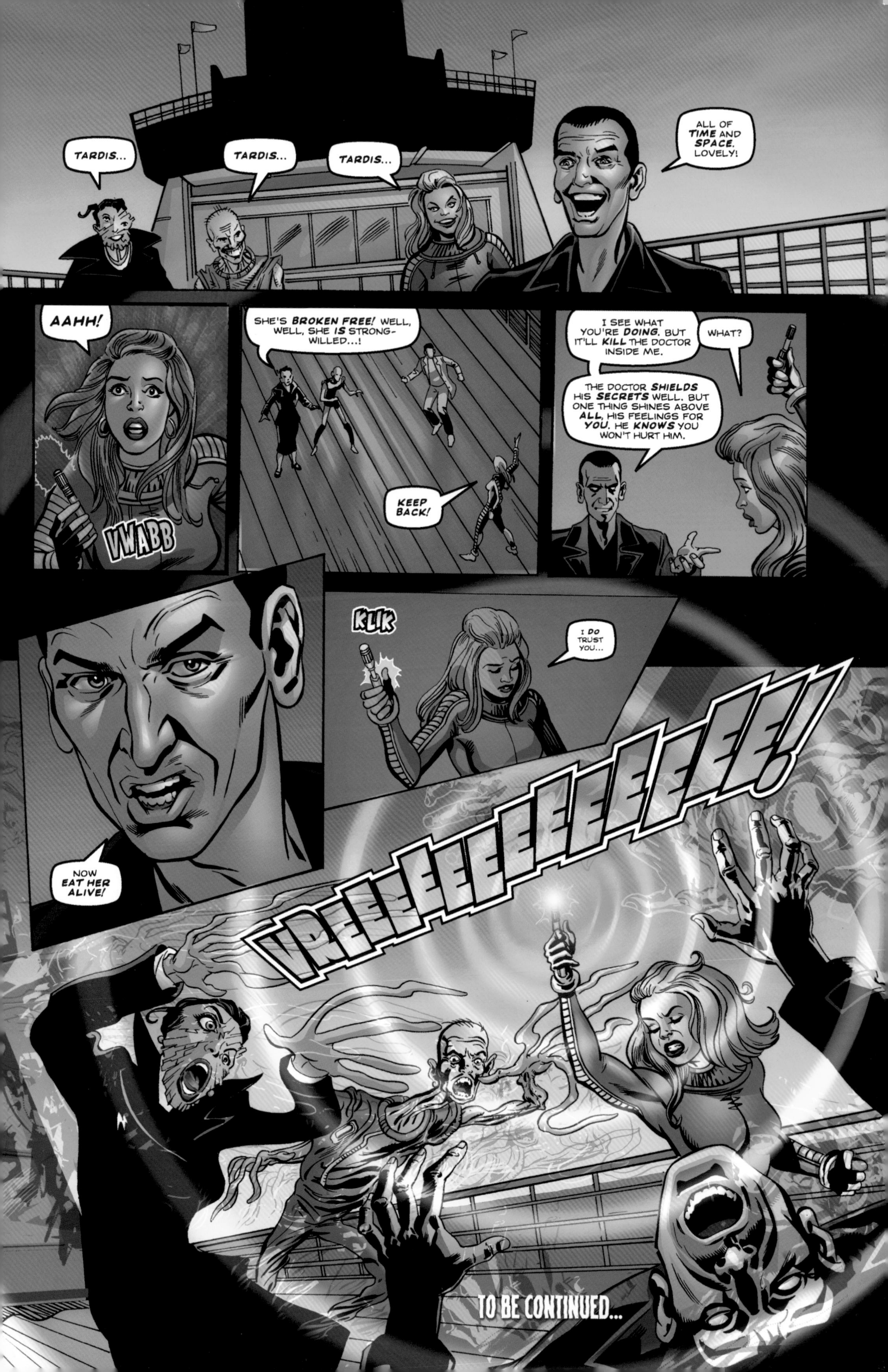
TARDIS...
TARDIS...
TARDIS...
ALL OF TIME AND SPACE. LOVELY!
AAHH!
VWABB
SHE'S BROKEN FREE! WELL, WELL, SHE IS STRONG-WILLED...!
KEEP BACK!
I SEE WHAT YOU'RE DOING, BUT IT'LL KILL THE DOCTOR INSIDE ME.
WHAT?
THE DOCTOR SHIELDS HIS SECRETS WELL. BUT ONE THING SHINES ABOVE ALL, HIS FEELINGS FOR YOU. HE KNOWS YOU WON'T HURT HIM.
NOW EAT HER ALIVE!
KLIK
I DO TRUST YOU...
VREEEEEEEEEEE...E...E!
TO BE CONTINUED...

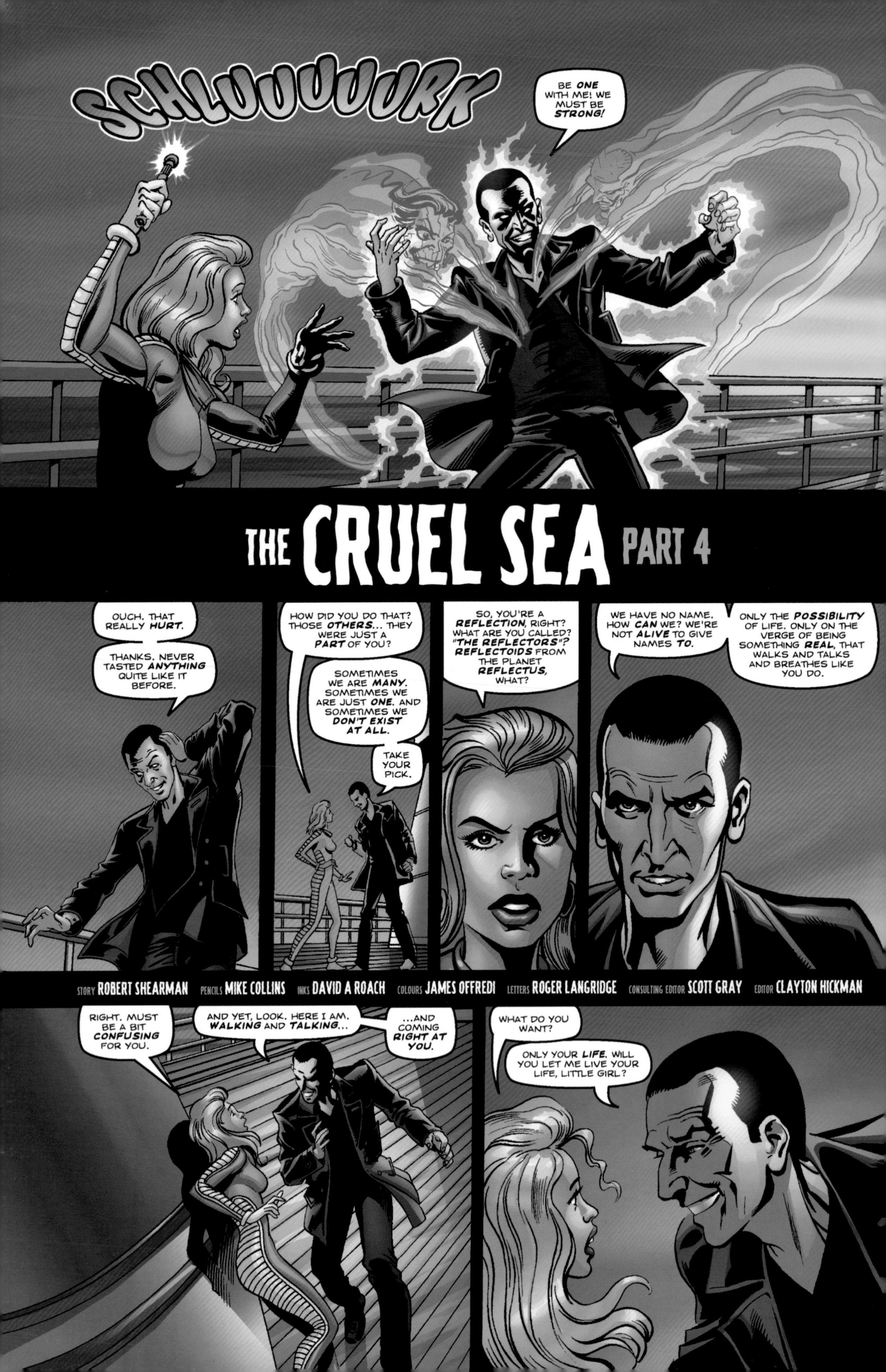
SCHLUUUUUURK
BE ONE WITH ME! WE MUST BE STRONG!
THE CRUEL SEA PART 4
OUCH. THAT REALLY HURT.
THANKS. NEVER TASTED ANYTHING QUITE LIKE IT BEFORE.
HOW DID YOU DO THAT? THOSE OTHERS... THEY WERE JUST A PART OF YOU?
SOMETIMES WE ARE MANY. SOMETIMES WE ARE JUST ONE. AND SOMETIMES WE DON'T EXIST AT ALL.
TAKE YOUR PICK.
SO, YOU'RE A REFLECTION, RIGHT? WHAT ARE YOU CALLED? "THE REFLECTORS"? REFLECTOIDS FROM THE PLANET REFLECTUS, WHAT?
WE HAVE NO NAME. HOW CAN WE? WE'RE NOT ALIVE TO GIVE NAMES TO.
ONLY THE POSSIBILITY OF LIFE. ONLY ON THE VERGE OF BEING SOMETHING REAL, THAT WALKS AND TALKS AND BREATHES LIKE YOU DO.
STORY ROBERT SHEARMAN PENCILS MIKE COLLINS INKS DAVID A ROACH COLOURS JAMES OFFREDI LETTERS ROGER LANGRIDGE CONSULTING EDITOR SCOTT GRAY EDITOR CLAYTON HICKMAN
RIGHT. MUST BE A BIT CONFUSING FOR YOU.
AND YET, LOOK. HERE I AM. WALKING AND TALKING...
...AND COMING RIGHT AT YOU.
WHAT DO YOU WANT?
ONLY YOUR LIFE. WILL YOU LET ME LIVE YOUR LIFE, LITTLE GIRL?

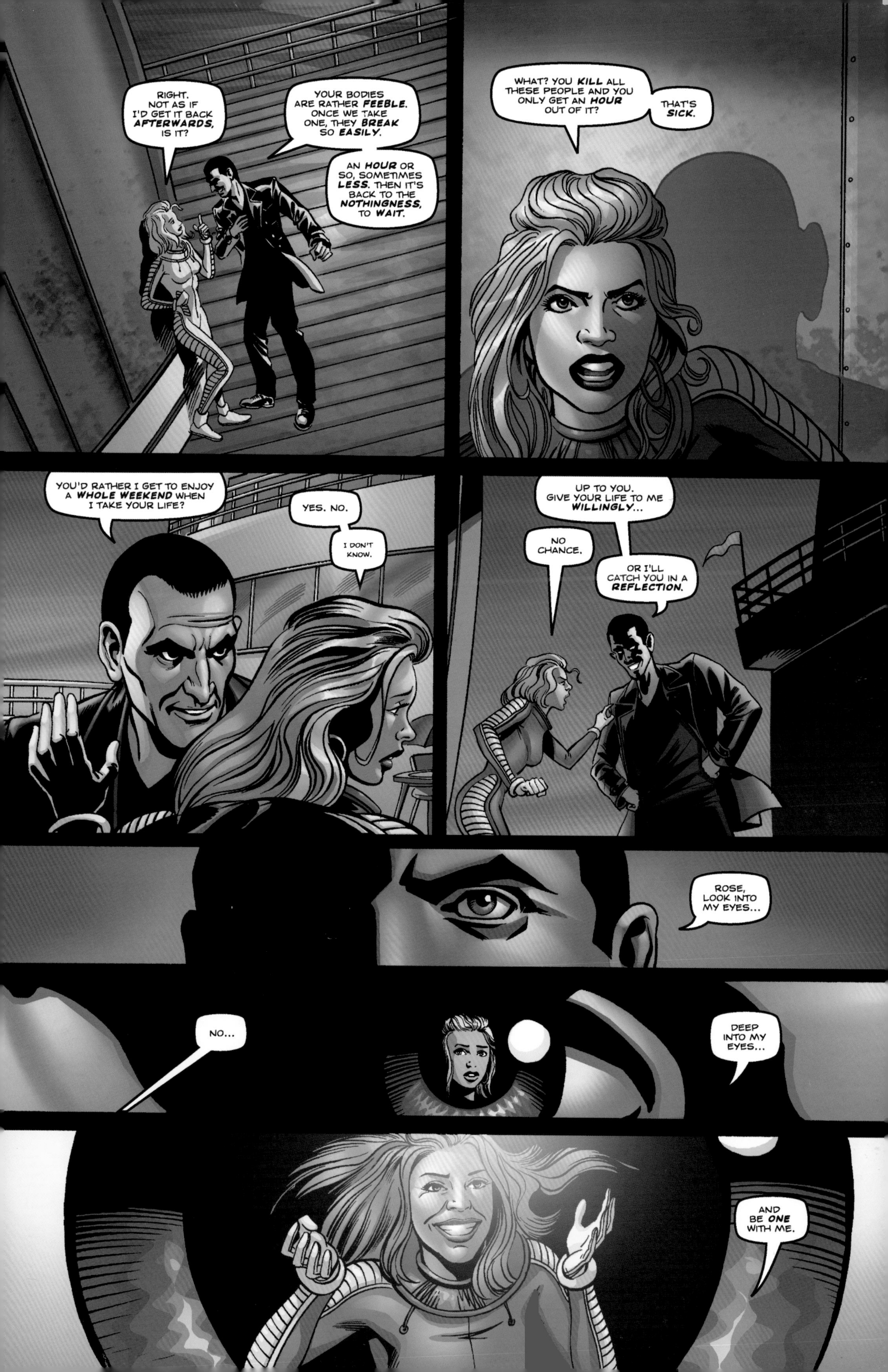
RIGHT. NOT AS IF I'D GET IT BACK AFTERWARDS, IS IT?
YOUR BODIES ARE RATHER FEEBLE. ONCE WE TAKE ONE, THEY BREAK SO EASILY.
AN HOUR OR SO, SOMETIMES LESS. THEN IT'S BACK TO THE NOTHINGNESS, TO WAIT.
WHAT? YOU KILL ALL THESE PEOPLE AND YOU ONLY GET AN HOUR OUT OF IT?
THAT'S SICK.
YOU'D RATHER I GET TO ENJOY A WHOLE WEEKEND WHEN I TAKE YOUR LIFE?
YES. NO.
I DON'T KNOW.
UP TO YOU. GIVE YOUR LIFE TO ME WILLINGLY...
NO CHANCE.
OR I'LL CATCH YOU IN A REFLECTION.
ROSE, LOOK INTO MY EYES...
NO...
DEEP INTO MY EYES...
AND BE ONE WITH ME.

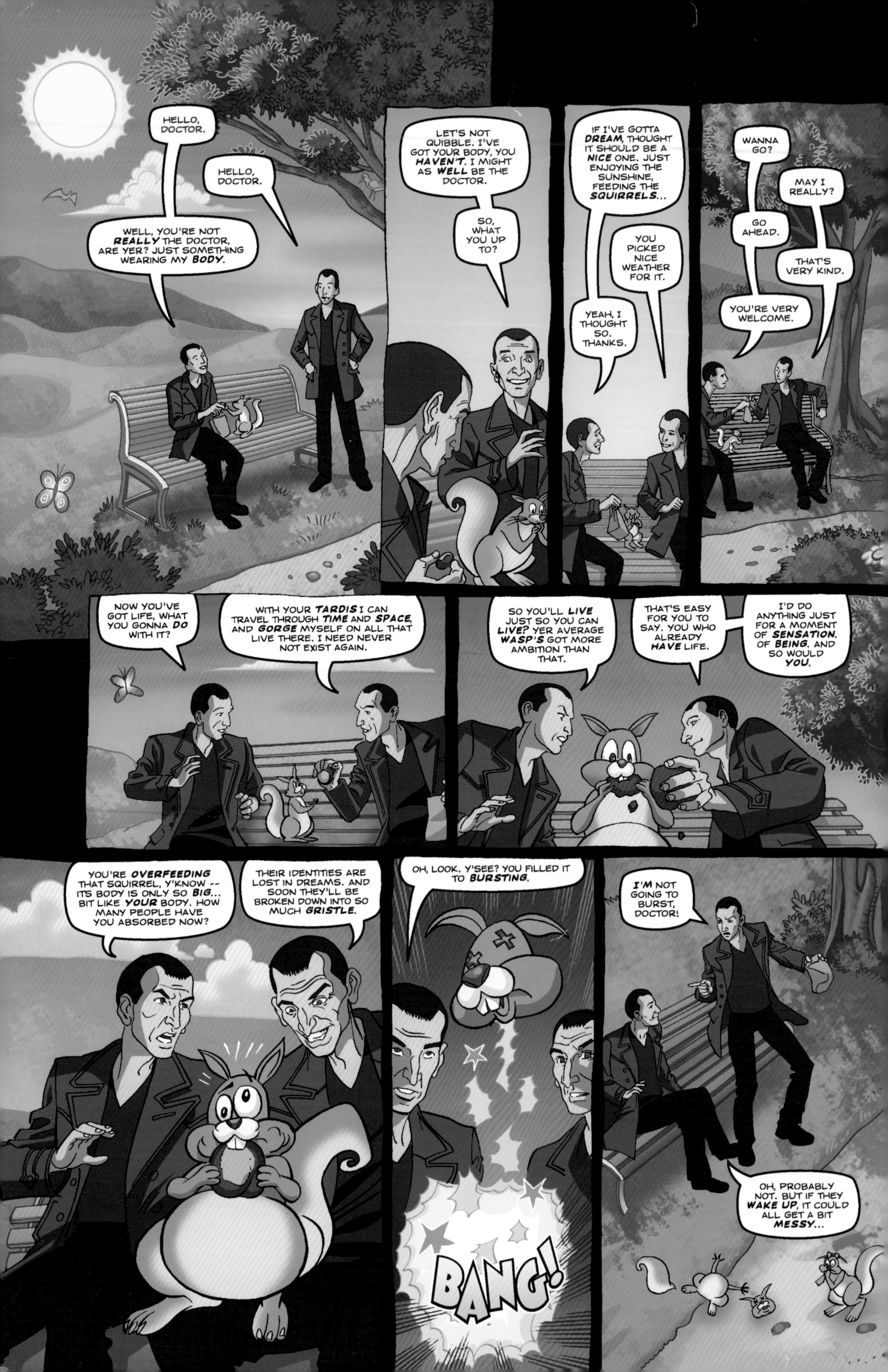
HELLO, DOCTOR.
HELLO, DOCTOR.
WELL, YOU'RE NOT REALLY THE DOCTOR, ARE YER? JUST SOMETHING WEARING MY BODY.
LET'S NOT QUIBBLE. I'VE GOT YOUR BODY, YOU HAVEN'T. I MIGHT AS WELL BE THE DOCTOR.
SO, WHAT YOU UP TO?
IF I'VE GOTTA DREAM, THOUGHT IT SHOULD BE A NICE ONE. JUST ENJOYING THE SUNSHINE, FEEDING THE SQUIRRELS...
YOU PICKED NICE WEATHER FOR IT.
YEAH, I THOUGHT SO. THANKS.
WANNA GO?
MAY I REALLY?
GO AHEAD.
THAT'S VERY KIND.
YOU'RE VERY WELCOME.
NOW YOU'VE GOT LIFE, WHAT YOU GONNA DO WITH IT?
WITH YOUR TARDIS I CAN TRAVEL THROUGH TIME AND SPACE, AND GORGE MYSELF ON ALL THAT LIVE THERE. I NEED NEVER NOT EXIST AGAIN.
SO YOU'LL LIVE JUST SO YOU CAN LIVE? YER AVERAGE WASP'S GOT MORE AMBITION THAN THAT.
THAT'S EASY FOR YOU TO SAY. YOU WHO ALREADY HAVE LIFE.
I'D DO ANYTHING JUST FOR A MOMENT OF SENSATION, OF BEING, AND SO WOULD YOU.
YOU'RE OVERFEEDING THAT SQUIRREL, Y'KNOW -- ITS BODY IS ONLY SO BIG... BIT LIKE YOUR BODY. HOW MANY PEOPLE HAVE YOU ABSORBED NOW?
THEIR IDENTITIES ARE LOST IN DREAMS. AND SOON THEY'LL BE BROKEN DOWN INTO SO MUCH GRISTLE.
OH, LOOK. Y'SEE? YOU FILLED IT TO BURSTING.
BANG!
I'M NOT GOING TO BURST, DOCTOR!
OH, PROBABLY NOT. BUT IF THEY WAKE UP, IT COULD ALL GET A BIT MESSY...

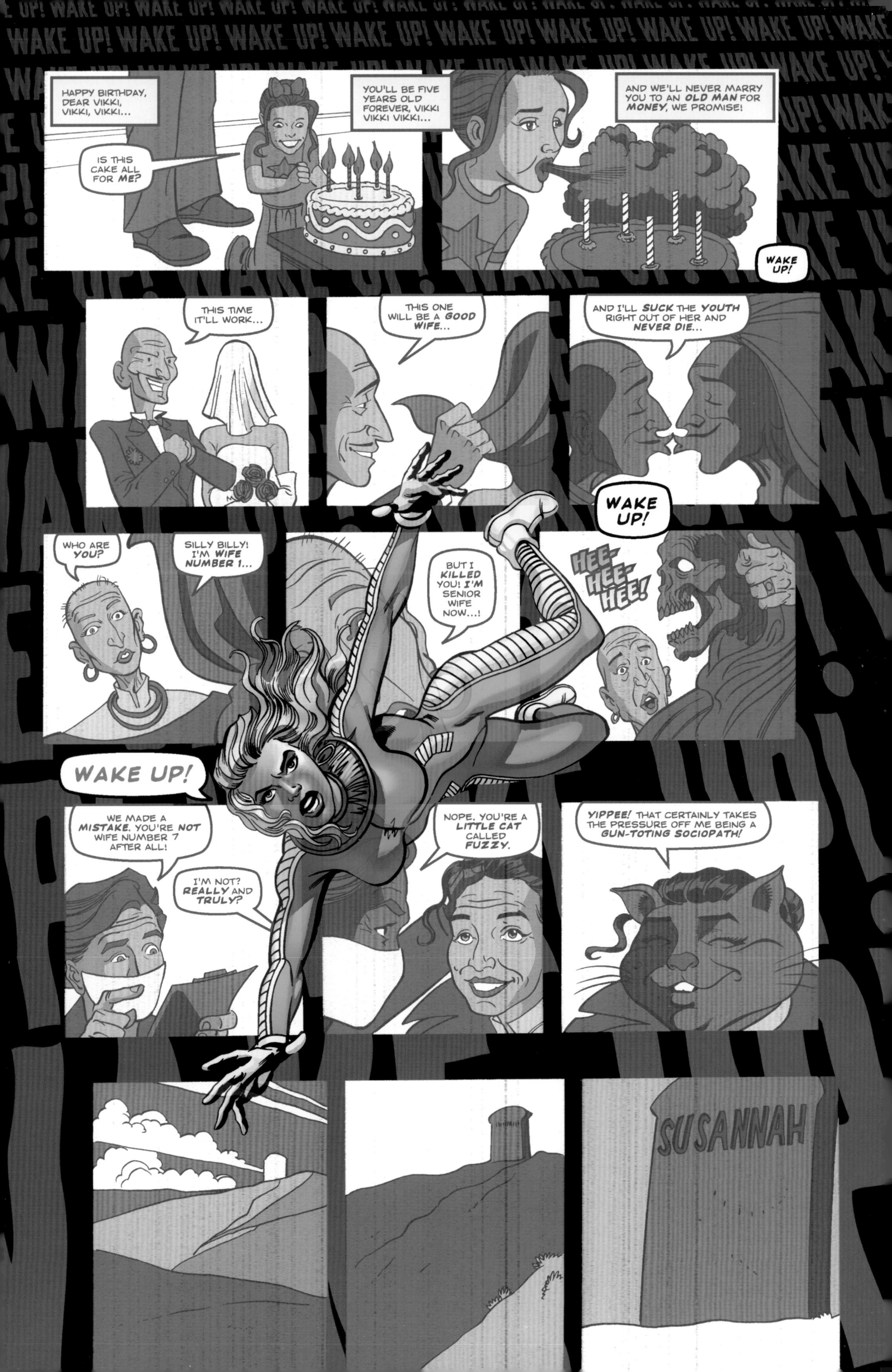
WAKE UP! WAKE UP! WAKE UP! WAKE UP! WAKE UP! WAKE UP! WAKE UP!
HAPPY BIRTHDAY, DEAR VIKKI, VIKKI, VIKKI...
IS THIS CAKE ALL FOR ME?
YOU'LL BE FIVE YEARS OLD FOREVER, VIKKI VIKKI VIKKI...
AND WE'LL NEVER MARRY YOU TO AN OLD MAN FOR MONEY, WE PROMISE!
WAKE UP!
THIS TIME IT'LL WORK...
THIS ONE WILL BE A GOOD WIFE...
AND I'LL SUCK THE YOUTH RIGHT OUT OF HER AND NEVER DIE...
WAKE UP!
WHO ARE YOU?
SILLY BILLY! I'M WIFE NUMBER 1...
BUT I KILLED YOU! I'M SENIOR WIFE NOW...!
HEE-HEE-HEE!
WAKE UP!
WE MADE A MISTAKE. YOU'RE NOT WIFE NUMBER 7 AFTER ALL!
I'M NOT? REALLY AND TRULY?
NOPE. YOU'RE A LITTLE CAT CALLED FUZZY.
YIPPEE! THAT CERTAINLY TAKES THE PRESSURE OFF ME BEING A GUN-TOTING SOCIOPATH!
SUSANNAH

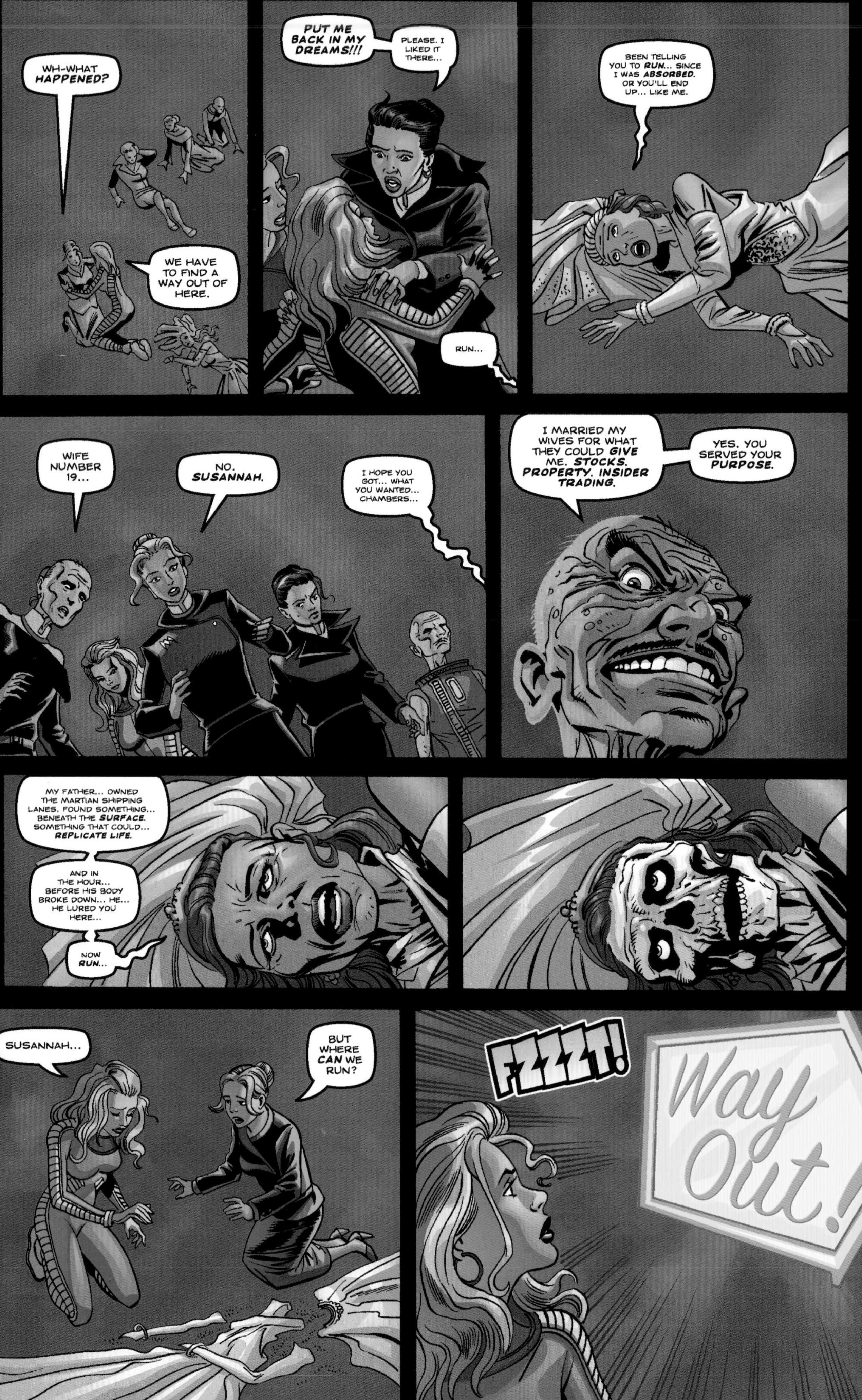

WH-WHAT HAPPENED?
WE HAVE TO FIND A WAY OUT OF HERE.
PUT ME BACK IN MY DREAMS!!!
PLEASE. I LIKED IT THERE...
RUN...
BEEN TELLING YOU TO RUN... SINCE I WAS ABSORBED. OR YOU'LL END UP... LIKE ME.
WIFE NUMBER 19...
NO. SUSANNAH.
I HOPE YOU GOT... WHAT YOU WANTED... CHAMBERS...
I MARRIED MY WIVES FOR WHAT THEY COULD GIVE ME. STOCKS. PROPERTY. INSIDER TRADING.
YES. YOU SERVED YOUR PURPOSE.
MY FATHER... OWNED THE MARTIAN SHIPPING LANES. FOUND SOMETHING... BENEATH THE SURFACE. SOMETHING THAT COULD... REPLICATE LIFE.
AND IN THE HOUR... BEFORE HIS BODY BROKE DOWN... HE... HE LURED YOU HERE...
NOW RUN...
SUSANNAH...
BUT WHERE CAN WE RUN?
FZZZT!
Way Out!

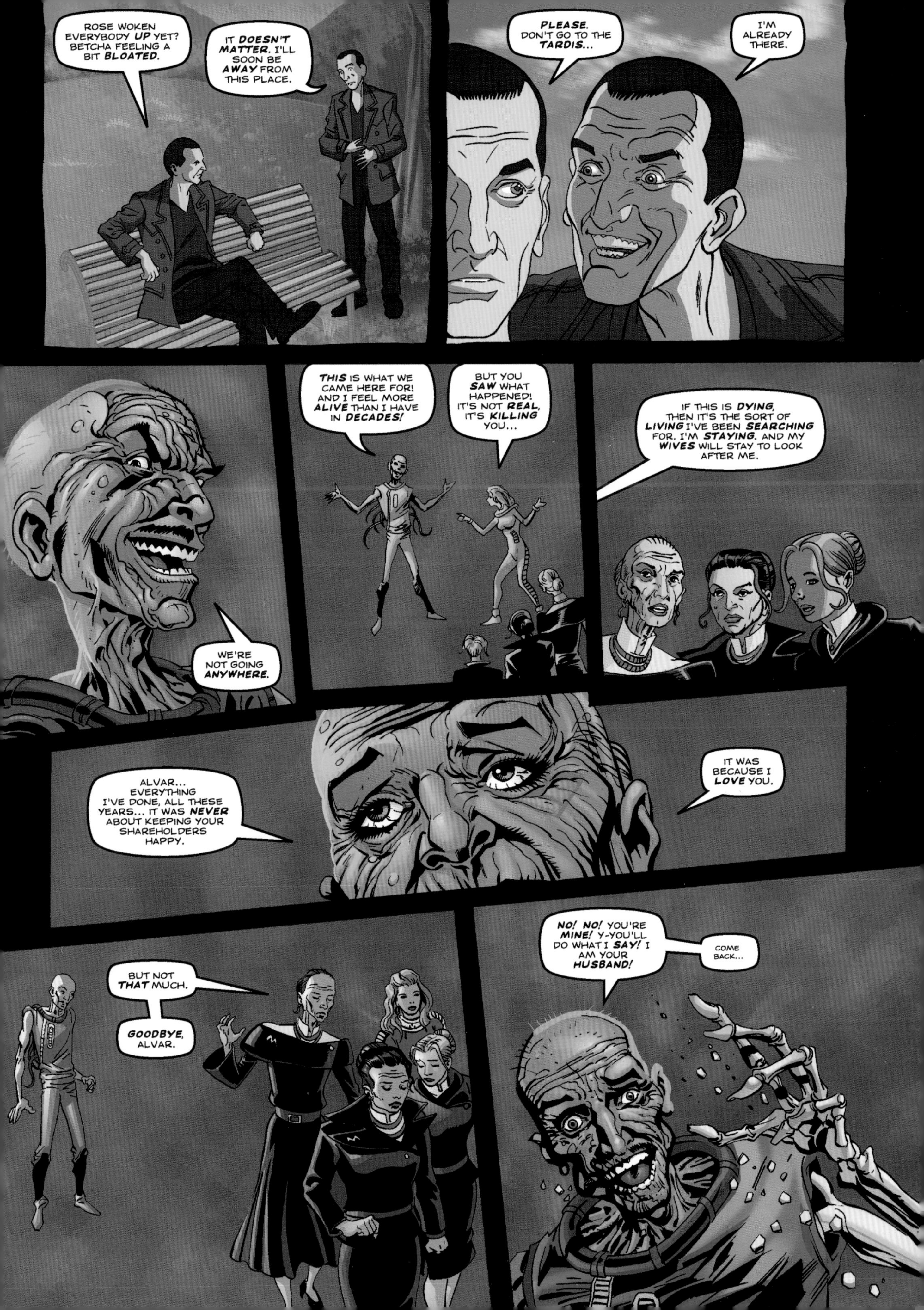
ROSE WOKEN EVERYBODY UP YET? BETCHA FEELING A BIT BLOATED.
IT DOESN'T MATTER. I'LL SOON BE AWAY FROM THIS PLACE.
PLEASE. DON'T GO TO THE TARDIS...
I'M ALREADY THERE.
WE'RE NOT GOING ANYWHERE.
THIS IS WHAT WE CAME HERE FOR! AND I FEEL MORE ALIVE THAN I HAVE IN DECADES!
BUT YOU SAW WHAT HAPPENED! IT'S NOT REAL, IT'S KILLING YOU...
IF THIS IS DYING, THEN IT'S THE SORT OF LIVING I'VE BEEN SEARCHING FOR. I'M STAYING. AND MY WIVES WILL STAY TO LOOK AFTER ME.
ALVAR... EVERYTHING I'VE DONE, ALL THESE YEARS... IT WAS NEVER ABOUT KEEPING YOUR SHAREHOLDERS HAPPY.
IT WAS BECAUSE I LOVE YOU.
BUT NOT THAT MUCH.
GOODBYE, ALVAR.
NO! NO! YOU'RE MINE! Y-YOU'LL DO WHAT I SAY! I AM YOUR HUSBAND!
COME BACK...

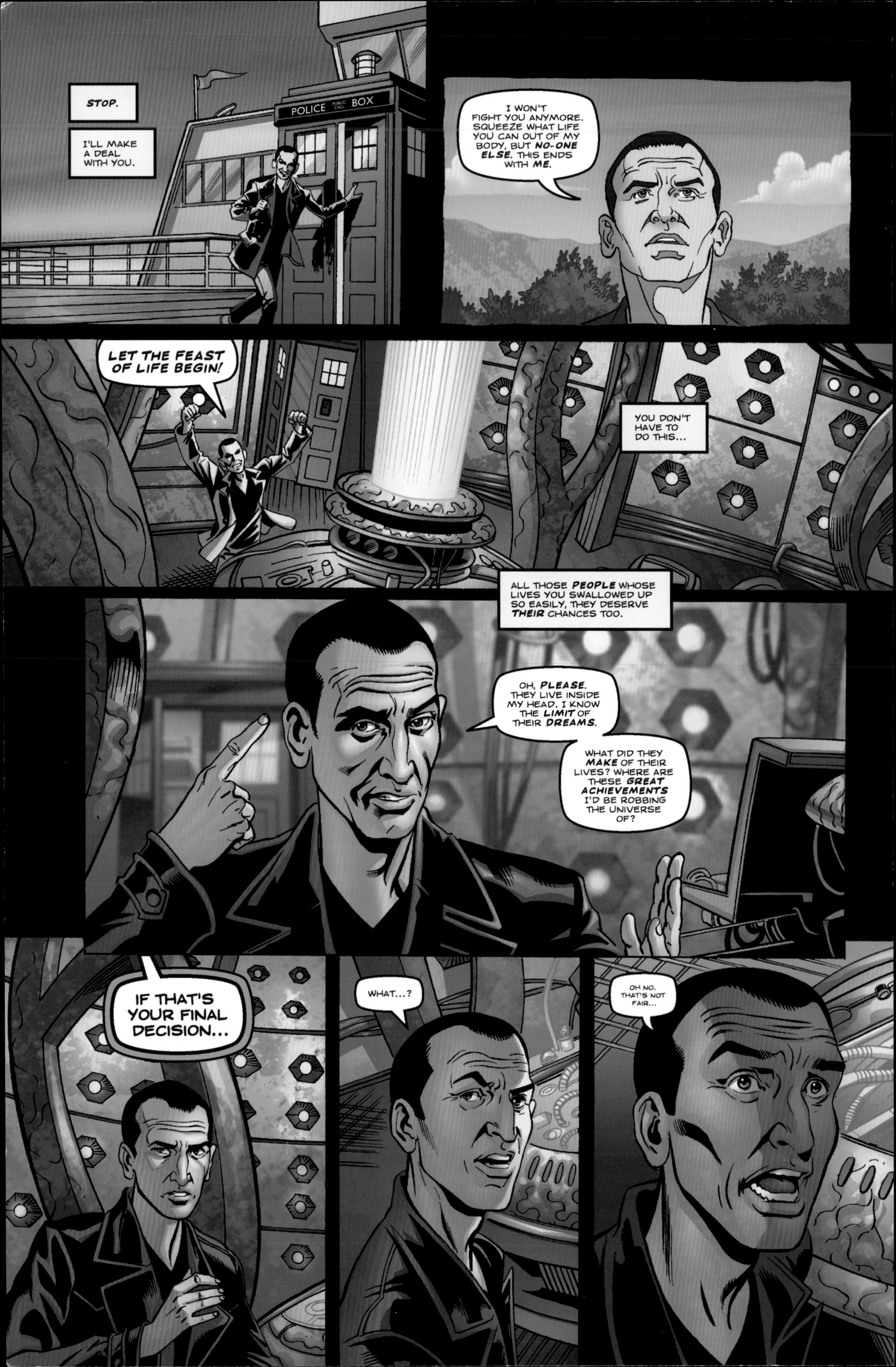
STOP.
I'LL MAKE A DEAL WITH YOU.
POLICE PUBLIC CALL BOX
I WON'T FIGHT YOU ANYMORE. SQUEEZE WHAT LIFE YOU CAN OUT OF MY BODY, BUT NO-ONE ELSE. THIS ENDS WITH ME.
LET THE FEAST OF LIFE BEGIN!
YOU DON'T HAVE TO DO THIS...
ALL THOSE PEOPLE WHOSE LIVES YOU SWALLOWED UP SO EASILY, THEY DESERVE THEIR CHANCES TOO.
OH, PLEASE. THEY LIVE INSIDE MY HEAD. I KNOW THE LIMIT OF THEIR DREAMS.
WHAT DID THEY MAKE OF THEIR LIVES? WHERE ARE THESE GREAT ACHIEVEMENTS I'D BE ROBBING THE UNIVERSE OF?
IF THAT'S YOUR FINAL DECISION...
WHAT...?
OH NO. THAT'S NOT FAIR...

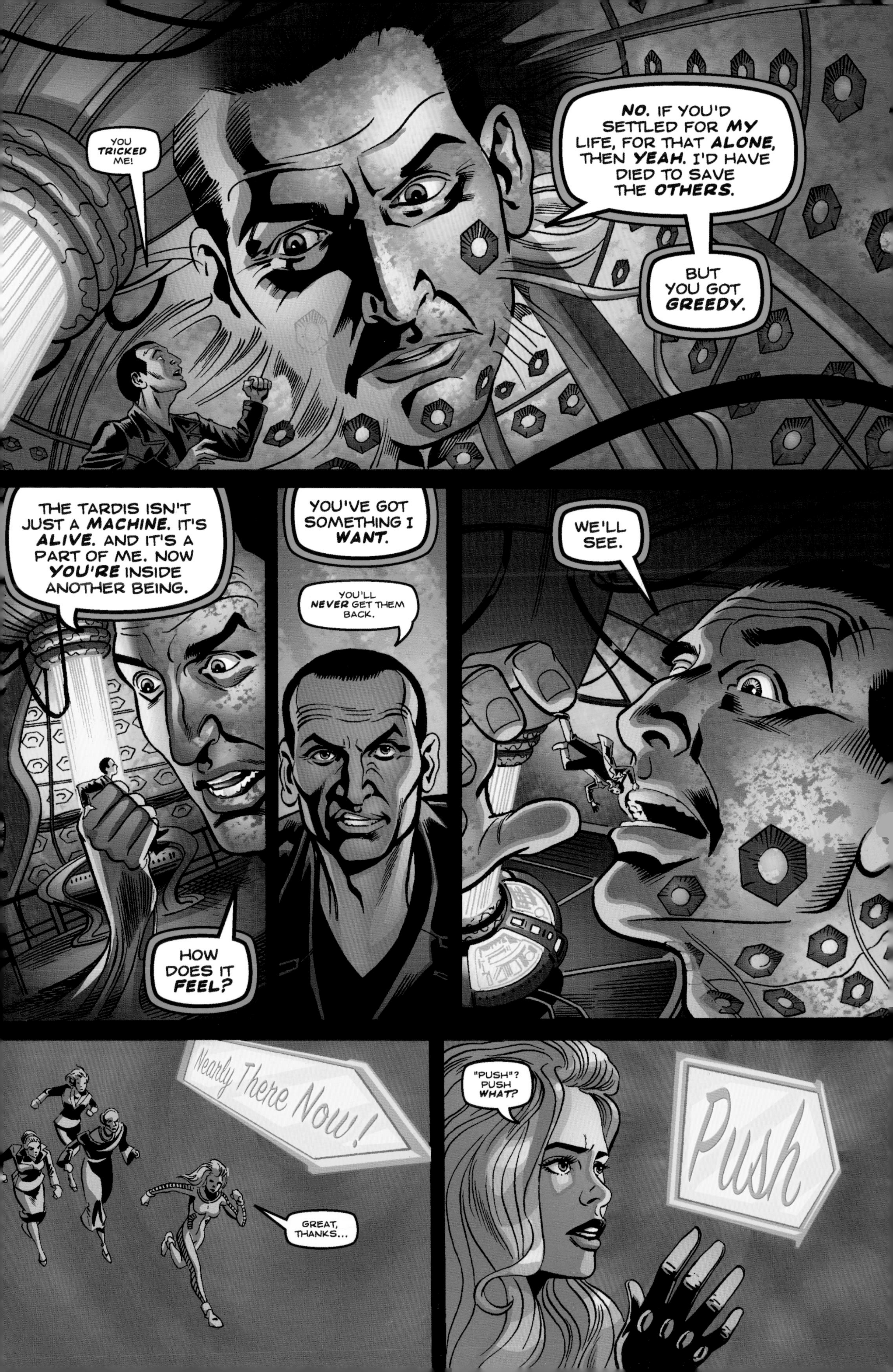
YOU TRICKED ME!
NO. IF YOU'D SETTLED FOR MY LIFE, FOR THAT ALONE, THEN YEAH. I'D HAVE DIED TO SAVE THE OTHERS.
BUT YOU GOT GREEDY.
THE TARDIS ISN'T JUST A MACHINE. IT'S ALIVE. AND IT'S A PART OF ME. NOW YOU'RE INSIDE ANOTHER BEING.
HOW DOES IT FEEL?
YOU'VE GOT SOMETHING I WANT.
YOU'LL NEVER GET THEM BACK.
WE'LL SEE.
Nearly There Now!
GREAT, THANKS...
"PUSH"? PUSH WHAT?
Push

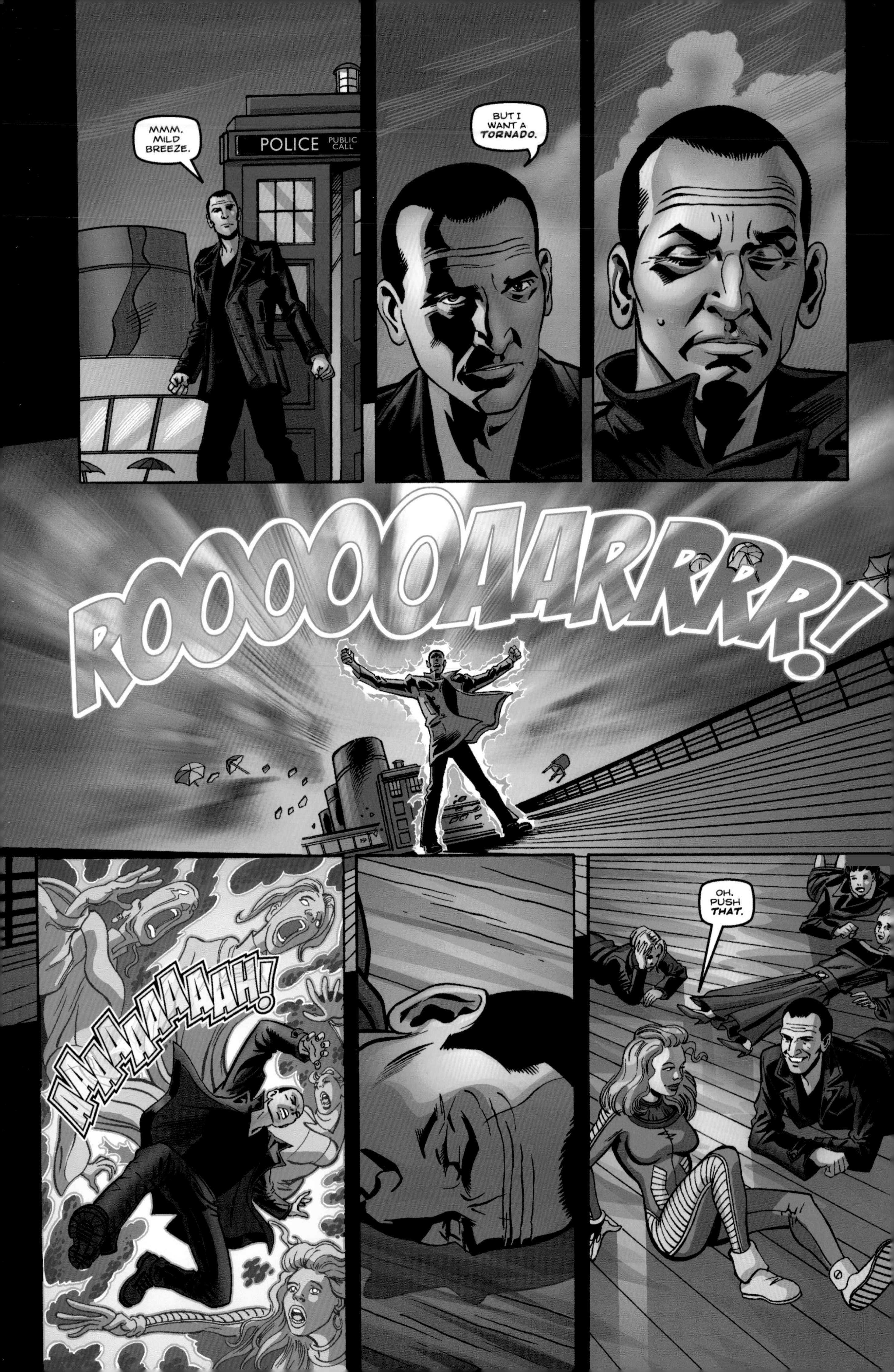

POLICE PUBLIC CALL
MMM. MILD BREEZE.
BUT I WANT A TORNADO.
ROOOOOAARRRR!
AAAAAAAAAH!
OH. PUSH THAT.

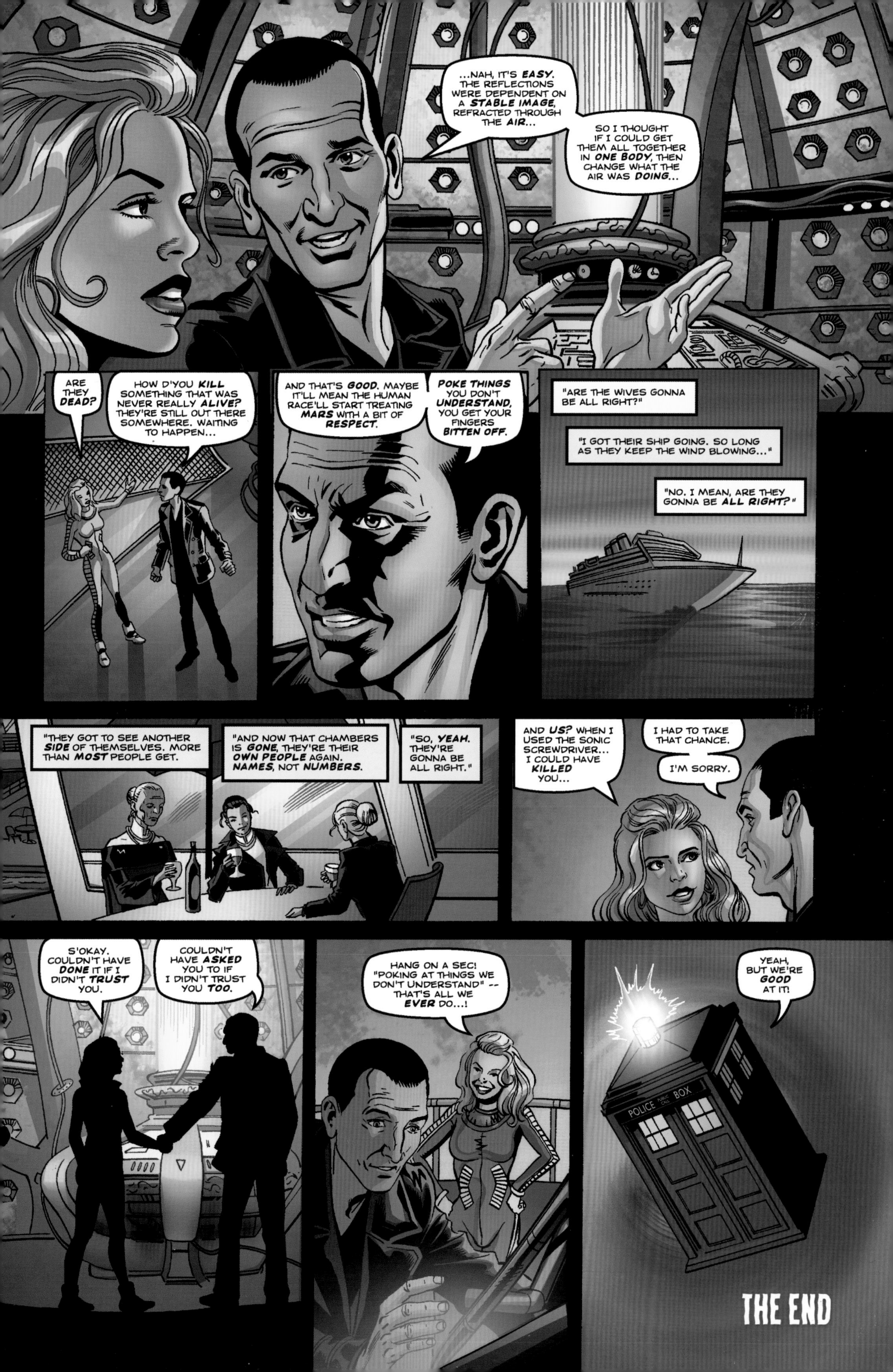
...NAH, IT'S EASY. THE REFLECTIONS WERE DEPENDENT ON A STABLE IMAGE, REFRACTED THROUGH THE AIR...
SO I THOUGHT IF I COULD GET THEM ALL TOGETHER IN ONE BODY, THEN CHANGE WHAT THE AIR WAS DOING...
ARE THEY DEAD?
HOW D'YOU KILL SOMETHING THAT WAS NEVER REALLY ALIVE? THEY'RE STILL OUT THERE SOMEWHERE. WAITING TO HAPPEN...
AND THAT'S GOOD. MAYBE IT'LL MEAN THE HUMAN RACE'LL START TREATING MARS WITH A BIT OF RESPECT.
POKE THINGS YOU DON'T UNDERSTAND, YOU GET YOUR FINGERS BITTEN OFF.
"ARE THE WIVES GONNA BE ALL RIGHT?"
"I GOT THEIR SHIP GOING. SO LONG AS THEY KEEP THE WIND BLOWING..."
"NO. I MEAN, ARE THEY GONNA BE ALL RIGHT?"
"THEY GOT TO SEE ANOTHER SIDE OF THEMSELVES. MORE THAN MOST PEOPLE GET.
"AND NOW THAT CHAMBERS IS GONE, THEY'RE THEIR OWN PEOPLE AGAIN. NAMES, NOT NUMBERS.
"SO, YEAH. THEY'RE GONNA BE ALL RIGHT."
AND US? WHEN I USED THE SONIC SCREWDRIVER... I COULD HAVE KILLED YOU...
I HAD TO TAKE THAT CHANCE.
I'M SORRY.
S'OKAY. COULDN'T HAVE DONE IT IF I DIDN'T TRUST YOU.
COULDN'T HAVE ASKED YOU TO IF I DIDN'T TRUST YOU TOO.
HANG ON A SEC! "POKING AT THINGS WE DON'T UNDERSTAND" -- THAT'S ALL WE EVER DO...!
YEAH, BUT WE'RE GOOD AT IT!
POLICE PUBLIC CALL BOX
THE END

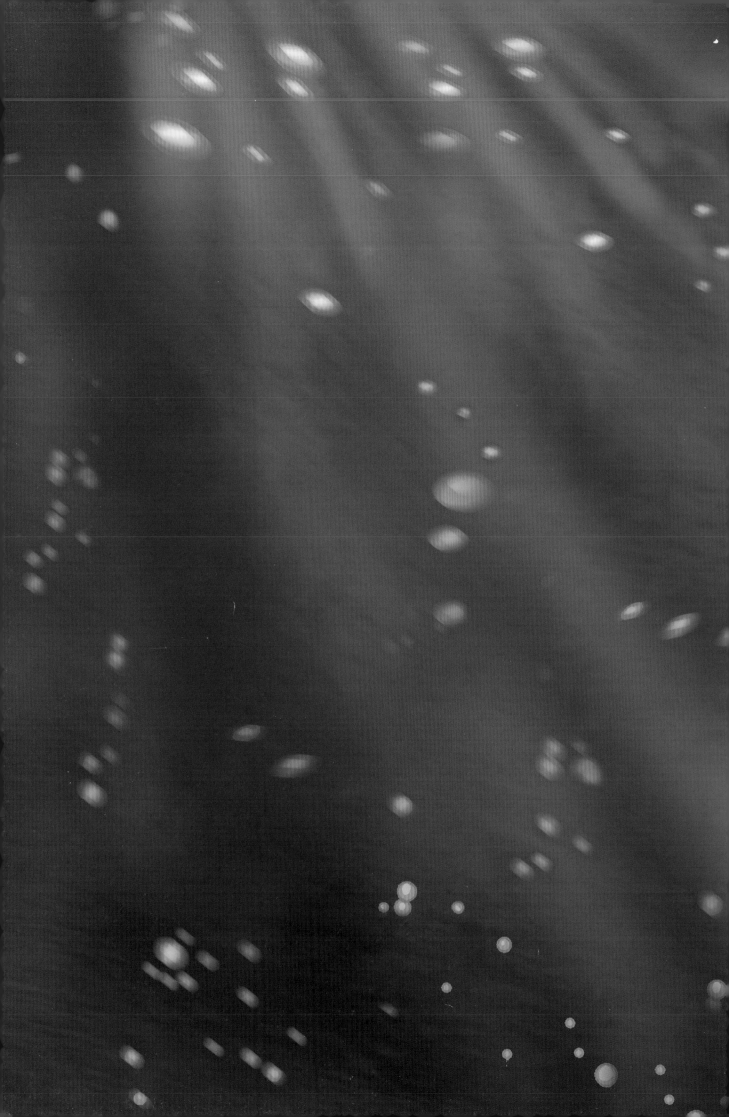

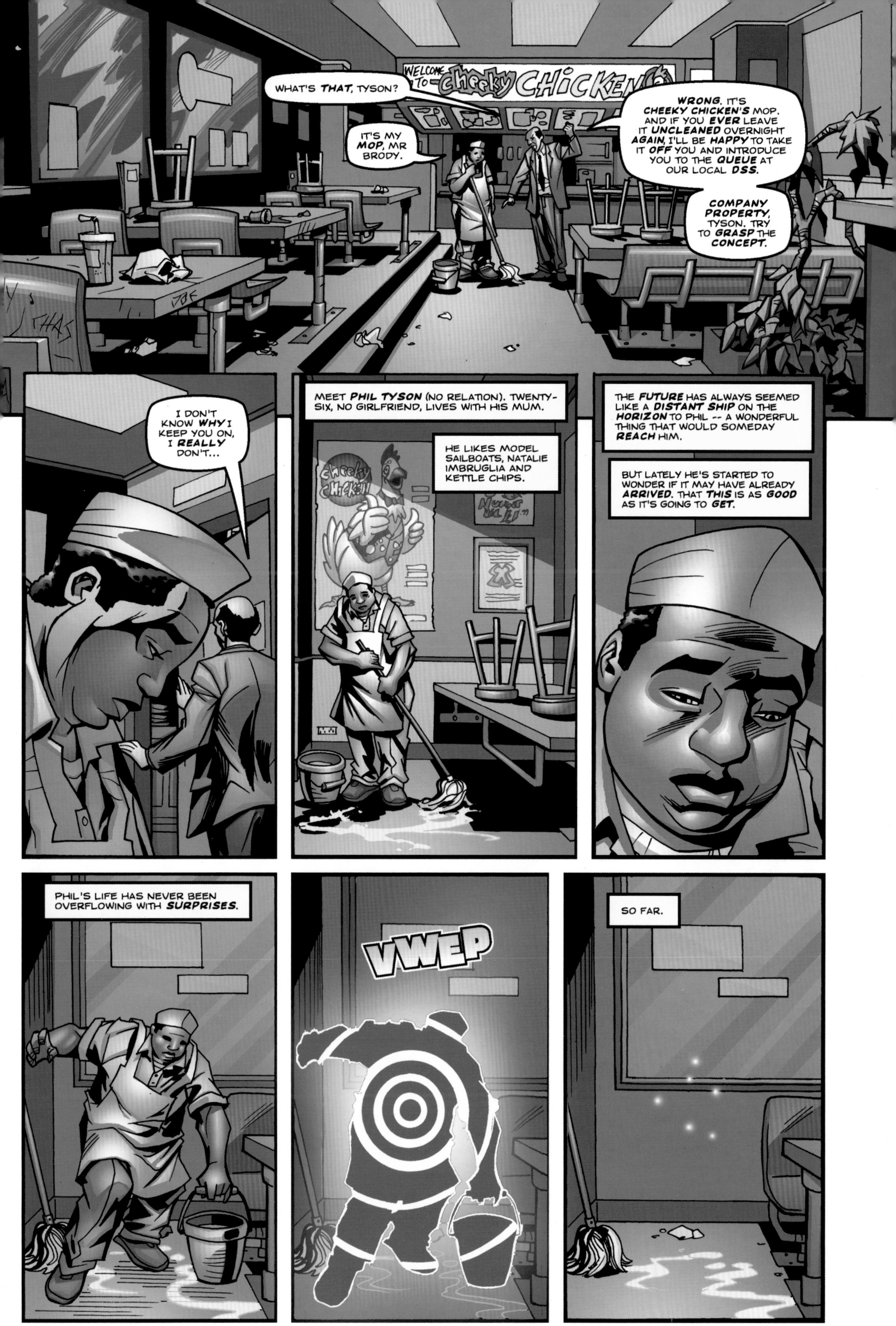
WELCOME TO cheeky CHICKEN
WHAT'S THAT, TYSON?
IT'S MY MOP, MR BRODY.
WRONG. IT'S CHEEKY CHICKEN'S MOP. AND IF YOU EVER LEAVE IT UNCLEANED OVERNIGHT AGAIN, I'LL BE HAPPY TO TAKE IT OFF YOU AND INTRODUCE YOU TO THE QUEUE AT OUR LOCAL DSS.
COMPANY PROPERTY, TYSON. TRY TO GRASP THE CONCEPT.
I DON'T KNOW WHY I KEEP YOU ON, I REALLY DON'T...
MEET PHIL TYSON (NO RELATION). TWENTY-SIX, NO GIRLFRIEND, LIVES WITH HIS MUM.
HE LIKES MODEL SAILBOATS, NATALIE IMBRUGLIA AND KETTLE CHIPS.
cheeky CHICKEN
THE FUTURE HAS ALWAYS SEEMED LIKE A DISTANT SHIP ON THE HORIZON TO PHIL -- A WONDERFUL THING THAT WOULD SOMEDAY REACH HIM.
BUT LATELY HE'S STARTED TO WONDER IF IT MAY HAVE ALREADY ARRIVED. THAT THIS IS AS GOOD AS IT'S GOING TO GET.
PHIL'S LIFE HAS NEVER BEEN OVERFLOWING WITH SURPRISES.
VWEP
SO FAR.

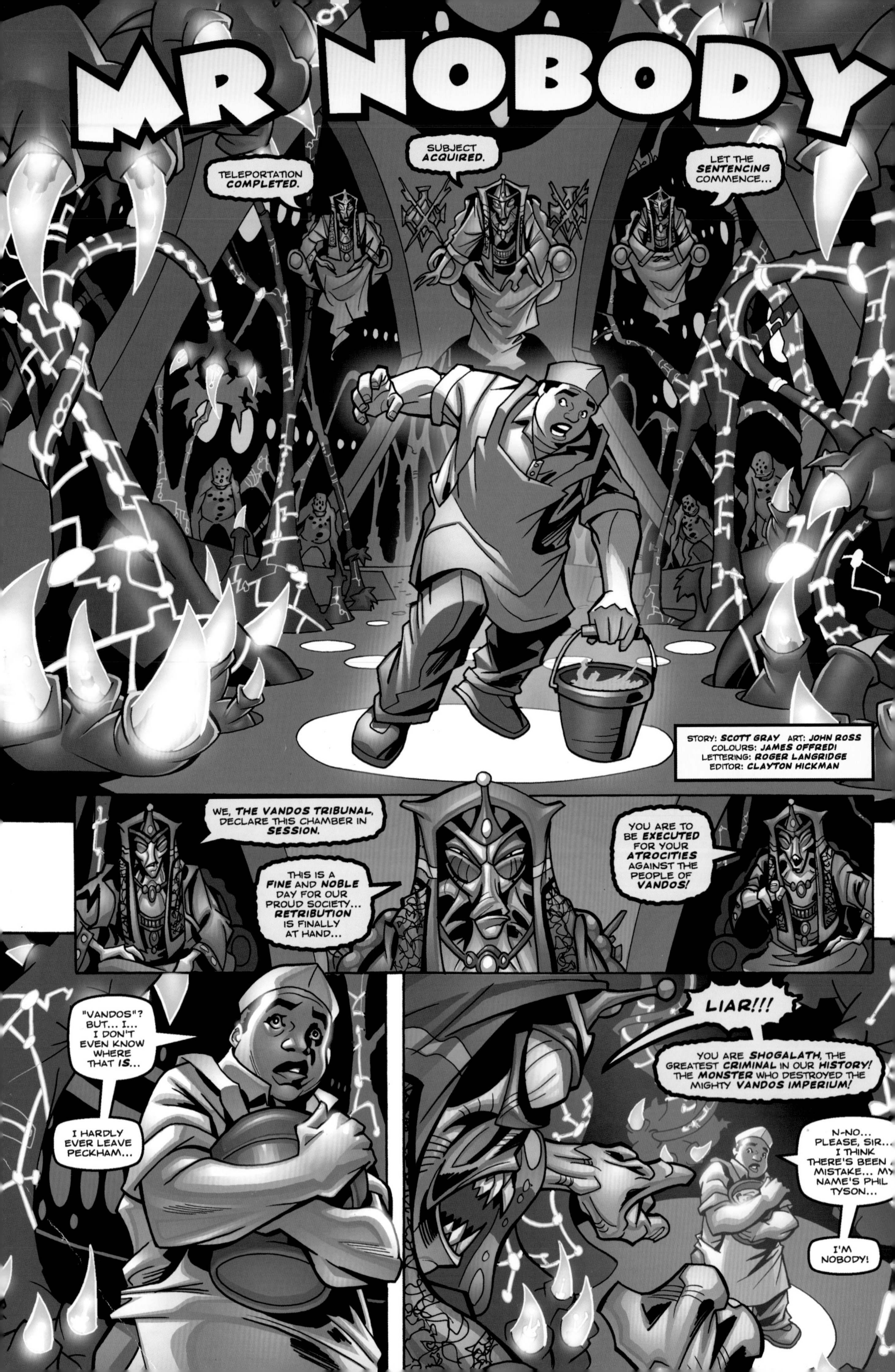
MR NOBODY
TELEPORTATION COMPLETED.
SUBJECT ACQUIRED.
LET THE SENTENCING COMMENCE...
STORY: SCOTT GRAY ART: JOHN ROSS
COLOURS: JAMES OFFREDI
LETTERING: ROGER LANGRIDGE
EDITOR: CLAYTON HICKMAN
WE, THE VANDOS TRIBUNAL, DECLARE THIS CHAMBER IN SESSION.
THIS IS A FINE AND NOBLE DAY FOR OUR PROUD SOCIETY... RETRIBUTION IS FINALLY AT HAND...
YOU ARE TO BE EXECUTED FOR YOUR ATROCITIES AGAINST THE PEOPLE OF VANDOS!
"VANDOS"? BUT... I... I DON'T EVEN KNOW WHERE THAT IS...
I HARDLY EVER LEAVE PECKHAM...
LIAR!!!
YOU ARE SHOGALATH, THE GREATEST CRIMINAL IN OUR HISTORY! THE MONSTER WHO DESTROYED THE MIGHTY VANDOS IMPERIUM!
N-NO... PLEASE, SIR... I THINK THERE'S BEEN A MISTAKE... MY NAME'S PHIL TYSON...
I'M NOBODY!

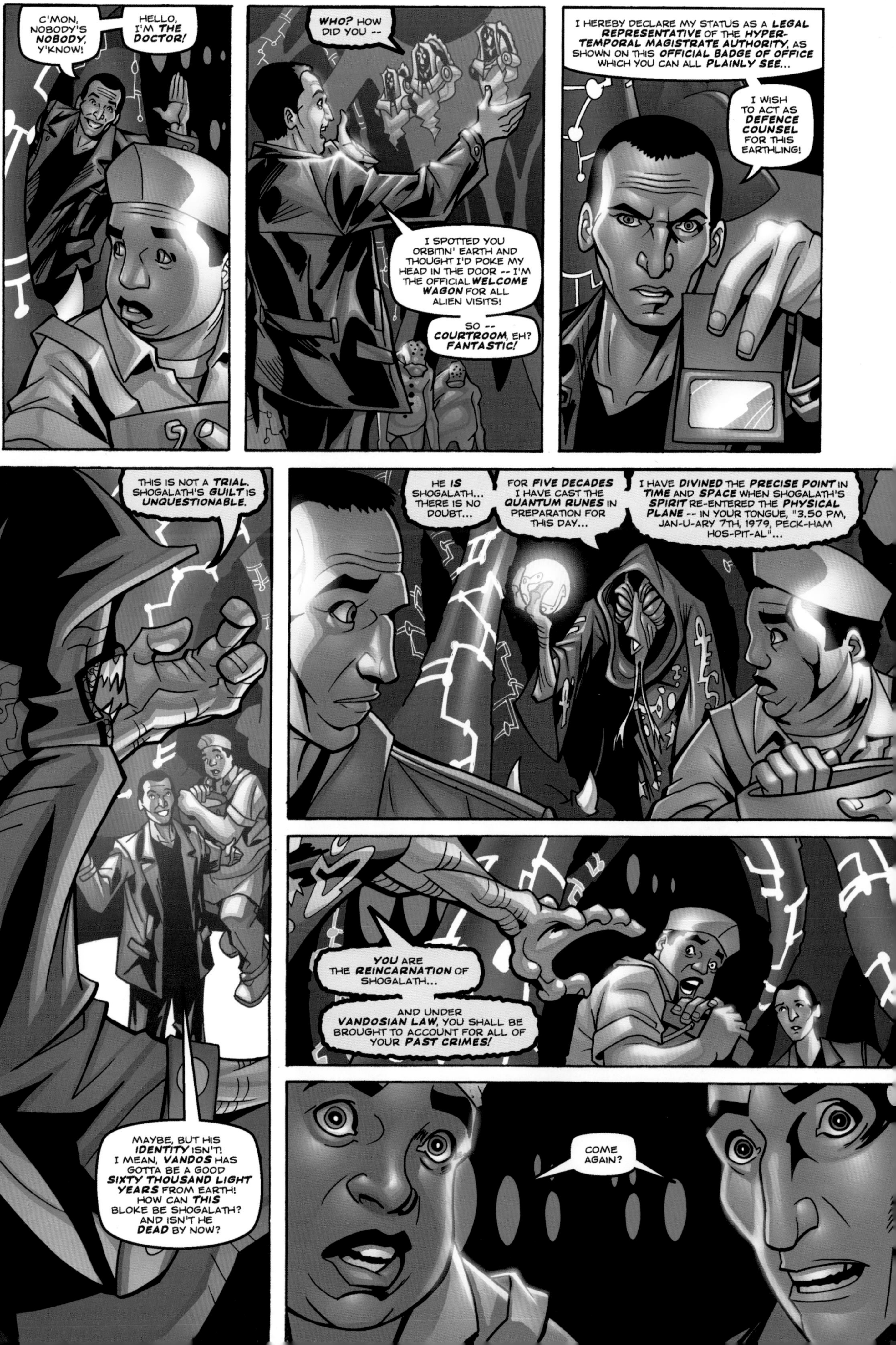
C'MON, NOBODY'S NOBODY, Y'KNOW!
HELLO, I'M THE DOCTOR!
WHO? HOW DID YOU --
I SPOTTED YOU ORBITIN' EARTH AND THOUGHT I'D POKE MY HEAD IN THE DOOR -- I'M THE OFFICIAL WELCOME WAGON FOR ALL ALIEN VISITS!
SO -- COURTROOM, EH? FANTASTIC!
I HEREBY DECLARE MY STATUS AS A LEGAL REPRESENTATIVE OF THE HYPER-TEMPORAL MAGISTRATE AUTHORITY, AS SHOWN ON THIS OFFICIAL BADGE OF OFFICE WHICH YOU CAN ALL PLAINLY SEE...
I WISH TO ACT AS DEFENCE COUNSEL FOR THIS EARTHLING!
THIS IS NOT A TRIAL. SHOGALATH'S GUILT IS UNQUESTIONABLE.
MAYBE, BUT HIS IDENTITY ISN'T! I MEAN, VANDOS HAS GOTTA BE A GOOD SIXTY THOUSAND LIGHT YEARS FROM EARTH! HOW CAN THIS BLOKE BE SHOGALATH? AND ISN'T HE DEAD BY NOW?
HE IS SHOGALATH... THERE IS NO DOUBT...
FOR FIVE DECADES I HAVE CAST THE QUANTUM RUNES IN PREPARATION FOR THIS DAY...
I HAVE DIVINED THE PRECISE POINT IN TIME AND SPACE WHEN SHOGALATH'S SPIRIT RE-ENTERED THE PHYSICAL PLANE -- IN YOUR TONGUE, "3.50 PM, JAN-U-ARY 7TH, 1979, PECK-HAM HOS-PIT-AL"...
YOU ARE THE REINCARNATION OF SHOGALATH...
AND UNDER VANDOSIAN LAW, YOU SHALL BE BROUGHT TO ACCOUNT FOR ALL OF YOUR PAST CRIMES!
COME AGAIN?

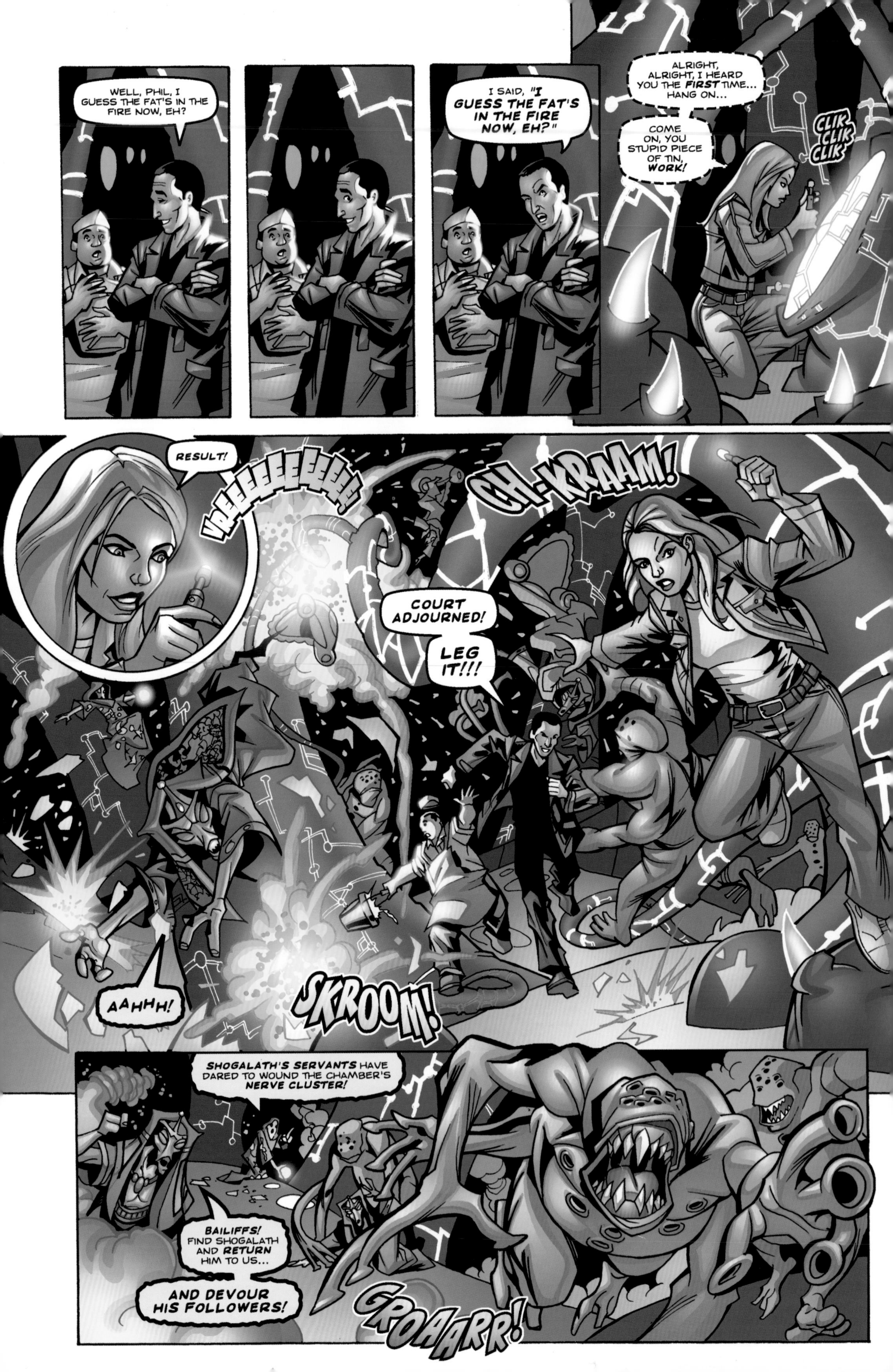
WELL, PHIL, I GUESS THE FAT'S IN THE FIRE NOW, EH?
I SAID, "I GUESS THE FAT'S IN THE FIRE NOW, EH?"
ALRIGHT, ALRIGHT, I HEARD YOU THE FIRST TIME... HANG ON...
COME ON, YOU STUPID PIECE OF TIN, WORK!
CLIK CLIK CLIK
RESULT!
VREEEEEEEEEEEE!
CH-KRAAM!
COURT ADJOURNED!
LEG IT!!!
AAHHH!
SKROOM!
SHOGALATH'S SERVANTS HAVE DARED TO WOUND THE CHAMBER'S NERVE CLUSTER!
BAILIFFS! FIND SHOGALATH AND RETURN HIM TO US...
AND DEVOUR HIS FOLLOWERS!
GROAARR!

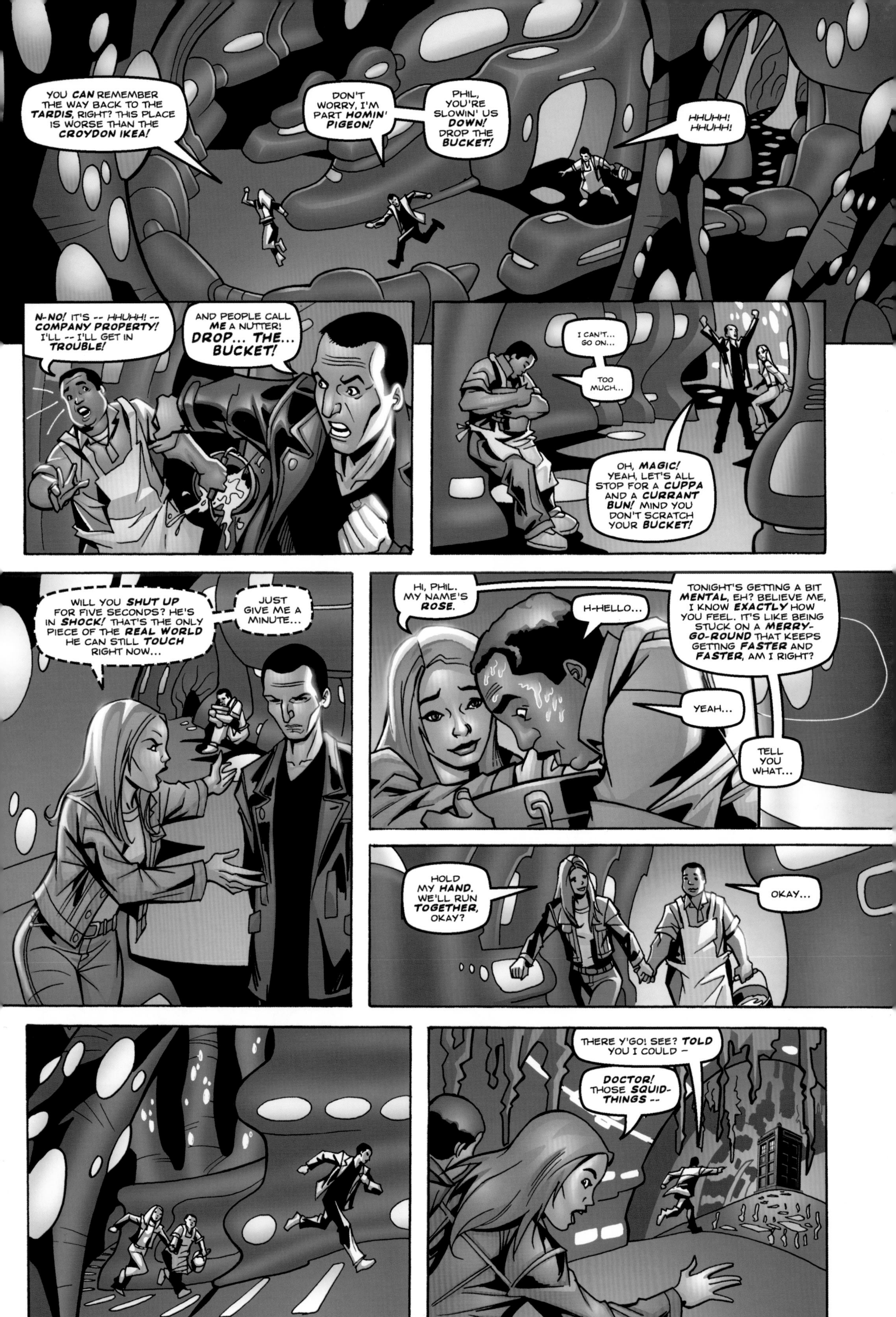
YOU CAN REMEMBER THE WAY BACK TO THE TARDIS, RIGHT? THIS PLACE IS WORSE THAN THE CROYDON IKEA!
DON'T WORRY, I'M PART HOMIN' PIGEON!
PHIL, YOU'RE SLOWIN' US DOWN! DROP THE BUCKET!
HHUHH! HHUHH!
N-NO! IT'S -- HHUHH! -- COMPANY PROPERTY! I'LL -- I'LL GET IN TROUBLE!
AND PEOPLE CALL ME A NUTTER! DROP... THE... BUCKET!
I CAN'T... GO ON...
TOO MUCH...
OH, MAGIC! YEAH, LET'S ALL STOP FOR A CUPPA AND A CURRANT BUN! MIND YOU DON'T SCRATCH YOUR BUCKET!
WILL YOU SHUT UP FOR FIVE SECONDS? HE'S IN SHOCK! THAT'S THE ONLY PIECE OF THE REAL WORLD HE CAN STILL TOUCH RIGHT NOW...
JUST GIVE ME A MINUTE...
HI, PHIL. MY NAME'S ROSE.
H-HELLO...
TONIGHT'S GETTING A BIT MENTAL, EH? BELIEVE ME, I KNOW EXACTLY HOW YOU FEEL. IT'S LIKE BEING STUCK ON A MERRY-GO-ROUND THAT KEEPS GETTING FASTER AND FASTER, AM I RIGHT?
YEAH...
TELL YOU WHAT...
HOLD MY HAND. WE'LL RUN TOGETHER, OKAY?
OKAY...
THERE Y'GO! SEE? TOLD YOU I COULD –
DOCTOR! THOSE SQUID-THINGS --

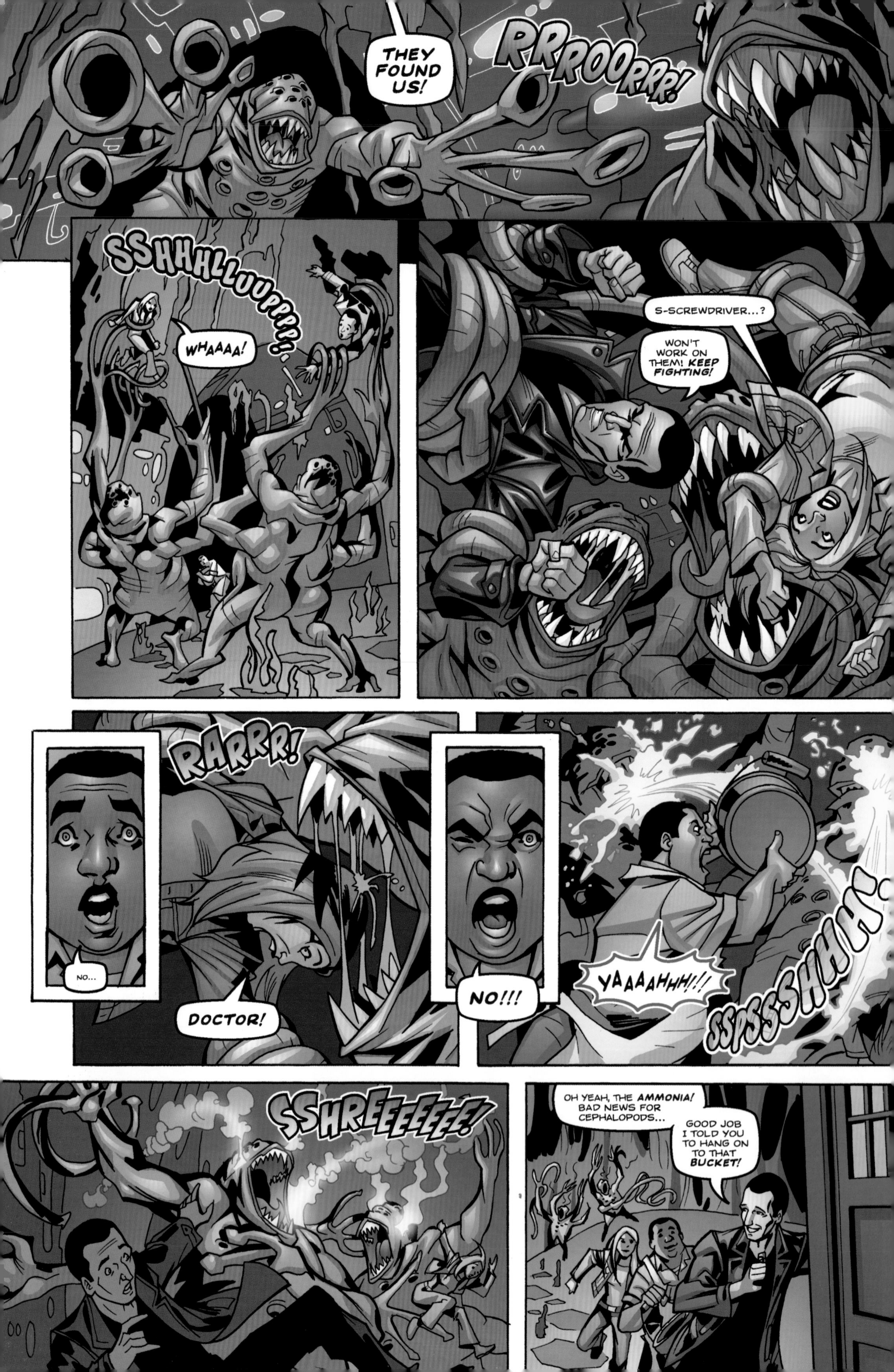

THEY FOUND US!
RRROORRR!
SSHHHLLUUPPPP!
WHAAAA!
S-SCREWDRIVER...?
WON'T WORK ON THEM! KEEP FIGHTING!
RARRR!
NO...
DOCTOR!
NO!!!
YAAAAHHH!!!
SSPSSSHHH!
SSHREEEEEEEE!
OH YEAH, THE AMMONIA! BAD NEWS FOR CEPHALOPODS...
GOOD JOB I TOLD YOU TO HANG ON TO THAT BUCKET!

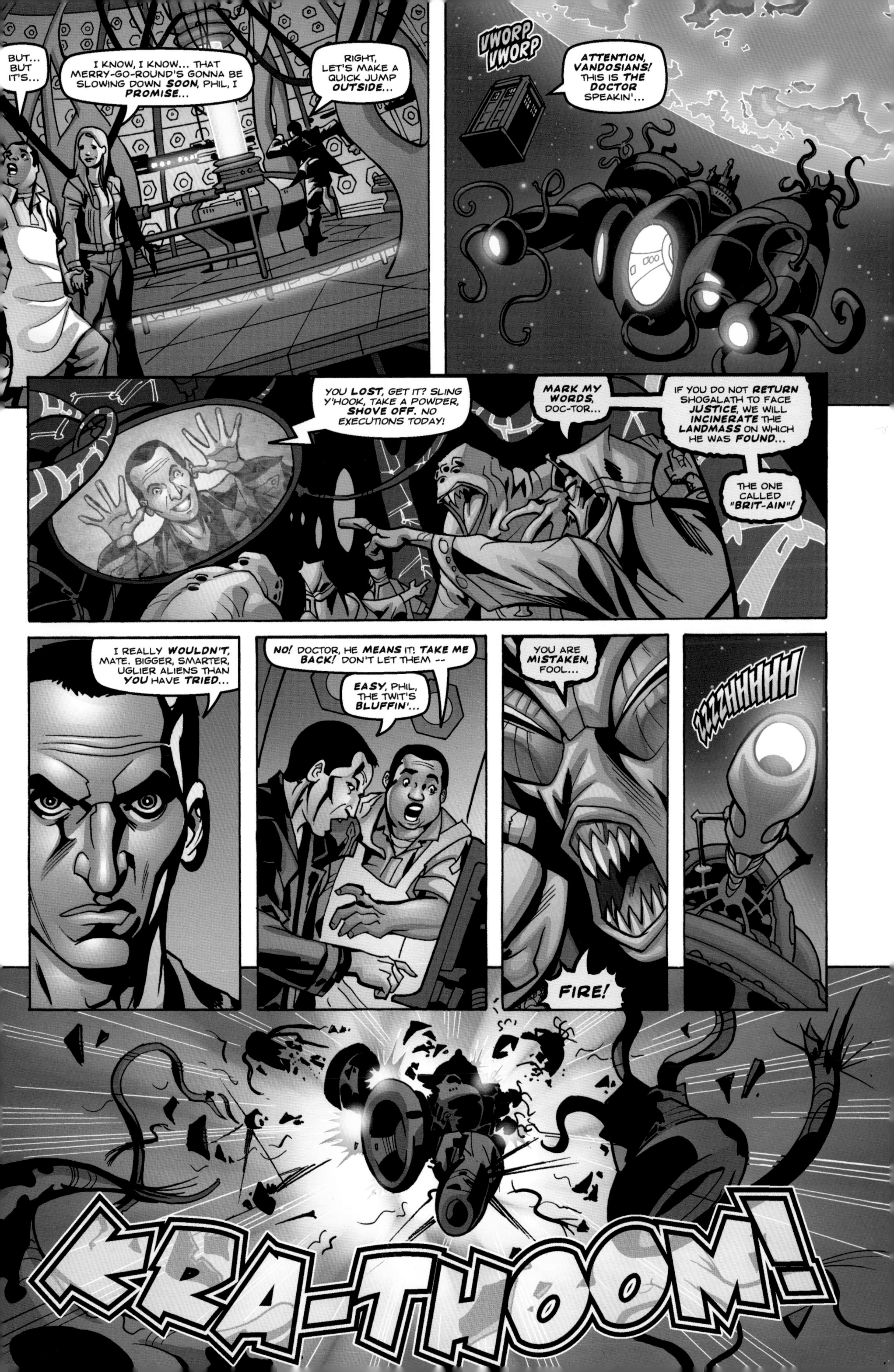
BUT... BUT IT'S...
I KNOW, I KNOW... THAT MERRY-GO-ROUND'S GONNA BE SLOWING DOWN SOON, PHIL, I PROMISE...
RIGHT, LET'S MAKE A QUICK JUMP OUTSIDE...
VWORP VWORP
ATTENTION, VANDOSIANS! THIS IS THE DOCTOR SPEAKIN'...
YOU LOST, GET IT? SLING Y'HOOK, TAKE A POWDER, SHOVE OFF. NO EXECUTIONS TODAY!
MARK MY WORDS, DOC-TOR...
IF YOU DO NOT RETURN SHOGALATH TO FACE JUSTICE, WE WILL INCINERATE THE LANDMASS ON WHICH HE WAS FOUND...
THE ONE CALLED "BRIT-AIN"!
I REALLY WOULDN'T, MATE. BIGGER, SMARTER, UGLIER ALIENS THAN YOU HAVE TRIED...
NO! DOCTOR, HE MEANS IT! TAKE ME BACK! DON'T LET THEM --
EASY, PHIL, THE TWIT'S BLUFFIN'...
YOU ARE MISTAKEN, FOOL...
FIRE!
ZZZHHHHHH
KRA-THOOM!

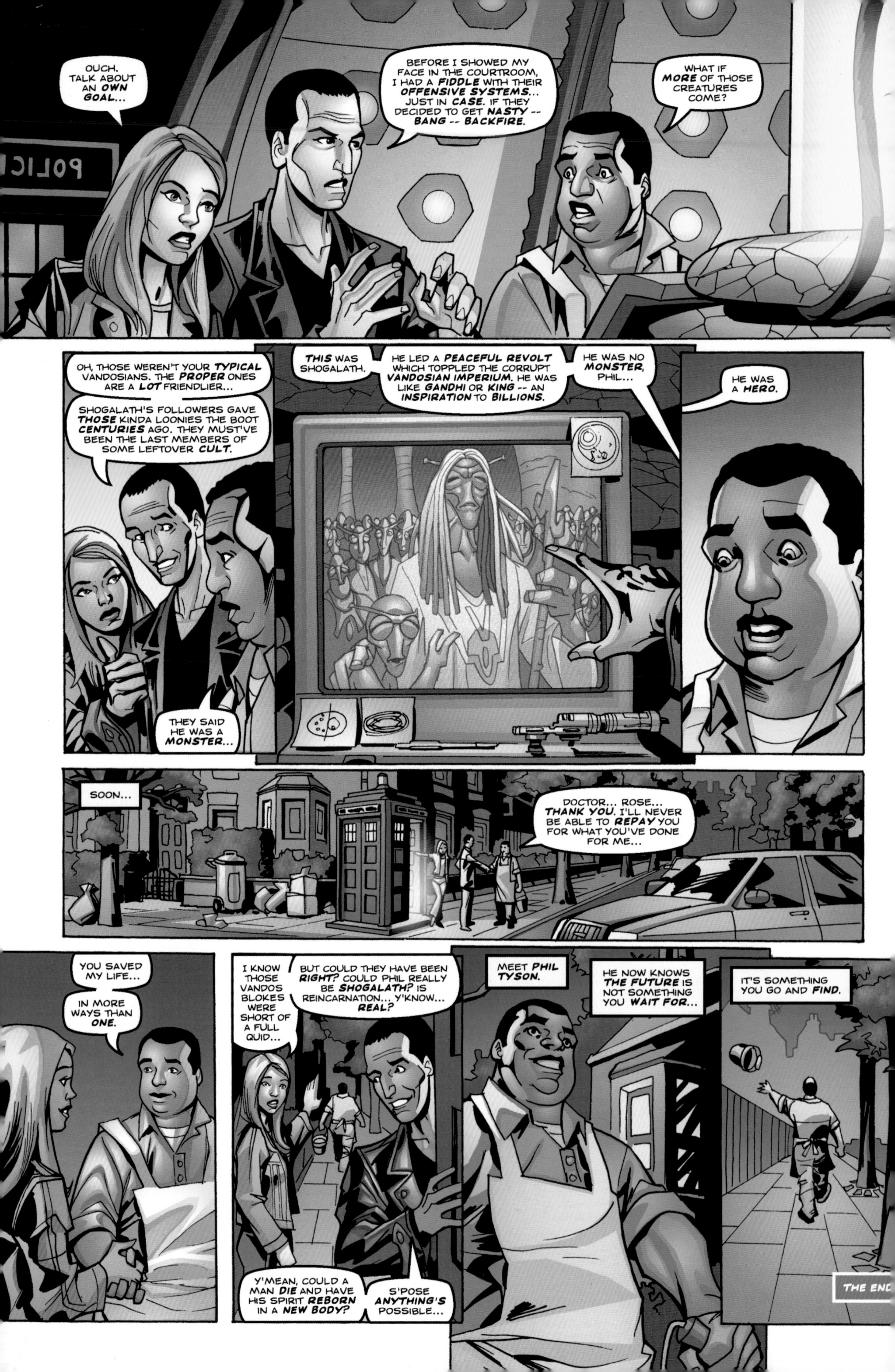

POLIC
OUCH. TALK ABOUT AN OWN GOAL...
BEFORE I SHOWED MY FACE IN THE COURTROOM, I HAD A FIDDLE WITH THEIR OFFENSIVE SYSTEMS... JUST IN CASE. IF THEY DECIDED TO GET NASTY -- BANG -- BACKFIRE.
WHAT IF MORE OF THOSE CREATURES COME?
OH, THOSE WEREN'T YOUR TYPICAL VANDOSIANS. THE PROPER ONES ARE A LOT FRIENDLIER...
SHOGALATH'S FOLLOWERS GAVE THOSE KINDA LOONIES THE BOOT CENTURIES AGO. THEY MUST'VE BEEN THE LAST MEMBERS OF SOME LEFTOVER CULT.
THEY SAID HE WAS A MONSTER...
THIS WAS SHOGALATH.
HE LED A PEACEFUL REVOLT WHICH TOPPLED THE CORRUPT VANDOSIAN IMPERIUM. HE WAS LIKE GANDHI OR KING -- AN INSPIRATION TO BILLIONS.
HE WAS NO MONSTER, PHIL...
HE WAS A HERO.
SOON...
DOCTOR... ROSE... THANK YOU. I'LL NEVER BE ABLE TO REPAY YOU FOR WHAT YOU'VE DONE FOR ME...
YOU SAVED MY LIFE...
IN MORE WAYS THAN ONE.
I KNOW THOSE VANDOS BLOKES WERE SHORT OF A FULL QUID...
BUT COULD THEY HAVE BEEN RIGHT? COULD PHIL REALLY BE SHOGALATH? IS REINCARNATION... Y'KNOW... REAL?
Y'MEAN, COULD A MAN DIE AND HAVE HIS SPIRIT REBORN IN A NEW BODY?
S'POSE ANYTHING'S POSSIBLE...
MEET PHIL TYSON.
HE NOW KNOWS THE FUTURE IS NOT SOMETHING YOU WAIT FOR...
IT'S SOMETHING YOU GO AND FIND.
THE END

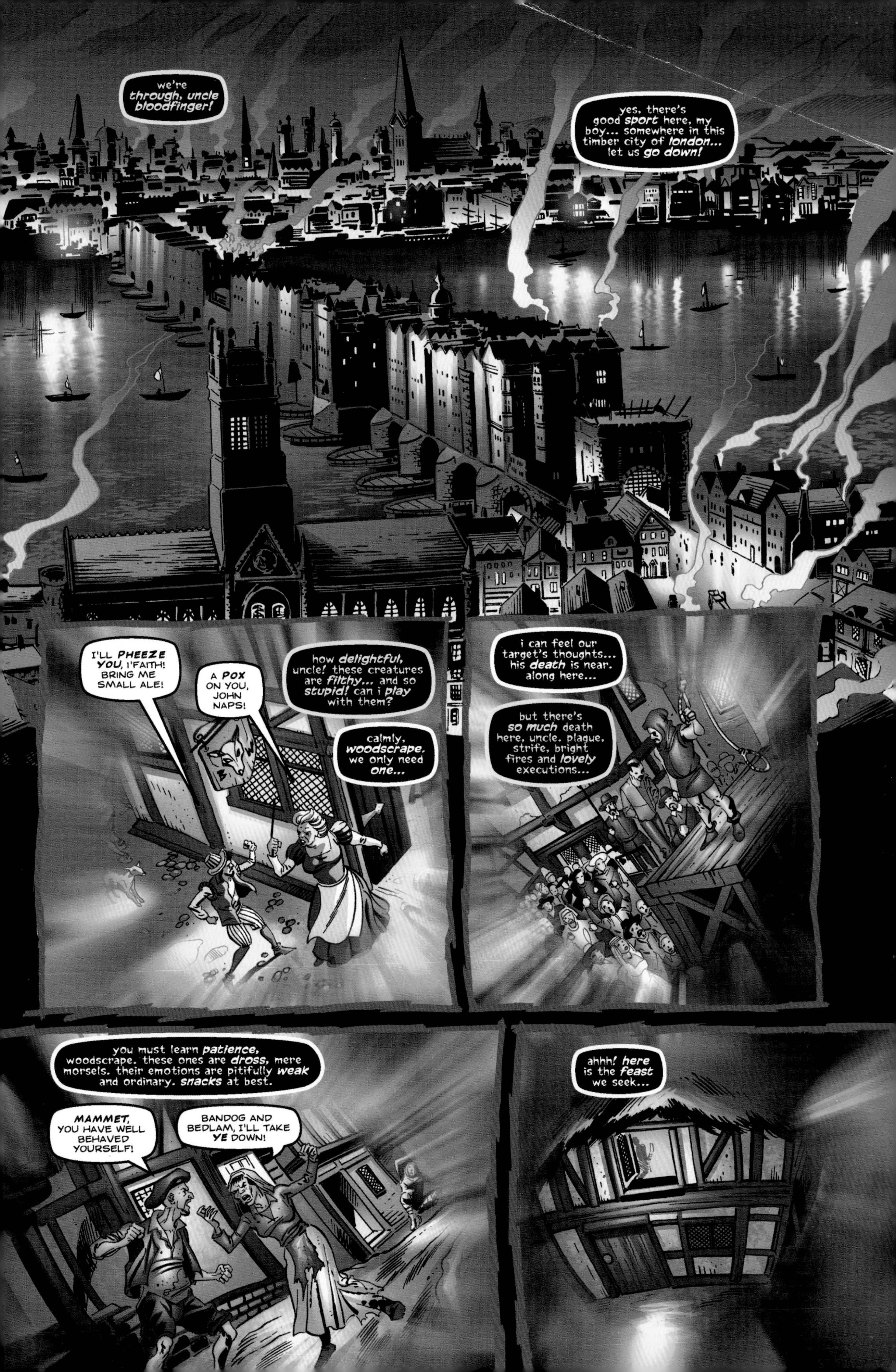
we're through, uncle bloodfinger!
yes, there's good sport here, my boy... somewhere in this timber city of london... let us go down!
I'LL PHEEZE YOU, I'FAITH! BRING ME SMALL ALE!
A POX ON YOU, JOHN NAPS!
how delightful, uncle! these creatures are filthy... and so stupid! can i play with them?
calmly, woodscrape. we only need one...
i can feel our target's thoughts... his death is near. along here...
but there's so much death here, uncle. plague, strife, bright fires and lovely executions...
you must learn patience, woodscrape. these ones are dross, mere morsels. their emotions are pitifully weak and ordinary. snacks at best.
MAMMET, YOU HAVE WELL BEHAVED YOURSELF!
BANDOG AND BEDLAM, I'LL TAKE YE DOWN!
ahhh! here is the feast we seek...

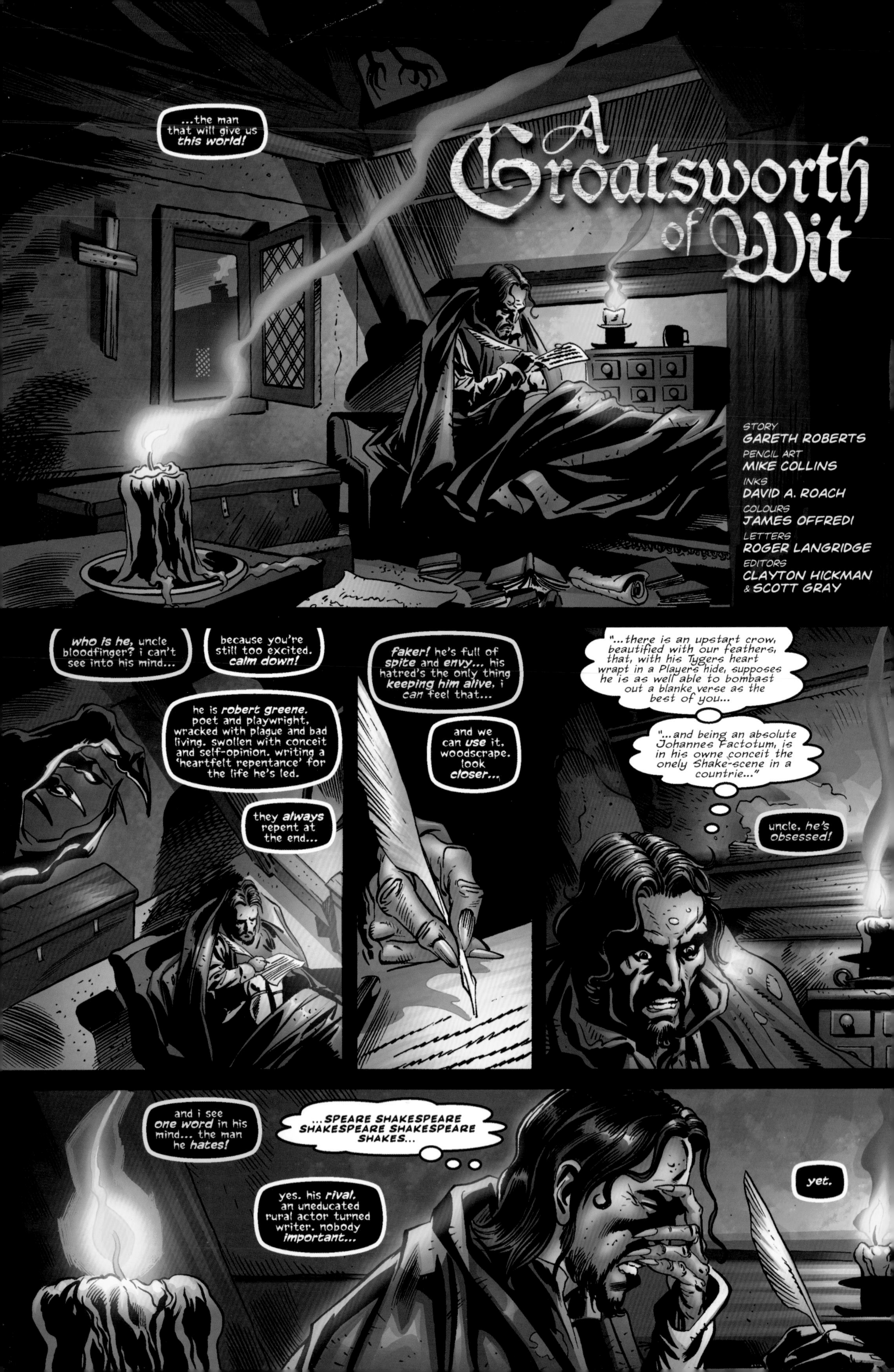

...the man that will give us this world!
A Groatsworth of Wit
STORY GARETH ROBERTS
PENCIL ART MIKE COLLINS
INKS DAVID A. ROACH
COLOURS JAMES OFFREDI
LETTERS ROGER LANGRIDGE
EDITORS CLAYTON HICKMAN & SCOTT GRAY
who is he, uncle bloodfinger? i can't see into his mind...
because you're still too excited. calm down!
he is robert greene, poet and playwright, wracked with plague and bad living. swollen with conceit and self-opinion. writing a 'heartfelt repentance' for the life he's led.
they always repent at the end...
faker! he's full of spite and envy... his hatred's the only thing keeping him alive, i can feel that...
and we can use it, woodscrape. look closer...
"...there is an upstart crow, beautified with our feathers, that, with his Tygers heart wrapt in a Players hide, supposes he is as well able to bombast out a blanke verse as the best of you...
"...and being an absolute Johannes Factotum, is in his owne conceit the onely Shake-scene in a countrie..."
uncle, he's obsessed!
and i see one word in his mind... the man he hates!
...SPEARE SHAKESPEARE SHAKESPEARE SHAKESPEARE SHAKES...
yes. his rival. an uneducated rural actor turned writer. nobody important...
yet.

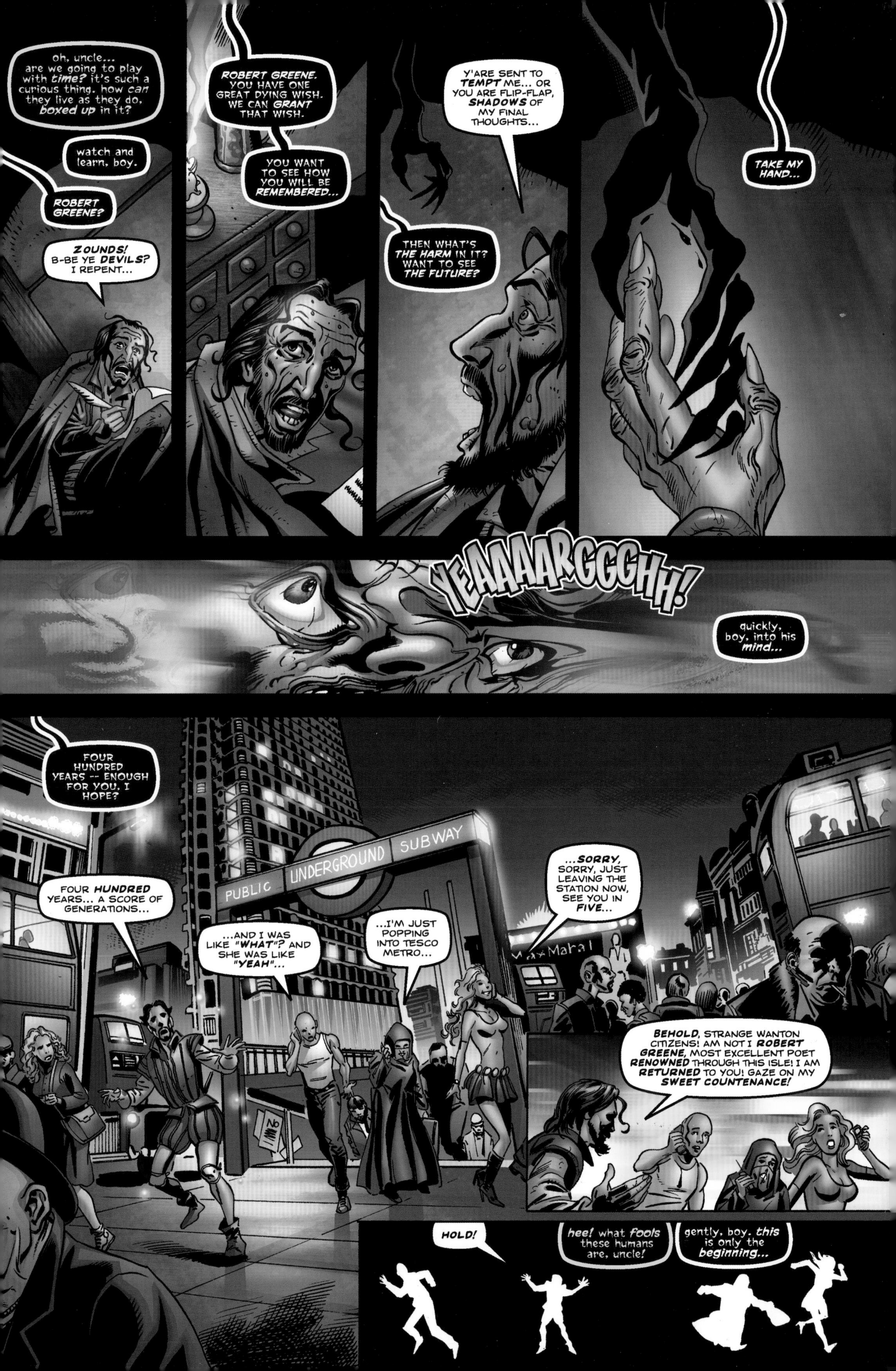
oh, uncle... are we going to play with time? it's such a curious thing. how can they live as they do, boxed up in it?
watch and learn, boy.
ROBERT GREENE?
ZOUNDS! B-BE YE DEVILS? I REPENT...
ROBERT GREENE. YOU HAVE ONE GREAT DYING WISH. WE CAN GRANT THAT WISH.
YOU WANT TO SEE HOW YOU WILL BE REMEMBERED...
Y'ARE SENT TO TEMPT ME... OR YOU ARE FLIP-FLAP, SHADOWS OF MY FINAL THOUGHTS...
THEN WHAT'S THE HARM IN IT? WANT TO SEE THE FUTURE?
TAKE MY HAND...
YEAAAARGGGHH!
quickly, boy, into his mind...
FOUR HUNDRED YEARS -- ENOUGH FOR YOU, I HOPE?
PUBLIC UNDERGROUND SUBWAY
FOUR HUNDRED YEARS... A SCORE OF GENERATIONS...
...AND I WAS LIKE "WHAT"? AND SHE WAS LIKE "YEAH"...
...I'M JUST POPPING INTO TESCO METRO...
...SORRY, SORRY, JUST LEAVING THE STATION NOW, SEE YOU IN FIVE...
BEHOLD, STRANGE WANTON CITIZENS! AM NOT I ROBERT GREENE, MOST EXCELLENT POET RENOWNED THROUGH THIS ISLE! I AM RETURNED TO YOU! GAZE ON MY SWEET COUNTENANCE!
HOLD!
hee! what fools these humans are, uncle!
gently, boy. this is only the beginning...

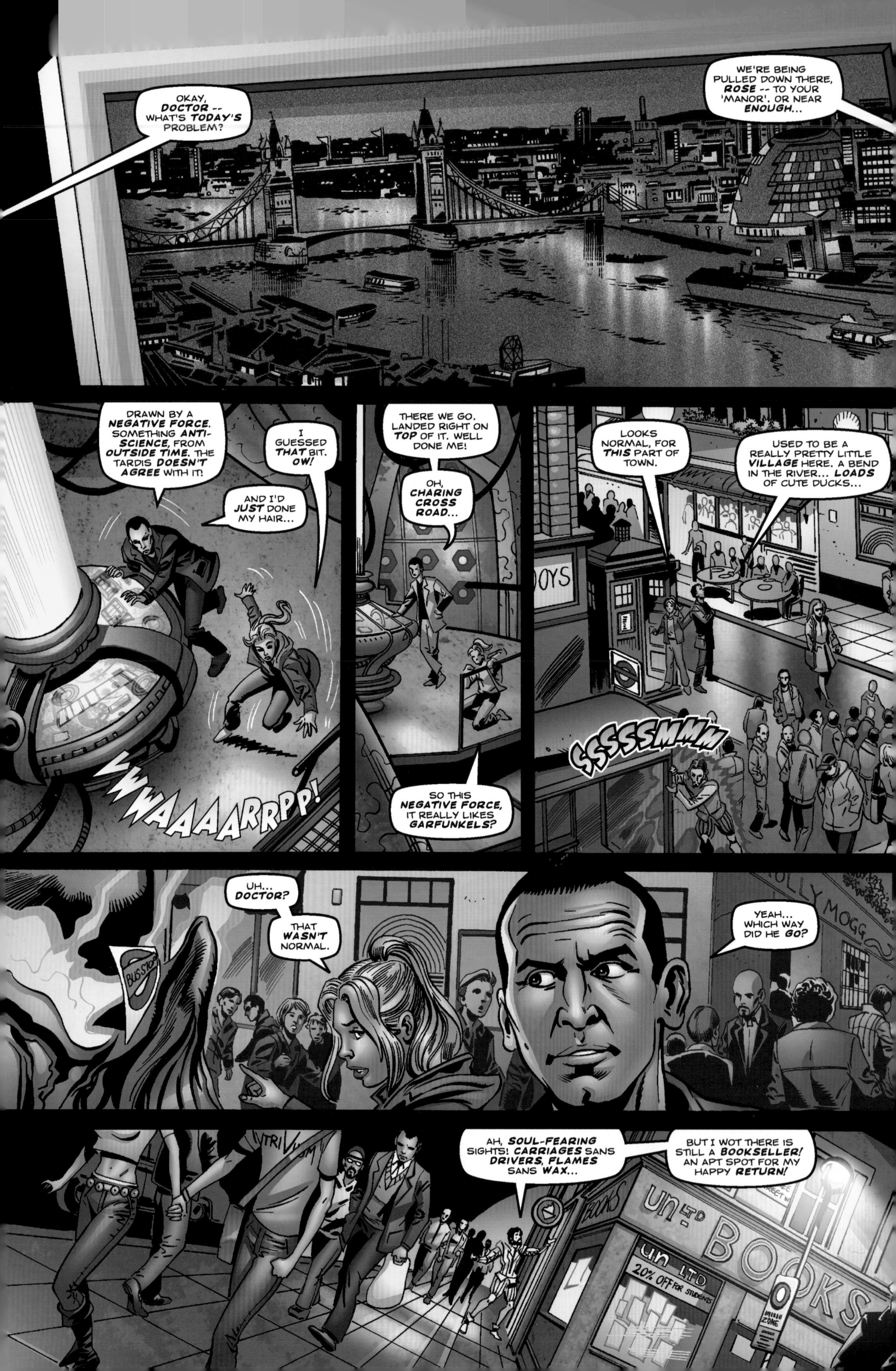
OKAY, DOCTOR -- WHAT'S TODAY'S PROBLEM?
WE'RE BEING PULLED DOWN THERE, ROSE -- TO YOUR 'MANOR'. OR NEAR ENOUGH...
DRAWN BY A NEGATIVE FORCE. SOMETHING ANTI-SCIENCE, FROM OUTSIDE TIME. THE TARDIS DOESN'T AGREE WITH IT!
I GUESSED THAT BIT. OW!
AND I'D JUST DONE MY HAIR...
VWWAAAARRPP!
THERE WE GO. LANDED RIGHT ON TOP OF IT. WELL DONE ME!
OH, CHARING CROSS ROAD...
SO THIS NEGATIVE FORCE, IT REALLY LIKES GARFUNKELS?
LOOKS NORMAL, FOR THIS PART OF TOWN.
USED TO BE A REALLY PRETTY LITTLE VILLAGE HERE. A BEND IN THE RIVER... LOADS OF CUTE DUCKS...
SSSSSMMM
UH... DOCTOR?
THAT WASN'T NORMAL.
YEAH... WHICH WAY DID HE GO?
BUS STOP
AH, SOUL-FEARING SIGHTS! CARRIAGES SANS DRIVERS, FLAMES SANS WAX...
BUT I WOT THERE IS STILL A BOOKSELLER! AN APT SPOT FOR MY HAPPY RETURN!
UN-LTD BOOKS
20% OFF FOR STUDENTS

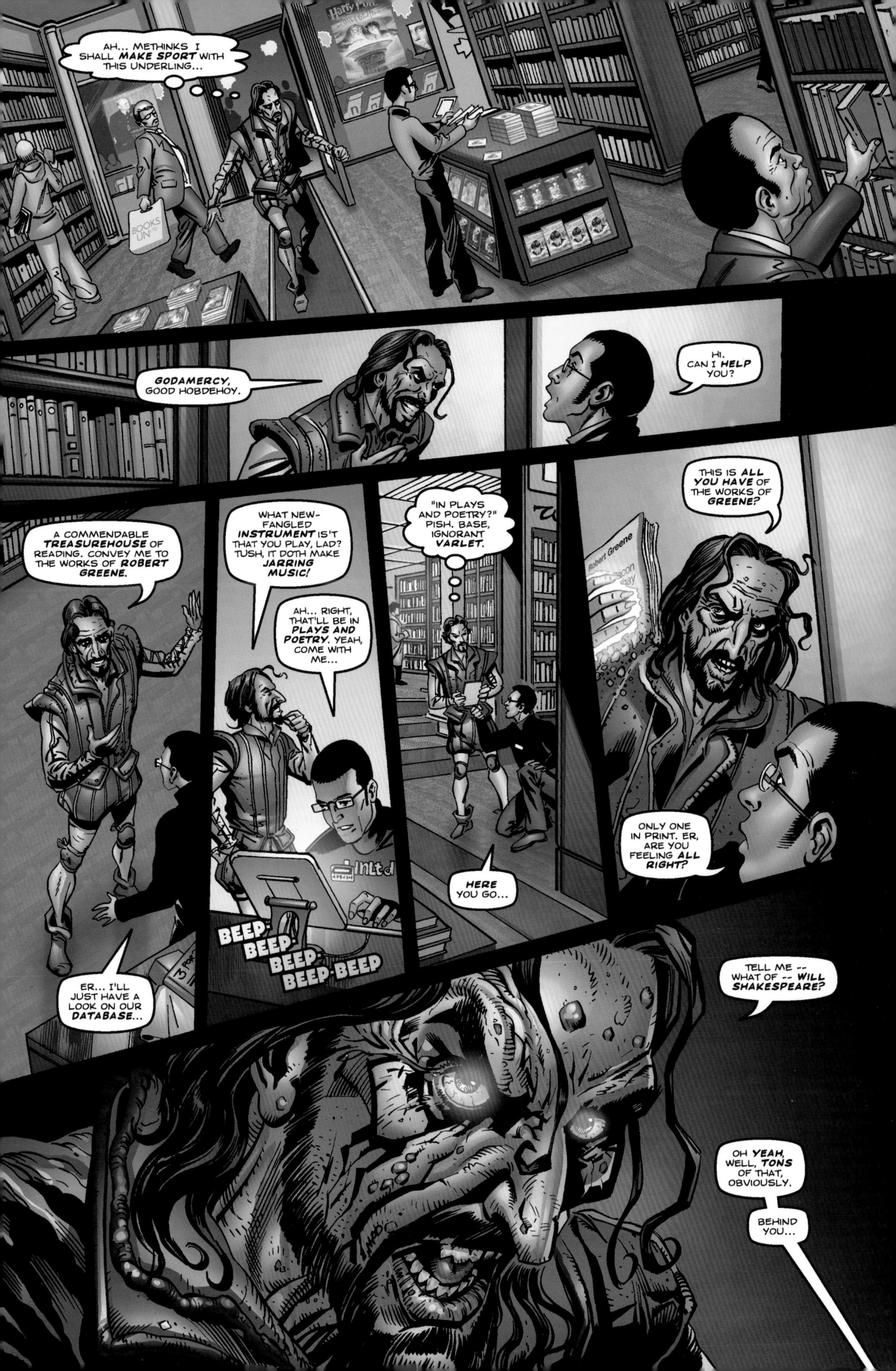

AH... METHINKS I SHALL MAKE SPORT WITH THIS UNDERLING...
BOOKS UN LTD.
GODAMERCY, GOOD HOBDEHOY.
HI. CAN I HELP YOU?
A COMMENDABLE TREASUREHOUSE OF READING. CONVEY ME TO THE WORKS OF ROBERT GREENE.
ER... I'LL JUST HAVE A LOOK ON OUR DATABASE...
WHAT NEW-FANGLED INSTRUMENT IS'T THAT YOU PLAY, LAD? TUSH, IT DOTH MAKE JARRING MUSIC!
AH... RIGHT, THAT'LL BE IN PLAYS AND POETRY. YEAH, COME WITH ME...
BEEP-BEEP-BEEP-BEEP-BEEP
"IN PLAYS AND POETRY?" PISH. BASE, IGNORANT VARLET.
HERE YOU GO...
Robert Greene
THIS IS ALL YOU HAVE OF THE WORKS OF GREENE?
ONLY ONE IN PRINT. ER, ARE YOU FEELING ALL RIGHT?
TELL ME -- WHAT OF -- WILL SHAKESPEARE?
OH YEAH, WELL, TONS OF THAT, OBVIOUSLY.
BEHIND YOU...

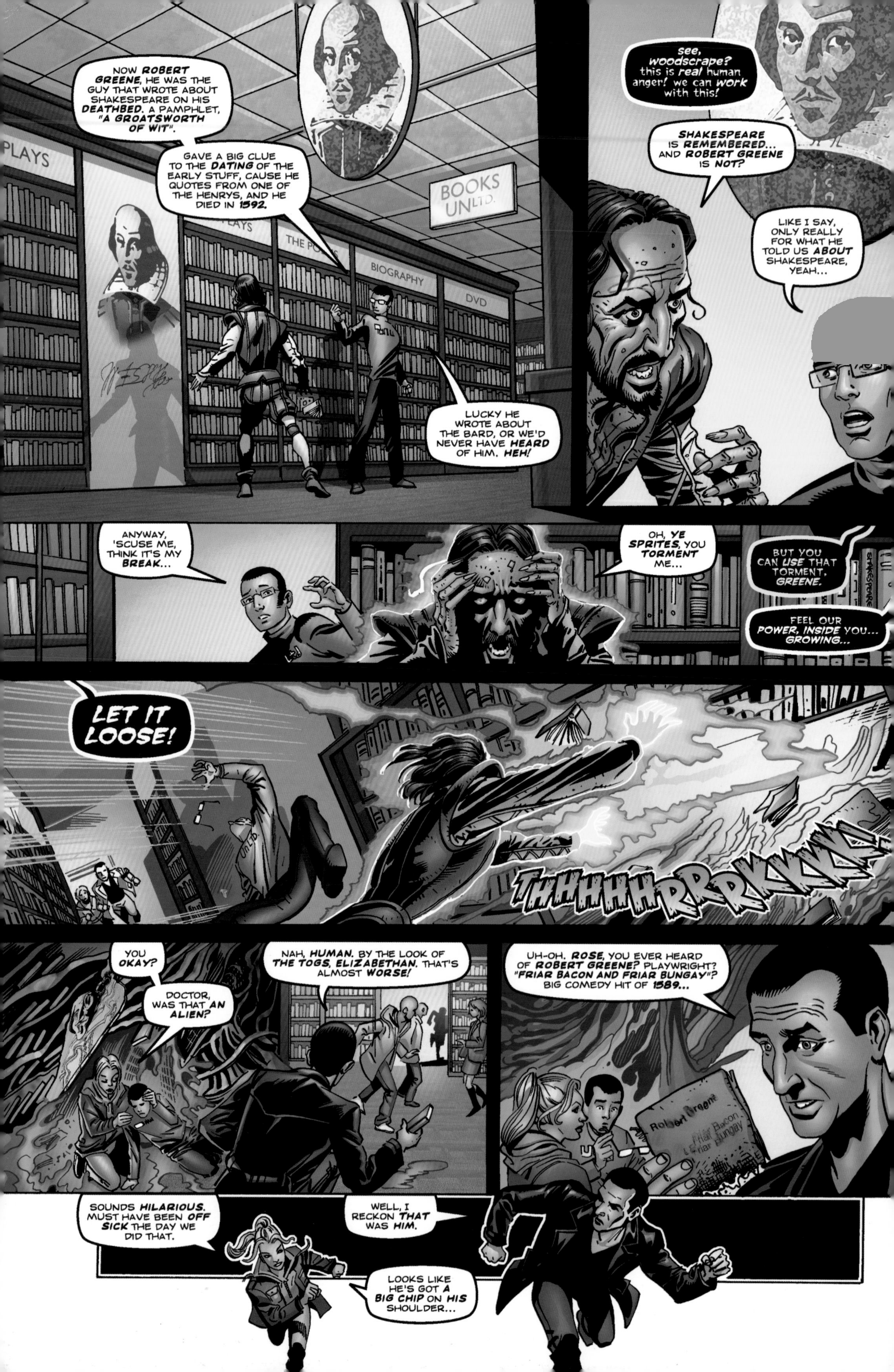
NOW ROBERT GREENE, HE WAS THE GUY THAT WROTE ABOUT SHAKESPEARE ON HIS DEATHBED. A PAMPHLET, "A GROATSWORTH OF WIT".
GAVE A BIG CLUE TO THE DATING OF THE EARLY STUFF, CAUSE HE QUOTES FROM ONE OF THE HENRYS, AND HE DIED IN 1592.
PLAYS
BOOKS UNLTD.
BIOGRAPHY
DVD
LUCKY HE WROTE ABOUT THE BARD, OR WE'D NEVER HAVE HEARD OF HIM. HEH!
see, woodscrape? this is real human anger! we can work with this!
SHAKESPEARE IS REMEMBERED... AND ROBERT GREENE IS NOT?
LIKE I SAY, ONLY REALLY FOR WHAT HE TOLD US ABOUT SHAKESPEARE, YEAH...
ANYWAY, 'SCUSE ME, THINK IT'S MY BREAK...
OH, YE SPRITES, YOU TORMENT ME...
BUT YOU CAN USE THAT TORMENT, GREENE.
FEEL OUR POWER, INSIDE YOU... GROWING...
LET IT LOOSE!
THHHHHRRRKKKK!
YOU OKAY?
DOCTOR, WAS THAT AN ALIEN?
NAH, HUMAN. BY THE LOOK OF THE TOGS, ELIZABETHAN. THAT'S ALMOST WORSE!
UH-OH. ROSE, YOU EVER HEARD OF ROBERT GREENE? PLAYWRIGHT? "FRIAR BACON AND FRIAR BUNGAY"? BIG COMEDY HIT OF 1589...
Robert Greene
Friar Bacon & Friar Bungay
SOUNDS HILARIOUS. MUST HAVE BEEN OFF SICK THE DAY WE DID THAT.
WELL, I RECKON THAT WAS HIM.
LOOKS LIKE HE'S GOT A BIG CHIP ON HIS SHOULDER...

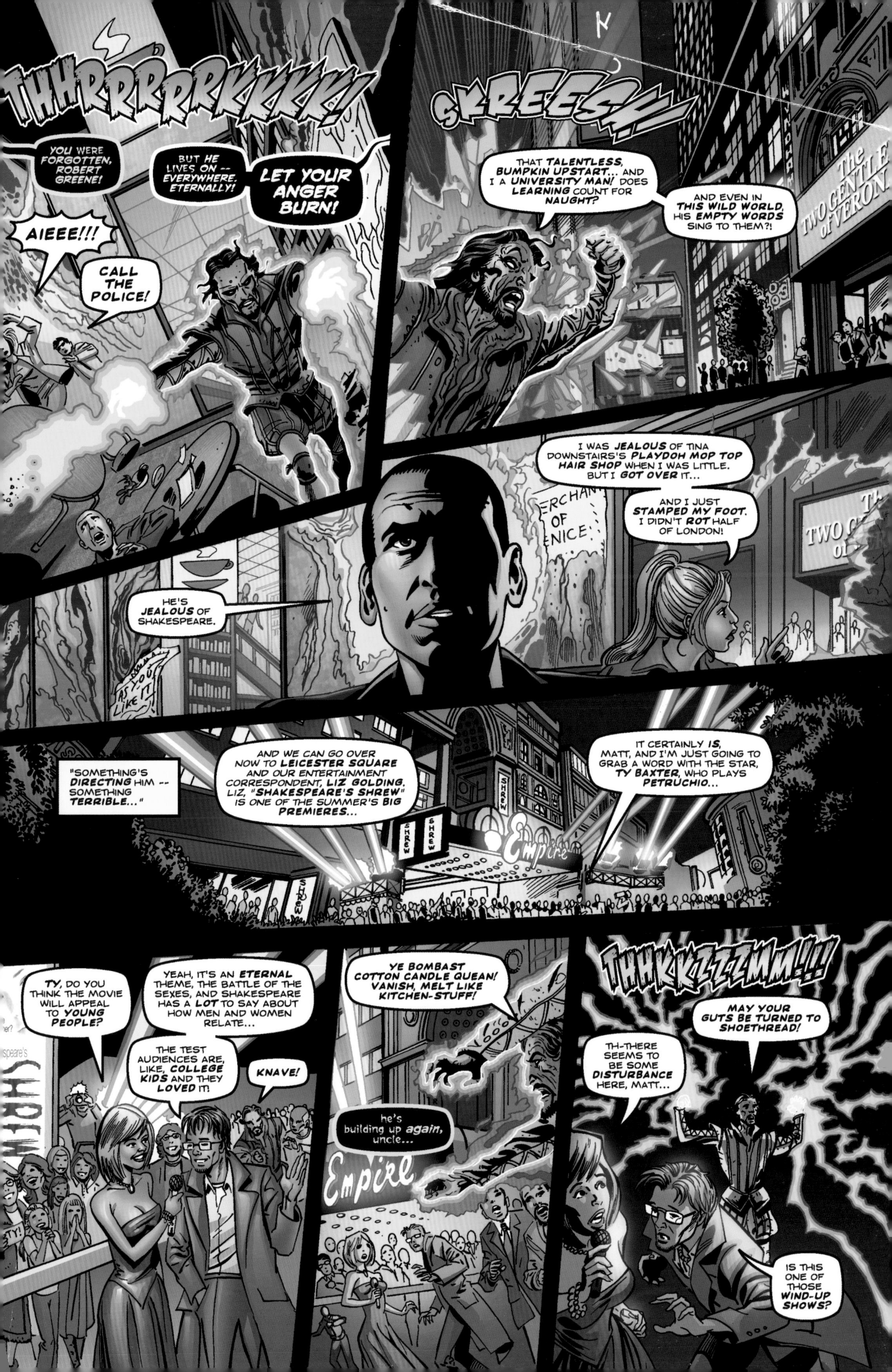
THHRRRRRKKKK!
YOU WERE FORGOTTEN, ROBERT GREENE!
BUT HE LIVES ON -- EVERYWHERE. ETERNALLY!
LET YOUR ANGER BURN!
AIEEE!!!
CALL THE POLICE!
SKREESH
THAT TALENTLESS, BUMPKIN UPSTART... AND I A UNIVERSITY MAN! DOES LEARNING COUNT FOR NAUGHT?
AND EVEN IN THIS WILD WORLD, HIS EMPTY WORDS SING TO THEM?!
The TWO GENTLE of VERON
HE'S JEALOUS OF SHAKESPEARE.
AS YOU LIKE IT
ERCHANT OF ENICE
I WAS JEALOUS OF TINA DOWNSTAIRS'S PLAYDOH MOP TOP HAIR SHOP WHEN I WAS LITTLE. BUT I GOT OVER IT...
AND I JUST STAMPED MY FOOT. I DIDN'T ROT HALF OF LONDON!
"SOMETHING'S DIRECTING HIM -- SOMETHING TERRIBLE..."
AND WE CAN GO OVER NOW TO LEICESTER SQUARE AND OUR ENTERTAINMENT CORRESPONDENT, LIZ GOLDING. LIZ, "SHAKESPEARE'S SHREW" IS ONE OF THE SUMMER'S BIG PREMIERES...
IT CERTAINLY IS, MATT, AND I'M JUST GOING TO GRAB A WORD WITH THE STAR, TY BAXTER, WHO PLAYS PETRUCHIO...
SHREW
Empire
TY, DO YOU THINK THE MOVIE WILL APPEAL TO YOUNG PEOPLE?
YEAH, IT'S AN ETERNAL THEME, THE BATTLE OF THE SEXES, AND SHAKESPEARE HAS A LOT TO SAY ABOUT HOW MEN AND WOMEN RELATE...
THE TEST AUDIENCES ARE, LIKE, COLLEGE KIDS AND THEY LOVED IT!
KNAVE!
SHREW
YE BOMBAST COTTON CANDLE QUEAN! VANISH, MELT LIKE KITCHEN-STUFF!
he's building up again, uncle...
Empire
THHKKZZZMM!!!
MAY YOUR GUTS BE TURNED TO SHOETHREAD!
TH-THERE SEEMS TO BE SOME DISTURBANCE HERE, MATT...
IS THIS ONE OF THOSE WIND-UP SHOWS?

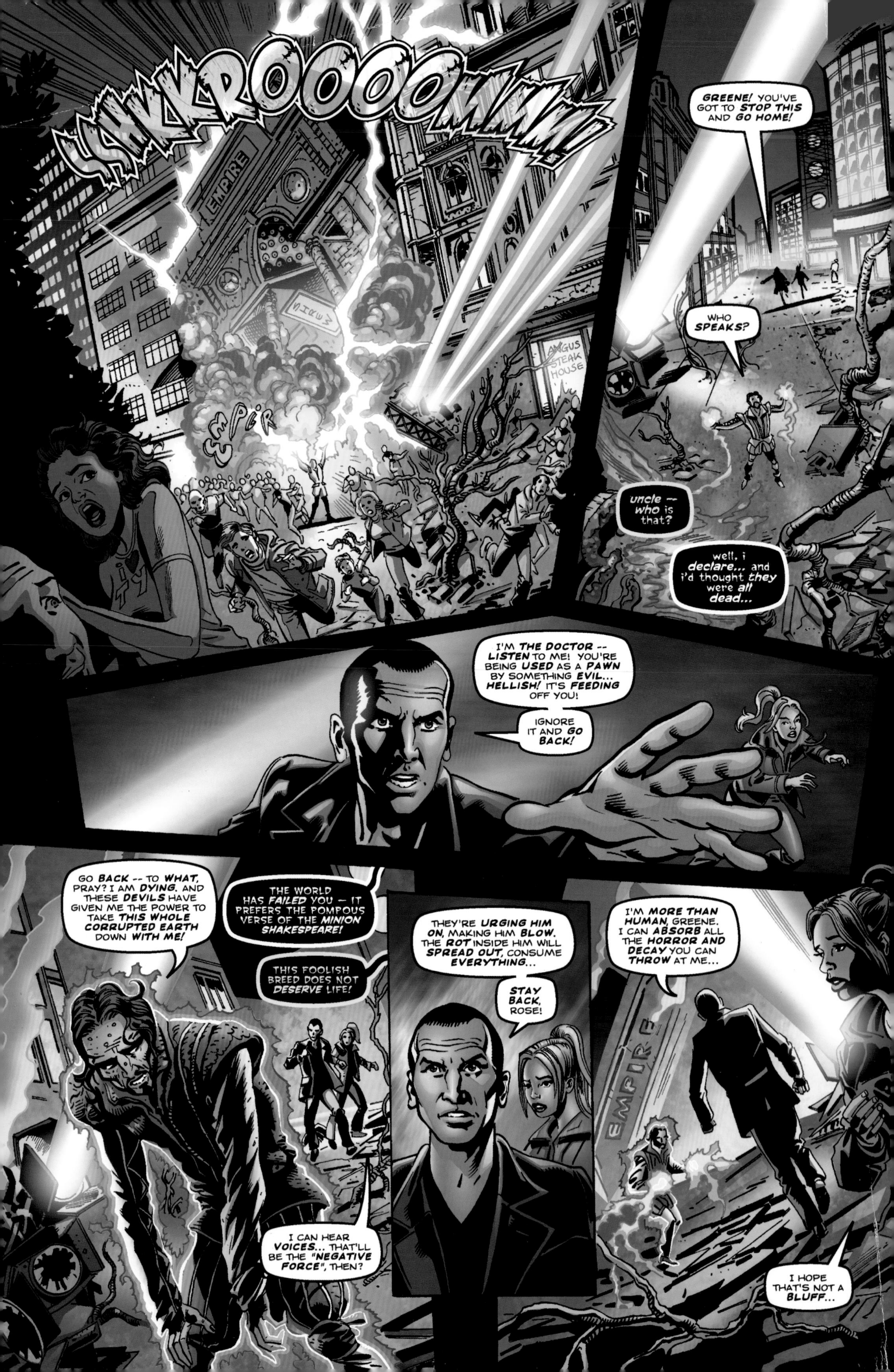
SHKROOOOOWWW!
EMPIRE
ANGUS STEAK HOUSE
GREENE! YOU'VE GOT TO STOP THIS AND GO HOME!
WHO SPEAKS?
uncle -- who is that?
well, i declare... and i'd thought they were all dead...
I'M THE DOCTOR -- LISTEN TO ME! YOU'RE BEING USED AS A PAWN BY SOMETHING EVIL... HELLISH! IT'S FEEDING OFF YOU!
IGNORE IT AND GO BACK!
GO BACK -- TO WHAT, PRAY? I AM DYING. AND THESE DEVILS HAVE GIVEN ME THE POWER TO TAKE THIS WHOLE CORRUPTED EARTH DOWN WITH ME!
THE WORLD HAS FAILED YOU — IT PREFERS THE POMPOUS VERSE OF THE MINION SHAKESPEARE!
THIS FOOLISH BREED DOES NOT DESERVE LIFE!
I CAN HEAR VOICES... THAT'LL BE THE "NEGATIVE FORCE", THEN?
THEY'RE URGING HIM ON, MAKING HIM BLOW. THE ROT INSIDE HIM WILL SPREAD OUT, CONSUME EVERYTHING...
STAY BACK, ROSE!
I'M MORE THAN HUMAN, GREENE. I CAN ABSORB ALL THE HORROR AND DECAY YOU CAN THROW AT ME...
EMPIRE
I HOPE THAT'S NOT A BLUFF...

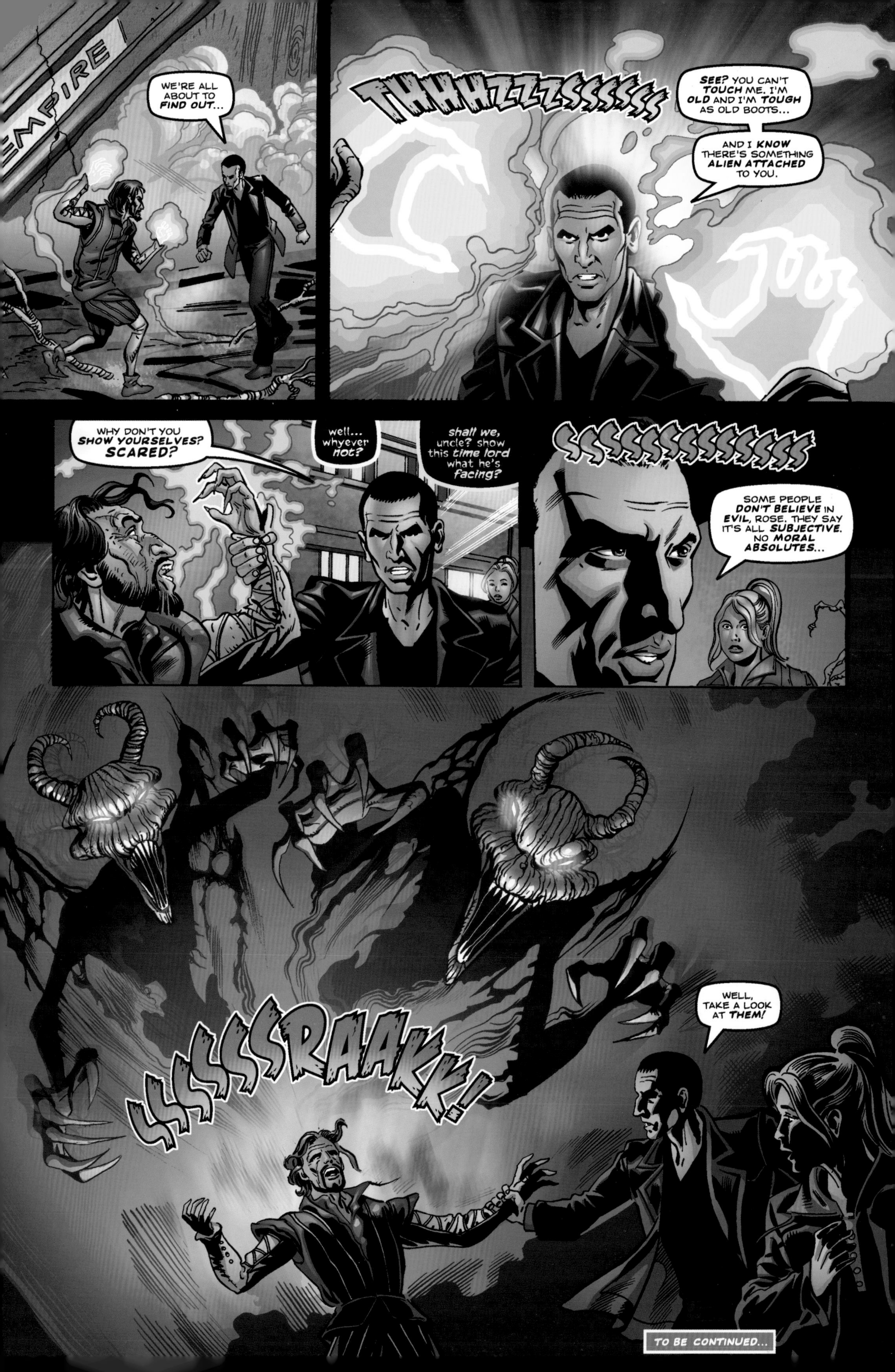
EMPIRE
WE'RE ALL ABOUT TO FIND OUT...
THHHZZZSSSSSS
SEE? YOU CAN'T TOUCH ME. I'M OLD AND I'M TOUGH AS OLD BOOTS...
AND I KNOW THERE'S SOMETHING ALIEN ATTACHED TO YOU.
WHY DON'T YOU SHOW YOURSELVES? SCARED?
well... whyever not?
shall we, uncle? show this time lord what he's facing?
SSSSSSSSSSSS
SOME PEOPLE DON'T BELIEVE IN EVIL, ROSE. THEY SAY IT'S ALL SUBJECTIVE. NO MORAL ABSOLUTES...
WELL, TAKE A LOOK AT THEM!
LLLSSSRAAKK!
TO BE CONTINUED...

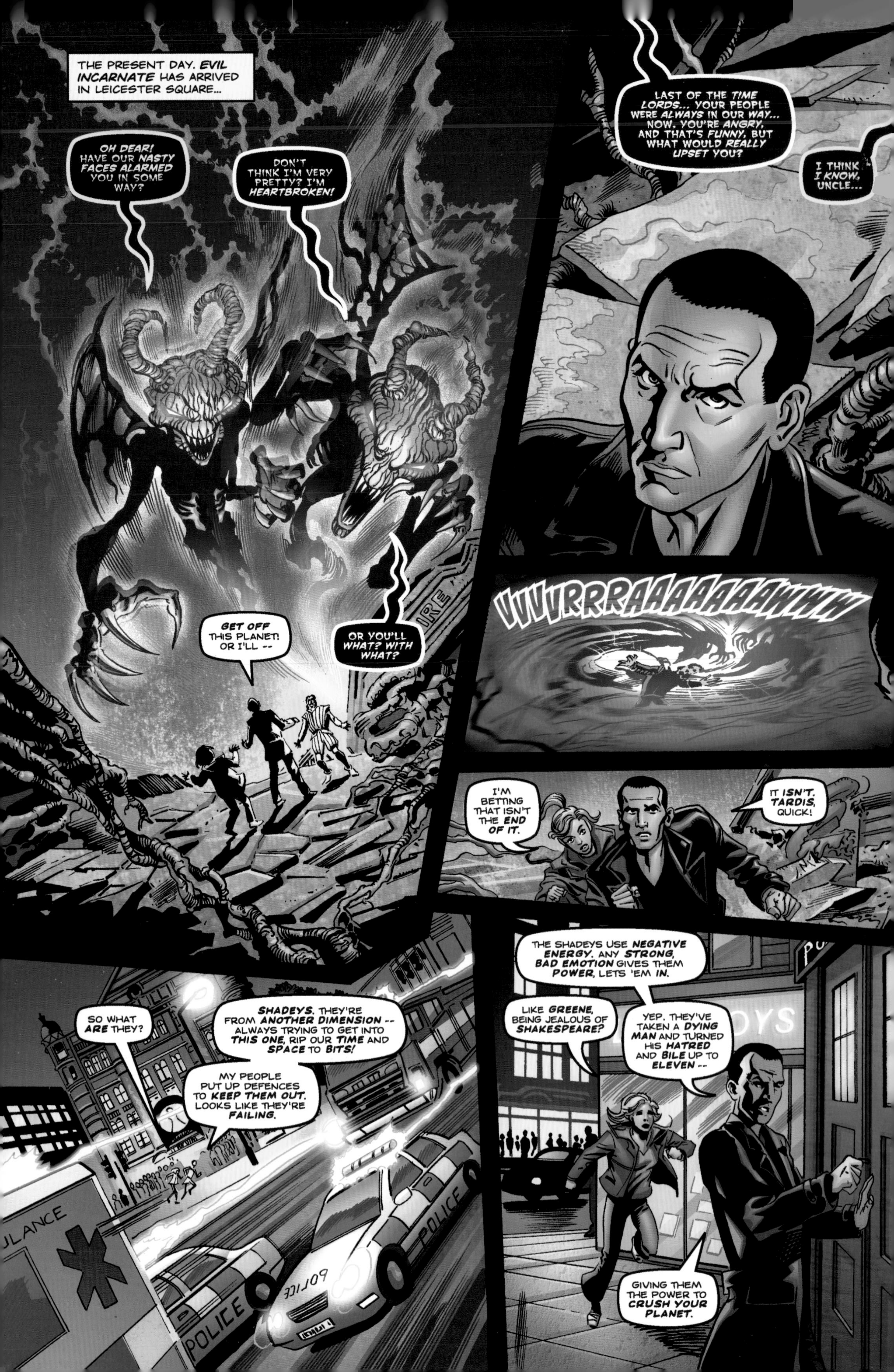
THE PRESENT DAY. EVIL INCARNATE HAS ARRIVED IN LEICESTER SQUARE...
OH DEAR! HAVE OUR NASTY FACES ALARMED YOU IN SOME WAY?
DON'T THINK I'M VERY PRETTY? I'M HEARTBROKEN!
GET OFF THIS PLANET! OR I'LL --
OR YOU'LL WHAT? WITH WHAT?
LAST OF THE TIME LORDS... YOUR PEOPLE WERE ALWAYS IN OUR WAY... NOW, YOU'RE ANGRY, AND THAT'S FUNNY, BUT WHAT WOULD REALLY UPSET YOU?
I THINK I KNOW, UNCLE...
VVVVRRRAAAAAAAWWWW
I'M BETTING THAT ISN'T THE END OF IT.
IT ISN'T. TARDIS, QUICK!
SO WHAT ARE THEY?
SHADEYS. THEY'RE FROM ANOTHER DIMENSION -- ALWAYS TRYING TO GET INTO THIS ONE, RIP OUR TIME AND SPACE TO BITS!
MY PEOPLE PUT UP DEFENCES TO KEEP THEM OUT. LOOKS LIKE THEY'RE FAILING.
THE SHADEYS USE NEGATIVE ENERGY. ANY STRONG, BAD EMOTION GIVES THEM POWER, LETS 'EM IN.
LIKE GREENE, BEING JEALOUS OF SHAKESPEARE?
YEP. THEY'VE TAKEN A DYING MAN AND TURNED HIS HATRED AND BILE UP TO ELEVEN --
GIVING THEM THE POWER TO CRUSH YOUR PLANET.

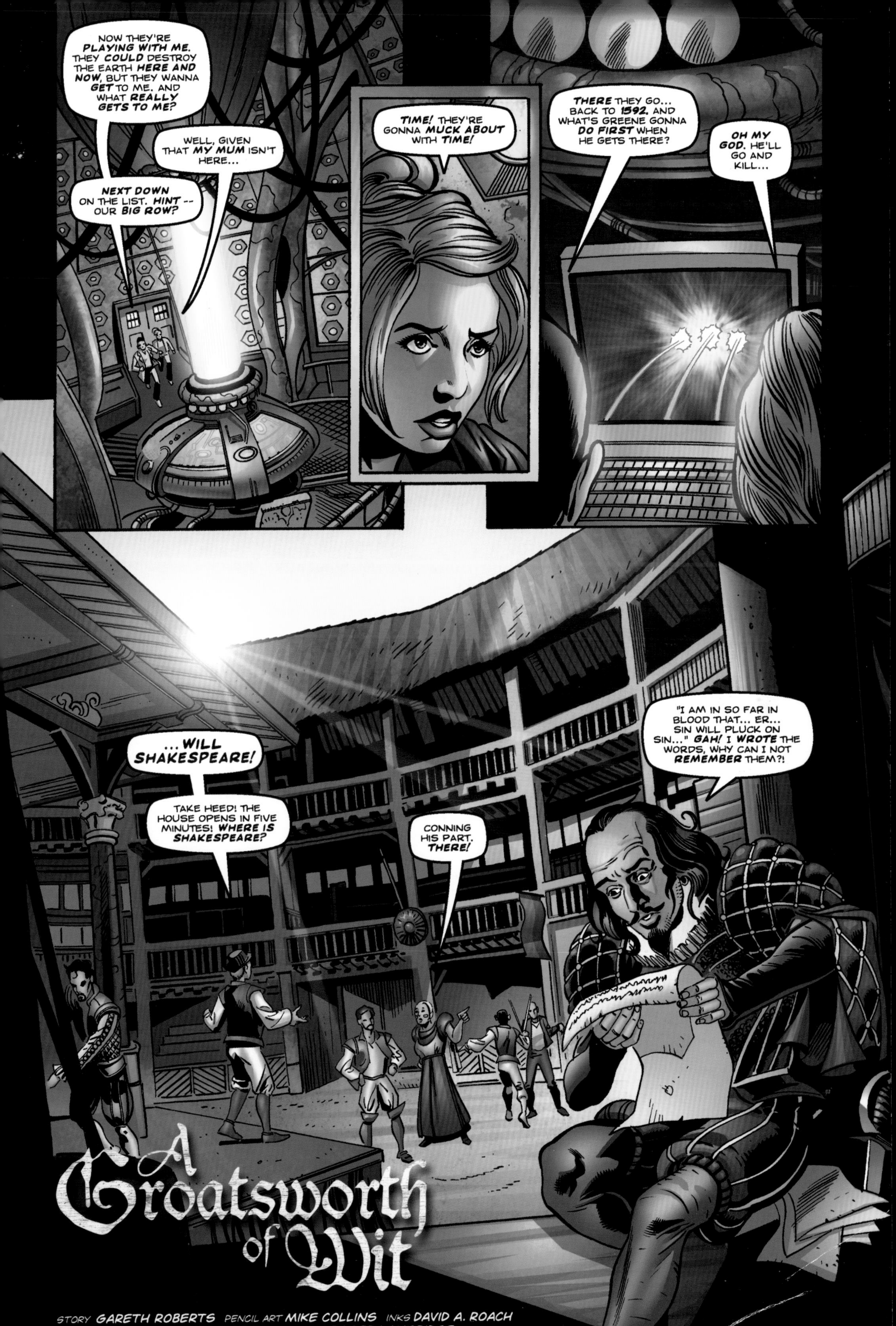
NOW THEY'RE PLAYING WITH ME. THEY COULD DESTROY THE EARTH HERE AND NOW, BUT THEY WANNA GET TO ME. AND WHAT REALLY GETS TO ME?
WELL, GIVEN THAT MY MUM ISN'T HERE...
NEXT DOWN ON THE LIST. HINT -- OUR BIG ROW?
TIME! THEY'RE GONNA MUCK ABOUT WITH TIME!
THERE THEY GO... BACK TO 1592. AND WHAT'S GREENE GONNA DO FIRST WHEN HE GETS THERE?
OH MY GOD. HE'LL GO AND KILL...
...WILL SHAKESPEARE!
TAKE HEED! THE HOUSE OPENS IN FIVE MINUTES! WHERE IS SHAKESPEARE?
CONNING HIS PART. THERE!
"I AM IN SO FAR IN BLOOD THAT... ER... SIN WILL PLUCK ON SIN..." GAH! I WROTE THE WORDS, WHY CAN I NOT REMEMBER THEM?!
A Groatsworth of Wit
STORY GARETH ROBERTS PENCIL ART MIKE COLLINS INKS DAVID A. ROACH
COLOURS JAMES OFFREDI LETTERS ROGER LANGRIDGE
EDITORS CLAYTON HICKMAN & SCOTT GRAY

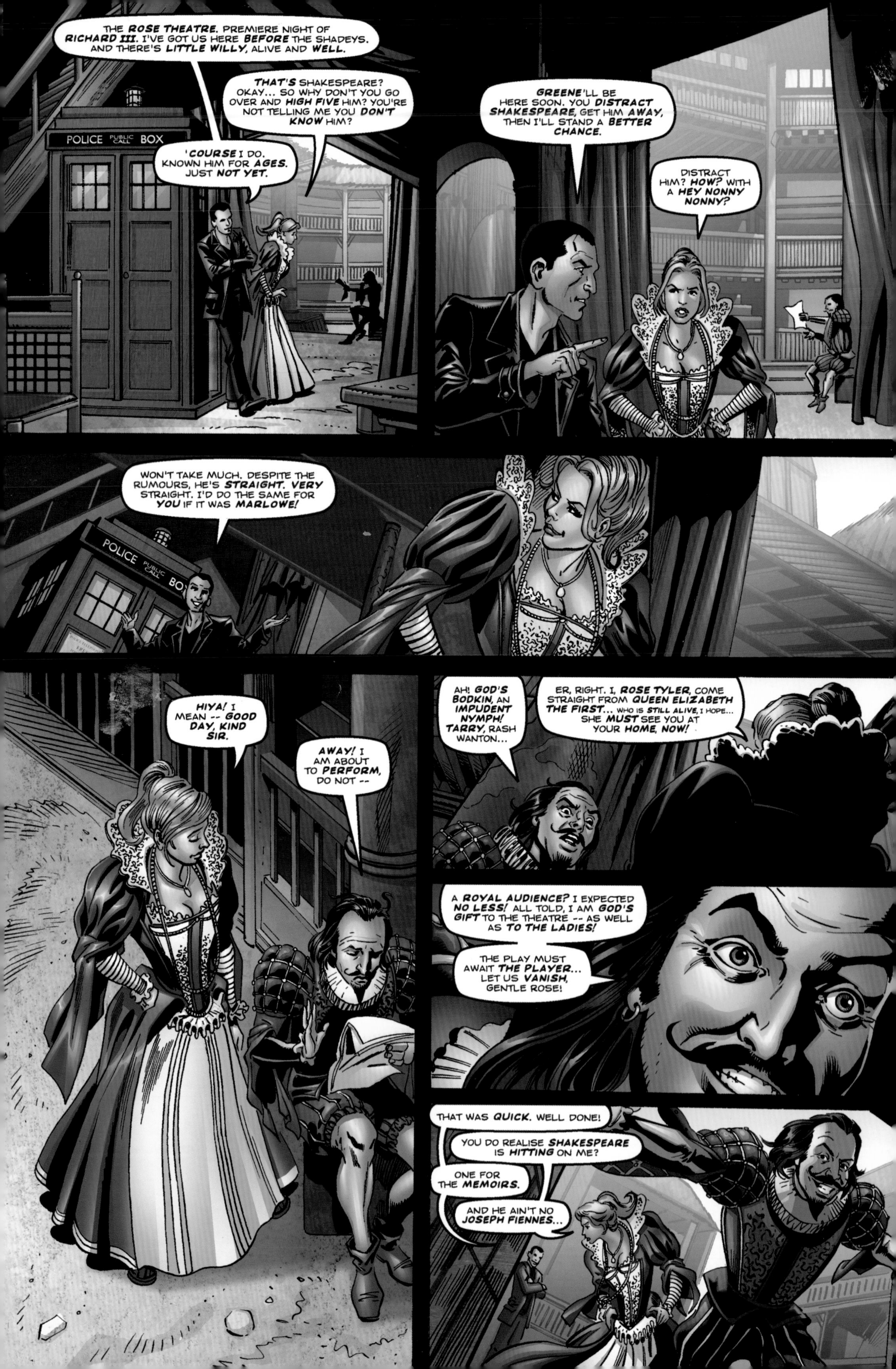
THE ROSE THEATRE. PREMIERE NIGHT OF RICHARD III. I'VE GOT US HERE BEFORE THE SHADEYS. AND THERE'S LITTLE WILLY, ALIVE AND WELL.
THAT'S SHAKESPEARE? OKAY... SO WHY DON'T YOU GO OVER AND HIGH FIVE HIM? YOU'RE NOT TELLING ME YOU DON'T KNOW HIM?
'COURSE I DO. KNOWN HIM FOR AGES. JUST NOT YET.
POLICE PUBLIC CALL BOX
GREENE'LL BE HERE SOON. YOU DISTRACT SHAKESPEARE, GET HIM AWAY, THEN I'LL STAND A BETTER CHANCE.
DISTRACT HIM? HOW? WITH A HEY NONNY NONNY?
WON'T TAKE MUCH. DESPITE THE RUMOURS, HE'S STRAIGHT. VERY STRAIGHT. I'D DO THE SAME FOR YOU IF IT WAS MARLOWE!
HIYA! I MEAN -- GOOD DAY, KIND SIR.
AWAY! I AM ABOUT TO PERFORM, DO NOT --
AH! GOD'S BODKIN, AN IMPUDENT NYMPH! TARRY, RASH WANTON...
ER, RIGHT. I, ROSE TYLER, COME STRAIGHT FROM QUEEN ELIZABETH THE FIRST... WHO IS STILL ALIVE, I HOPE... SHE MUST SEE YOU AT YOUR HOME, NOW!
A ROYAL AUDIENCE? I EXPECTED NO LESS! ALL TOLD, I AM GOD'S GIFT TO THE THEATRE -- AS WELL AS TO THE LADIES!
THE PLAY MUST AWAIT THE PLAYER... LET US VANISH, GENTLE ROSE!
THAT WAS QUICK. WELL DONE!
YOU DO REALISE SHAKESPEARE IS HITTING ON ME?
ONE FOR THE MEMOIRS.
AND HE AIN'T NO JOSEPH FIENNES...

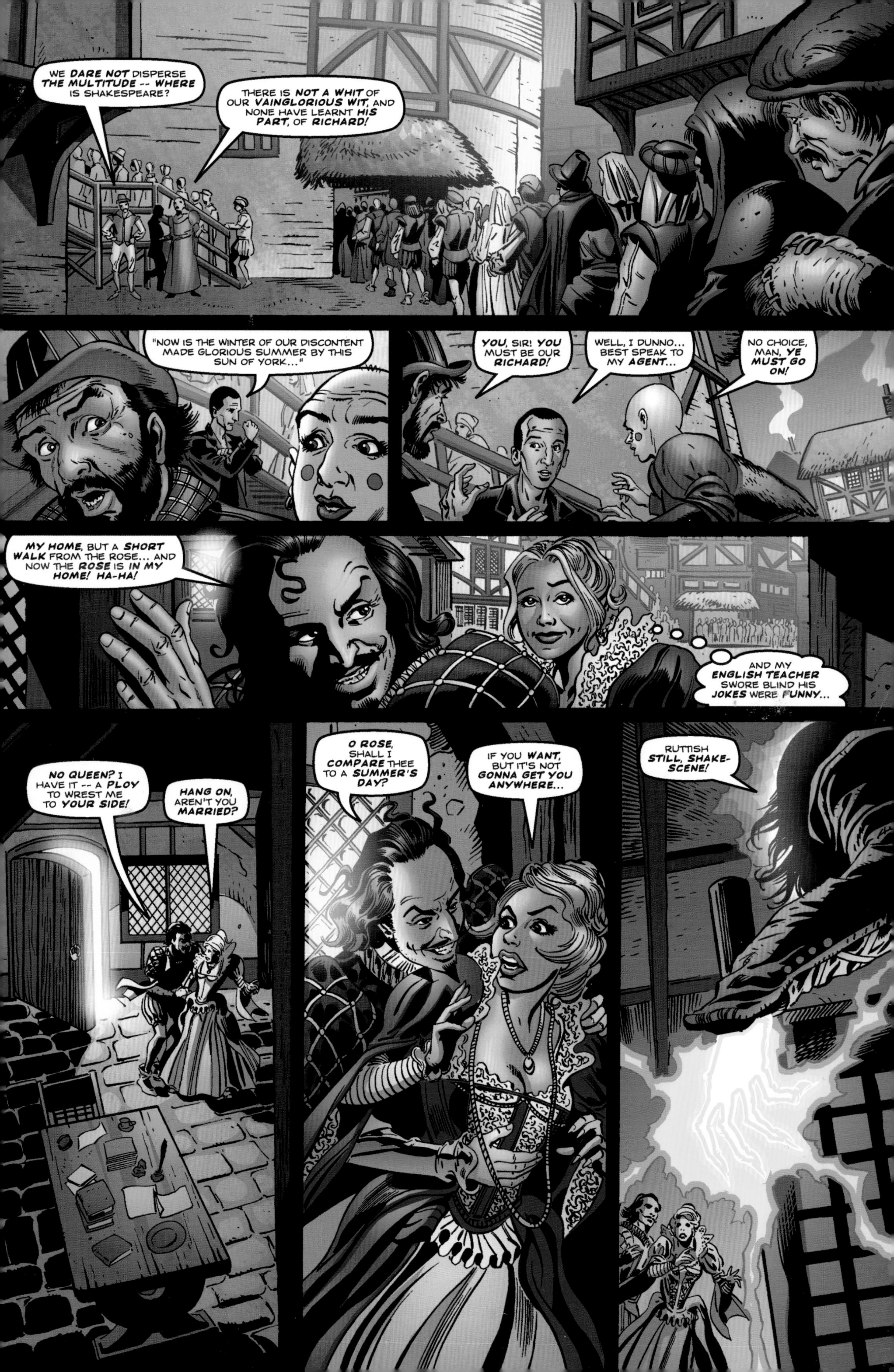
WE DARE NOT DISPERSE THE MULTITUDE -- WHERE IS SHAKESPEARE?
THERE IS NOT A WHIT OF OUR VAINGLORIOUS WIT, AND NONE HAVE LEARNT HIS PART, OF RICHARD!
"NOW IS THE WINTER OF OUR DISCONTENT MADE GLORIOUS SUMMER BY THIS SUN OF YORK..."
YOU, SIR! YOU MUST BE OUR RICHARD!
WELL, I DUNNO... BEST SPEAK TO MY AGENT...
NO CHOICE, MAN, YE MUST GO ON!
MY HOME, BUT A SHORT WALK FROM THE ROSE... AND NOW THE ROSE IS IN MY HOME! HA-HA!
AND MY ENGLISH TEACHER SWORE BLIND HIS JOKES WERE FUNNY...
NO QUEEN? I HAVE IT -- A PLOY TO WREST ME TO YOUR SIDE!
HANG ON, AREN'T YOU MARRIED?
O ROSE, SHALL I COMPARE THEE TO A SUMMER'S DAY?
IF YOU WANT, BUT IT'S NOT GONNA GET YOU ANYWHERE...
RUTTISH STILL, SHAKE-SCENE!

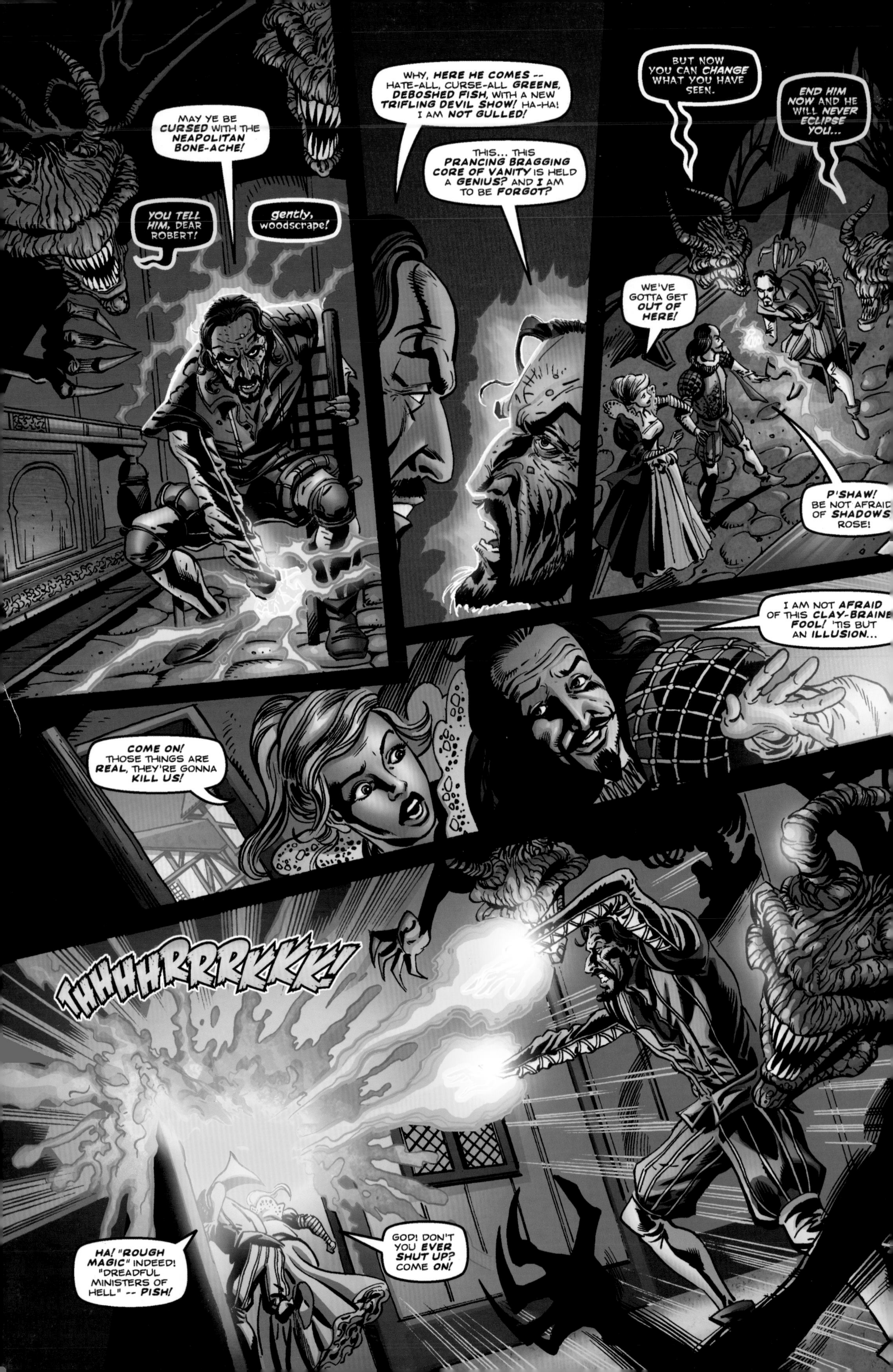
MAY YE BE CURSED WITH THE NEAPOLITAN BONE-ACHE!
YOU TELL HIM, DEAR ROBERT!
gently, woodscrape!
WHY, HERE HE COMES -- HATE-ALL, CURSE-ALL GREENE, DEBOSHED FISH, WITH A NEW TRIFLING DEVIL SHOW! HA-HA! I AM NOT GULLED!
THIS... THIS PRANCING BRAGGING CORE OF VANITY IS HELD A GENIUS? AND I AM TO BE FORGOT?
BUT NOW YOU CAN CHANGE WHAT YOU HAVE SEEN.
END HIM NOW AND HE WILL NEVER ECLIPSE YOU...
WE'VE GOTTA GET OUT OF HERE!
P'SHAW! BE NOT AFRAID OF SHADOWS ROSE!
I AM NOT AFRAID OF THIS CLAY-BRAINE FOOL! 'TIS BUT AN ILLUSION...
COME ON! THOSE THINGS ARE REAL, THEY'RE GONNA KILL US!
THHHHRRRKKK!
HA! "ROUGH MAGIC" INDEED! "DREADFUL MINISTERS OF HELL" -- PISH!
GOD! DON'T YOU EVER SHUT UP? COME ON!

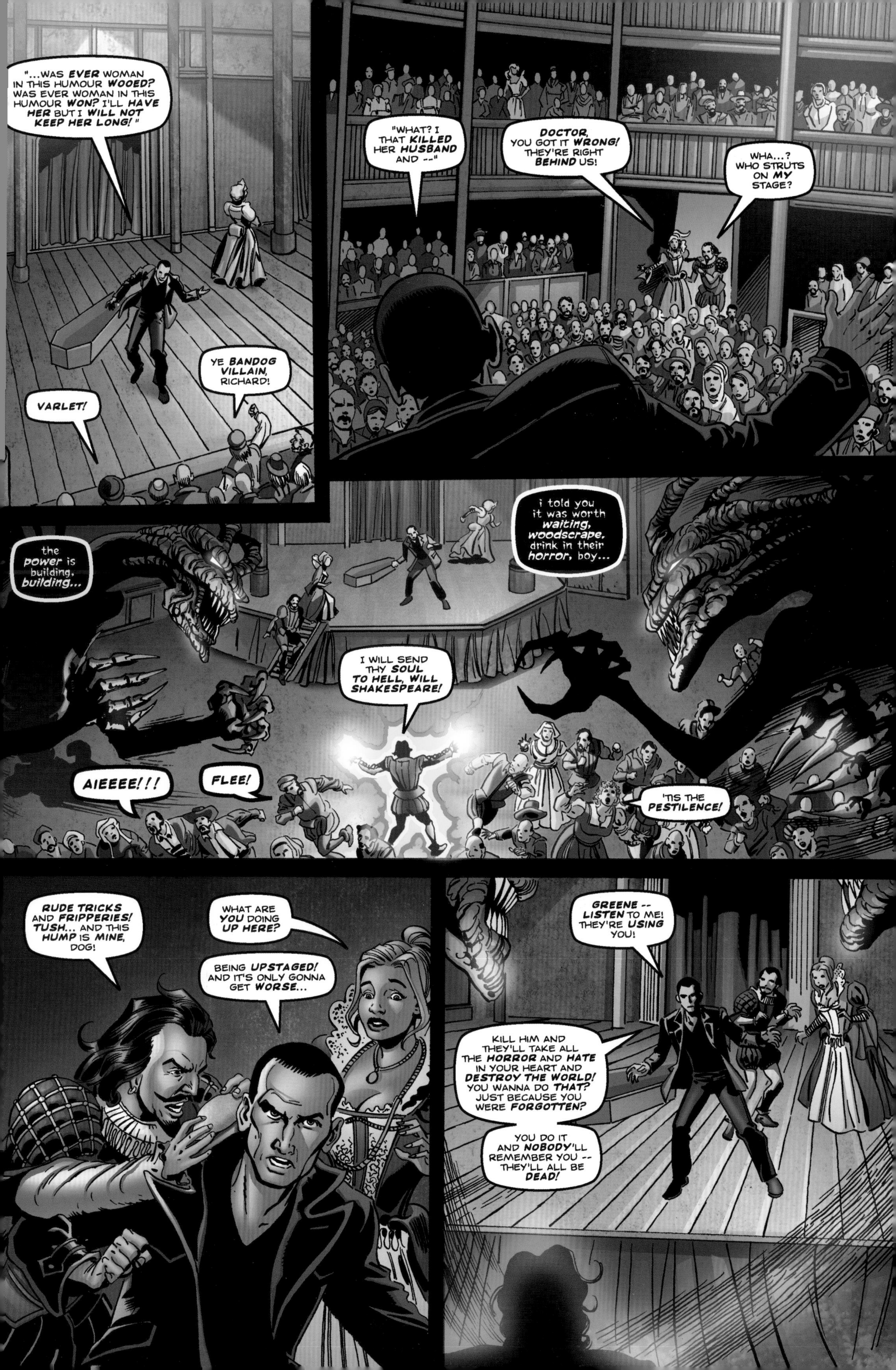
"...WAS EVER WOMAN IN THIS HUMOUR WOOED? WAS EVER WOMAN IN THIS HUMOUR WON? I'LL HAVE HER BUT I WILL NOT KEEP HER LONG!"
YE BANDOG VILLAIN, RICHARD!
VARLET!
"WHAT? I THAT KILLED HER HUSBAND AND --"
DOCTOR, YOU GOT IT WRONG! THEY'RE RIGHT BEHIND US!
WHA...? WHO STRUTS ON MY STAGE?
the power is building, building...
i told you it was worth waiting, woodscrape, drink in their horror, boy...
I WILL SEND THY SOUL TO HELL, WILL SHAKESPEARE!
AIEEEE!!!
FLEE!
'TIS THE PESTILENCE!
RUDE TRICKS AND FRIPPERIES! TUSH... AND THIS HUMP IS MINE, DOG!
WHAT ARE YOU DOING UP HERE?
BEING UPSTAGED! AND IT'S ONLY GONNA GET WORSE...
GREENE -- LISTEN TO ME! THEY'RE USING YOU!
KILL HIM AND THEY'LL TAKE ALL THE HORROR AND HATE IN YOUR HEART AND DESTROY THE WORLD! YOU WANNA DO THAT? JUST BECAUSE YOU WERE FORGOTTEN?
YOU DO IT AND NOBODY'LL REMEMBER YOU -- THEY'LL ALL BE DEAD!

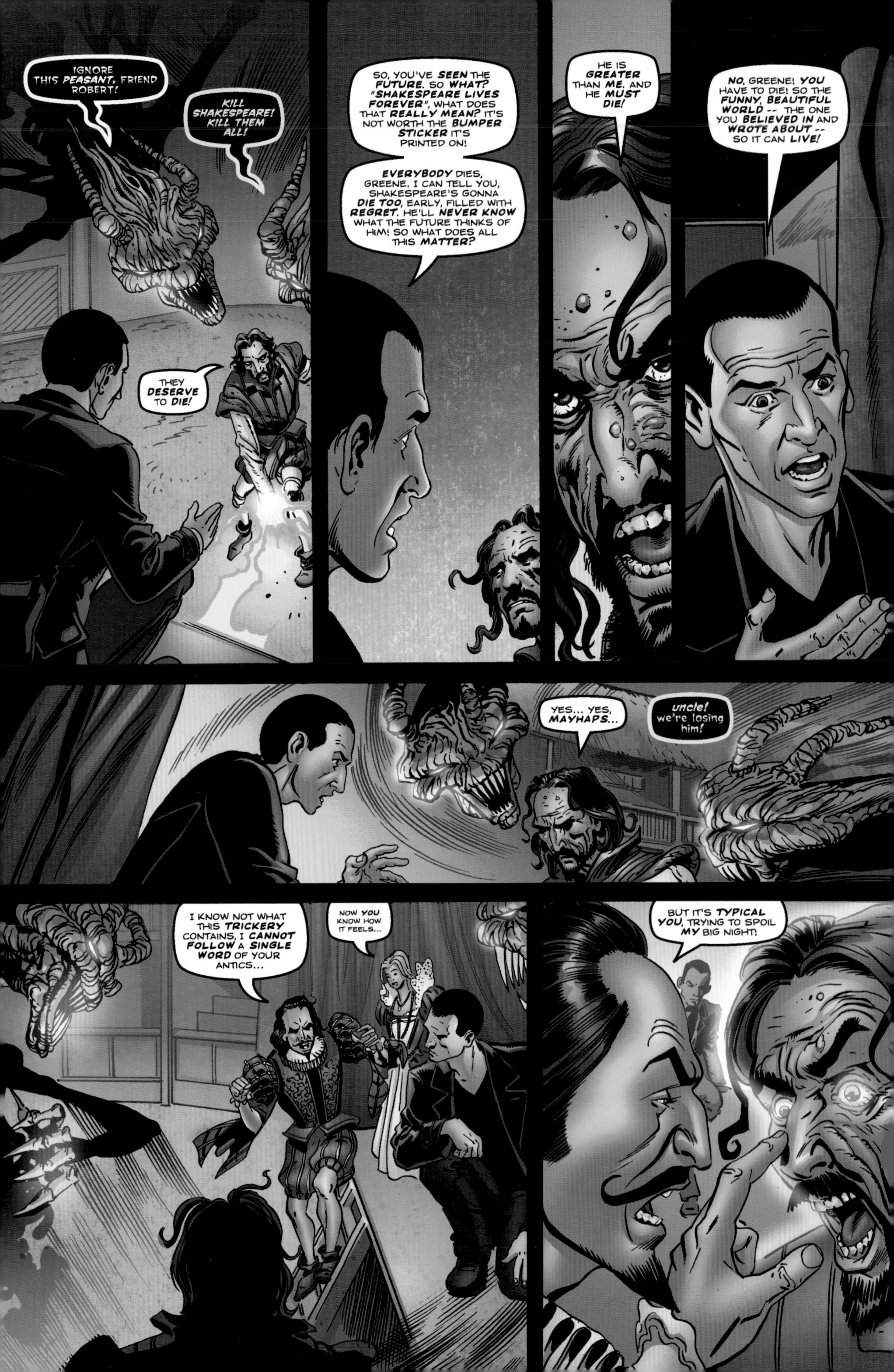
IGNORE THIS PEASANT, FRIEND ROBERT!
KILL SHAKESPEARE! KILL THEM ALL!
THEY DESERVE TO DIE!
SO, YOU'VE SEEN THE FUTURE. SO WHAT? "SHAKESPEARE LIVES FOREVER", WHAT DOES THAT REALLY MEAN? IT'S NOT WORTH THE BUMPER STICKER IT'S PRINTED ON!
EVERYBODY DIES, GREENE. I CAN TELL YOU, SHAKESPEARE'S GONNA DIE TOO, EARLY, FILLED WITH REGRET. HE'LL NEVER KNOW WHAT THE FUTURE THINKS OF HIM! SO WHAT DOES ALL THIS MATTER?
HE IS GREATER THAN ME, AND HE MUST DIE!
NO, GREENE! YOU HAVE TO DIE! SO THE FUNNY, BEAUTIFUL WORLD -- THE ONE YOU BELIEVED IN AND WROTE ABOUT -- SO IT CAN LIVE!
YES... YES, MAYHAPS...
uncle! we're losing him!
I KNOW NOT WHAT THIS TRICKERY CONTAINS, I CANNOT FOLLOW A SINGLE WORD OF YOUR ANTICS...
NOW YOU KNOW HOW IT FEELS...
BUT IT'S TYPICAL YOU, TRYING TO SPOIL MY BIG NIGHT!

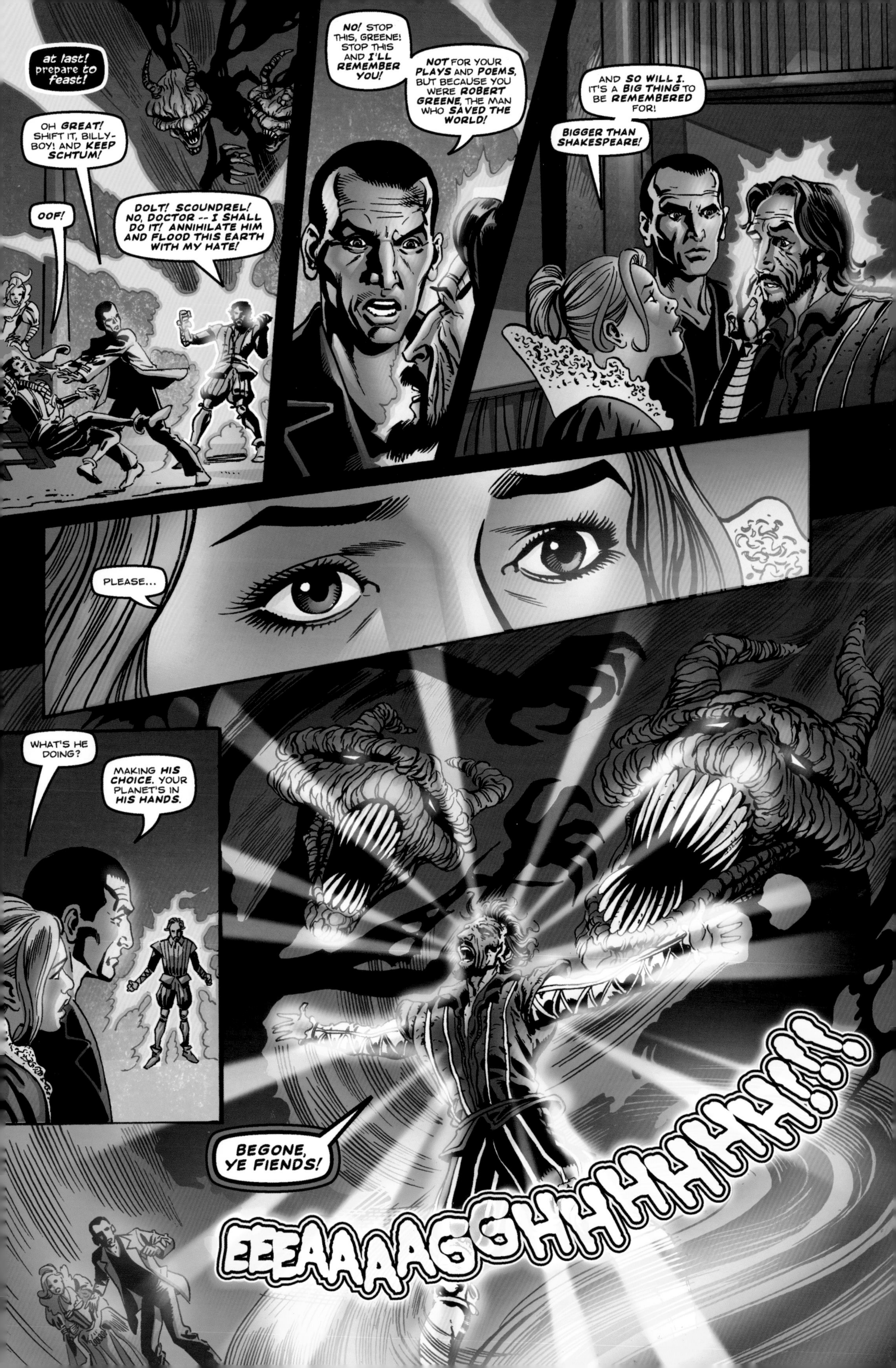
at last! prepare to feast!
OH GREAT! SHIFT IT, BILLY-BOY! AND KEEP SCHTUM!
OOF!
DOLT! SCOUNDREL! NO, DOCTOR -- I SHALL DO IT! ANNIHILATE HIM AND FLOOD THIS EARTH WITH MY HATE!
NO! STOP THIS, GREENE! STOP THIS AND I'LL REMEMBER YOU!
NOT FOR YOUR PLAYS AND POEMS, BUT BECAUSE YOU WERE ROBERT GREENE, THE MAN WHO SAVED THE WORLD!
AND SO WILL I. IT'S A BIG THING TO BE REMEMBERED FOR!
BIGGER THAN SHAKESPEARE!
PLEASE...
WHAT'S HE DOING?
MAKING HIS CHOICE. YOUR PLANET'S IN HIS HANDS.
BEGONE, YE FIENDS!
EEEAAAAAGGHHHHHHHH!!!!

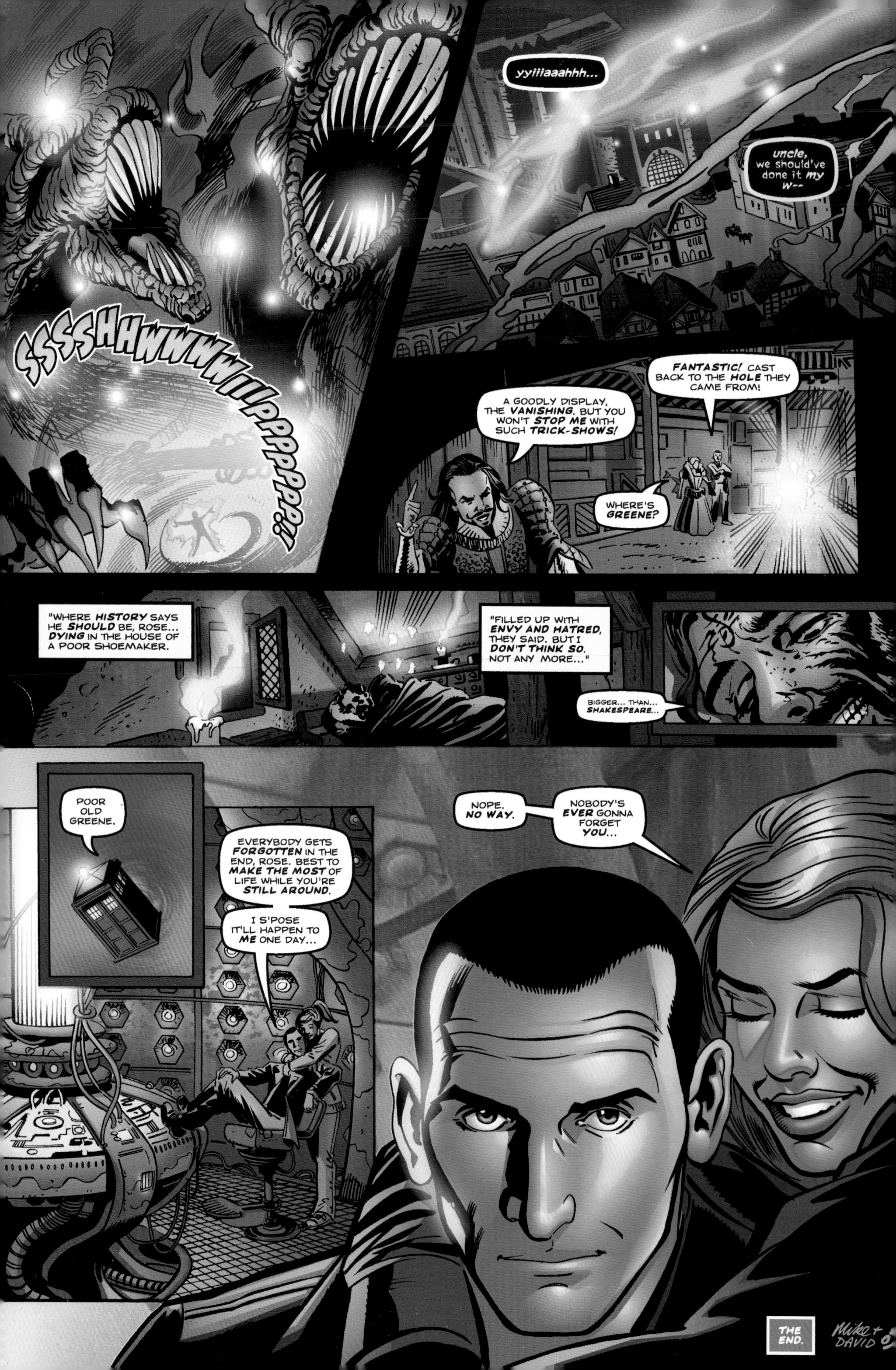
SSSSHHWWWWIIIPPPPPP!!
yyiiiaaahhh...
uncle, we should've done it my w--
A GOODLY DISPLAY, THE VANISHING. BUT YOU WON'T STOP ME WITH SUCH TRICK-SHOWS!
FANTASTIC! CAST BACK TO THE HOLE THEY CAME FROM!
WHERE'S GREENE?
"WHERE HISTORY SAYS HE SHOULD BE, ROSE... DYING IN THE HOUSE OF A POOR SHOEMAKER.
"FILLED UP WITH ENVY AND HATRED, THEY SAID. BUT I DON'T THINK SO. NOT ANY MORE..."
BIGGER... THAN... SHAKESPEARE...
POOR OLD GREENE.
EVERYBODY GETS FORGOTTEN IN THE END, ROSE. BEST TO MAKE THE MOST OF LIFE WHILE YOU'RE STILL AROUND.
I S'POSE IT'LL HAPPEN TO ME ONE DAY...
NOPE. NO WAY.
NOBODY'S EVER GONNA FORGET YOU...
THE END.
Mike + DAVID

What I Did On My Christmas Holidays
by SALLY SPARROW

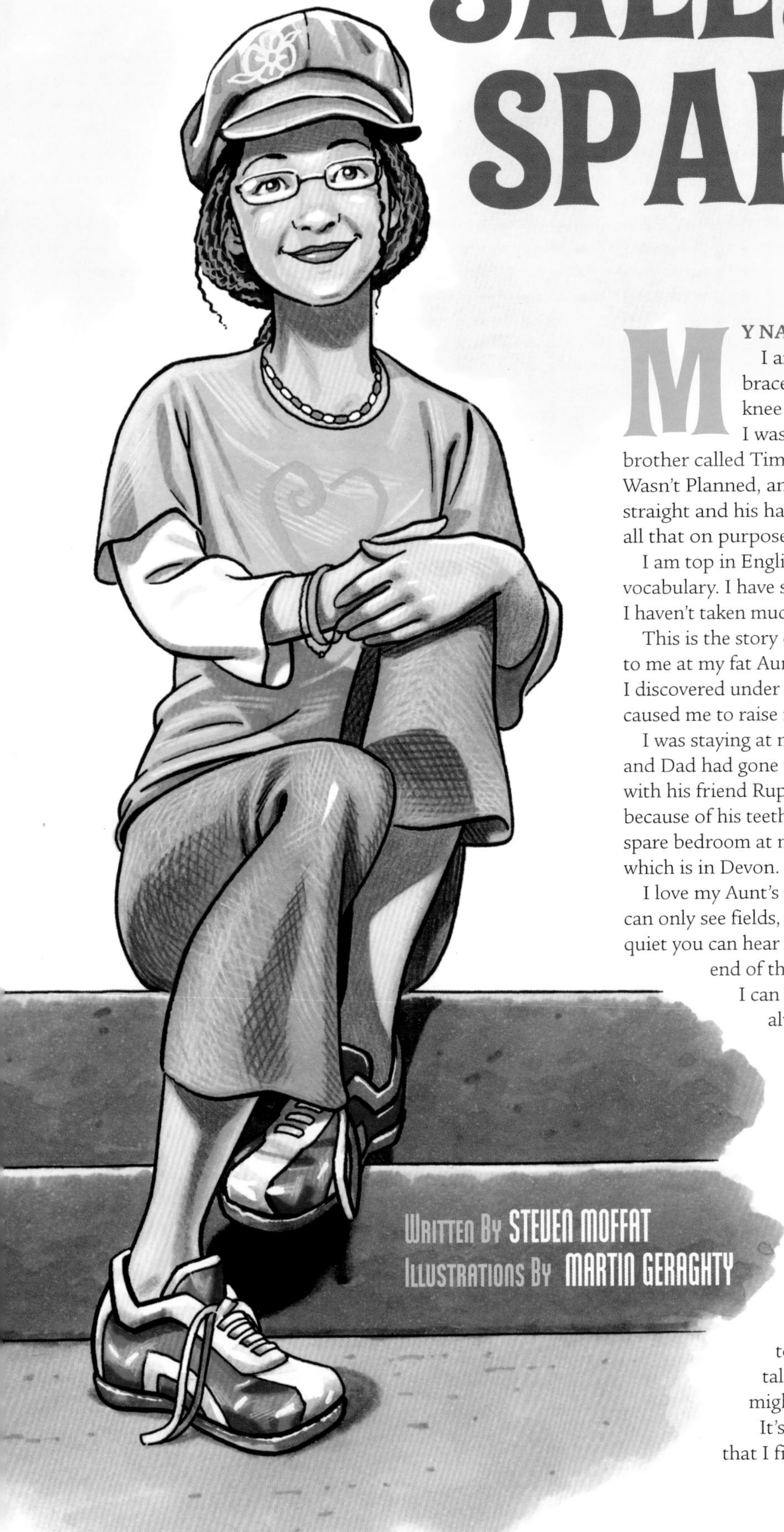

Written By **STEVEN MOFFAT**
Illustrations By **MARTIN GERAGHTY**

MY NAME IS SALLY SPARROW. I am 12 years old, I have auburn hair, braces you can hardly see, a dent in my left knee from where I fell off a bicycle when I was ten, and parents. I also have a little brother called Tim. My Mum told Mrs Medford that Tim Wasn't Planned, and you can tell because his nose isn't straight and his hair sticks up and I can't believe you'd do all that on purpose. Or his ears.

I am top in English, and Miss Telfer says I have an excellent vocabulary. I have sixteen friends who are mainly girls. I haven't taken much interest in boys yet, because of the noise.

This is the story of the mysterious events that happened to me at my fat Aunt's cottage at Christmas and what I discovered under the wallpaper of my bedroom, which caused me to raise my eyebrows with perplexity.

I was staying at my fat Aunt's cottage because my Mum and Dad had gone on a weekend away. Tim was staying with his friend Rupert (who I don't think was planned either because of his teeth) and I found myself once more in the spare bedroom at my Aunt's cottage in the countryside, which is in Devon.

I love my Aunt's cottage. From her kitchen window you can only see fields, all the way to the horizon, and it's so quiet you can hear water dripping off a leaf from right at the end of the garden. Sometimes, when I lie in bed, I can hear a train far away in the distance and it always fills me with a big sighing feeling, like sadness, only nice. It's good, my bedroom at my aunt's. Really big, with a wardrobe that rattles its hangers when you walk past it and huge yellow flowers on the wallpaper. When I was little I used to sit and stare at those flowers and when no-one was looking I'd try to pick them, like they were real flowers. You can still see a little torn bit where I tried to peel one off the wall when I was three, and every time I go into the room, the first thing I do is go straight to that flower and touch it, just remembering and such. I've talked about it with my Dad and we think it might be Nostalgia.

It's because of that flower and the Nostalgia that I first met the Doctor.

IT WAS THREE DAYS BEFORE CHRISTMAS. I'D JUST arrived at my fat Aunt's house, and as usual, I'd hugged her and run straight upstairs to my room, to hang all my clothes in the rattley wardrobe. And as usual I'd gone straight to the torn yellow flower on the wall, and knelt beside it (I'm bigger now) and touched it. But this time, I did something different. I don't know why. I heard my Aunt calling from downstairs that I shouldn't be too long, because she'd cooked my favourite and it was on the table, and usually I'd have run straight down. Maybe it was because I knew she'd want to talk about school and sometimes you don't want to talk about school (sorry, Miss Telfer) especially if you've got braces and frizzy hair and people can be a bit silly about that kind of thing, even if they're supposed to be your friends. Maybe it was because I was thinking about being three, and how much smaller the flowers looked now. Actually I think it was because Mary Phillips had made up a song about my hair and I was feeling a bit cross and my eyes were all stingy and blurry the way they get when you know you're going to cry if you don't really concentrate. Anyway, my fingers were resting right on the torn bit, and I was thinking about the song, and frizziness and such, and suddenly it was like I just didn't care! And I started to tear the paper a little bit more! Just a tiny bit at first, I just sort of tugged it to see what would happen. And I kept going! And you know sometimes it's like you're in a dream – you're doing something, but it doesn't feel like you're *doing* it, more like you're just watching? Well, I went right on and peeled the whole flower off the wall. A whole streak of wallpaper and I just ripped it right off!

And then, oh my goodness me! I just stared!

I once read in a story about a girl who got a fright and the writer said she felt her hair stand on end. I thought that was rubbish and would look really stupid, like my brother. I thought the writer was probably making that bit up, because it couldn't happen. But I was wrong. I could feel it happening now, starting up my neck, all cold, then all my scalp just fizzing and tingling.

And here is what was written under the wallpaper. 'Help me, Sally Sparrow'.

I looked closer, trying to work out if it was a trick, and noticed something else. More words, written just under those ones, but still covered by the wallpaper. Well, I thought, I'd already ruined it so I had nothing to lose. As carefully as I could, I tore off another strip. Beneath the words was just a date. 24/12/85.

Twenty years ago, someone in this room, asked for my help. Eight years before I was even born!

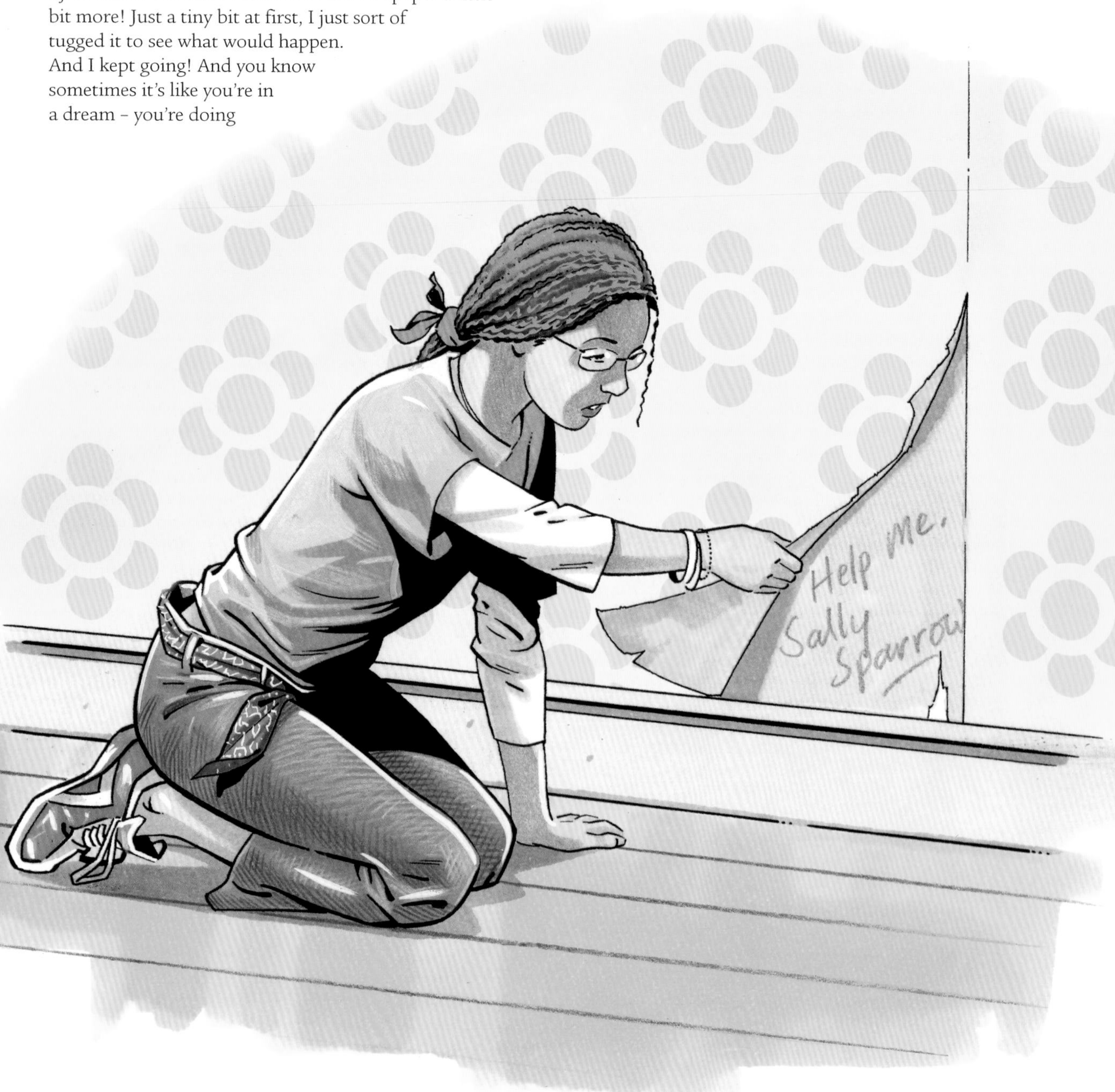
Help me,
Sally
Sparrow

'CHRISTMAS EVE, 1985? SORRY LOVE, I DON'T really remember.' My Aunt was frowning at me across the dinner table, trying to think.

'Can you really try, please? It's ever so important. Maybe you had guests, or friends staying or something? Maybe in my room.'

'Well we always had Christmas parties, when your uncle was still alive.'

'He *is* still alive, he's living in Stoke with Neville.'

'You could check in the shed.'

'Why would he be in the shed, Auntie, he's very happy with –'

'For the *photographs*.' She was looking at me, all severe now. 'If we had a party we always had photographs. I always keep photographs, I'll have a look around.'

'Thanks, Auntie!'

'What does it matter though? Why so interested?'

I nearly told her, but I knew she'd laugh. Because really, if you think about it, there was only one explanation. Coincidence. There must have been another Sally in the family I'd never heard about, and whoever had written that on the wall twenty years ago, they hadn't meant *me*, they'd meant *her*. They'd meant that mysterious other Sally from twenty years ago. I wondered what she was like. I wondered where she was now, and if her hair was frizzy. And I wondered most of all why she'd been kept a dark secret all these many years. Perhaps she'd been horribly murdered for Deadly Reasons!

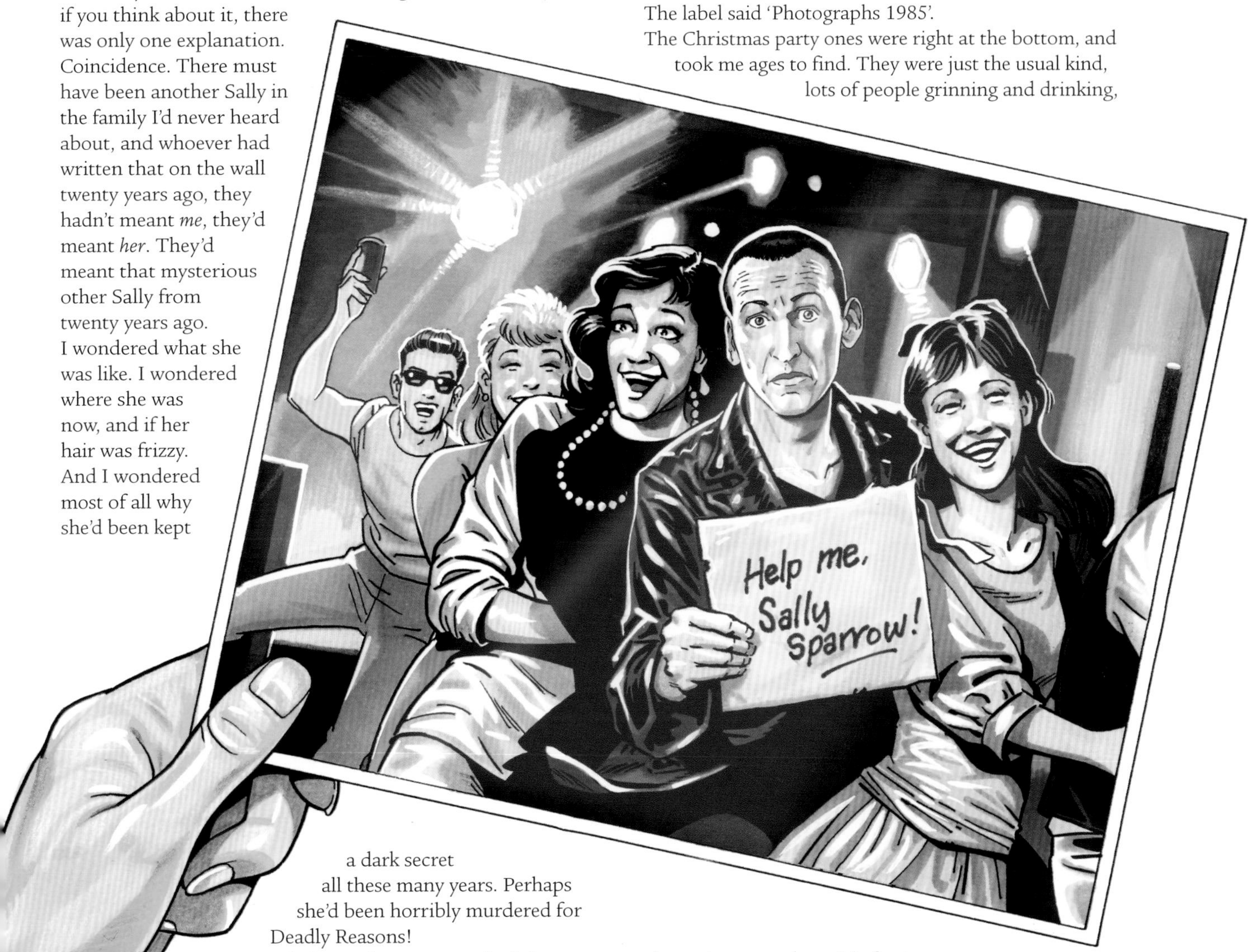
Help me, Sally Sparrow!

As I was about to go to bed, I looked hard at my Aunt – the way I do when I'm warning adults not to lie to me – and asked, 'There was another Sally Sparrow, wasn't there, Auntie? I'm not the first, am I?'

My Aunt looked at me really oddly for a moment. I half expected her to stagger back against the mantelpiece, all pale and clutching at her bosom, and ask in quivery tones how I had uncovered the family secret and have terrible rending sobs. But no, she just laughed and said 'No, of course not! One Sally Sparrow is quite enough. Now off to bed with you!'

I lay in my bed but I couldn't sleep! There had to be another Sally, there just *had* to be. Otherwise someone from twenty years ago was trying to talk to me from under the wallpaper and that was just stupid!

When my Aunt came in to kiss me goodnight (I always pretend to be asleep but I never am), I heard her put something on my bedside table. As soon as I heard her bedroom door close, I jumped and switched the light on! Maybe this was it! Maybe this was her dark confession – the truth about the other Sally Sparrow, and her Dreadful Fate. Sitting on my bedside table was a box. I gasped horrendously! I wondered how big a box would have to be to contain human remains! I narrowed my eyes shrewdly (and also bravely) and looked at the label on the lid (though I did think labelling murdered human remains would be a bit of an obvious mistake).

The label said 'Photographs 1985'.

The Christmas party ones were right at the bottom, and took me ages to find. They were just the usual kind, lots of people grinning and drinking, and wearing paper hats. My fat Aunt was there, still with Uncle Hugh, and my Mum and Dad too looking all shiny and thin. And then I saw it! My eyebrows raised in perplexity again, slightly higher this time. Because standing right in the middle of one of the photographs was a man with a leather jacket and enormous ears. He was in the middle of a line of grown-ups laughing and dancing, but he was looking right at the camera and holding up a piece of paper like a sign. And on the sign it said 'Help me, Sally Sparrow!'

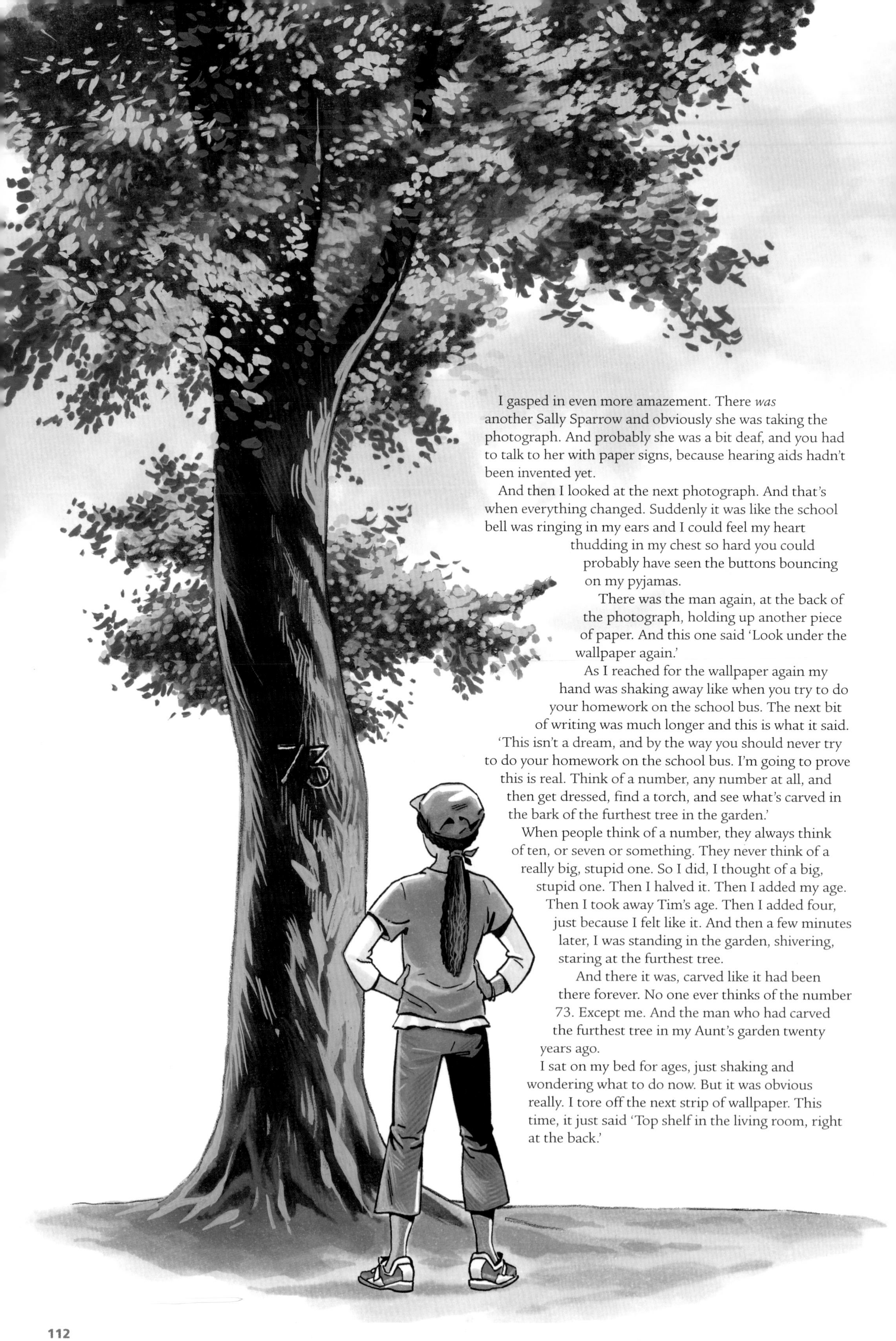
73

I gasped in even more amazement. There *was* another Sally Sparrow and obviously she was taking the photograph. And probably she was a bit deaf, and you had to talk to her with paper signs, because hearing aids hadn't been invented yet.

And then I looked at the next photograph. And that's when everything changed. Suddenly it was like the school bell was ringing in my ears and I could feel my heart thudding in my chest so hard you could probably have seen the buttons bouncing on my pyjamas.

There was the man again, at the back of the photograph, holding up another piece of paper. And this one said 'Look under the wallpaper again.'

As I reached for the wallpaper again my hand was shaking away like when you try to do your homework on the school bus. The next bit of writing was much longer and this is what it said. 'This isn't a dream, and by the way you should never try to do your homework on the school bus. I'm going to prove this is real. Think of a number, any number at all, and then get dressed, find a torch, and see what's carved in the bark of the furthest tree in the garden.'

When people think of a number, they always think of ten, or seven or something. They never think of a really big, stupid one. So I did, I thought of a big, stupid one. Then I halved it. Then I added my age. Then I took away Tim's age. Then I added four, just because I felt like it. And then a few minutes later, I was standing in the garden, shivering, staring at the furthest tree.

And there it was, carved like it had been there forever. No one ever thinks of the number 73. Except me. And the man who had carved the furthest tree in my Aunt's garden twenty years ago.

I sat on my bed for ages, just shaking and wondering what to do now. But it was obvious really. I tore off the next strip of wallpaper. This time, it just said 'Top shelf in the living room, right at the back.'

The top shelf was where my Aunt kept all her videos. She hardly ever watched television, never mind videos, so they were all very dusty. And right at the back, jammed half way down the gap at the back of the shelf, was a tape that looked like it had been there for a long time. And stuck on it, a post-it. It said 'FAO Sally Sparrow'.

I slipped it into the VCR and kept the television volume really low, so as not to wake my Aunt.

And there, grinning like a loon from the television, was the man from the photographs. 'Hello, Sally Sparrow! Any questions?'

He was sitting in my bedroom! Only the walls were bare, and there was a pair of ladders in the middle of the room, like someone was decorating. I could hear party music coming from somewhere downstairs, and I wondered if it was the party in 1985.

'Well, come on, Sally!' the man was saying, 'You've gotta have questions. *I* would.'

I frowned. Not a lot of point in asking questions when the man you're asking can't hear them!

'Who says I can't hear you?' grinned the man.

I stared! I think I probably gasped. My eyebrows were practically bursting out of the top of my head. It was ridiculous, it was *impossible*. I hadn't even said that *out loud*.

'No, you didn't,' said the man, checking on a piece of paper, 'You just thought that.' He glanced at the paper again. 'Oh, and yeah, you did gasp.'

'Who are you?' I blurted.

'That's more like it, now we're cooking. I'm the Doctor. I'm a time traveller and I'm stuck in 1985, and I need your help.'

I had so many questions racing round my head I didn't know which one to pick.

'How did you get stuck?' I said.

'Parked my time machine in your Aunt's shed. Was just locking up, and it... well... *burped*.'

'Burped??'

'Yeah, burped. Shot forward twenty years, I hate it when that happens.'

I looked out the window to where my Aunt's shed stood at the end of the garden. And I noticed there was something glowing at the windows. Suddenly, I was just a little bit afraid. 'So it's *here* then?'

'Exactly. Nip out to your Aunt's shed, you'll find a big blue box, key still in the door. Could just stick around for twenty years and pick it up myself but I don't want it falling into the wrong hands.' He leaned forward to the camera, and his eyes just *burned* at me. 'And I know *you're* not the wrong hands, Sally Sparrow. So I want you to fly it back to me!'

I swallowed hard. This was totally freaky.

He glanced at his paper again. 'You've got another question, I think.'

He was right. 'You're just on video tape. How can you *hear* me??'

He smiled. 'Actually, I can't. Can't hear a thing. I just happen to know everything you and me are gonna say in this whole conversation.'

'How??'

'Cos Mary Phillips made up a song about your hair.'

I could hardly breathe for all the gasping.

'And you punched her, didn't you, Sally Sparrow? And then you got a punishment?'

My face was burning. How did he know all this? I hadn't even told my Mum and Dad.

'You got Christmas homework. An essay about what you did over the Christmas holidays.' He grinned. 'And I've got a copy!'

And this is freakiest part of all. Because he held a copy of the actual essay I'm writing right now!!

'I know everything you're gonna ask when you see this tape, cos I've read the essay you wrote about it. That's how I knew what to write on the wall – you'll have to show me exactly where, by the way – and that's how I knew what number you were thinking of.'

'But... but...' I could hardly think for my mind racing. 'How did you get a copy of my Christmas homework! I haven't even written it yet!!'

'Told you, I'm a time traveller. I got it in the future. From a beautiful woman on a balcony in Istanbul.' He smiled, like it was happy memory. 'She was some sort of spy, I think. Amazing woman! I'd just had a sword fight on the roof with two Sontarans, and she saved me from the second one. Then she gave me your Christmas homework and told me to keep it on me at all times, cos I'd need it one day.' He grinned. 'She was right!'

A spy, in the future, was going to have a copy of my Christmas homework? Talk about pressure!

He was looking at his watch. 'Okay, that's just about time up. Gonna need you to go to the time machine, and fly it here.'

'I can't fly a time machine. I had stabilisers on my bike till I was *nine*!!'

'Sally, I absolutely know that you can do this. And do you know how?'

'How?'

'Because I've read to the end of the story.' He laughed. 'Also – you hear that noise?'

Coming from the television, a terrible wheezing and groaning.

'What's that??'

He was still grinning.

'That's you!'

Behind the man, a huge blue box just appeared out of thin air. I stared at it. There were words over the door and I squinted closer to read them.

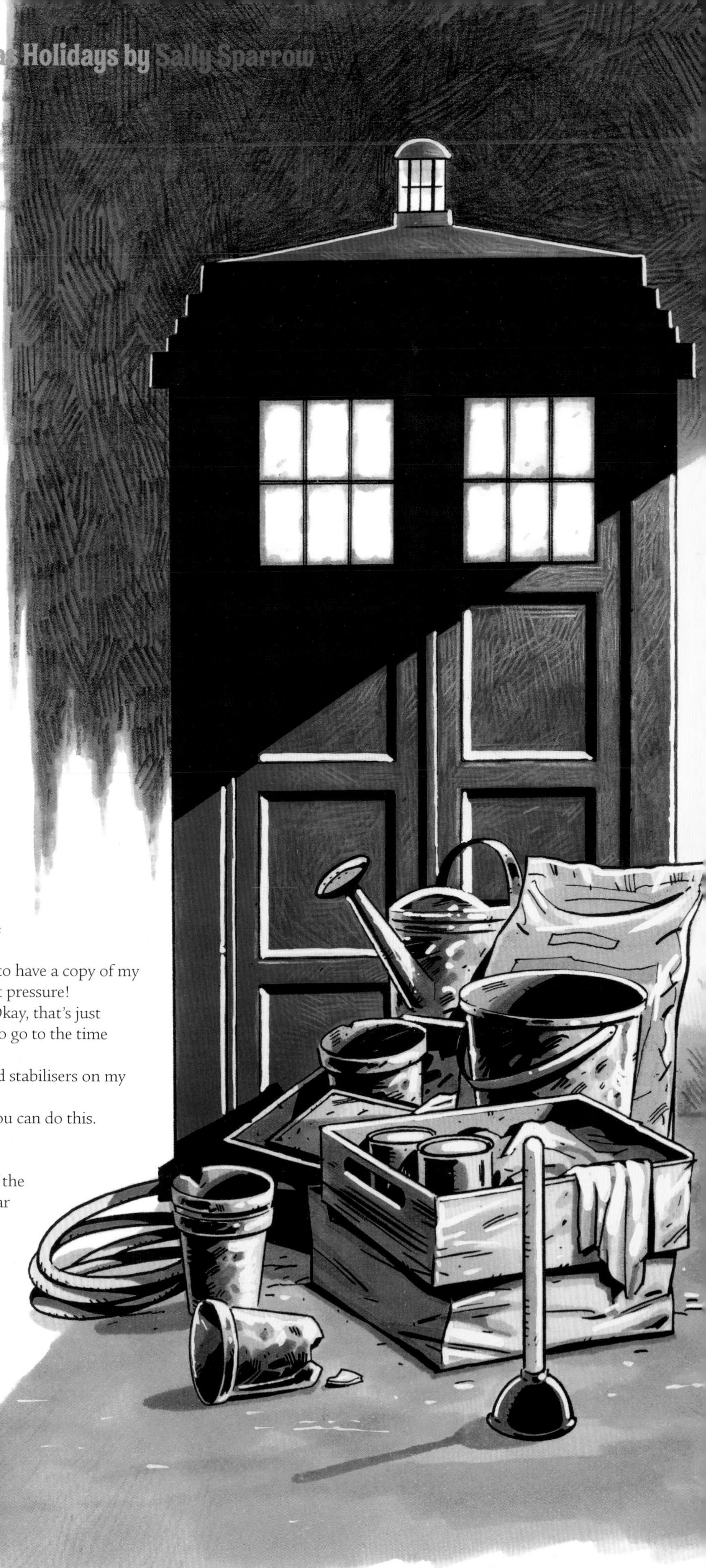

I should've known. He looked like a policeman

'That's your time machine?'

'Yep. Like it?'

'But who flew it there?'

You could almost get tired of that grin. 'You did!'

The doors on the big blue box were opening. And then the most amazing thing ever. *I stepped out of the box!!* Me! Sally Sparrow! Another me stepped out of the time machine and waved at the camera.

'Hello, Sally Sparrow, two hours ago!' said the other me. 'It's great in there, you're going to love it. It's bigger on the inside!'

'See?' said the man. 'Told you you could fly a time machine.'

'Yeah, it's easy!' said the other Sally. 'It homes in on his watch, anyway. You just have to press the reset button next to the phone.'

'Who told you that?' I asked her.

A frown clouded her face. 'I did,' she said, and looked puzzled.

The man looked a little cross about that.

'Yeah, well before you set off any more time paradoxes... Sally Sparrow!' he gave me a Teacher look from the television. 'Go and do your homework!'

'Yeah!' said the other Sally, 'You've got to write the essay before you can fly the time machine. It'll take you about two hours.'

'That's enough, both of you!' said the man, 'Got enough paradoxes going on here, without you pair having a chat!'

'But, listen, it's going to be *great!*' said the other Sally. And she gave me the biggest, most excited smile ever.

And oh goodness! You *can* see my braces!

AND SO HERE I AM, FINISHING MY ESSAY. It's nearly two o'clock in the morning, and in a minute I'll be fetching the shed key from the kitchen drawer and setting off across the garden on the trip of a lifetime.

A big, amazing adventure. And not my last one either, oh no! Just the first of lots and lots, for the rest of my life probably. Suddenly I don't care what my Aunt is going to say about the torn wallpaper or what Mary Phillips thinks about my hair.

I'll go back to school after the holidays and just be nice to her, and she can make up all the songs she wants. I'll join in, if it makes her happy.

You see, I know the best thing in the world. I know what's coming. I asked the man one more question before the end of the tape. I asked how a beautiful woman spy in the future could have a copy of my Christmas homework.

'Can't you guess?' he smiled. Not grinned, smiled. 'Her name,' he continued, 'Was Sally Sparrow.'

The big blue box is waiting in the shed at the end of the garden. And I've finished my homework. ●

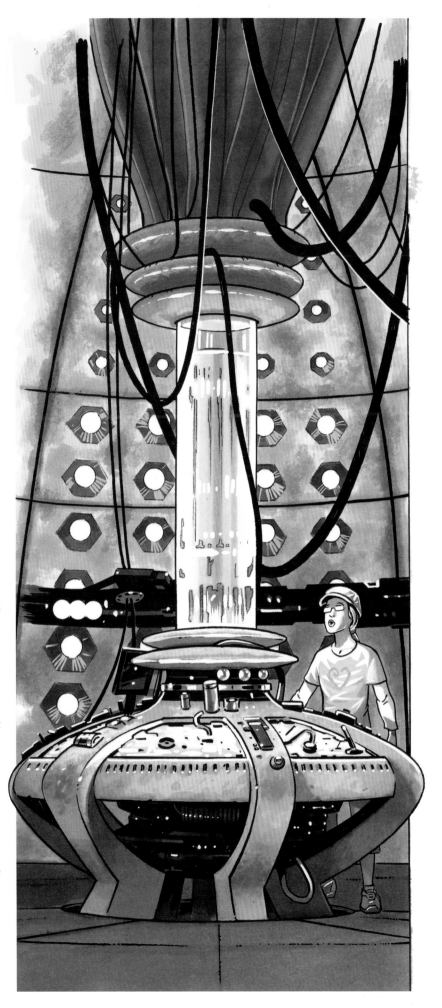

Fantastic Journey

Inside The Ninth Doctor Comic Strips

By Clayton Hickman (DWM Editor 2002-07)

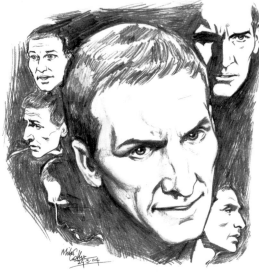

Visualise a crumpled copy of **Doctor Who Magazine**, probably the one with a Sontaran dressed as Anne Robinson on the cover. Over this, scrolling text in an almost unreadably small point size, intoned by someone who sounds like Tom Baker. Probably Jon Culshaw:

*Through the wilderness years, the **DWM** staff of Panini led a life of peace and ordered calm, protected against any threat of cancellation by their great and loyal subscriber base and the fact that nobody was actually very interested in* Doctor Who*, least of all their BBC licensors. But this was to change. Suddenly and wonderfully, **Doctor Who Magazine** faced the most unexpected challenge in its long history...*

Right & below: Mike Collins' initial character sketches of the Ninth Doctor.

Yes, in 2003, against all the odds, *Doctor Who* was back BACK *BACK!* The new TV series we fans had dreamed of for 16 years was about to become a reality. I'd joined **DWM** in the space-year 2000, taking over as editor two years later. Although the magazine had survived, even thrived, during *Doctor Who*'s long absence from our screens, we really were in need of something fresh. The history of the show had already been meticulously detailed in our pages, and almost everyone involved with it tracked down and rigorously interviewed. There was only our coverage of books and audio plays to fill the 'newness' quotient each month.

So the announcement that the series was to return as a bold, exciting, primetime drama, under the stewardship of Russell T Davies and with the full weight of the BBC behind it, was a dream come true. It *could* easily have become a nightmare come true, however, what with the full glare of a galvanized BBC Worldwide suddenly turned upon our previously-ignored little magazine. But Russell was a **DWM** reader from the start, and loyally smoothed over any potential problems, protecting us and making us feel we were a proper part of his new production team. He kept us updated, arranged interviews, set visits, script access and news exclusives, and month-in, month-out emailed us with praise for each new issue.

Especially the comic strip.

DWM had kept *Doctor Who* alive in comic form since 1979. Despite his short TV tenure, the Eighth Doctor's strip incarnation, under the guidance of my predecessors Gary Gillatt and Alan Barnes, had enjoyed a long and successful run, marking one of the real high points in *Doctor Who* comics history. One of my favorite parts of the job was working with writer Scott Gray on his stunning run of Eighth Doctor strips. Now, with a new Doctor on the horizon at last, we planned a big 'season finale' for Paul McGann's Time Lord in an epic Cyberman tale called *The Flood.*

Then Russell made Scott and me a completely unexpected offer: there was to be no regeneration in the TV series, so would we like to show the transformation from the Eighth to the Ninth Doctor in the **DWM** strip? We were completely floored. What an honour!

Sadly, things didn't work out in the end (and you can read the full story in *The Flood* graphic novel, probably still available in all good bookshops), but the upshot was that we couldn't show the Ninth Doctor before he appeared on TV, and couldn't show the Eighth Doctor once the new series began. This meant that the McGann-to-Eccleston transformation was impossible to depict. We were sad to lose such an iconic moment, not to mention the 'canonisation' of our beloved strip, but very soon we realised that, as an adjunct to a huge new flagship BBC show, the **DWM** strip needed to change alongside the magazine itself. We should be reflecting what a new generation of fans would soon be enjoying each Saturday night: the Ninth Doctor and Rose Tyler having fantastic adventures together. And, let's be honest, we'd have been 'de-canonised' eventually by Paul McGann's triumphant return in *The Night of the Doctor*, not to mention John Hurt's incarnation, so it probably all worked out for the best in the end.

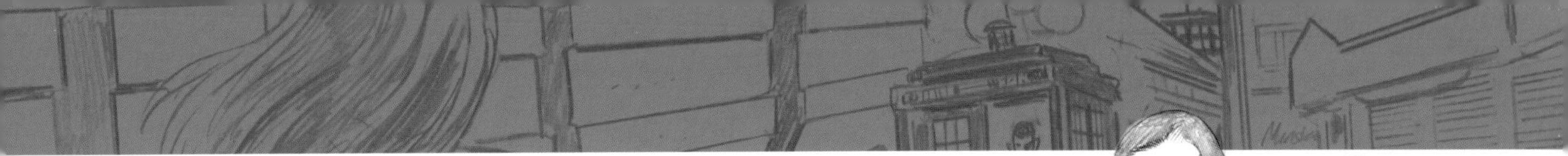

Having sustained an epic run of stories, Scott Gray decided to step down as writer, but he joined me as the strip's co-editor and we began to plan our new era. Russell's generosity with set and script access meant that we had a pretty good idea of what the new TV series was going to be like, and we wanted to reflect that tone in the strip. To help with this, Russell selflessly offered to personally check over our scripts, which was invaluable, especially early on where we had little to go on in terms of performances. In anticipation of a new, younger readership brought to **DWM** by the TV series (children's comic *Doctor Who Adventures*, with its own comic strip aimed specifically at the young 'uns, didn't arrive until 2006), we initially decided to skew our Ninth Doctor stories a little younger. We had recently cleaned up the entire run of **Doctor Who Weekly** Fourth Doctor strips, illustrated by Dave Gibbons, for the first of our graphic novels, and their approach was a big influence on us – witty, accessible, memorable stories, but with a scope and visual clout that a TV budget couldn't match.

We even tried to get Dave Gibbons back to draw a story, which would probably have been the final Ninth Doctor strip and written by Russell himself. Although he was enthusiastic and proclaimed himself 'a great fan of Russell's', Dave had to decline, being under exclusive contract to DC Comics in the US. But all was not lost as the basic story Russell had worked out eventually ended up on TV as *Love & Monsters*, and the **Weekly** strips themselves were commemorated by mention of Kronkburgers (from *The Iron Legion*) in the TV episode *The Long Game*.

But I'm getting ahead of myself. As early as August 2004, with the TV series only a few weeks into production, Russell was thinking ahead, strips-wise. He suggested a potential launch strip for the Ninth Doctor, to be written by him and illustrated by Brian Hitch, an esteemed comics artist who had also been supplying concept art for the new series. Hectic work schedules eventually made this impossible, so I turned to Gareth Roberts, a TV writer with a long history of *Doctor Who* strips and novels, to pen the new Doctor's début.

Martin Geraghty had been *the* artist during the Eighth Doctor's run of strips, but he was still busy on the final episodes of *The Flood* and we needed to get going on the new stuff right away, so I brought in Mike Collins. I'd long admired Mike's work, especially an old Seventh Doctor strip, *The Good Soldier*, and had recently invited him back into the **DWM** fold for an Eighth Doctor strip, also by Gareth Roberts, called *The Nightmare Game*. And 'nightmare' is what I put poor Mike through as we geared up for the Ninth Doctor's introduction.

Above & bottom left: Mike's pencils for the 2006 *Doctor Who Magazine Collected Comics*.

Below: More Ninth Doctor pencil sketches from Mike.

Doctor Who was now a big TV show with big stars, and Christopher Eccleston and Billie Piper both had likeness approval over all merchandise, which included their comic strip selves. Photos were thin on the ground at this point, being jealously guarded by the publicity department. We scrimped and scraped up as much reference material as we could, and set Mike to work on a sort of 'character reference sheet' for the Doctor and Rose, which we could send to the actors for approval. Mike caught Billie straight away, but we went back and forth with the Ninth Doctor, being guided by Russell who knew what Chris would be looking for. Initially Mike had 'heroed up' his depiction, flattening out a lot of the interesting and striking aspects of Chris' face, but Russell knew that, unlike many actors, flattery was not what Chris would respond well to. So Mike went back to the drawing board. Many times. In fact, it wasn't until late February 2005, barely a month before *Rose* was due to air, that we got word that Chris and Billie had approved their likenesses.

Then it was all systems go, with Mike burning the midnight oil to meet the magazine's deadlines. His dazzling visuals saw the Ninth Doctor through the whole of his comic strip run (with a brief detour for the *Doctor Who Annual 2006* when Scott Gray and artist John Ross teamed up for *Mr Nobody*), and I honestly don't know how we'd have coped without his tireless enthusiasm.

But Mike's work wasn't over yet. Only a month after Christopher Eccleston had given the thumbs-up to his comic strip self, the news broke that he would be leaving *Doctor Who* after his first season. Mike would have to get sketching the next Doctor, a young actor (and another **DWM** reader) by the name of David Tennant...

So, just as he burned brightly but briefly on TV, Christopher Eccleston's Doctor notched up a short but sweet run of five Panini strips. But in those ten short months he packed in trips to Earth in the 1600s, the 1960s and the 21st century, an art gallery in space, a devastated planet, a Martian cruise ship, and a disturbingly sinister dream world. I hope you enjoy revisiting them all in the company of the Ninth Doctor. He really was fantastic.

Clayton Hickman
April 2014

Right: Mike Collins' design layout for the opening page of *The Love Invasion*.

Below: Mike's sketches for Igrix.

Opposite above: The more 'gawky' version of the Ninth Doctor that was approved.

Opposite right: Original pencil art of Charlotte Cobb.

Opposite below: More layout pages.

THE LOVE INVASION

Gareth Roberts Writer

In 1996 I was being tempted to 'come over'. The mysterious Nuala Buffini, which I had thought until then was a pasta dish, was courting me, hoping I'd write for the new *Doctor Who* range at BBC Books. The BBC had rescinded Virgin's publishing license, after umpteen years, in a morally exemplary way. As a stalwart and sometime employee of Virgin, with seven *New* and *Missing Adventures* novels under my belt, I could not compromise my integrity. Until a very small sum of money was mentioned. At which point I spontaneously came up with an idea called *The British Invasion*, in which the Eighth Doctor would be pitted against girl singers in the Tin Pan Alley of 1966. Because, camp old laugh. But before I could fire up my Amstrad, the arch-enemies of the BBC, Granada TV, egged on by the soon-to-be-regretful Russell T Davies, had poached me for an enormous sum of money to work on *Coronation Street*. So *The British Invasion*, inspired by 60s girl singers with amazing names like Tammy St John and Glo Macari, joined *Doctor Who and the Clock* and *Way Down Yonder* in Doc's Lost Dumper.

Imagine my delight when, eight years later, Clayton Hickman asked me to write the first **DWM** comic strip for the new TV Doctor Christopher Eccleston. *The British Invasion* could be revived – but there was one big proviso. There could be no singing. Particularly involving Rose Tyler, as in another life she had sung her way to the top of the hit parade for no other reason than because she wanted to. So the girls became the glamorous dolly-bird employees of the Helping Hands Agency. Because, camp old laugh.

Russell had liked my recent Eighth Doctor strip *The Nightmare Game*, so it seemed wise to continue in that vein with a bright, breezy story with lots happening in every panel. I was keen that the strip should feel like the new TV series, with nothing too off-puttingly 'way out'. I think I succeeded, but it was strange to find myself writing the *final* Ninth Doctor comic strip just a few weeks later.

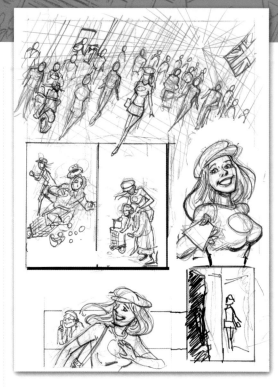

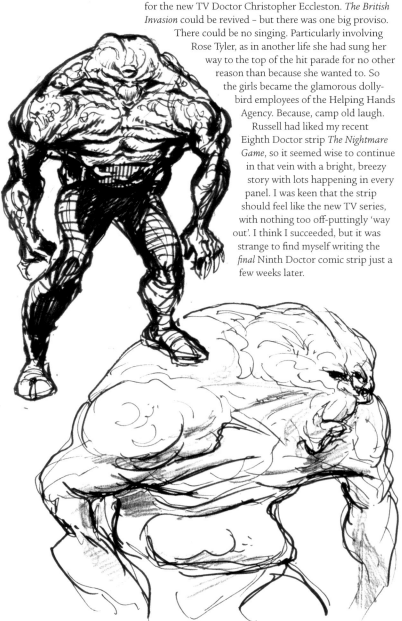

Mike Collins Artist

2005 – the new series of *Doctor Who* premières, and hot on its heels, the new comic strip! Or actually, almost not. You nearly didn't get the sweet and sleek volume you now hold. After years of almost uninterrupted strips featuring the good Doctor, this one almost died before being born. And it would've been my fault.

I'd been working exclusively for US comics for most of the 90s and early 2000s, with occasional work for *2000 AD*. Long time *Doctor Who* inker, and sometime studio mate David Roach asked me out of the blue what I thought about drawing a football comic strip. I said I'd be interested but in what context? Turned out it was a Paul McGann *Doctor Who* strip set in the 70s, *The Nightmare Game*. I had a lot of fun researching the time period detail and the *Who* story was a riot. I told Clayton any time he needed more from me to drop me a call. He obliged, giving me spot illos for the magazine, while I carried on with my American work, and storyboarding for television.

And then, in 2003 we all heard the astonishing news that *Doctor Who* was to return to our screens. The stalwarts of the strip – Scott Gray and Martin Geraghty – were orchestrating their grand conclusion to years of fabulous work in the seminal *The Flood*. Both saw it as a stepping off (or at least, stepping *back*) point. So there it was – a new series. Really. Not a 'well, maybe', but an honest to Gallifrey new show. And to be made in Cardiff of all places. *Where I live*. The stars aligned. It had to be. Knowing that Martin was going, I threw my hat in the ring. I was, frankly, a tart about the whole thing. But I never got into comics for the self respect, after all, and this was *DOCTOR WHO*.

Amazingly, they agreed. After all, I'd drawn *Doctor Who* in the past, and had for years drawn for various licensed books for Marvel and DC featuring all shades of *Star Trek*, *Babylon 5* and even (appropriately) the adaptation of *The Time Machine*. I did likenesses. The writers of this first story were to be Clayton and Gareth, the writers of my *Nightmare Game* story, and again, it was to be a period piece, 60s rather than 70s. It all just seemed so *right*.

What could go wrong?

But this was a new BBC too: over the years, contracts had improved for actors – no longer were they at the whim of licensees creating barely recognisable merchandise featuring them. If they were to be utilised in other media – toys, lunchboxes, whatever – they had to sign off on it. This included comics. Now, this wasn't new to me as I'd

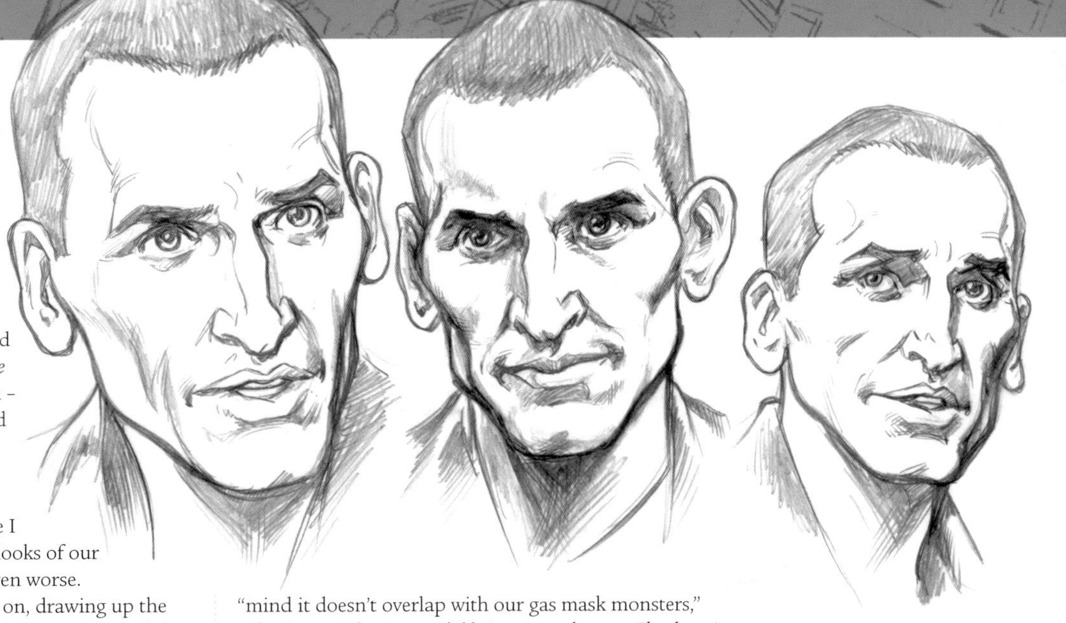

had to do audition sheets for the various US projects I'd been involved in. You did your best likenesses, flattered the talent, and voila, you were drawing the Enterprise, or Babylon 5 or whatever, on a glorious four-colour romp. So that's what I did. I surrounded myself with pre-release publicity session pics provided by the BBC, and DVDs of Christopher Eccleston – *The Second Coming* was key amongst them – and crafted my audition pieces. Word came back: 'no'.

The **DWM** team was perplexed, I was utterly banjaxed. Okay, maybe I hadn't got his face quite right, maybe I hadn't emphasised the rugged good looks of our now-Northern hero. I tried again. Even worse.

In the meanwhile, I'd been getting on, drawing up the first episode, leaving the headshots of Christopher lightly pencilled... our deadline was fast approaching, any lead time we thought we had being eaten up. Clayton took it on himself to find out where I'd gone wrong, and the answer was stupidly obvious. I'd gotten it wrong because I had been working in *American* comics. I had been used to the *glamorisation* and idolisation of actors. So that's what I'd done here. Christopher Eccleston had a very clear idea of how he looked, and told us that if he was himself as a comic character – it was Plug out of the *Bash Street Kids*. Newly armed with this knowledge I did a further set of illos, showing him gawky, big eared, a big Adam's apple... and he signed off.

Conversely, Clayton showed Billie Piper my art, and she approved on the spot – Clayton immediately texted me her comment, verbatim: "Ooo, he's given me hips and tits, I like it!" That's on my CV.

The story was (despite that early panic) a fabulous one to start on – a vibrant, bright romp fully in the spirit of the new TV episodes. Just like *The Nightmare Game*, Gareth and Clayton's script gave me the opportunity to indulge in copious research and adding all kinds of period detail. I got to 'cast' a young Charlotte Rampling as our scientist, and indulge my fascination with 60s fashion. Interestingly several threads from this story made it to TV – the sonic screwdriver being mistaken for a toothbrush; the Doctor saving himself from poisoning by eating; the Doctor riding a scooter. As a tip of the hat to **DWM** history, the scooter I branded as a Gibbo, as a tribute to old Mod and originator of the Marvel/Panini strip, Dave Gibbons.

Clayton Hickman Editor

I worked with Gareth on *The Love Invasion* as we needed to start on it as early as possible and the scripts for the new TV series were still top secret. Having read them, I was there to steer things in the right direction. Not that I need have worried – Gareth's style and wit was a perfect match for Russell's vision of the show, so we hit the ground running. Russell was delighted when I sent over the script for Part One, enthusing: "Brilliant, I love it. Gareth has got the Ninth Doctor's dialogue 100 percent right. Fact!" Regarding Charlotte's face-mask gassings, Russell did caution us: "mind it doesn't overlap with our gas mask monsters," referring to *The Empty Child*. So we made sure Charlotte's mask was more of the dentist sort.

I also helped out with the shape of the story. Gareth had a great opening for *The Love Invasion*, but things petered out as it went on, so we shored up the details of the alien's plan together. I liked the idea of a monster who really *was* making things 'better' for the human race, even though his motives weren't as noble as they first appeared. I also suggested the TARDIS landing next to a real police box, as it was something I'd long had in the back of my mind if we ever did a 1960s-set story, plus I thought it would help new readers understand what this strange blue thing used to represent. In the final part I couldn't resist adding Ben and Polly – mid-proposal – in the Post Office Tower restaurant, as this was where it all started for them in *The War Machines*. I'd always loved the pair of them and wanted to give them a happy ending. Well, happier than just buggering off at Gatwick Airport anyway.

The Love Invasion eventually provided a scene for Gareth's 2008 TV story *The Unicorn and the Wasp*, where the Tenth Doctor cures himself of poisoning with a bizarre range of foodstuffs, just as his Ninth self does at the start of Part Two. And if you held a gun to my head, and I was in the right mood, I'd have to say that Rose's little sigh when she hears a huge 'NEIGHH!' outside the pub, is the moment that has made me laugh most in all *Doctor Who*.

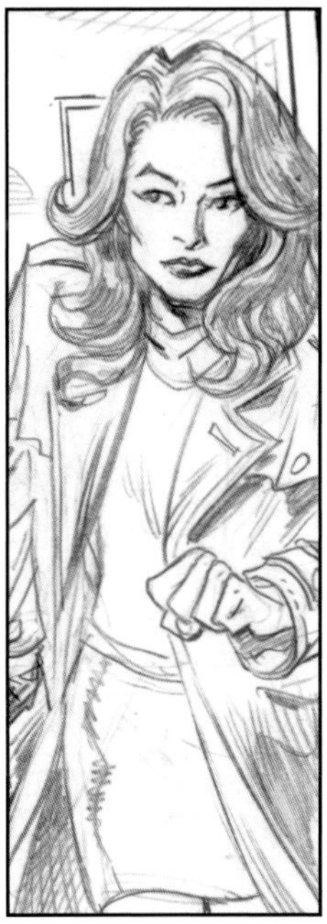

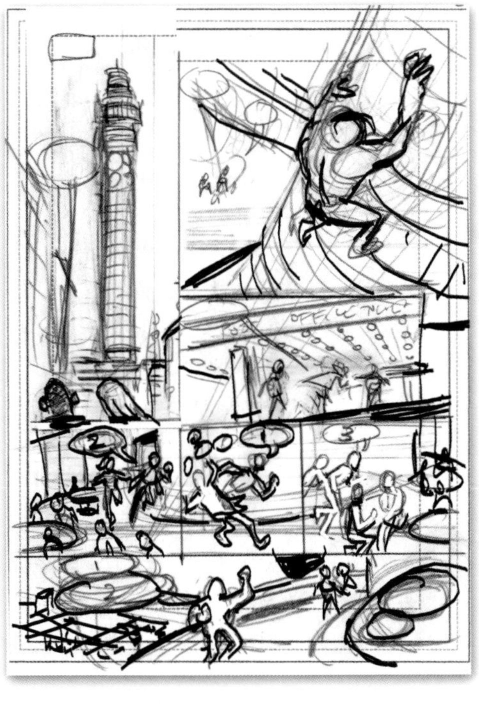

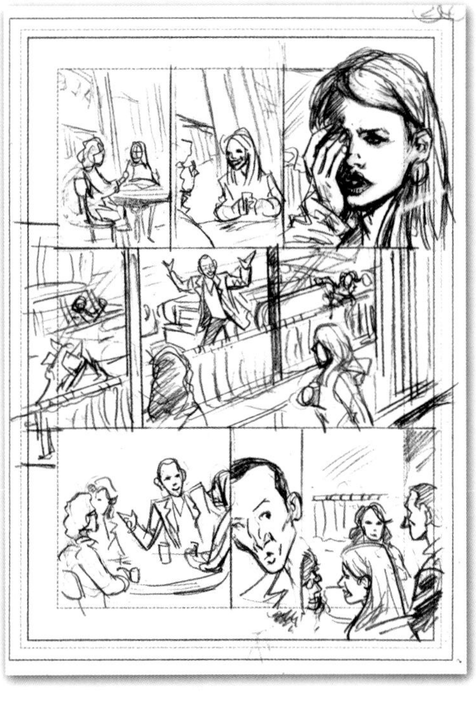

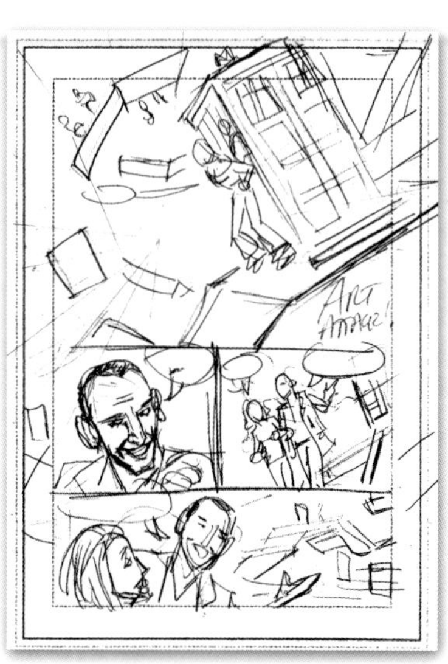

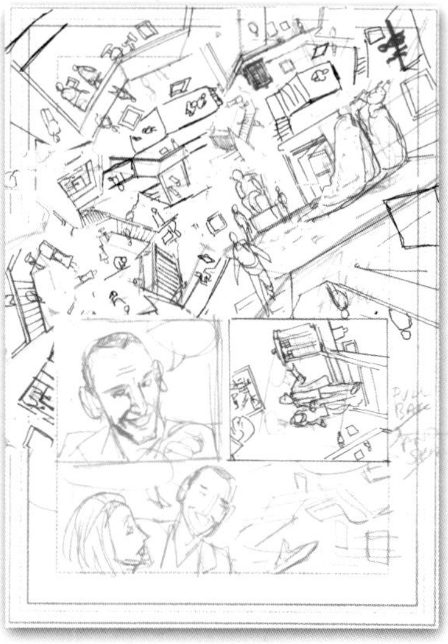

Above: The initial layout of the title page for *Art Attack*, and the more complex version that followed.

Below: Cazkelf the Transcendant in pencil form by Mike Collins.

Art Attack

Mike Collins Writer and Artist

Part of the deal Clayton offered me when I took over the art on the strip was that I'd have a chance to write the occasional story too – I've written *Doctor Who* for longer than I've drawn it (John Ridgway and Kev Hopgood did fabulous work on the 80s strip tales *Profits of Doom* and *Claws of the Klathi* for me, better than I'd have done) – so I jumped at the chance, only... this wasn't old-style *Who*, this was something newly minted and breathless. At this point I'd only seen *Rose* and *The End of the World*, so I based my approach on those examples: breakneck speed in storytelling – the whole piece unravelling before your eyes, *You Are There*.

I sent a whole stack of ideas in, one of which was based on an aspect of *Doctor Who* that had always nagged me: why was no-one ever concerned about the companions who'd left Earth? Didn't that leave a hole in their lives? I reasoned there were 'chronal cuckoos' who slipped in, filling the time that the Doctor's assistants were away, to all intents and purposes, living their lives for them. When (in my story) Rose returned, she found no-one had missed her, and – in fact – *she was still there*.

Normally, when the rightful owner of the timeline returned, the cuckoo would automatically leave, blending back into the time-stream... but that was before the Time War, and this cuckoo had become sentient and didn't want to return to chaos. Conflict, agony, regret, two Roses, and a tearful conclusion. All in nine action-packed pages. The BBC wouldn't let us do it, and wouldn't tell me why... and when *Aliens of London* appeared, the penny dropped – Russell had obviously *also* been nagged by that historic oversight but came up with a brilliantly funny/heartfelt way of dealing with it.

No idea goes unused though, and the temporal levelling got reshaped to the Hajor in my Tenth Doctor *Futurists* story, semi-sentient 'righters' of the timelines who decided to take it on themselves to clean up the Time Lords' messes.

Taking the lead from Russell's vision of the Doctor as more your mate than your crazy bookish uncle, I had the idea that he'd want to show off to Rose. She asks to see the Mona Lisa and instead of just taking her to the Louvre, he takes her to a far future gallery. I was shamelessly thinking how Mike-the-Artist could have fun with an Escher landscape and random artworks and aliens scattered about.

My one contribution to the *Who* mythos happens in this story – I have Rose mention a school trip to Paris where she and a mate bunked off to Parc Asterix rather than go to an art gallery. I picked Parc Asterix because I prefer it to Disneyland Paris, blissfully unaware at the time of RTD's love of the tiny Gaul. When Russell wrote Rose's timeline for the *2006 Annual* he included the bunking off as an event, which gave me the excuse to grin stupidly for longer than usual.

Originally titled *The Atrocity Exhibition* as a nod to JG Ballard, it got the far more family friendly title (and call back to top TV kids art show hosted by Neil Buchanan) of *Art Attack*... which actually was more on-the-nose than I'd originally intended. The idea that the alien was an artist rather than a warrior appealed to me (they're always warriors aren't they?), and the means he'd find to lead himself home was based on the shared experience of an art 'installation' struck me as more in tune with this new version of *Doctor Who*. The daft Damien Hurst jokes, the Doctor's incessant bragging about historical figures he knew, I felt fitted in with the vibe I got from *The End of the World*. And the bittersweet ending when he finds that all he's striven for for so long is a world of ashes, struck the note of melancholy that underpins that whole Christopher Eccleston season of *Doctor Who*. A tip of the hat to Scott for turning my very dark ending around by having the gallery patrons embrace Cazkelf at the end and have his art be his continuing reason to exist, to celebrate his culture in memoriam.

I like the idea that straight afterwards Rose did indeed drag the Doctor on the rides at Parc Asterix...

I think my story suffered coming between Gareth and Clayton's giddy, glorious 60s romp, and the simply mesmerising Mars-set psychodrama of Rob Shearman's *The Cruel Sea*. If you treat it as a silly sweet palette cleanser between courses, I quite understand.

As always with my stories (going right back to *Profits of Doom*), there's Welsh language sneaking in. Here, the pan-dimensional gallery is called Oriel which is simply Welsh for, well, *gallery*. The alien's name is a phonetic version of 'cas celf' which is Welsh for 'nasty art'.

As to the look of the strip – I wanted to keep it all open and multi-layered, a reaction to the deep, detailed shots of 60s London I'd done on the previous tale. One of the appeals of working on *Doctor Who*, is that each story is a new experience, almost a new strip entirely. The look of Cazkelf is actually based on a mix of Laurence Llewelyn-Bowen, who never seemed to be off our screens at the time, and the bizarre barrel-chested figure wearing a crown and a sash I remember from the back of Pork Scratchings bags I had in the Black Country, growing up in the 70s. I've not managed to find a picture to substantiate my mental image, so you'll just have to trust me on this. Or not.

Clayton Hickman Editor

Given his crazy schedule at this point, I can't quite believe Mike Collins had the time or the inclination to add scripting to his ever-increasing workload, but he must've done, given that *Art Attack* exists.

It was a fun story, particularly in Cazkelf's very Laurence Llewelyn-Bowen inspired look, and was a smooth and hassle-free experience in all. Mike's professionalism and dedication in writing as well as pencilling made me eager to give him a shot at a longer strip, eventually bearing fruit in the Tenth Doctor's era, starting with *The Futurists*. I was especially pleased that Mike later got his five minutes of fame on the CBBC spin-off show *Totally Doctor Who*, when host Barney Harwood visited Mike's studio in Cardiff for a quick drawing lesson.

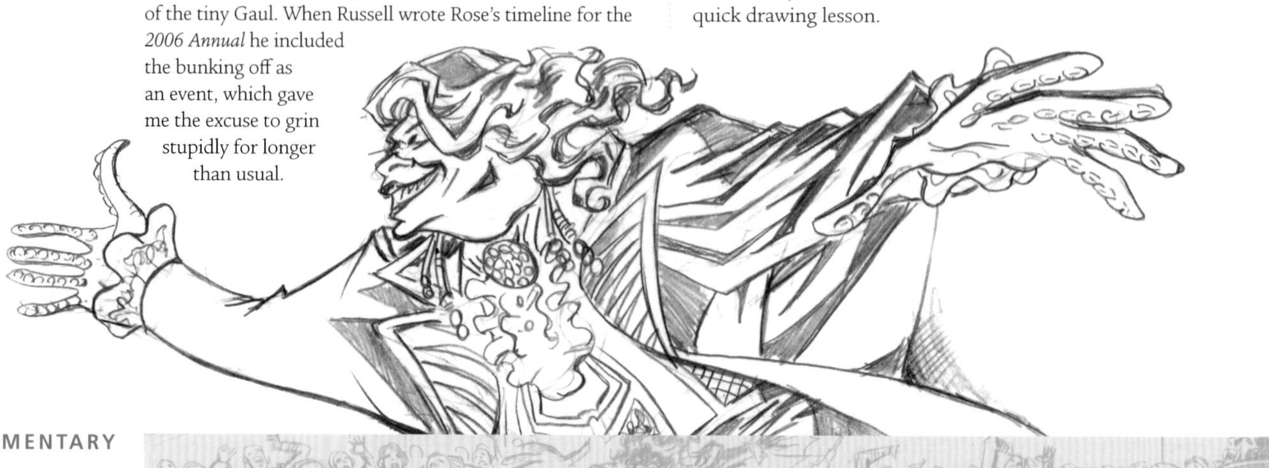

Above: *The Cruel Sea* – from layout to pencils to finished inks: Rose is swallowed by her own reflection.

Below: Mike's design sketch of Rose in her spacesuit.

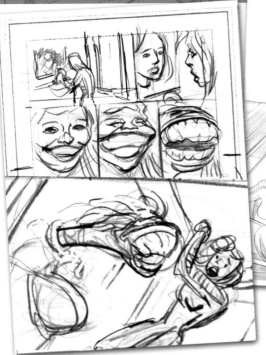

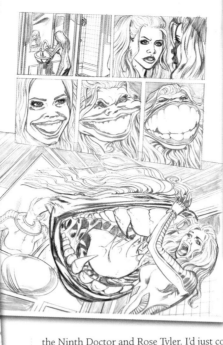

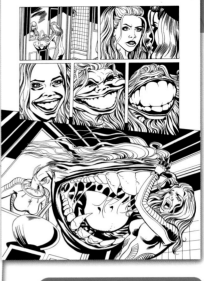

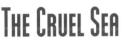

THE CRUEL SEA

Robert Shearman Writer

I can't draw. I can't paint. At school, I couldn't even do colouring in without going over the borders. Undeterred by this, when I was eight years old I set to work writing and illustrating my very first 'graphic novel' – not that I would have termed it that at the time. It ran for 100 A4 pages exactly, and featured the adventures of Bert travelling around the world trying to escape the clutches of some bank robbers. If I'm required to draw a man I still draw him like Bert – a big round head, and arms sticking out of the stomach.

When Clayton Hickman asked if I would like to write a comic strip for **Doctor Who Magazine**, I did try to point out that my single experience with the form hadn't produced any earth-shattering results. My own (rather nervous) condition was that everybody more expert in such matters would help me along the way. The truth was, I was somewhat intimidated. I'd been reading Scott Gray's extraordinary stint on the Eighth Doctor strips, and it seemed to me as questing and as fresh as *Doctor Who* had ever been; I admired the extraordinary range of the episodes he came up with each and every month. Had I not felt I was following in Scott's footsteps, I would have been much happier with the commission. It was all Scott Gray's fault.

And I wasn't a great comics reader. I'd never got into the superhero stuff that was imported from the States; as a kid I'd read *Asterix the Gaul* and a little bit of *Peanuts*. My one regular exposure to an adventure strip had been in the pages of **Doctor Who Monthly**, and I used to marvel in particular at the tales featuring some shapeshifting penguin called Frobisher, and wondered how the television series at the time and the comic could be so tonally at variance. At university a friend had forced me to read Neil Gaiman's *Sandman* series, and I fell in love with it, and thought then that it was a masterpiece of literature. But it didn't persuade me to try any other comics. The problem I had – and I accept this sounds a bit stupid – was that I never quite understood what I should be looking at first. Should I read the speech bubble, then look at the picture – or should it be the other way round? Either way, somehow, seemed wrong.

The reason I agreed to write a *Doctor Who* strip – and in four parts too, just like it used to be on the telly! – was because there was an opportunity once more to write for the Ninth Doctor and Rose Tyler. I'd just come off my stint writing *Dalek* for the TV show, and it was that funny thing – it was perhaps only as I was on my final drafts that I felt I tapped properly into Russell T Davies' voice for the show and the full potential of the characters. And the *style* of the show too – what I particularly loved was the way Russell wanted to write about pioneers, that this was an account of the history of humanity with all its ingenuity and zeal. The idea of putting Chris' Doctor on to another planet – and Mars, moreover, why not! – and presenting it as something rare and magical, that was what got my imagination going.

I'd somehow thought that writing a comic strip would be a little like writing a TV screenplay. That it would be visual storytelling, but that rather than have the camera *move* through the action, we'd be taking static snapshots of it at key moments. I remember thinking as I wrote *The Cruel Sea* that it'd be as if John Cura was taking telesnaps of some long wiped 1960s adventure! And although it wasn't an unhelpful thing to think of when writing the script – I was still completely off the mark. Comic writing is not screenplay writing with lots more descriptive bits for the artist to fill in. If only. That would be easy. Instead it requires an economical exactness which is the polar opposite of my usual style, where characters chat too much and too rapidly. Writing *Dalek* had made me learn that, unlike in theatre or radio, there must be a precise *need* for every scene – *The Cruel Sea* made me realise that the same thing was true for each and every word a character spoke. And every single frame had to flow naturally from the one before, whilst offering something new and contrasting. Dialogue had to be brief enough to fit inside the bubble, and yet still appear to have the breezy eccentricity you expect from *Doctor Who*.

I was incredibly lucky that Mike Collins was there to translate my words into horrifyingly beautiful art. As the months went by, I began to learn how to write from studying Mike's interpretation of what I'd been up to, and realised

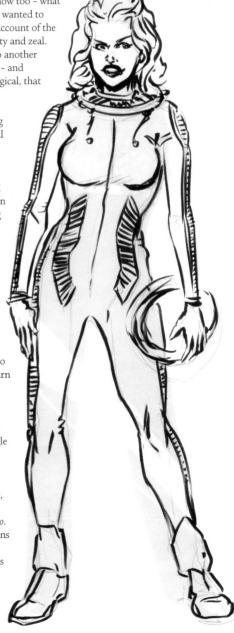

The Cruel Sea

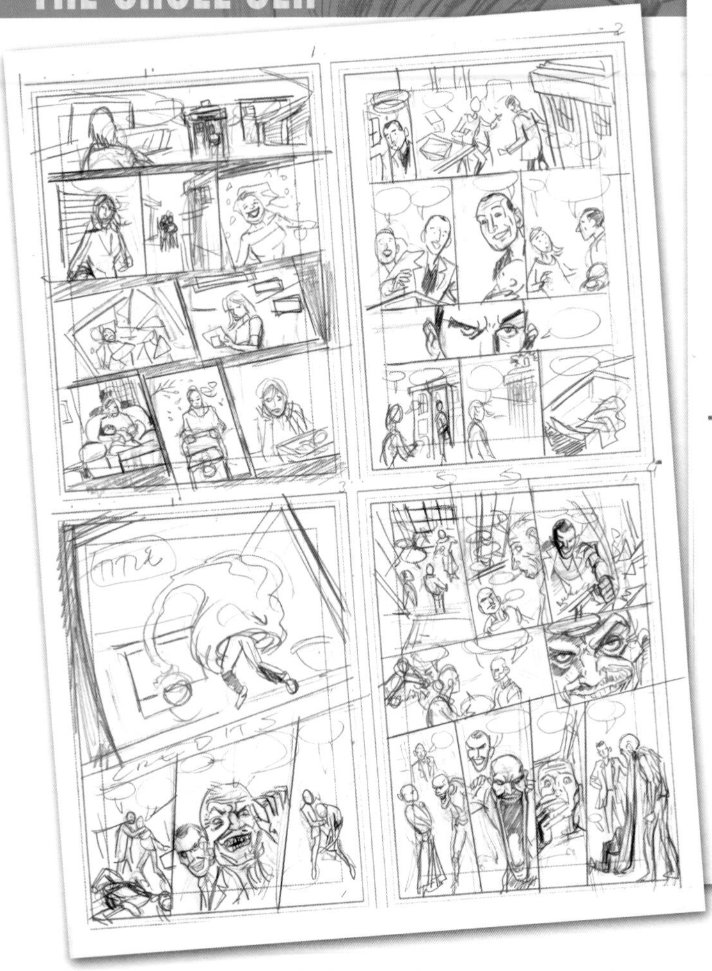

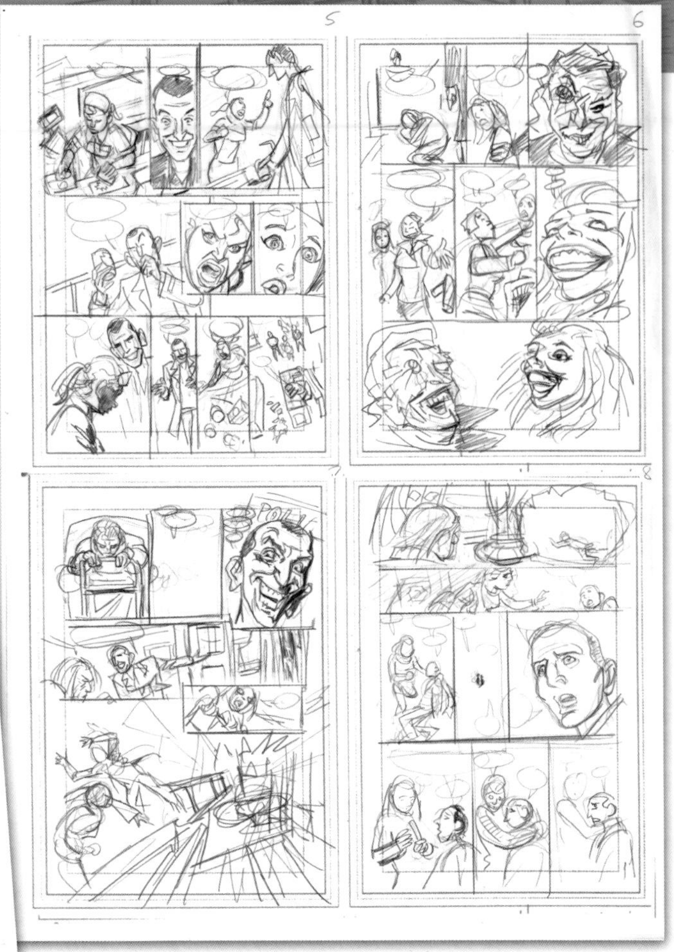

Above: Mike's initial layouts.

Below: A preliminary design of the 'cracked face' mirror woman.

that he wasn't there to serve me, I was there to serve him. Before writing the story I had experimented by reading some manga horror, and had devoured all three volumes of Junji Ito's *Uzumaki*. It remains the most frightening thing I've ever read. *The Cruel Sea* is hugely inspired by the madness of it, especially in sequences where characters crawl into distended mouths – what I love so much about Mike's work is that he took my influences and made them seem pure *Doctor Who*. And he put in exploding squirrels too, just for fun.

I'm very fond of *The Cruel Sea*. I think the third episode in particular is rather good – by that point I felt I was starting to get the hang of it, and Mike's work that month was outstanding. And there aren't many trips Chris Eccleston got to take in the TARDIS – I'm very proud that I was able to give him another.

Mike Collins Artist

There have been very few stories where I've had problems with *Doctor Who* scripts – there's always been something for me to get a handle on, some aspect of storytelling, or a landscape I've not encountered before. I always find something to challenge me, to satisfy me artistically.

And then there's *The Cruel Sea*.

In all the years I've been drawing comics (and it's a few), I've never encountered a script like *The Cruel Sea*. I still cannot believe this is the first and only strip Rob has written. It is just the most brilliant use of the comics medium I've ever come across. The sequence where the world becomes less 'real' rendered as different styles of comics storytelling is simply genius. Forget your Grant Morrison meta-frippery – *this* is genuinely groundbreaking storytelling.

Now it'd be enough that Rob had come up with this technique but he grounds it in a fabulous tale of loss, regret and venal and corrupt figures. It has a sheen of modern body horror, and the chance for me to draw some truly nasty and bizarre graphics. The standout images here have to be the mirror-Rose swallowing the real Rose, and the ex-wife crawling into Alvar's mouth. The shattered face of the mirror woman was a joy to create.

It's interesting, from an artistic standpoint, because it's probably the only *Doctor Who* story I've ever drawn with a cast list of less than a dozen. It meant I could focus on the situations, on the staging.

As well as the more bizarre elements (I thought he was joking when Rob texted me 'do you have any issues about drawing exploding squirrels?'), the scenes of a middle-aged Rose working in a supermarket made a fantastic counterpoint to the spare and sparse Mars sequences.

A special note must go to the new addition to our art team; James Offredi. The first two stories were coloured by fellow Cardiffian Dylan Teague and he did a brilliant job (especially considering the insane demands I made on him with my Escher-esque space art gallery), but he ended up going back to *2000 AD* (where he's done some of the best work in that comic in the last ten years), so we needed someone up to his standard. James hit the ground running. The opening shot of the cruiseliner on the Martian ocean was as stunning an introduction as anyone could make. Jaw-dropping stuff.

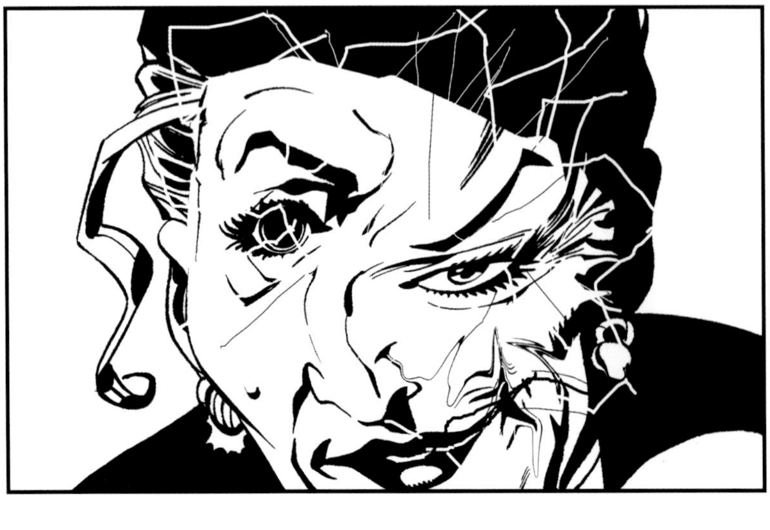

If folks ask me what my favourite comics jobs are, *The Cruel Sea* is always at the top of that list. I measure every job since against it. Some have moments where I feel I've achieved something special but – due in no small part to Rob's generous, endlessly inventive script – this one is the whole package for me.

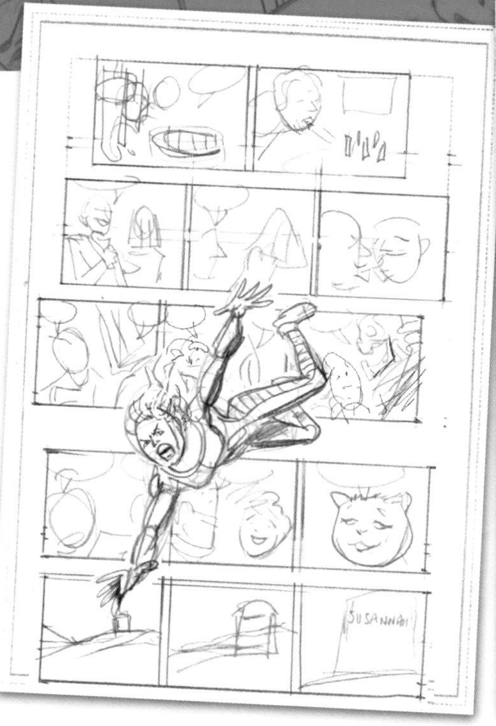

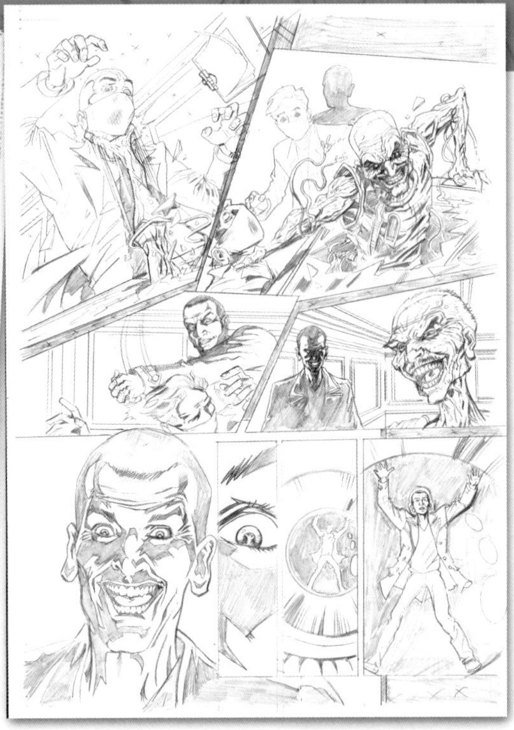

Clayton Hickman Editor

It was a great coup for the comic strip that we were able to get one of the actual *Doctor Who* TV writers to contribute to it, and Rob Shearman delivered a twisted, nightmarish *tour-de-force* in *The Cruel Sea*.

It was, I think I'm right in saying, Rob's first ever comic strip, and he was a complete dream to work with. He really did his homework, studying some of Scott's old scripts to really get a handle on the way that comics work. Combined with his brilliant ear for dialogue and all the deliciously dark twists that exemplified his work for Big Finish, Rob's scripts were some of my favourites to work on.

It was smooth sailing on the first three parts, but there was a bit of concern with the original ending, which Russell feared might be too dark and grotesque – plus I recall it portrayed the Doctor using a weapon, which was strictly verboten. I was initially worried that Rob might be put out about changing things, but being just about the nicest, least precious man in the world, Rob obliged, and with a few tweaks the story concluded in fine style.

The Cruel Sea also saw James Offredi's début as regular colourist, and much as I liked Dylan Teague's work on the preceding stories, James brought a depth and vibrancy to his colouring that I honestly think has rarely been bettered in British comics. The gorgeous reds and pinks of the underwater scenes, the flat kids-cartoon look of the Doctor's nightmare, and the spot-on recreation of the neon greens and warm browns of the TARDIS control room, all married to some of the best – and most terrifying – visuals Mike Collins has ever produced, really make *The Cruel Sea* stick in the memory.

And, hang on... the Doctor pitted against a deadly water-based foe running rampant on a futuristic version of the planet Mars? Where else have I seen that? Say, four years later? On BBC One? Hmmm...

Above: Mike's layout of Rose's surreal journey and a finished pencilled page.

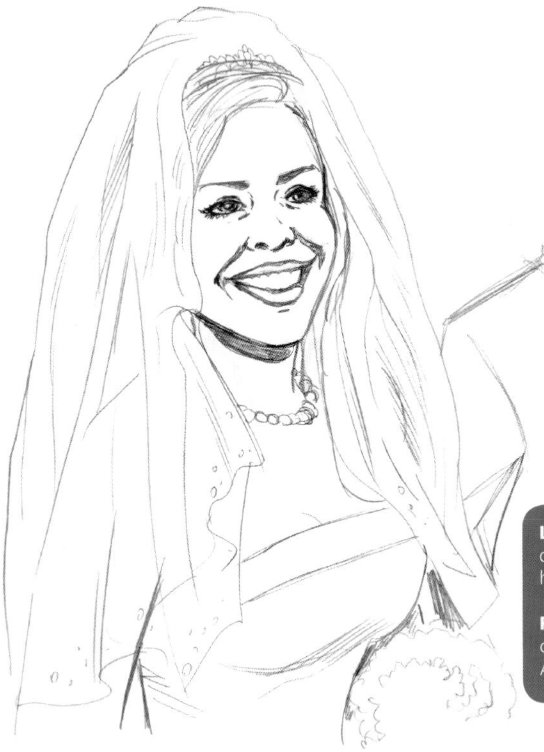

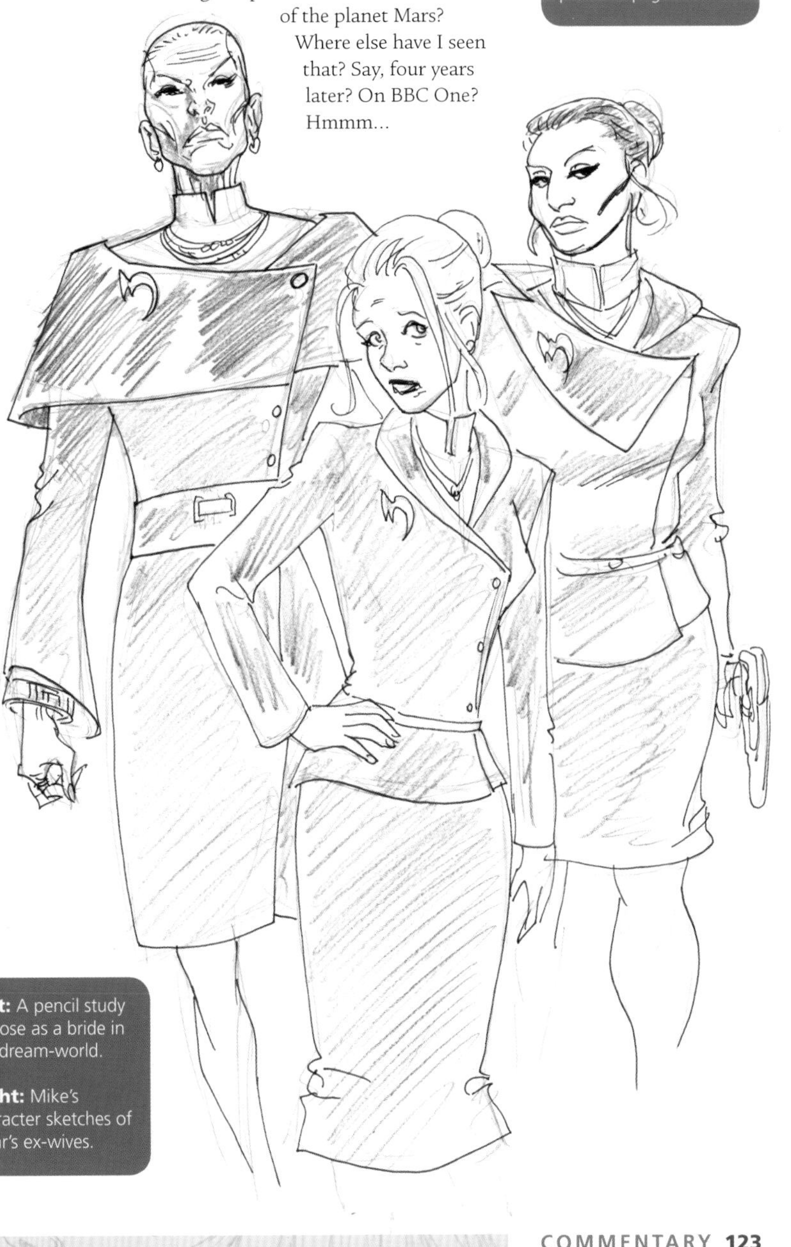

Left: A pencil study of Rose as a bride in her dream-world.

Right: Mike's character sketches of Alvar's ex-wives.

MR NOBODY

Scott Gray Writer

I have a tough time remembering dates and times and places and names and faces and conversations, but apart from that my memory is pretty good. 2005 was certainly a memorable year, for me and every other *Doctor Who* fan. I had completed a lengthy run writing the **DWM** comic strip. Artist Martin Geraghty and I had sent the Eighth Doctor strolling off into the sunset with the Cyberman story *The Flood* – a big crowd-pleasing invasion-of-Earth extravaganza. I had decided to sit back and enjoy the new Doctor's comic adventures from the safety of the editor's chair instead. Easy! (Well, eas-*ier*, anyway.)

But then scripts from the new television series started to arrive in the office. *Rose. The End of the World. Dalek. Aliens of London.* Oh, blimey, they were *really* good. This was a new super-charged version of *Doctor Who*: pacey and funny and shocking. It seemed clear that if the production could cope with the cinema-sized demands the scripts were making (the spaceship hits *Big Ben?!*), then the reborn *Doctor Who* was going to be a huge success. And right in the centre of it all was the new Doctor. I thought he was fascinating – an angry, vulnerable figure, but one enriched with a sense of wonder and a desire to make things right. A tragic hero, wounded by guilt and loss but still looking to the future with hope in his hearts. I wanted to have a crack at him. Just once would be enough!

Then rumours started to do the rounds that Christopher Eccleston would only be appearing in the first year of the show, which took everyone by surprise. When the rumours were confirmed, and the news came through that a new Doctor would most likely be débuting at Christmas, I realised that the Ninth Doctor would only be appearing in the **DWM** comic strip for a mere ten issues. If I didn't jump in quickly I'd miss my chance forever.

Luckily there was another option: the *Doctor Who Annual 2006*. I absolutely love that book, I think it's the best *Doctor Who* Annual ever published. I'm very proud to have been a part of it. There was that superb frontispiece by Alister Pearson. So many great short stories, all by the writers of the TV series. *Meet the Doctor* by Russell T Davies! *Robot Rose* by (it can now be revealed) Gareth Roberts! That beautiful introduction to the history of *Doctor Who* by Philip MacDonald. It's the kind of book I would have devoured when I was eight. We all knew it was going to be materialising under the Christmas trees of a brand-new generation of *Doctor Who* fans, hungry for more information and further adventures. I think we did them proud. (Somewhere there's a parallel Earth where Panini retained the rights to publish the Annuals and we kept on producing them to that standard – what a collection that must be, stacked up on a shelf in some corner of the multiverse.)

I had had a story premise in my head for some time that I hadn't yet used: a person is charged with a crime committed by someone else – and his accusers are from a culture with an absolute belief in reincarnation. It was the kind of bizarre pseudo-logic that powers a lot of British science-fiction, and I knew I could get a story out of it. But who to put on trial?

Above & below: John Ross' sketches of Rose and Phil Tyson.

Right: *Mr Nobody*'s title page pencilled by John Ross.

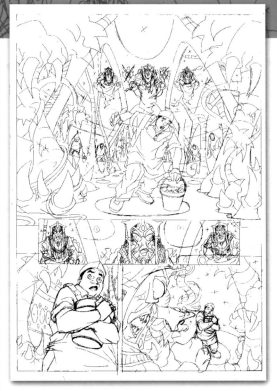

The new *Doctor Who* series was very much grounded in the real world, and seemed to be championing the common man (or woman) in a very upfront way: it's shop-girl Rose Tyler who saves the world in the opening episode. Small-time wheeler-dealer Pete Tyler sacrifices his life to repair history in *Father's Day*. Mechanic Micky Smith defeats the Slitheen in *World War Three*. All of them find an inner strength of which they were previously unaware, and are changed forever by the experience. The message at the heart of the new *Doctor Who* was as simple as it was wonderful: nobody is really 'ordinary' – we all have the potential to be amazing. With that in mind, I put the spotlight on Phil Tyson: a lonely bloke with no belief in himself and no ability to improve his life. And of course, the ending presented itself straight away – Phil would learn that the person he had supposedly been in a past life was a hero to millions. Whether Phil really had been Shogalath or not was immaterial: he'd have found the strength of will to get his life moving at last.

I remember writing the script just after *Rose* had aired. I'd originally had the Doctor bluff the Vandosians by showing them his membership card for the *Captain Video* fan club (an American sci-fi TV series from the 1950s). Then *The End of the World* was broadcast and I was reminded that he now had a clever new device which got him past most layers of officialdom: psychic paper!

We were lucky enough to get John Ross to illustrate *Mr Nobody*. John is a tremendous talent, one of a rare breed of artists who don't seem to have any weak areas. Some artists can provide atmospheric scenes of the highest order, but give them an action sequence and they freeze up. Others are brilliant illustrators but have difficulty with coherent panel-to-panel storytelling. John, however, is a writer's dream: he ticks every box: dynamic layouts, a strong understanding of perspective, terrific anatomy, a wide range of expressions. There's a great sense of muscularity to John's characters: everyone has real weight to their frames. His command of body language is superb too – just look at the scene where Rose gives the Doctor an earful, then comforts Phil. Remove the dialogue and it's still as clear as day. It was no surprise when the younger readers title *Doctor Who Adventures* recruited him as its regular comic artist.

We were equally lucky to get James Offredi to collaborate with John. James has been colouring the **DWM** comic strip for many years, and I count my lucky stars every day a piece of his art pings into my inbox. Colouring is an invisible artform in comics, akin to music in television. It enhances the mood and flavours the atmosphere of every scene on a near-subliminal level. I see James as the comic strip's equivalent of composer Murray Gold on TV *Doctor Who*. He always makes subtle, intelligent choices. The courtroom scene is a beautiful example. John had provided us with these terrific teeth/claw shapes growing out of the environment. James turned them into light sources, giving the setting a translucent quality. It looked like an aquarium at night: eerie, yet magical!

Mr Nobody is no epic. It doesn't tie itself into TV continuity or bring back a classic enemy or reveal some shocking truth about the Doctor's past. But it does have a point to make, plus exciting artwork, some sparky dialogue, a nice twist and a solid ending. It remains one of my favourites of the *Doctor Who* stories I've written.

Not bad for eight pages!

John Ross Artist

It's always great to get a call from Scott Gray. I've worked with Scott on lots of different projects over the years (one of my favourite jobs of all time was working on the moody and atmospheric *Me and My Shadow* for **DWM**), and his energy and endless enthusiasm is ideal for getting me revved up for action. So, when I got the script for *Mr Nobody*, I was fired up and ready to go. I loved Phil (who really represents all of us) and wanted the readers to love him too. I used all the tools I had to get across in the artwork exactly who he was by using body language and facial expression. He was a lot of fun to draw.

There was something else that particularly attracted me to this strip... the little matter of the Ninth Doctor. And Rose. I hadn't drawn that many *Doctor Who* strips at that time but I knew that being one of the first artists to draw the new Doctor would be cool. And it was. As it turned out, I was one of the *few* artists to draw him in comics, so I'm pretty glad I was in the right place at the right time to pick up that accolade.

Also, this was the first time I would go through the process of submitting new Doctor and companion sketches to the branding people at the BBC. They needed to see head shots of both characters before I started the strip. I was a bit nervous actually – I'm not really a great 'likeness' kind of artist (and therefore a strange choice for *Doctor Who* some might say!), but my second attempts at the Doctor and Rose were approved and I was able to get to work on *Mr Nobody*. Technically, it was a bit of a learning curve but I'm pretty happy with my representation of the Ninth Doctor and Rose. I'd get to practice more on my version of Rose in the *Doctor Who Adventures* magazine but that was the extent of my involvement with the Christopher Eccleston Doctor – short and sweet – but I'm extremely proud to have been able to illustrate such a brilliant Doc.

Clayton Hickman Editor

I was so pleased that Scott agreed to write the comic strip for our first – and, as it turned out, only – *Doctor Who Annual*, and was again astounded by how masterfully he managed to pack a proper story full of big ideas and emotional wallops into a mere eight pages.

With the *Annual* we were aiming squarely at the mainstream, and the kids' end of it to boot, and Scott was the safest pair of hands. Again, with Mike Collins busy on **DWM** duties, we needed a new artist and John Ross' gorgeous work on *Mr Nobody* cemented him as my favourite of our regular irregulars.

With the astronomical sales of the *Annual* – which, ironically, contributed to its demise as a Panini publication once Penguin Books got in on the act – it's probably fair to say that *Mr Nobody* might well be the most widely-read comic strip we've ever published. Couldn't have happened to a nicer story!

A Groatsworth Of Wit

Gareth Roberts Writer

This story was *not* to be a camp old laugh. It was a serious, stirring idea – Robert Greene brought into the twenty-first century – which I'd had years before but hadn't found a way to use. I tried on *Brookside*, but Phil Redman said no.

I thought Chris Eccleston was a marvellous Doctor Who, and I wanted to do him proud. I was inspired by *The Screwtape Letters* and by my own love of Shakespeare (being, frankly, amazed that the Doctor had never met Shakespeare on-screen in the television series), and wanted to deliver an emotional story, full of heart and humour, which would prove to me, and I hope to other people, that I wasn't just about those camp old laughs.

A Groatsworth of Wit certainly made an impression in all the right places at BBC Wales, as just a few weeks later I found myself writing that first television meeting between the Doctor and William Shakespeare.

Mike Collins Artist

After the scaled back, limited cast and controlled environments of the *Cruel Sea*, here I was confronted with

Above: Mike Collins' thumbnail sketches for *A Groatsworth of Wit*'s opening.

Below: A finished pencilled page from Part One.

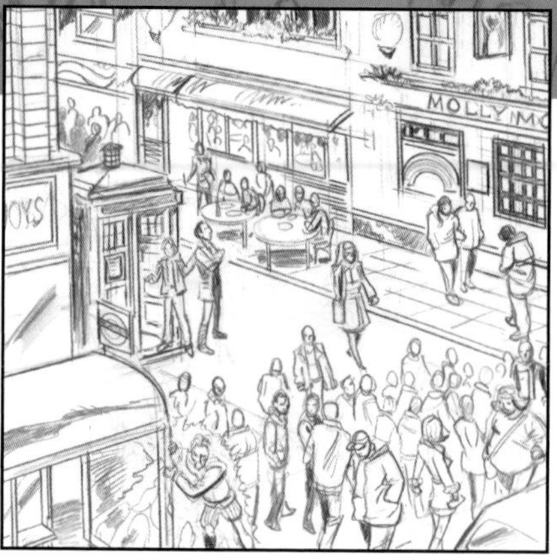

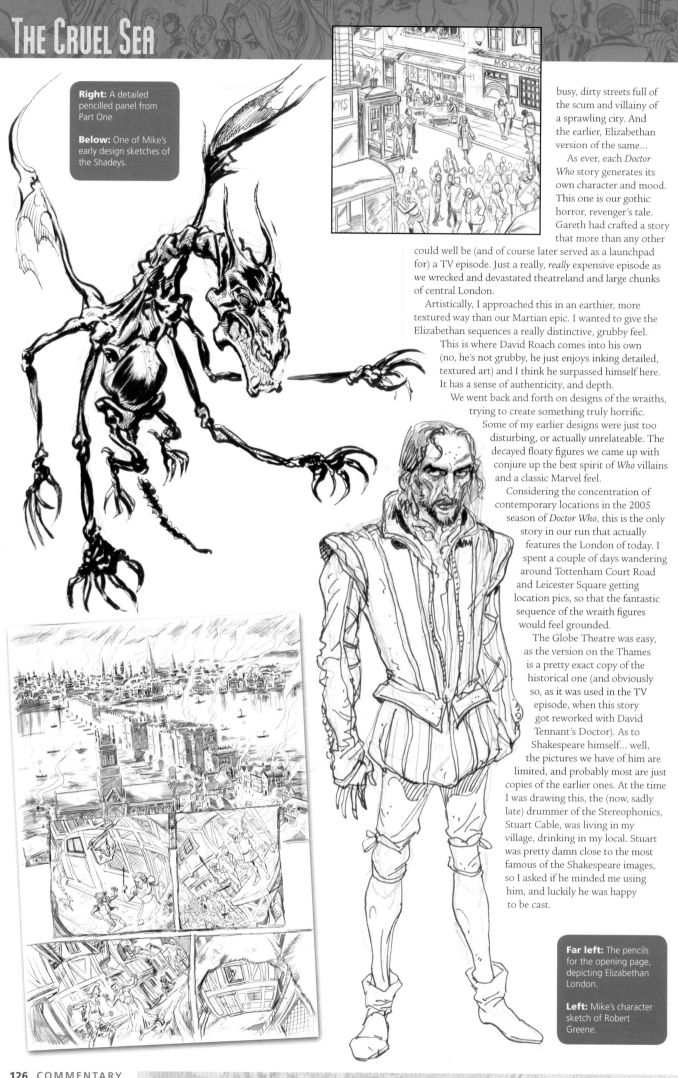

Right: A detailed pencilled panel from Part One.

Below: One of Mike's early design sketches of the Shadeys.

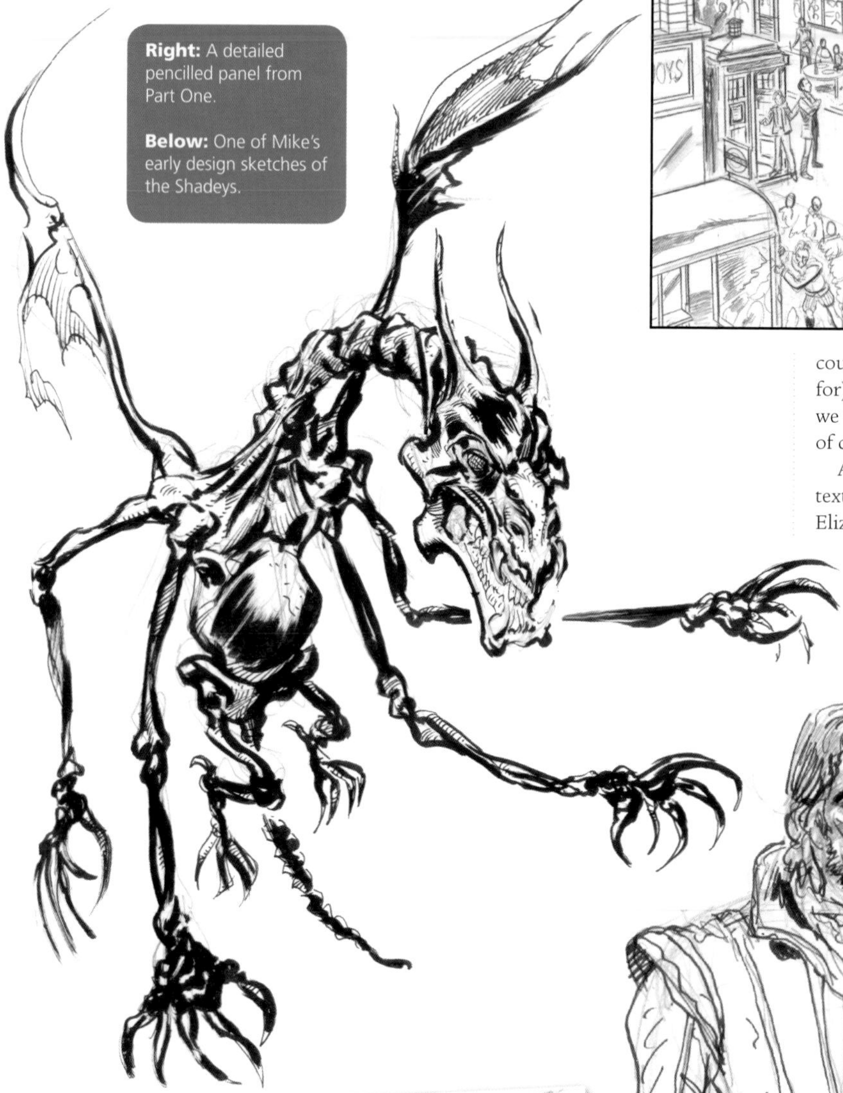

busy, dirty streets full of the scum and villainy of a sprawling city. And the earlier, Elizabethan version of the same...

As ever, each *Doctor Who* story generates its own character and mood. This one is our gothic horror, revenger's tale. Gareth had crafted a story that more than any other could well be (and of course later served as a launchpad for) a TV episode. Just a really, *really* expensive episode as we wrecked and devastated theatreland and large chunks of central London.

Artistically, I approached this in an earthier, more textured way than our Martian epic. I wanted to give the Elizabethan sequences a really distinctive, grubby feel. This is where David Roach comes into his own (no, he's not grubby, he just enjoys inking detailed, textured art) and I think he surpassed himself here. It has a sense of authenticity, and depth.

We went back and forth on designs of the wraiths, trying to create something truly horrific. Some of my earlier designs were just too disturbing, or actually unrelateable. The decayed floaty figures we came up with conjure up the best spirit of *Who* villains and a classic Marvel feel.

Considering the concentration of contemporary locations in the 2005 season of *Doctor Who,* this is the only story in our run that actually features the London of today. I spent a couple of days wandering around Tottenham Court Road and Leicester Square getting location pics, so that the fantastic sequence of the wraith figures would feel grounded.

The Globe Theatre was easy, as the version on the Thames is a pretty exact copy of the historical one (and obviously so, as it was used in the TV episode, when this story got reworked with David Tennant's Doctor). As to Shakespeare himself... well, the pictures we have of him are limited, and probably most are just copies of the earlier ones. At the time I was drawing this, the (now, sadly late) drummer of the Stereophonics, Stuart Cable, was living in my village, drinking in my local. Stuart was pretty damn close to the most famous of the Shakespeare images, so I asked if he minded me using him, and luckily he was happy to be cast.

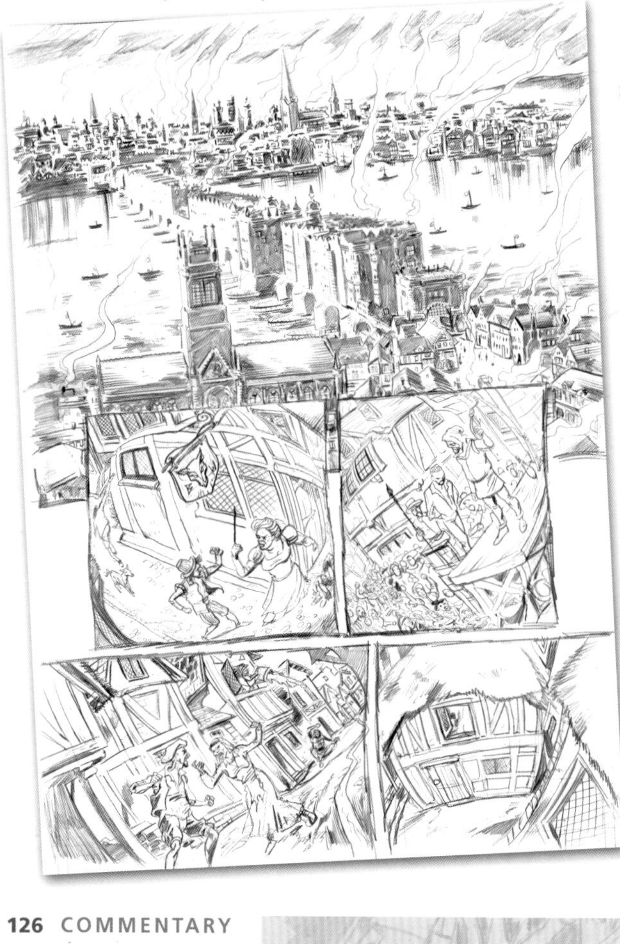

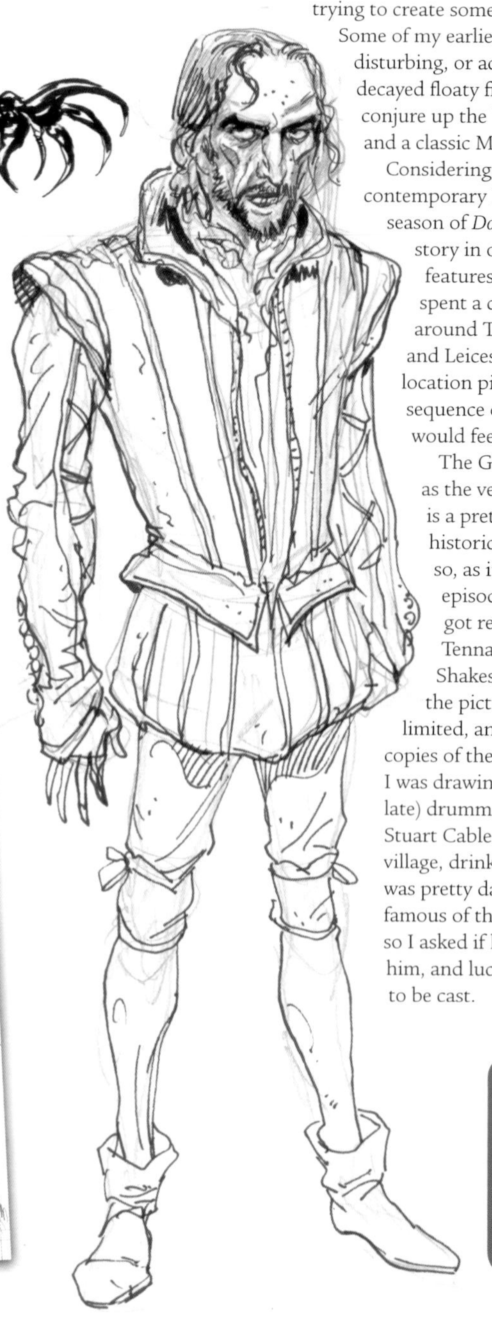

Far left: The pencils for the opening page, depicting Elizabethan London.

Left: Mike's character sketch of Robert Greene.

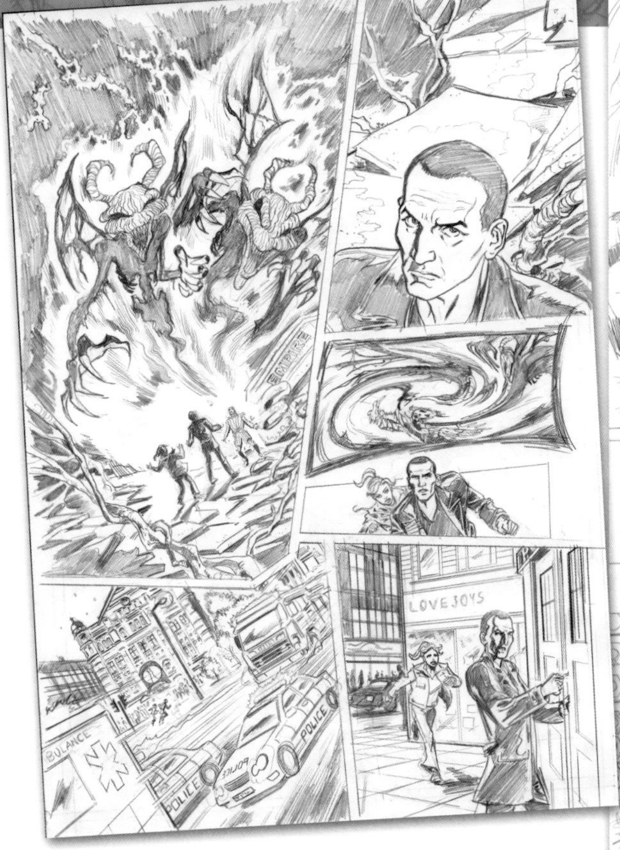
LOVEJOYS
POLICE
POLICE

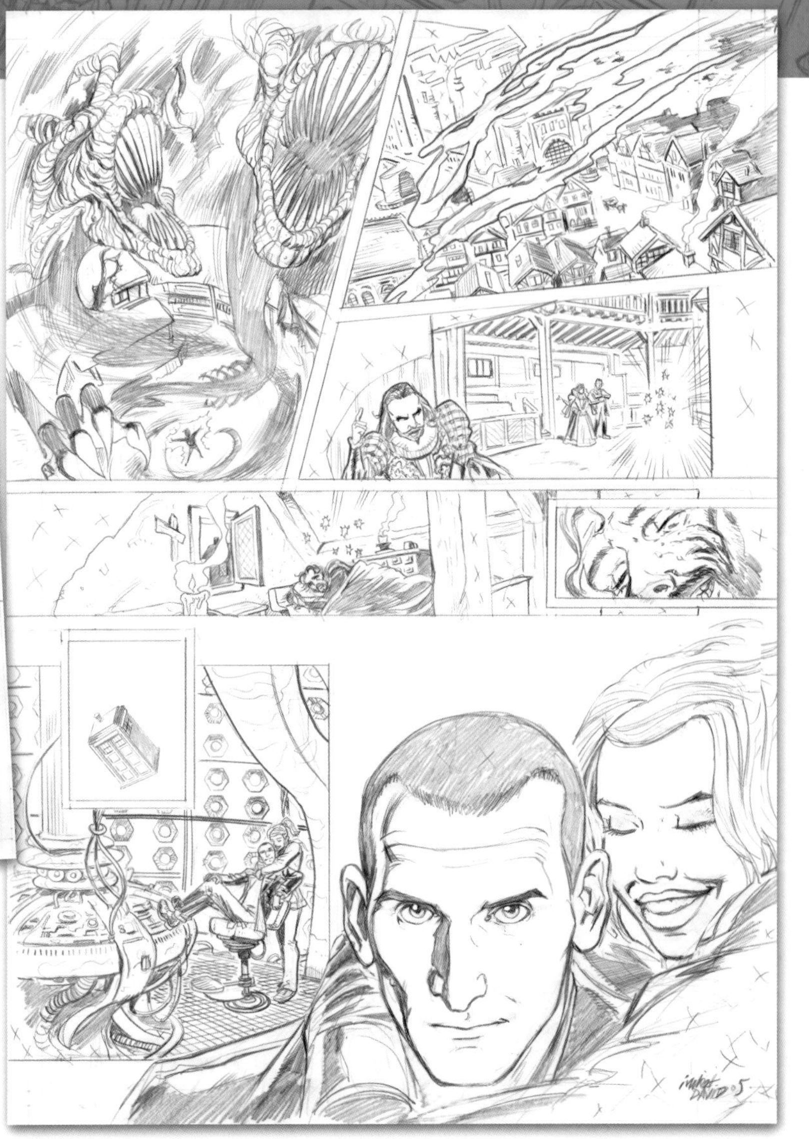

This is also the story where we said goodbye to Christopher Eccleston's Doctor. Gareth wrote a fabulous final adventure, utilizing the best of his character. Towards the end of episode one of this story, I finally felt I'd nailed down his likeness. If he had lasted another season I'd have been really acing his image regularly.

I actually drew the last page, of Rose and the Doctor looking up at us early on, not wanting to rush our goodbye image. It's a sweet farewell to a brilliant character.

Clayton Hickman Editor

Gareth flew solo for the final Ninth Doctor strip, *A Groatsworth of Wit*, which saw the Doctor meet Shakespeare and owed a debt to CS Lewis' *The Screwtape Letters* which Gareth had recently encouraged me to read.

Russell himself admitted that Gareth's work on these **DWM** strips, along with his excellent Ninth Doctor novel *Only Human*, so impressed him that they helped Gareth onto the writing team for the TV show. Additionally, *Groatsworth* heavily influenced Gareth's first *Doctor Who* TV script, *The Shakespeare Code*, which also featured the Immortal Bard, the Globe, and a whirlwind of floating, demonic aliens. Later, of course, another of Gareth's **DWM** strips, *The Lodger*, was adapted for TV in its entirety, featuring Matt Smith's Doctor. Now that *is* canonisation!

What I Did On My Christmas Holidays By Sally Sparrow

Clayton Hickman Editor

It was always a source of pride for me that **DWM** was seen as kosher enough to be able to call on the considerable talents of *Doctor Who*'s TV writers for content, with Paul Cornell, Rob Shearman, Mark Gatiss, Tom MacRae, Gareth Roberts and many more contributing both to the magazine and to our yearly not-quite-an-Annual publication *The Doctor Who Storybook*, which ran throughout David Tennant's tenure in the TARDIS.

But the first of these hardback collections, for Christmas 2005, really *was* an Annual, and featured the same illustrated short stories and comic strip as the later books, alongside some fun features and puzzles, plus intriguing biographies of the Doctor and Rose courtesy of Russell T Davies – especially notable for being the first time the words 'You Are Not Alone' were uttered, a good while before they were finally explained on TV in the form of Derek Jacobi's enigmatic Professor Yana.

Perhaps its most notable inclusion came from another of the TV show's most prominent writers, Steven Moffat, a few years before his elevation to *Doctor Who* showrunner and co-creator of the only telly series to give *Doctor Who* a real run for its money in the hilarious-yet-clever-yet-moving-yet-nailbiting stakes, *Sherlock*. His story, featuring the sort of brilliant timey-wimey plotting he would become famous for, was loosely adapted for the TV show in 2007 as the award-winning *Blink*. Although they both feature cryptic scrawls under the wallpaper, video messages from the past, and a character by the name of Sally Sparrow, the original tale is conspicuous by its lack of Weeping Angels, perhaps the most brilliant creations of the BBC Wales era.

Nonetheless, it's a wonderful story, enhanced by some charming illustrations courtesy of Martin Geraghty, and it's lovely to think that one of *Doctor Who*'s greatest successes started life in the pages of our Annual. That's a Christmas gift that keeps on giving. ●

Above: Two of Mike's pencilled pages from Part Two.

Below: The one and only Ninth Doctor Annual, published by Panini in 2005.

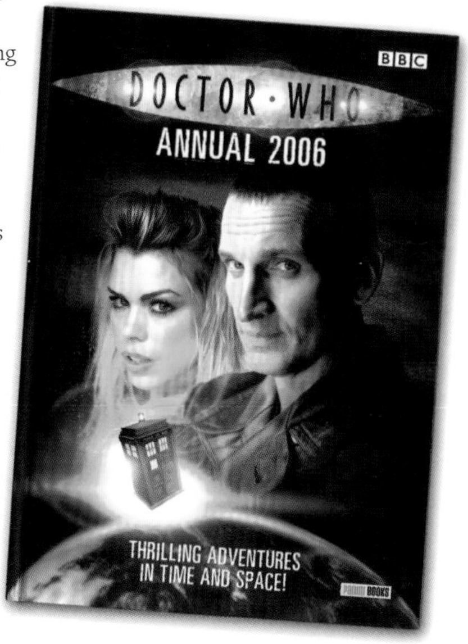
BBC
DOCTOR·WHO
ANNUAL 2006
THRILLING ADVENTURES IN TIME AND SPACE!
PANINI BOOKS

DOCTOR WHO COMIC COLLECTIONS

CLASSIC STRIP ADVENTURES

DAVE GIBBONS
MILLS & WAGNER
STEVE MOORE
DOCTOR WHO
THE IRON LEGION
A PANINI BOOKS GRAPHIC NOVEL

Volume One of the Fourth Doctor's comic strip adventures, containing five digitally restored stories:

THE IRON LEGION, **CITY OF THE DAMNED**, **THE STAR BEAST**, **THE DOGS OF DOOM** and **THE TIME WITCH!**

Featuring work from **Dave Gibbons**, **Pat Mills**, **John Wagner** and **Steve Moore**

164 pages | b&w | softcover
£14.99 | $24.95
ISBN 1-9041 59-37-0

DAVE GIBBONS
STEVE PARKHOUSE
STEVE MOORE
DOCTOR WHO
DRAGON'S CLAW
A PANINI BOOKS GRAPHIC NOVEL

Volume Two of the Fourth Doctor's comic strip adventures, containing 10 digitally restored stories:

DRAGON'S CLAW, **THE COLLECTOR**, **DREAMERS OF DEATH**, **THE LIFE BRINGER**, **WAR OF THE WORDS**, **SPIDER-GOD**, **THE DEAL**, **END OF THE LINE**, **THE FREE-FALL WARRIORS**, **JUNKYARD DEMON** and **THE NEUTRON KNIGHTS**!

164 pages | b&w | softcover
£14.99 | $24.95
ISBN 1-9041 59-81-8

DAVE GIBBONS
STEVE PARKHOUSE
MICK AUSTIN
STEVE DILLON
DOCTOR WHO
THE TIDES OF TIME
A PANINI BOOKS GRAPHIC NOVEL

The Fifth Doctor's complete comic strip run, containing six digitally restored stories:

THE TIDES OF TIME, **STARS FELL ON STOCKBRIDGE**, **THE STOCKBRIDGE HORROR**, **LUNAR LAGOON**, **4-DIMENSIONAL VISTAS** and **THE MODERATOR**!

Featuring art from **Dave Gibbons**

228 pages | b&w | softcover
£14.99 | $24.95
ISBN 1-9041 59-92-3

JOHN RIDGWAY
STEVE PARKHOUSE
ALAN McKENZIE
DOCTOR WHO
VOYAGER
A PANINI BOOKS GRAPHIC NOVEL

Volume One of the Sixth Doctor's comic strip adventures containing seven digitally restored adventures:

THE SHAPE SHIFTER, **VOYAGER**, **POLLY THE GLOT**, **ONCE UPON A TIME LORD**, **WAR-GAME**, **FUNHOUSE** and **KANE'S STORY/ABEL'S STORY/ THE WARRIOR'S STORY/ FROBISHER'S STORY**!

172 pages | b&w softcover
£15.99 | $31.95
ISBN 978-1-905239-71-9

JOHN RIDGWAY
GRANT MORRISON
JAMIE DELANO
DOCTOR WHO
OUT OF PRINT
THE WORLD SHAPERS
A PANINI BOOKS GRAPHIC NOVEL

Volume Two of the Sixth Doctor's comic strip adventures containing the following digitally restored adventures:

EXODUS, **REVELATION!**, **GENESIS!**, **NATURE OF THE BEAST**, **TIME BOMB**, **SALAD DAZE**, **CHANGES**, **PROFITS OF DOOM**, **THE GIFT** and **THE WORLD SHAPERS**!

188 pages | b&w | softcover
£15.99 | $31.95
ISBN 978-1-905239-87-0

DOCTOR·WHO
A COLD DAY IN HELL!

Volume One of the Seventh Doctor's comic strip adventures containing 11 digitally restored stories:

A COLD DAY IN HELL!, **REDEMPTION!**, **THE CROSSROADS OF TIME**, **CLAWS OF THE KLATHI!**, **CULTURE SHOCK!**, **KEEPSAKE**, **PLANET OF THE DEAD**, **ECHOES OF THE MOGOR!**, **TIME AND TIDE**, **FOLLOW THAT TARDIS!** and **INVADERS FROM GANTAC!**

PLUS an introduction and commentary by former strip editors **Richard Starkings** and **John Freeman**

188 pages | b&w | softcover
£15.99 | $31.95 | ISBN 978-1-84653-410-2

BBC
DOCTOR WHO
DW
Richard Starkings John Tomlinson Lee Sullivan John Ridgway
NEMESIS OF THE DALEKS

Volume Two of the Seventh Doctor's complete comic strip adventures from the pages of **Doctor Who Magazine** and *The Incredible Hulk Presents*. Contains 14 complete stories:

NEMESIS OF THE DALEKS, **STAIRWAY TO HEAVEN**, **ONCE IN A LIFETIME**, **HUNGER FROM THE ENDS OF TIME!**, **WAR WORLD!**, **TECHNICAL HITCH**, **A SWITCH IN TIME!**, **THE SENTINEL!**, **WHO'S THAT GIRL!**, **THE ENLIGHTENMENT OF LI-CHEE THE WISE**, **SLIMMER!**, **NINEVEH!**, **TRAIN-FLIGHT**, **DOCTOR CONKERER!**
and also the adventures of Abslom Daak in **ABSLOM DAAK... DALEK KILLER** and **STAR TIGERS!**

PLUS a massive behind-the-scenes feature, including commentaries from the writers, artists and editors, cut scenes, pencil art, design sketches, and much, much more.

196 pages | b&w | softcover
£16.99 | $24.99 | ISBN 978-1-84653-531-4

These titles are available now from all good bookshops, specialist comic shops and online retailers

Panini COMICS

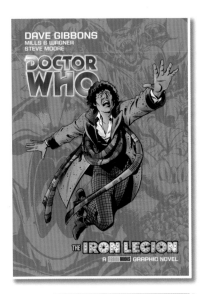

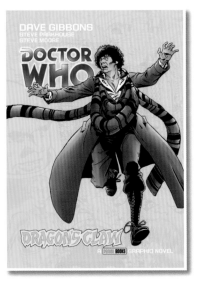

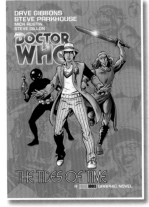

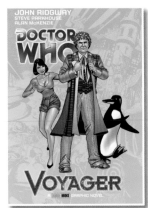

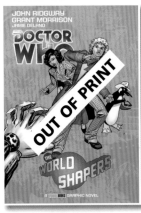

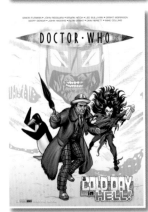

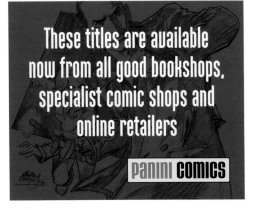

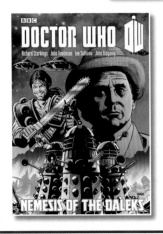

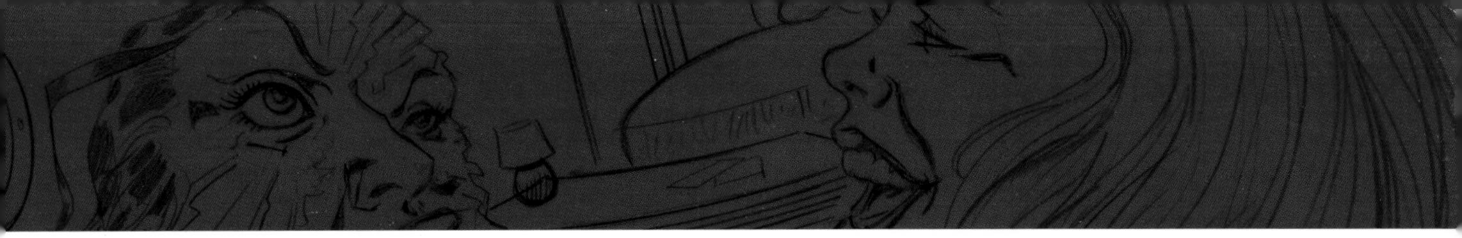

THE COMPLETE EIGHTH DOCTOR

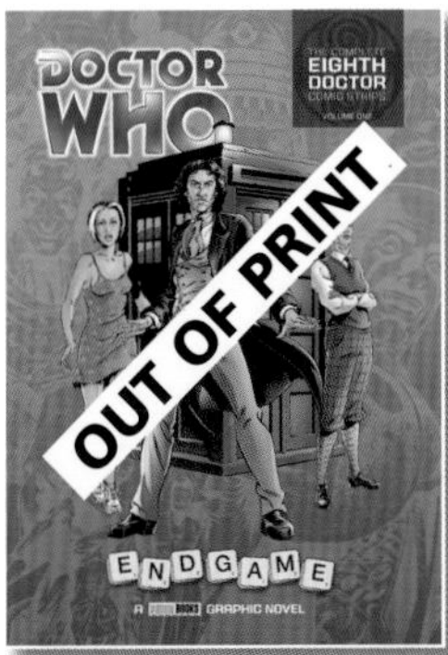
DOCTOR WHO
OUT OF PRINT
ENDGAME

Volume One of the Eighth Doctor's complete comic strip adventures, containing eight digitally restored stories: **ENDGAME**, **THE KEEP**, **FIRE AND BRIMSTONE**, **TOOTH AND CLAW**, **THE FINAL CHAPTER**, **WORMWOOD**, **A LIFE OF MATTER AND DEATH** and **BY HOOK OR BY CROOK**!

PLUS a 16-page behind-the-scenes feature with unused story ideas, character designs and an authors' commentary on all the strips!

228 pages | b&w | softcover
£14.99 | $24.95 | ISBN 1-9052 39-09-2

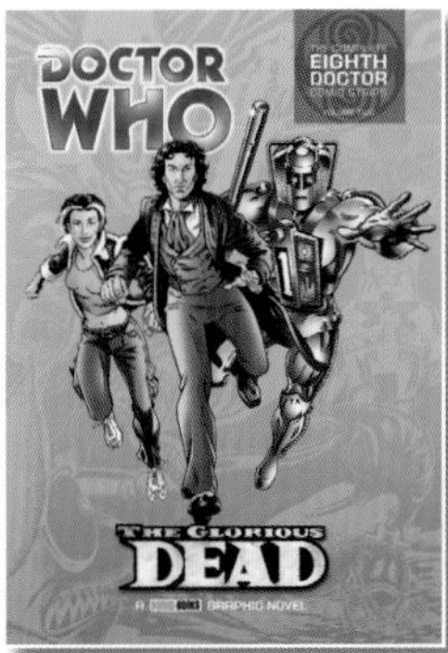
DOCTOR WHO
THE GLORIOUS DEAD

Volume Two of the Eighth Doctor's complete comic strip adventures, containing eight digitally restored stories: **THE FALLEN**, **UNNATURAL BORN KILLERS**, **THE ROAD TO HELL**, **COMPANY OF THIEVES**, **THE GLORIOUS DEAD**, **THE AUTONOMY BUG**, **HAPPY DEATHDAY** and **TV ACTION**!

PLUS a six-page behind-the-scenes feature and two classic 1980s strips featuring Kroton the Cyberman: **THROWBACK** and **SHIP OF FOOLS**!

244 pages | b&w | softcover
£15.99 | $26.50 | ISBN 1-9052 39-44-0

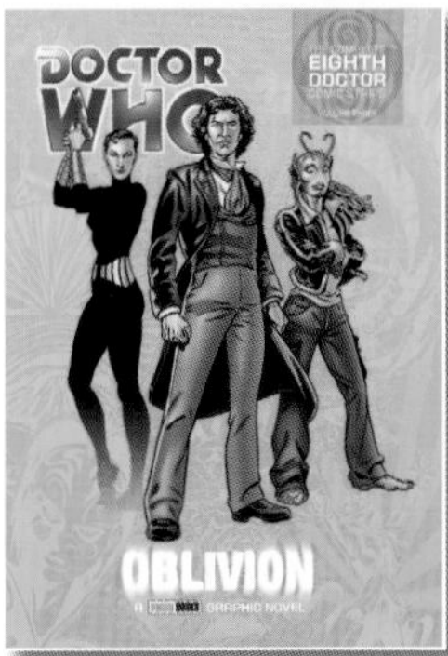
DOCTOR WHO
OBLIVION

Volume Three of the Eighth Doctor's complete comic strip adventures, containing eight digitally restored stories: **OPHIDIUS**, **BEAUTIFUL FREAK**, **THE WAY OF ALL FLESH**, **CHILDREN OF THE REVOLUTION**, **ME AND MY SHADOW**, **UROBOROS** and **OBLIVION**!

PLUS a massive 22-page behind-the-scenes feature, bonus strip **CHARACTER ASSASSIN** and a newly-extended conclusion to Dalek strip **CHILDREN OF THE REVOLUTION**!

228 pages | full colour | softcover
£15.99 | $26.50 | ISBN 1-905239-45-9

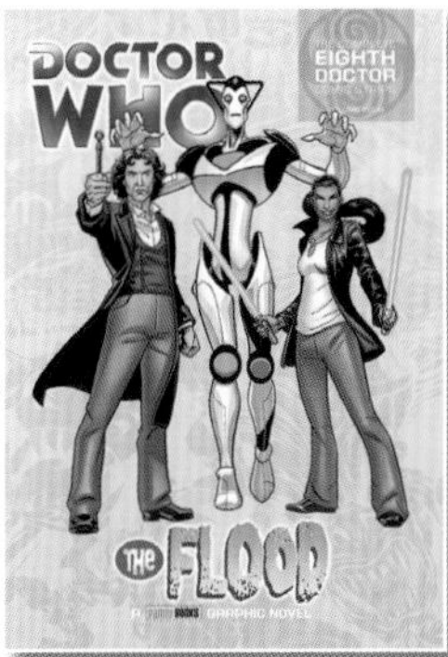
DOCTOR WHO
THE FLOOD

Volume Four of the Eighth Doctor's complete comic strip adventures, containing eight digitally restored stories: **WHERE NOBODY KNOWS YOUR NAME**, **THE NIGHTMARE GAME**, **THE POWER OF THOUERIS!**, **THE CURIOUS TALE OF SPRING-HEELED JACK**, **THE LAND OF HAPPY ENDINGS**, **BAD BLOOD**, **SINS OF THE FATHERS** and **THE FLOOD**!

PLUS a massive 28-page behind-the-scenes feature, and a newly-extended conclusion to **THE FLOOD!**

228 pages | full colour | softcover
£15.99 | $26.50 | ISBN 978-1-905239-65-8

THE COMPLETE TENTH DOCTOR

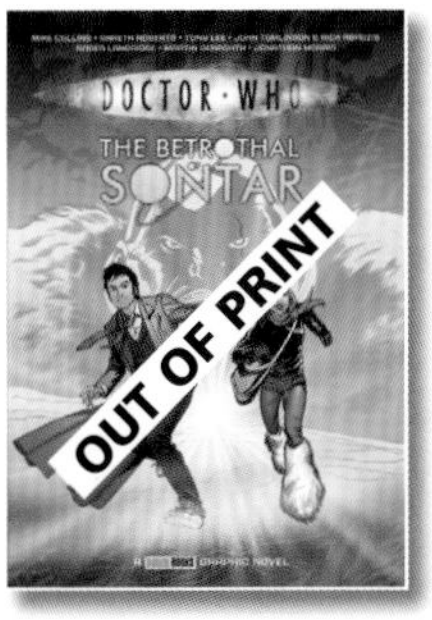
DOCTOR WHO
THE BETROTHAL OF SONTAR
OUT OF PRINT

Volume One of the Tenth Doctor's comic strip adventures from the pages of **Doctor Who Magazine**, containing eight complete stories:

THE BETROTHAL OF SONTAR, **THE LODGER**, **F.A.Q.**, **THE FUTURISTS**, **INTERSTELLAR OVERDRIVE**, **OPERA OF DOOM!**, **THE GREEN-EYED MONSTER** and **THE WARKEEPER'S CROWN**!

PLUS a massive behind-the-scenes feature, including commentaries from the writers and artists, design sketches and more.

180 pages | full colour softcover
£15.99 | $31.95 | ISBN 978-1-905239-90-0

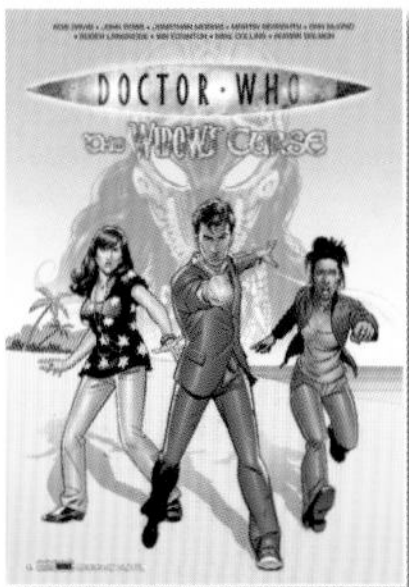
DOCTOR WHO

Volume Two of the Tenth Doctor's comic strip adventures from the pages of **Doctor Who Magazine**, containing nine complete stories:

THE WOMAN WHO SOLD THE WORLD, **BUS STOP!**, **THE FIRST**, **SUN SCREEN**, **DEATH TO THE DOCTOR!**, **UNIVERSAL MONSTERS**, **THE WIDOW'S CURSE**, **THE IMMORTAL EMPEROR** and **THE TIME OF MY LIFE**!

PLUS a massive behind-the-scenes feature, including commentaries from the writers and artists, design sketches and more.

220 pages | full colour | softcover
£15.99 | $31.95 | ISBN 978-1-84653-429-4

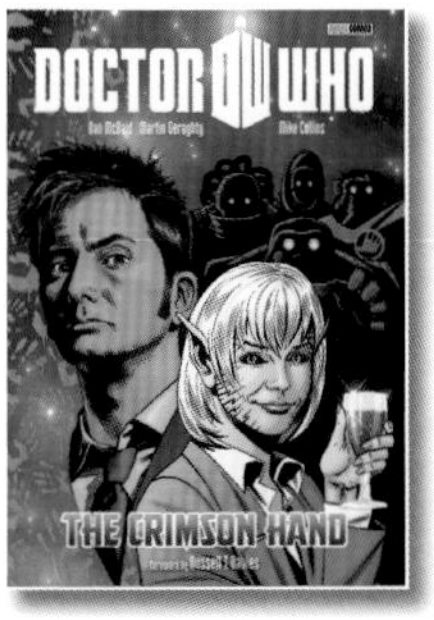
DOCTOR WHO
THE CRIMSON HAND

Volume Three of the Tenth Doctor's comic strip adventures from the pages of **Doctor Who Magazine**, containing ten complete stories:

HOTEL HISTORIA, **SPACE VIKINGS!**, **THINKTWICE**, **THE STOCKBRIDGE CHILD**, **MORTAL BELOVED**, **THE AGE OF ICE**, **THE DEEP HEREAFTER**, **ONOMATOPOEIA**, **GHOSTS OF THE NORTHERN LINE** and **THE CRIMSON HAND**!

PLUS a massive behind-the-scenes feature, including commentaries from the writers and artists, design sketches and more.

260 pages | full colour | softcover
£15.99 | $31.95 | ISBN 978-1-84653-451-5

THE COMPLETE ELEVENTH DOCTOR

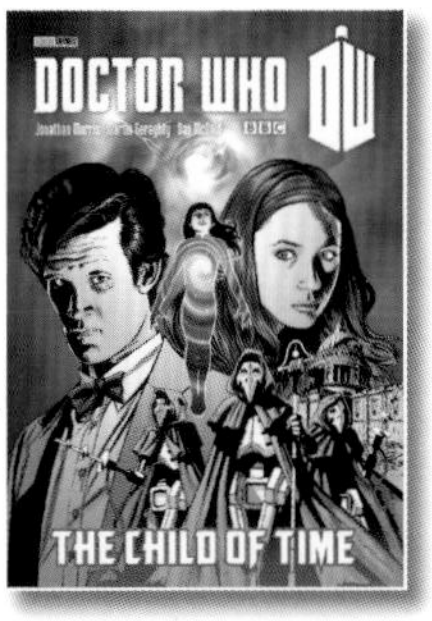
DOCTOR WHO
THE CHILD OF TIME

Volume One of the Eleventh Doctor's comic strip adventures from the pages of **Doctor Who Magazine**, containing nine complete stories:

SUPERNATURE, **PLANET BOLLYWOOD!**, **THE GOLDEN ONES**, **THE PROFESSOR, THE QUEEN AND THE BOOKSHOP**, **THE SCREAMS OF DEATH**, **DO NOT GO GENTLE INTO THAT GOOD NIGHT**, **FOREVER DREAMING**, **APOTHEOSIS** and **THE CHILD OF TIME**!

PLUS a massive behind-the-scenes feature from the creators of the strips with design sketches and more.

244 pages | full colour | softcover
£16.99 | $24.99 | ISBN 978-1-84653-460-7

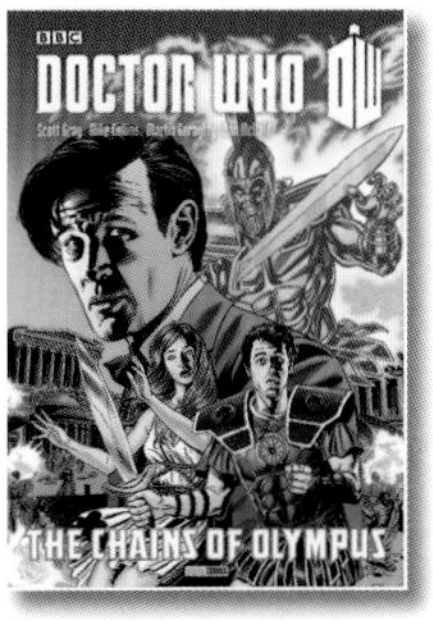
BBC
DOCTOR WHO
THE CHAINS OF OLYMPUS

Volume Two of the Eleventh Doctor's comic strip adventures from the pages of **Doctor Who Magazine**, containing three complete stories:

THE CHAINS OF OLYMPUS, **STICKS AND STONES** and **THE CORNUCOPIA CAPER**!

PLUS a massive behind-the-scenes feature, including commentaries from the writers and artists, design sketches and more.

132 pages | full colour | softcover
£12.99 | $18.99 | ISBN 978-1-84653-558-1

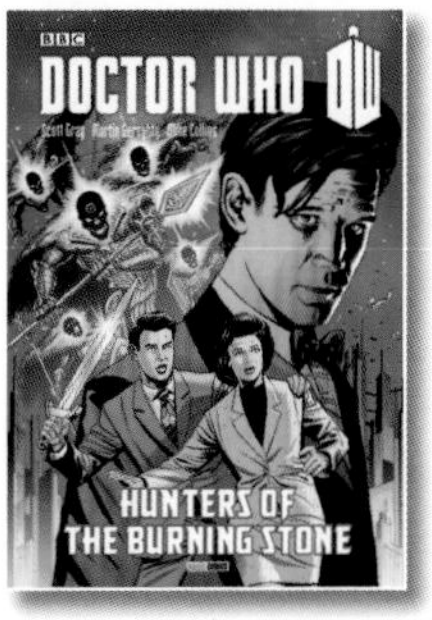
BBC
DOCTOR WHO
HUNTERS OF THE BURNING STONE

Volume Three of the Eleventh Doctor's comic strip adventures from the pages of **Doctor Who Magazine**, containing three complete stories:

THE BROKEN MAN, **IMAGINARY ENEMIES** and **HUNTERS OF THE BURNING STONE**!

PLUS a massive behind-the-scenes feature, including commentaries from the writers and artists, design sketches and more.

164 pages | full colour | softcover
£13.99 | $19.99 | ISBN 978-1-84653-545-1

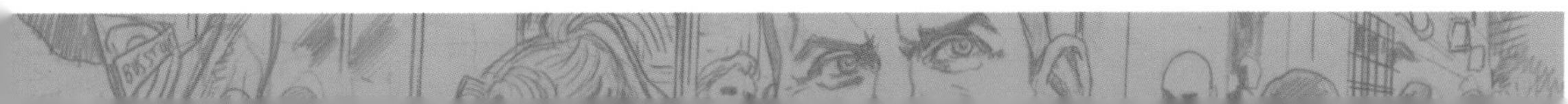

COMING SOON...

THE BLOOD OF AZRAEL

THE FINAL ELEVENTH DOCTOR COMIC COLLECTION!

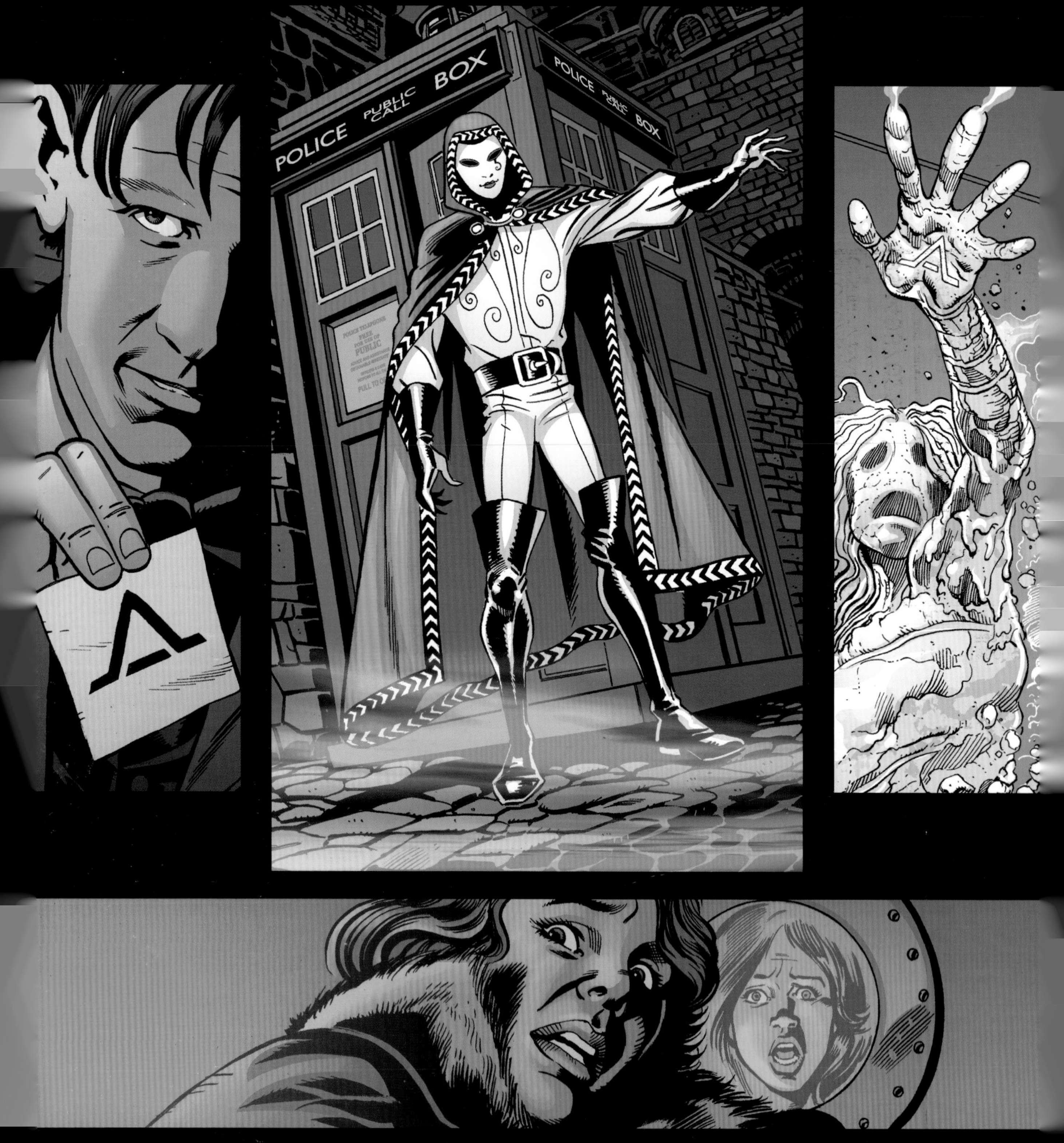
POLICE PUBLIC CALL BOX
POLICE PUBLIC CALL BOX

A BUMPER VOLUME OF AMAZING COMIC STRIP ADVENTURES FROM